LOUIS
XIV

ALSO BY JOSEPHINE WILKINSON

Richard III: The Young King to Be

Mary Boleyn: The True Story of Henry VIII's Favourite Mistress

Anne Boleyn: The Young Queen to Be

*The Princes in the Tower: Did Richard III Murder His Nephews,
Edward V and Richard of York?*

Katherine Howard: The Tragic Story of Henry VIII's Fifth Queen

EDITED BY JOSEPHINE WILKINSON

Anne Boleyn by Paul Friedmann

LOUIS XIV

The Power and the Glory

Josephine Wilkinson

PEGASUS BOOKS
NEW YORK LONDON

LOUIS XIV

Pegasus Books, Ltd.
148 West 37th Street, 13th Floor
New York, NY 10018

First Pegasus Books paperback edition December 2020
First Pegasus Books cloth edition March 2019

Interior design by Maria Fernandez

Library of Congress Cataloging-in-Publication Data is available.

ISBN: 978-1-64313-592-2

10 9 8 7 6 5 4 3 2 1

Printed in the United States of America
Distributed by Simon & Schuster
www.pegasusbooks.com

CONTENTS

PROLOGUE

I t is perhaps only fitting that the story of the most legendary king ever to sit on the throne of France should itself begin with a legend. It opens on a bleak December day in 1637 when a small company of riders thunders through the narrow streets of Paris. They have just left the small hunting lodge of Versailles and are now making their way towards Saint-Mandé, on the eastern edge of the city. As they ride along the rue Saint-Antoine, one of them suddenly signals his desire to stop, and the small party comes to a halt outside the convent of the Visitation. The man dismounts and enters the building while the others wait patiently outside.

Within, all is peace and tranquillity, while the unassuming design and austere décor contribute to the general atmosphere of no-non-sense solemnity. The man crosses the floor, making his way towards a wooden door whose only feature is a grille closed from the inside.

No one approaches him or tries to impede his progress in any way, for he is a regular visitor to the convent and well known to the nuns. Besides, few would be so bold as to challenge the king of France, who has come to see a close friend, to discuss his problems, and receive her wise counsel.

Out of courtesy, a small stool is placed before the door; he sits and patiently awaits his friend's arrival. Suddenly the grille slides open and the king looks upon the familiar, exquisite face of the novice. She smiles in greeting. She knows why Louis has come, and she listens with a serenity that belies her youth as he confides to her his secret worries about the state, his dealings with his ministers, and, most poignantly, his difficult relationship with his queen. She offers her advice as best she can, but most of the time she merely allows him to unburden himself. Then, at a carefully chosen point in their conversation, she takes the opportunity to urge him, as she has done so many times before, to reconcile with the queen, for France is very much in need of a dauphin.

After a time, Louis XIII takes leave of his friend and steps into the street to discover that the storm which had been threatening all afternoon has finally broken. Undaunted, he mounts his horse, and the small party resumes its journey amid the gathering darkness. They do not travel very far before the weather, already bad, has deteriorated markedly. The cold and drenching rains whiten into a heavy sleet, which in turn gives way to driving snow, while the blustering winds make it impossible to keep the torches lit. Guitaut, the trusted captain of the king's guard, suggests that it would be folly to go any farther, and that it might be better to spend the night at the Louvre. This makes sense. The Louvre is still only a short ride away; it is warm and dry, and the hunting party could resume its excursion in the morning. The king, however, is reluctant. He knows the queen is in residence at the Louvre, but they have been estranged for some time; besides, he is expected at Saint-Mandé, and his bed and other necessities have been sent on ahead, while his hosts are awaiting his arrival, as are his servants. Louis looks at the sky and assures Guitaut that the storm will soon pass and they should continue on their way.

Before long, however, it becomes obvious that the storm is growing yet more violent. Guitaut speaks up again, reiterating his proposal that they go to the Louvre for the night. Again the king protests, pointing out that the queen takes her supper and retires too late for him. Guitaut assures his master that she would conform to the king's wishes in this respect, and Louis, reluctantly, indicates his consent.

As the small company retraces its steps and makes its way towards the Louvre, Guitaut rides ahead to alert the queen of the king's imminent arrival and state the time at which he would like to take his supper. The queen issues orders to serve the king his favorite dish, and the royal couple shares a warming meal. They then withdraw for the night, and Louis finds that his pillow has been placed on the queen's bed. Nine months later, the queen, Anne of Austria, gives birth to their son, the dauphin of France. The child is named Louis, but at his formal baptism he will be given a second name, one that reflects the miraculous nature of his arrival: Dieudonné, for Louis XIV of France truly was a gift from God.[1]

As with all legends, this one has some basis in fact, but not much. However, its author, the Abbé Griffet, was correct to portray the coming of the dauphin as a prodigious event, for the fact was that Louis XIV was born at a time when France had every reason to give up hope that her king would ever produce a much-desired heir—and the circumstances of Louis XIV's conception and birth are every bit as dramatic as the legend.

LOUIS
XIV

ONE

A Gift from God

I t was a charming scene. In the fairy-tale château at Burgundy, the bride and groom, both of whom were only fourteen years old, came together for the formal solemnization of their marriage. Anne of Austria was "as beautiful as the day,"[1] tall, with large blue eyes, luxuriant chestnut hair, and long white hands of which she was especially proud. She wore a velvet gown of royal purple powdered with golden fleur-de-lis, the symbol of her new country. Louis was quite plump and spoke with a stammer; he was "handsome and very well made," and his appearance "did not displease the queen."[2] His dark hair and deep brown eyes were perfectly set off by a suit of white satin embellished with gold embroidery and a large ruff.[3] They exchanged gifts, Louis presenting Anne with a plume from his hat, while she gracefully acquiesced to his request for one of the bows that bound her hair.

The wedding festivities would continue into the night, but first the royal couple was ceremonially put to bed as other members of the royal family and courtiers looked on and a priest blessed the marriage bed in the hope that God would help the couple produce an heir. Where the bride and groom were children, this symbolic "consummation" was all that was required, and the groom, having been placed in the bed beside his wife before witnesses, would then be removed and taken away to his own chamber. The young couple would then continue to live in separate households until it was decided that they were old enough to begin their married life together in the fullest sense. However, Louis and Anne, despite their youth, were deemed old enough to begin living together as husband and wife immediately, and it was here that the problems began.

At the time of his wedding to Anne of Austria,[4] Louis XIII of France already had a highly developed aversion towards women. This was largely the result of the schemes and conspiracies of his mother, Marie de Médicis, who proved reluctant to relinquish the power she had exercised as regent, and who had always favored her younger son, Gaston, duc d'Orléans, at the expense of the king. Now, as he stood on the threshold of manhood, Louis appeared disinclined to consummate his marriage.

At five thirty in the afternoon, Louis announced that the wedding ceremonies had tired him out, and he retired to his room. No amount of persuasion would induce him to change his mind, and when his courtiers regaled him with lurid sex stories, they seemingly made a bad situation worse. However, the king's behavior was merely artifice, part of a larger ritual designed for such a momentous occasion.

When, after almost two hours, Louis had still not emerged from his chamber, Marie de Médicis entered and, as his companions looked on, announced, "My son, it's not all done in getting married; you have to come to see the queen your wife, who awaits you." Louis replied, "Madame, I was only waiting for your command. I'm happy to set out with you to find her." The nervous bridegroom allowed himself to be led by his mother to Anne's chambers, to find her sitting up in bed. "My daughter," said Marie, "here is your husband whom I bring to you; receive him into your bosom and love him well, I beseech you." Anne expressed her eagerness to please Their Majesties,[5] before the young king and queen were left in the care of two royal nurses. The sumptuous curtains were drawn around the bed and, after a little over two hours, Louis called for his slippers and dressing gown. He withdrew to his own chamber, announcing that he had done his duty twice.

As it happens, there is some dispute as to whether or not Louis and Anne consummated their marriage that night. Marie de Médicis claimed to have discovered stains on the blankets, which suggested that they had, but rumor had it that the king had been incapable of fully performing his conjugal duty; whatever the case, so distasteful did Louis find the physical side of married life that he left Anne alone thereafter.

No attempt to induce Louis to fulfill his royal responsibility and produce a dauphin seemed to work. A story later told by the Venetian ambassador had it that Louis was invited to the bedroom of his half sister upon her marriage to the duc d'Elbeuf and allowed to watch as they made love several times in the hope that he would be inspired to do the same with the queen. It was to no avail, and the now nineteen-year-old king eventually had to be carried, literally kicking and screaming, to Anne's bed, when the full consummation of their marriage finally took place.[6]

The problem was not so much personal dislike for his bride but his aversion to women in general; moreover, Louis had long harbored a deep distrust of the Spanish, which in turn influenced his attitude towards his new queen. This could only make a difficult situation worse, for Louis and Anne were not really compatible. He was reserved and deeply pious. He had received a broad education designed to prepare him for kingship, and he was intelligent, but not an intellectual. Instead of occupying himself with philosophy and political theory, he preferred gardening and sports. A soldier at heart, Louis spent a lot of his time practicing with weaponry of all kinds. His preferred pastime, however, was hunting, and he kept several lodges throughout the Île de France, although none could match his favorite, Versailles, which nestled among the marshes and wild forests of the Val de Gallie.

For her part, Anne was also deeply pious, but she was also fun-loving, with "a fascinating gift for coquetry and an alarming lightness of behavior."[7] Sociable, she indulged a love of gambling and enjoyed parties and being surrounded by her friends, not all of whom exercised a favorable influence on her. The most notorious of her companions was the exquisitely beautiful Marie de Rohan, in turn duchesse de Luynes and duchesse de Chevreuse, who was already well known for the intrigues and conspiracies that would see her exiled from court, and even from France, on several occasions.

Notwithstanding their differences, Louis did manage to do his duty by his queen and his country, and Anne became pregnant more than once. Her first pregnancy ended in miscarriage when, upon returning to the Louvre from a party late one night with her friends, one of whom was La Rohan, she frolicked through the darkened corridors of the château. Slipping on the highly polished floor, Anne crashed in an undignified heap and lost her baby shortly afterwards.[8] When another three pregnancies also ended in miscarriage, the king's distrust of his queen deepened, and he would usually console himself by going to the hunt with an intimate group of favorites, leaving the government of the country to his chief minister and éminence grise, Cardinal Richelieu.

While Louis occupied himself with the chase, Anne had distractions of her own. Several men paid court to her, among them the duc de Bellegarde, an older gentleman who responded to Anne's beauty as her husband never could. This was nothing more than the innocent flirtation that belonged to the realm of courtly love; however, the attentions of two of the queen's admirers would be more significant. The first was Cardinal Richelieu, who, among his many other duties, served in Anne's household as almoner.

More distinguished than good-looking and pressed by burning ambition, Richelieu made it his business to ingratiate himself into Anne's favor as a means of further advancing his own career. His tactics had succeeded once before, when he had found favor with the queen mother. Now he turned his attention to Anne, with overtures that he described as "fatherly efforts to show her kindness." The queen was not impressed, but urged by her friend Marie de Rohan, she tricked the cardinal into dancing the fandango while wearing a green costume, complete with bells. Humiliated by their laughter, he never forgot this assault on his dignity, nor could he ever forgive the queen. Anne had made an enemy of him, and thereafter he took every opportunity to discredit her with the king.[9]

Much later, Anne was pursued by a man who would break all the rules of courtly love and threaten seriously to compromise her virtue—George Villiers, Duke of Buckingham. The handsome and chivalrous duke first came into Anne's life in 1623 when he and Prince Charles, the future king of England, travelled incognito through France on their way to Spain. Buckingham was enchanted by Anne, and, when he returned to France two years later to accompany Charles's queen, Henriette, to England, he took full advantage of his mission to renew his attentions to her. The court travelled with Henriette and her gallant escort as they began their journey to Calais, but the queen mother became ill, and the party was obliged to find lodgings so she could rest for a few days. One evening, as Anne was strolling in the garden with her coterie of friends, Buckingham approached and asked to speak to her. Anne's companions maintained a respectful distance as she and the duke walked along in private conversation. The path led them into a part of the garden that was hidden by shrubbery, and Anne, alarmed to find herself suddenly alone with her English admirer, cried out and brought servants and friends rushing to her aid.

When the court took leave of Henriette, Buckingham bent to kiss the hem of Anne's gown as she sat in the front of her coach, taking care to hide his face so as to conceal his tears. The two parties went their separate ways, the French court making their way back to Fontainebleau, while Henriette and Buckingham journeyed on towards Calais. Buckingham, however, was tortured by an irresistible urge to see Anne once again and, pretending he had received fresh orders from his master, left his charge at Boulogne and caught up with the French court at Compiègne. Finding Anne in bed and attended by a few of her ladies, he threw himself onto his knees next to the bed and kissed the sheets. Anne, embarrassed and a little annoyed, was unable to speak, and it was left to her lady-of-honor to announce sharply to the duke that such behavior was not the custom in France and that he should rise. Buckingham reasoned that, since he was not a Frenchman, he was not bound to observe French customs; he then spoke tenderly to Anne, but she merely complained of his boldness and ordered him to leave. Yet it was obvious to all that Anne was not as angry with the duke as she pretended to be, and, as he left for England, he announced his intention to return to France as soon as he could.[10] Anne later confessed that if a virtuous woman could love a man other than her husband, Buckingham would be the only one who could have pleased her.[11]

Louis, too, enjoyed tender moments when he became strongly attracted to Marie de Hautefort, a young woman who had recently joined his mother's household. Known as l'Aurore, the Goddess of the Dawn, she was fourteen years old and highly spirited, with large blue eyes, golden hair, and a dewy complexion; although the king fell in love with her, he continued to admire her from a distance, much to the amusement of his queen and her friends.[12]

For her part, Mlle de Hautefort was not too impressed with her royal devotee. Although she agreed to spend time with him, she was sorry to report that all the king did was talk about hunting and dogs. On occasion, he would confide his woes about the queen to her, only for her to chide him for treating Anne so badly.

One who noticed Marie de Hautefort's power over Louis was Cardinal Richelieu, who befriended the favorite with a view to using her to influence the king. Marie, however, would have none of it. She rejected Richelieu's overtures, rebuking him instead for his ill-treatment of the queen.[13]

The friendship between Louis and Marie de Hautefort continued for some five years until he became attracted to Louise de La Fayette. She was the queen's maiden-of-honor, and she possessed every accomplishment that fitted her for the position: she was seventeen and very pretty, with a good singing voice and a talent for dancing; but what attracted the king was her love of outdoor pursuits, especially hunting. Louis and La Fille, as he called her, would often go riding together, when he would regale her with tales of his success on the hunting grounds. Louise had a charming and easy manner, and Louis genuinely fell in love with her, much to the astonishment of the court, for Louis was not the man to take mistresses. The king felt comfortable enough with Louise to confide to her his hopes and worries, and he would discuss everything from the progress of the Franco-Spanish War to his dealings with Richelieu.

Much to Louis's sorrow, however, the young maiden-of-honor was more devoted to God than to a life at court. He was heartbroken when, after four years of devoted attachment, Louise announced her intention to follow her true vocation, which was to retire from court and enter the Convent of the Visitation as a novice. Reluctantly, Louis let her go, but as he watched her leave, he at least had the consolation of being able to visit her at the convent whenever he liked; during these visits, Louise would urge the king to be kind to his wife so that France might have an heir.[14]

The personal difficulties between the king and queen might have been alleviated by these diversions, but they did nothing to address what was now becoming a very real problem: France still lacked a dauphin. Until Louis and Anne produced a son, the heir presumptive was Gaston d'Orléans, whose ambition to become king, coupled with his penchant for conspiracies and disreputable associates, made him a very dangerous man. Worse, Gaston had no sons, meaning that upon his death the throne would go to their cousins, the Condés, who wished to drag France back into feudalism, an equally undesirable scenario. At one point, Gaston became involved in a plot to murder Cardinal Richelieu, depose Louis, and force him to annul his marriage, while Queen Anne would marry Gaston, who would then become king. Despite the involvement of her friend Marie de Rohan, Anne was merely a blameless pawn in the conspiracy, but Louis would never be entirely persuaded of her innocence.

Louis's suspicions seemed to be justified when Anne withdrew to the convent of the Val-de-Grâce. While this had long been her practice, on this occasion she was discovered to be holding secret correspondence with her brothers, Philip IV of Spain, and the cardinal-infante, who was in command of troops in the Spanish Netherlands. The letters, which were passed into Spain through an underground network, were uncovered by Richelieu's spies; with France and Spain still at war, he felt justified in raiding the queen's apartments, where more letters were found. Most of these were uncompromising, the natural correspondence of a sister and brother; however, in one, Anne had mentioned a certain monk whom Richelieu planned to send to Spain as an agent. Richelieu viewed Anne's actions as treason and sent her to Chantilly while her fate was being decided.

Richelieu now had the perfect excuse to finally be rid of a woman he had long regarded as his enemy, an ambition that could only be helped by the fact that she and Louis had been married for twenty-two years and had not yet managed to produce an heir. Anne was acutely aware of her situation, and she had often expressed her fears that she might be repudiated. However, despite his personal feelings, Richelieu knew that the best interests of France could be served only by reconciliation between the king and queen. Taking the matter into his own hands, he confronted Anne with her treason, pointing out the seriousness of her activities and warning her of the consequences both to herself and to France should she persist. He then offered his forgiveness and promised to solicit the king to pardon her, and so Louis and Anne were reconciled.

The king and queen resided at Saint-Germain for three weeks in November 1637 before Anne went to the Louvre, while Louis left to go on a hunting expedition. His first stop was Crosne before moving on to Versailles, where he was installed by December 5. It was during this period that Louis XIV was conceived. An announcement published in the *Gazette* at the end of January promised good news to come: "All the princes, lords, and people of fashion went to congratulate their majesties at Saint-Germain on their hopes of a happy event, which with God's help, we will tell you about soon."[15]

It was, of course, essential that Anne's child should be a boy. Although daughters made useful pawns for political alliances, they could not succeed to the throne. With this in mind, Louis requested special novenas to be said in the hope that God would bless France with a dauphin. He also placed France into the hands of the Blessed Virgin and issued orders that the Feast of the Assumption[16] should be celebrated each year.

Elsewhere, spiritual assistance was offered by Jean-Jacques Olier, founder of Saint-Sulpice, who took to scourging himself regularly, while Jeanne de Matel of l'Institut du Verbe Incarné prophesied that Queen Anne's child would be a boy.[17] A discalced Augustine, Father Fiacre, urged the queen to make novenas at each of three churches dedicated to the Virgin,[18] while the Carmelite Marguerite of the Blessed Sacrament, who claimed to have been visited several times by the Virgin, knew weeks before anyone else that Anne was pregnant.[19]

Formal confirmation of the happy event came when the *Mercure Français* announced that "France has hopes of the greatest happiness so far in this august and marvellous reign, namely the birth of a dauphin, destined by God to take place this year."[20] When Anne felt the baby stir for the first time, a fireworks display was held at the Arsenal in Paris to celebrate. As the summer wore on, the queen sent for a precious relic, a fragment of the holy girdle worn by the Virgin as she gave birth. Gifts arrived for the new baby, including a layette and other garments from Pope Urban VIII, while greetings were sent from King Philip of Spain; notwithstanding that their two counties were at war, he was, after all, the baby's uncle.

A team of wet nurses was engaged, as well as midwives and the royal accoucheur, or obstetrician, Dame Peronne. There was a heightened sense of excitement when Louis returned from the front in August to attend the imminent birth of his first child. However, when Anne had still not given birth by the nineteenth of the month, he grew impatient and angrily wrote to Richelieu stating that he wished he had not arrived so early and that he would prefer still to be with his army in Picardy. He then announced his intention to go to Versailles for two or three days, having found "the female sex as senseless and impertinent as ever" and expressing his desire to "be away from all these women."[21]

By August 28, the baby was considered overdue and prayers were said in Paris, while the Blessed Sacrament was displayed in the churches. Anne had already withdrawn to the Château-Neuf of Saint-Germain, the smaller and more comfortable of the two châteaux, for her lying-in. A week later, towards midnight, she went into labor surrounded by her attendants, while witnesses watched her at every moment. Chief among these was Gaston d'Orléans, who had arrived at Saint-Germain in the middle of August; with the integrity of the succession at stake, witnesses ensured that the queen's child was not substituted for another—a boy exchanged for a girl, or a living baby to take the place of one born dead.

At 11:20 in the morning of Sunday, September 5, the future Louis XIV was born. He was a healthy baby, weighing nine pounds. Upon seeing the child who now took his place in the succession, Gaston retired to his estates and "complained of his misfortune with thousands of tears."[22] Meanwhile, the gentlemen of the court threw their hats into the air as a signal to everyone that the queen had given birth to a boy. Louis fell to his knees and thanked God for the blessing bestowed upon him, although he forgot to kiss his wife until it was pointed out to him that he ought to.

The birth of the dauphin was seen as nothing short of a miracle. For Montglat, the baby appeared to have come from the hand of God.[23] Mme de Motteville also credited divine intervention through the medium of the king's friend, Louise de La Fayette, for Louis, "having stayed with her too late to return to Saint-Germain for the night as he intended, he was constrained to go to the Louvre and share the bed of the queen, who had come to Paris for affairs of no importance; and so it is said that this gave us the king reigning today."[24] This short passage would provide the basis of Griffet's legend.

The baby was taken and *ondoyé*; that is, given his first, informal baptism by Dominique Séguier, the king's chaplain. This was a necessary precaution in times of tragically high infant mortality; it meant that should the baby die, his soul would immediately be admitted into heaven. The child was named Louis after the saintly King Louis IX and Clovis, who had united the tribes to form the country now known as France;[25] and his own father, Louis XIII. The king was proud of his son; upon showing him to the Venetian ambassador, he said, "Here is the miraculous result of the grace of Almighty God, for what else may describe such a beautiful child after twenty-two years of marriage and my wife's four miscarriages."[26]

France greeted the new dauphin with rejoicing and celebration. At Saint-Germain, four silver dolphins spewed an endless flow of wine; the air rang with the sound of church bells; in each church the *Te Deum* was sung and the Blessed Sacrament exposed; cannon were fired in salute and lanterns brightened the windows of every house. On Monday, all the shops remained closed so that everyone might enjoy a holiday.

On the following day, the tiny dauphin held his first audience when representatives of the sovereign courts accepted the king's invitation to come to the Château-Neuf of Saint-Germain and offer their compliments. The secretary of state then escorted the magistrates into the dauphin's bedchamber so they could look upon the new infant. Mathieu Molé recalled that the child's governess, Madame de Lansac, "held the sleeping M. le Dauphin, his face uncovered, on a pillow of white satin and showed him, and said that he would open his eyes to see his faithful servants."[27]

Horoscopes were drawn up as attempts were made to determine the character and destiny of the future king.[28] It was noted that the dauphin's constellation was composed of nine stars, signifying "great genius." Among these were Pegasus, "the puissant cavalier"; Sagittarius, "the infantry"; Aquarius, for "naval power"; and the Swan, or Cygnus, signifying that "poets, historians and orators would sing his praises." That the constellation touched the equator signified "justice." Being born on a Sunday, "the Dauphin, like the sun, by his warmth and light will be the happiness of France and her allies."

In a departure from usual royal protocol, Anne of Austria insisted upon keeping the Dauphin Louis with her at all times, although she did not nurse him. The baby's voracious appetite showed itself early, when he went through several wet nurses, an uncomfortable experience for them, since he had been born with two teeth. Still resident at Saint-Germain, high above the Seine looking down on Paris, Anne was often found wheeling her son around in his carriage. Meanwhile, the young Louis performed his first official function when, at only sixteen months old, he received a napkin from the *maître d'hotel* and handed it to the king.

It was at about this time that Anne found herself pregnant again, but the king was now greatly concerned about her influence over their firstborn. Writing to Richelieu, he announced that he was "most displeased with my son. As soon as he sets eyes on me, he yells as if he were looking at the devil and always cries for his mother. He must be cured of these tantrums and taken away from the Queen's side as soon as possible."[29]

A few days later, Louis noted that "thanks to the good offices of Mme de Lansac my son begged my forgiveness on his knees and played with me for an hour and more." The next day he wrote again, reporting that the child "cannot bear to leave me, he tries to follow me everywhere. I fondle him as much as I can. I think that a little speech I made in front of some people who were sure to pass it on, and the offices of Mme de Lansac have contributed to this change." Louis had told his household that his son was in the company of too many women, and that they were trying to make the child afraid of men. He had then threatened to remove all the child's attendants except Mme de Lansac if the tantrums continued, for "I wanted him to see nothing but men from now on."[30] The dauphin was barely two years old.

Anne gave birth to her second child, Philippe de France, on September 21, 1640. The king was even more pleased with his second son than he had been with the dauphin because, as he said, he had not expected the great happiness of being the father of two children, when he had feared he would have no children at all.

Louis, however, continued to be concerned about the attention Anne was lavishing on his sons. On one occasion he arrived home from the hunt and changed into his nightclothes early. The three-year-old dauphin, unaccustomed to seeing his father in a nightcap, took fright and began to cry. The king flew into a rage, chiding the queen for bringing up the child in aversion for his person and threatening once again to take both boys away from her.[31]

However, Louis XIII was now very ill; the tuberculosis that would kill him within two years was quite advanced, and it did nothing to calm his increasingly irascible temper. Nevertheless, as he prepared to go on a journey with the marquis de Cinq-Mars, his new favorite, he bade farewell to the queen, urging her to take care of his children and never to leave them. The young marquis appears to have brought out a gentler side to Louis's character.

In time, it became clear that the king was dying. In April 1643, he suffered a "hepatitic flux with a species of slow fever"[32] and was put to bed. He was concerned that the dauphin had not yet been christened, and this was rectified in a service at Saint-Germain on April 21, with the princesse de Condé as godmother and Jules Mazarin, Richelieu's pro-tégé, as godfather. The child was described as "beautiful as an angel, manifesting in all this action a modesty and a self-control extraor-dinary for one of his age"[33] and given the name Louis-Dieudonné, Louis the God-given. A story later told that, when the ceremony was ended, the boy, still wearing his gown of silver taffeta, went to his father's bedside. "What is your name now?" the king asked him. "Louis the Fourteenth," the child replied. "Not yet, my son," the king sighed, "but you will be soon, if that is God's will."[34]

When the king asked how long he had to live, he was told "two or three hours at the most." He joined his hands in prayer, saying that he consented to it with all his heart. Then he ordered the curtains sur-rounding his bed to be drawn aside so he could look out the window. Gazing at the distant spire of Saint-Denis, the traditional final resting place of the kings of France, he whispered, "There is where I will go soon, and where I will stay for a long time."[35] Shortly afterwards, he died. It was May 14, 1643, and the long reign of Louis XIV had begun.

TWO

To Educate a Living God

Threep he little boy's face was that of a cherub, round and pale with bright blue eyes framed by blond curls[1] tied in ribbons and a lace cap complete with an ostrich feather. Over a floor-length gown, he wore a white apron trimmed with lace and adorned by a sky blue ribbon of the Ordre du Saint-Esprit. A blue mantle powdered with golden fleur-de-lis was placed upon his shoulders as Anne of Austria knelt before him in homage. He was only four and a half years old, but Louis XIV was king of France.

It was a new dawn; the rising sun brought with it a renewed hope, filled with promise, but Louis was not safe. He was surrounded by ill-wishers who looked for, and were ready to exploit, any weakness in the new regime. Some were to be found among the gloriously robed magistrates, who concealed their ambition behind smiling expressions of love and oaths of loyalty. Then there was the nobility, whose lineages were at least as long as Louis's, men who saw their families as the foundation upon which France rested.

These men represented danger enough, but even more treacherous were the princes of the blood, the king's own relatives who sought to usurp the power that had devolved upon him by an accident of birth. Of these, Gaston d'Orléans posed the greatest threat. A foppish and unscrupulous bon vivant whose ambition had driven him on numerous occasions to agitate against his brother, the late king, Gaston had been heir presumptive for many years before the Dieudonné came. No less dangerous was Henri II de Bourbon, prince de Condé. An intriguer and rebel, his mutinous spirit was calmed for a time by Richelieu, who arranged for Condé's son and heir to be married to his niece. Finally, there was César, duc de Vendôme, an illegitimate son of Henri IV by his mistress, Gabrielle d'Estrées. He had once joined Condé in rebellion, but his main threat lay in his son, François, duc de Beaufort. Thirty years old, tall, and possessing the blond beauty of a Viking, Beaufort was a hotheaded adventurer, but he was popular with the people, especially the women. This gallant had once praised Queen Anne's beautiful hands, a sure route to her heart, and she, fearing a coup d'état, now engaged his services in order to protect the young king. Beaufort and a detail of Cent-Suisses formed a cordon around Louis. Anne had ensured her son's safety in the face of his enemies, but she also saved him from himself: a dark story had it that, as the court waited for Louis XIII to die, a gentleman usher asked the young dauphin if he wished to be king. The child cried, "Non! I do not wish to be king. If he dies, I shall throw myself in the moat of the château."[2] Anne could take no chances.

On May 15, 1643, the court left Saint-Germain, abandoning the dead king to the care of priests, embalmers, and history. Louis XIV made his entrance into Paris, his cortège surrounded by musketeers commanded by M. de Tréville. The journey, which would take about

an hour under normal circumstances, took seven. The royal progress was stopped at every turn by endless speeches made by various
dignitaries, while the ecstatic crowds pressed on all sides to catch a
glimpse of their child-king, to touch his hair and kiss his clothes as
he passed. One witness, the magistrate and royal councillor Olivier
Lefèvre d'Ormesson, wrote in his *Journal* that the crowd was enchanted
by Louis and his brother, Philippe, and could not agree which child
was the more beautiful.[3]

Louis was unconcerned about all the adulation shown to him. He
behaved with astonishing maturity, possessing the gravity and poise
of a much older person. Well coached by his mother and his godfather,
Mazarin, in the correct way to perform in public, it was frequently
noted that he rarely laughed and barely moved.[4]

The royal family took up residence in the Louvre. The palace, which
dated back to the twelfth century, had grounds that sprawled onto the
right bank of the Seine. It was still undergoing the renovation work
that Louis's grandfather, Henri IV, had begun almost fifty years before.
Once the king and Philippe were settled into their apartments, the first
order of business was to summon *parlement*, and the date was set for
Monday, May 18. Its purpose would be to discuss the late king's will
and his carefully laid plans for the regency. Initially, Louis XIII had
debarred Gaston from the regency council and would have excluded
Anne too, had he not been prevented from doing so by tradition, which
granted queens regency powers upon the accession of a minor king.
However, he could restrict her power, and, as death approached, he
revised his will, appointing Gaston to the council as lieutenant-general
of the realm and Cardinal Mazarin as president. A final clause decreed
that decisions reached by the regency council would be binding upon
Anne, who would be obliged to act upon their recommendations.
Anne would be regent, but her powers would be severely restricted.

Louis XIII had satisfied the basic requirements of a king: he had left
a son and heir to reign after him; he had appointed a regency council
to rule until the young king attained his majority; he had done so

while restricting the powers of a wife and queen he had never fully come to trust, yet without breaking with the cherished traditions of the realm. One thing Louis had not taken into consideration was the understanding that kings could not rule from beyond the grave; his will was valid only for as long as he lived.

Anne spent the next two days meeting ambassadors and holding discussions with various officials. She discussed the regency, the composition of the council, and her place in it. The agreements that were reached would be announced at the next day's *lit de justice* before being registered by the parlement.[5]

The *lit de justice* was a solemn session of parlement originally devised to enforce the registration of a decree or edict that otherwise would have been disputed on the grounds that it was felt to be contrary to the laws and traditions of France. The *lit* was literally a pile of cushions upon which Louis would be seated. On the morning of May 18, he and his mother, accompanied by the princesse de Condé, the duchesse de Longueville, and Louis's governess, Madame de Lansac, left the Louvre. The route, lined all the way by cheering crowds hedged by French guards and Cent-Suisses, took Louis across the Pont Neuf before turning towards the Palais de la Cité on the Île de la Cité.

Louis, tiny though he was, was magnificent in the violet robes of royal mourning, their ermine trimming set off by the sky blue cordon of the Ordre du Saint-Esprit. He arrived just after nine o'clock and immediately made his way to the Sainte-Chapelle to attend the mass celebrated by the bishop of Beauvais. At the same time, the gentlemen of the parlement, dressed in the long red robes of their office, had begun to take their seats. They were joined by the prince de Condé and his younger son, the prince de Conti, followed by the chancellor, Pierre Séguier.

Outside the Sainte-Chapelle, four présidents à mortier (second presidents) and eight councillors waited to escort their king and his suite into the Grand Chambre, the entourage being led by guards, with members of the nobility following behind. Louis was carried to the *lit de justice* by the duc de Joyeuse and supported by the comte de Charost, the captain of the guards, a ritual that served to emphasize the king's status as a child.

Louis was seated on the *lit de justice* with the queen regent and the princes of the blood to his right, while the bishop of Beauvais sat to his left. At the king's feet was his great chamberlain, the duc de Chevreuse, while four captains of the guards took their seats further down. Facing them were the gentlemen of the parlement. Once everyone was in his place, Mme de Lansac lifted Louis onto his throne before one of the captains of the guard called for silence. All eyes were now fixed on the small boy, who, "with a grace uncommon to those of his years," addressed the assembly. His words were well rehearsed: "Messieurs, I have come to testify my affection and my good will towards my parlement. My chancellor will tell you the rest."[6] The king then stole a glance towards his mother, who smiled her approval.

Omer Talon, the avocat-général, was the first to rise. He likened Louis's throne to that of the Living God and begged him to consider that the honor and respect the estates of his realm rendered to him were as that to a visible divinity.[7] Chancellor Séguier spoke next, urging parlement to overturn the late king's will and confirm Anne of Austria as regent. As it was, Anne had already secured her position by promising the magistrates that she would grant them automatic ennoblement within eighteen months if they would agree to the suppression of her late husband's will. She had also come to an understanding with the duc d'Orléans and Condé, who now publicly pledged their loyalty and devotion. Anne then assured the regency council that she would be happy to receive their advice on all occasions.[8] With that the business of the day was done. Louis, Anne, and their entourage made their way back to the Louvre, the air filled with acclamations of "Vive le roi."[9] Louis XIV had completed his first official ceremony as king.

A medal commemorating Louis's accession was designed, bearing the legend FRANCORUM SPES MAGNA: Louis was the "Great Hope of the French."[10] A few days later, news arrived that the duc d'Enghein,

Condé's eldest son, had defeated the Spanish at the battle of Rocroi. The news crowned the dawn of the reign of Louis XIV with glory.

Seated on the throne of the living God he might have been, but Louis XIV was still a child and too young to govern. Anne of Austria immediately began the process of arranging the regency council to suit her own needs. Out went Richelieu's creatures, Claude Bouthillier and his son, Léon de Chavigny, and in came Nicolas de Bailleul, a président à mortier of the Parlement of Paris, [11] while the marquise de Seneçay replaced Mme de Lansac as Louis's governess. Cardinal Mazarin, who had been Richelieu's protégé, also expected to be dismissed and was already packing his bags in readiness for his return to Rome when the marquis de Chouppes knocked on his door. The marquis tried to assure his friend that the queen mother would not let him leave, but Mazarin felt certain that she meant to replace him with the bishop of Beauvais, a favorite for whom she had already requested a cardinal's hat. At that moment, Beauvais arrived and Mazarin braced himself for bad news, but he was to be surprised. Beauvais announced that he had come from the queen with the message that "Her Majesty offers Your Eminence the only post befitting his dignity, that of Prime Minister."[12]

Mazarin met Anne of Austria in 1631 during his first visit to Paris. Richelieu introduced him to the queen with the observation, "Madame, you will like him well, he resembles Buckingham."[13] Indeed, Anne did like the handsome and personable man who was about the same age as her, and this did not go unnoticed by Richelieu, who sought to control her through him.[14]

It is true that there was some resemblance between Mazarin and Buckingham, and Richelieu's insolent remark has inspired historians to question the true nature of the relationship that formed between the queen and the future cardinal, but any suggestion that they were lovers, or even that they married, remains unfounded.[15] Anne's own words, spoken to Mme de Brienne, show the true depth of feeling she had for Mazarin: "I grant you that I like him, and I may even say tenderly, but the affection I bear him does not go so far as love, or if it does so without my knowledge it is not my senses which are involved but only my mind, which is charmed by the beauty of his."[16] The attraction was obvious: Mazarin was a capable diplomat and administrator dedicated to the service of his adopted country. He and Anne shared much in common, most importantly the duty to preserve the security and integrity of the kingdom inherited by Louis XIV.

Anne of Austria did not feel secure in her role as regent, and she attempted to buy support with favors, governorships, and appointments. This greatly alarmed Mazarin, who quickly grasped her political naïveté and susceptibility to flattery; he warned her that such actions could result in factionalism because "a favor granted to one meant the enmity of the other."[17] Mazarin advised Anne to recall from exile her old friend Mme de Chevreuse, to neutralize any intrigue that might arise. Although Anne no longer had any love for her former companion, she agreed. Meanwhile, the cardinal educated Anne in politics, and they would convene each evening to discuss the business of the day. During their meetings, which lasted half an hour or more, they might have been out of earshot of Anne's ladies, but they were never out of sight.

Mazarin's perceived influence over Anne aroused jealousy in those who had hoped that the death of Louis XIII and Richelieu would signal their return to power. A cabal formed, led by the duc de Beaufort, who, worryingly, was soon joined by Mme de Chevreuse. Another who joined their ranks was the duchesse de Longueville, Condé's brilliant, beautiful, and scheming daughter. Their haughtiness led them to be labelled the Cabale des Importants, and their plan was as dangerous as it was ambitious: to assassinate Mazarin and exert their own influence over the queen regent. Their one opportunity to execute their plan failed because the cardinal happened to be travelling in a coach with Gaston, who would have regarded any violence against his passenger as an affront to his honor. The conspiracy having been uncovered, the leaders were rounded up and imprisoned or sent into exile.

It has sometimes been said that Louis had an unhappy childhood, one marked by neglect,[18] but there is no evidence to support this. There are, however, numerous accounts describing Louis's hauteur and pride, although few realized that such traits masked shyness. On September 5, 1643, Angelo Contarini, envoy extraordinary of the Republic of Venice, saw the king, who was celebrating his fifth birthday. Contarini left a pen portrait praising Louis's alert mind and "the beauty of his disposition," which he saw as "an indication of high qualities as yet undeveloped." He continued:

> He is of sturdy build and has an animated if rather serious expression, but it is a seriousness full of charm. He rarely laughs, even at play. He insists that his three-year-old brother, the duc d'Anjou, shall show him respect and obedience. He knows and understands that he is King and intends to be treated as such. And when, occasionally, the Queen his mother reproves him, he replies that the time is coming when he will be master. When the Ambassadors talk to the Regent, he does not listen, but when they address him he is very attentive . . . In short, unless his life and education play him false, he promises to be a great King.[19]

A few days later, Louis attended a special ceremony in Paris to congratulate his cousin, the duc d'Enghein, upon the capture of Thionville.[20] The town, which had been besieged since 1639, had finally capitulated during the summer, one of several towns to do so in a year that had seen mixed fortunes for the French forces. Yet while these victories added to the glory of the new reign, they did nothing to end the ongoing war. The financial burdens caused by the conflict fell heaviest upon the poor, and this led inevitably to unrest. The peasants of the Rouergue were the first to rise up, followed by those of Aunis and Saintonge, where the people were joined by the local nobility. The revolt was swiftly and brutally put down by the marquis d'Aumont, but Mazarin opposed such harsh measures. He persuaded Anne that concord would come only through leniency and compassion, and together they prepared a royal proclamation. In this, the earliest such declaration to be signed by Louis XIV, the king assured his subjects that "the rapidity with which the said provinces have been reduced to submission has led me, on the advice of my Mother, the Queen Regent, to overlook their misdemeanors."[21] Louis was learning a valuable lesson: that the highest attribute of princes was mercy towards those he saw as misguided and unfortunate.

The following day, Louis reviewed his troops for the first time. The occasion had more the air of a family outing than the formal royal duty it actually was. Louis, accompanied by his mother and a small party, sat in a coach in the Bois de Boulogne, to the west of Paris, and watched the Cent-Suisses performing maneuvers.[22] The king was expected to be as much a military leader as a political one, and good relations with his troops were vital. This event, the first of many, reinforced Louis's emerging interest in all things military. Already his play had a distinct martial flavor. He was surrounded by *enfants d'honneur*, children his own age specially selected from noble families, who would share his games and, later, his lessons. Among these were Louis-Henri Loménie, the future comte de Brienne, who would recall Louis playing with wooden swords and toy guns and banging his drum to the rhythm of the march of the Cent-Suisses.[23]

At this point Louis was still living at the Louvre, but in early October Anne moved her family into a new home, the nearby Palais-Cardinal. Originally built in the 1630s for Cardinal Richelieu and situated opposite the Louvre in the rue Saint-Honoré, the palace was spacious and filled with light, and it boasted beautiful gardens for the boys to play in. Renamed the Palais-Royal, it would become Louis's main residence in Paris for the rest of the regency. Mazarin, meanwhile, took over three neighboring mansions, transforming them into a magnificent, ostentatiously decorated residence filled with the minister's art collection and other treasures.

Louis's relationship with his mother was unusually close, and he and Philippe would spend most of their day with her, except for playtimes. Considered too young to eat with her, they would nevertheless sit with her while she ate. In the morning, Louis was always present at Anne's *lever*, or her rising and dressing ceremony, at which he handed her the chemise in a ritual that should have been allowed to a favored lady.[24]

At seven, Louis attained the "age of reason," when he was deemed capable of discerning right from wrong, mature and responsible in thought and action. Now he was taken out of his skirts and dressed in male clothing; at the same time, he was removed from the care of women and placed under the tutelage of men.

Anne wanted her sons to be "instructed in all knowledge."[25] Latin was considered desirable, though not essential, for the education of princes, but history was seen as indispensable, for it "will show them examples, and give them views by which to govern great kingdoms, to control by the same laws people of different natures, to maintain them in peace with their neighbors, and make them feared by their enemies." Such vital learning as this, however, could not be taught, but must come through experience.

Anne could think of no better instructor for Louis than Mazarin, whom she appointed superintendent of the government and of the conduct of the king, but he could not work alone. He selected Nicolas de Neufville, marquis de Villeroy as governor of the king's person, while Hardouin de Péréfixe was appointed director of studies. Péréfixe taught the king history and the liberal arts, and attempted to instill in his pupil a desire for peace over war. However, under Péréfixe's guiding hand, Louis would come to believe that God "made me out of nothing and drew me up out of nothingness where I was, to give me being, life, my kingdom and all the advantages I now possess."[26] It was all heady stuff for so young a person, and the origins of Louis's self-identification as a divinely appointed king. Focusing on more mundane subjects, other teachers would instruct Louis in writing, reading, arithmetic, and drawing, as well as Spanish and Italian. Latin was not neglected, however, and Louis was made to translate the *Commentaries of Caesar*.

Louis's schooling was not entirely of an intellectual nature, for he received lessons in fencing, horsemanship, and, most important of all, dancing. As it was, his first chance to show off his dancing skills came when he made his debut appearance at a ball held at the Palais-Royal. Here, the seven-year-old king partnered his cousin, Mlle de Montpensier, "with a grace characteristic of all his actions, but unusual in this respect that it caused everyone to wonder at the way in which this young prince, combining so charmingly dignity with pleasure, comported himself as a king even while dancing."[27]

There was one area of her son's life where Anne refused to relinquish control: religion. She "took great care to maintain in the soul of the young king those sentiments of virtue, honor, and piety, which she had instilled in him from infancy."[28] Anne, with Louis and Philippe in tow, visited churches in Paris and beyond, but perhaps the most important of these was the Val-de-Grâce, her own establishment, which she had renovated as thanksgiving for the birth of the king.

Anne's faith was deep and sincere, and it was marked by the rigorous and ostentatious observances she had learned as a child in Spain; but hers was a simple faith, which did not require the application of intellectual study. This approach she passed on to Louis, who would always prefer to be guided by carefully selected chaplains rather than his own reading of the Bible and theological works.

When he was six, Louis began to spend his autumns at Fontaine-bleau, the beautiful château built by François I upon an older structure, much as Louis himself was to do with Versailles. Initially, these sojourns were a means to escape the stifling heat of the Parisian summer, but they had now become a regular feature of the king's calendar. The royal family would enjoy entertainments in the park and the vast forest that surrounded the château, but most of the time they would don their long gray shifts and bathe in the cool waters of the Seine.[29]

Of course, the business of the court continued, and Fontainebleau provided the setting for diplomatic audiences and royal visits. One special guest was Charles, prince of Wales, who came in 1645.[30] Charles had fought alongside his father and had been appointed nominal leader of the royal forces in England's West Country. By this time, however, it was becoming clear that the war was not going well for the royalists, and the exile of the young prince grew imperative. At first Charles withdrew to the Scilly Isles before moving on to Jersey and then to France. Here, he was united with his mother, Henriette-Marie, and lived at the expense of the French court.

Despite his presence in France for several weeks, it was not until August 14 that Charles was formally presented to King Louis at Fontainebleau amid elaborate ceremony. Charles was given the honor of riding in the same coach as Louis, on the same side as the king and at his right hand. Royal protocol, however, went only so far, and Charles was accorded no more than the customary three days at court.[31]

The two cousins met again the following March at the Palais-Royal, where three days of festivities had been laid on for Shrovetide. Already Louis was developing a love of theater, much to the indignation of the rector of Saint-Germain, who thought such amusement to be "a mortal sin and ought not to be permitted."[32] On this occasion, Mazarin offered a spectacular play, complete with moving scenery, magnificent costumes, and "music in the Italian fashion."[33]

The high point of the celebrations was a ball held in one of the chambers of the palace, "gilded and lined with great frames in which were pictures painted in perspective."[34] At one end of the hall stood a throne, over which was draped a fringed cloth of estate in shimmering silver and gold. Louis appeared wearing a suit of black satin heavily embroidered with gold and silver thread. His costume was enhanced with cherry-colored plumes and ribbons, which showed off the beauty of the eight-year-old king, with his pale complexion, blond hair, and blue eyes that were marked by a seriousness unusual in one so young.[35]

As a courtesy to Charles, Louis did not take the throne, offering it instead to his cousin, the duchesse de Montpensier. There was an ulterior motive: some attempt was being made to secure a match between the duchess and Charles, although, by this stage it was becoming obvious to all that neither party was very excited at the prospect.[36]

Everyone was aware of the troubles in England, but France was enjoying great victories in the field; the duc d'Enghien had just won the Battle of Nordlingen, and he would make further gains in the coming weeks. The continuing war weighed heavily on the treasury, and a *lit de justice* was held on Louis's seventh birthday, September 5, 1645, to raise taxes still further.[37] The parlement, however, was increasingly hostile towards the regency government, a sentiment driven in no small part by the members' disdain for Mazarin as a low-born Italian, as well as the fact that promises to ennoble them within eighteen months showed no sign of being fulfilled. At first, parlement attempted to prevent Anne from enforcing edicts in a *lit de justice*, saying she had no right to do so. Anne, however, pointed out that her right was founded on precedent, that of Marie de' Médicis.[38] To ensure the success of her appeal, Anne waited for the duc d'Orléans to return to Paris.

The last time Louis held a *lit de justice*, he was carried into the chamber; this time, he walked in, holding his mother's hand. When he finished speaking, the *parlementaires* applauded him, but their adulation did not prevent their regaling the child and his ministers with terrible reports of poverty-stricken peasants and the wretchedness that reigned throughout the kingdom. In the end, the edicts were passed, but it was becoming clear to Louis, young though he was, that all was not well in his kingdom.

In the summer of 1647, Louis was taken on a journey to the frontier, where the town of Armentières was currently under siege. This was a vital role for the king, whose presence boosted the morale of his men and the local citizenry, and served to encourage new recruits. The first stop was Amiens, where Louis wrote to his brother, Philippe, signing himself off with "your affectionate and kind *petit papa*, Louis."[39]

On one occasion, Louis misbehaved and his mother threatened to spank him, telling him that it was she who had the authority, not him, and that "it is too long since you have had a beating. I will show you that you can be spanked at Amiens as well as in Paris." Louis, angry and resentful, wept for quite some time before throwing himself on his knees before Anne, saying, "Maman, I ask your pardon. I promise never to have any other will but yours." Anne's heart softened; she kissed her beloved son and the two were friends again.[40]

The next stop was Abbeville, from which the royal party expected to go on to Rouen. However, this leg of the journey was abandoned because Rouen was found to be "insensible to the honor of the king."[41] Instead, Louis travelled on to the coastal town of Dieppe, where he stayed three days. Here, he inspected a large ship, a gift from Queen Christina of Sweden. A mock naval battle was held, lasting several hours and culminating in the French striking their victory colors, much to the delight of the king.

The people of Dieppe continued to cherish the memory of Louis's grandfather, Henri IV, and now they were honored with the responsibility of guarding Louis. Everywhere he went, Louis was followed by throngs of his subjects, who boasted that "there were no Ravaillacs among them,"[42] while the women poured out endless benedictions on the king.

During his stay at Dieppe, Louis received officials from the parlement of Normandy, the Cour des Aides, and the Chambre des Comptes, but the occasion was overshadowed by a tragic incident. The chief judge of Rys, a man of about sixty and said still to be in good health, took ill as he was leaving the royal presence. Hearing the commotion, Louis rushed out to find the man prostrate on the floor. His efforts to make the man take some remedy were in vain, for he had died instantly.

Having been on progress for much of the summer, the court made its way back to Paris, where it arrived in late August, but it moved on to Fontainebleau after only three weeks. Once again, the court was joined by Prince Charles, whose unhappy state of affairs "made every one regard him with the tenderness that accompanies pity."[43] The king and the prince were awkward together, as though embarrassed by each other's presence, a state of affairs that was not helped by their shyness and the lack of "freedom of spirit which intercourse with the world gives to private individuals." Louis, who never lost his serious demeanor, said little "from fear of not speaking well."[44]

Shortly after the court returned to Paris, Louis, whose health had previously been good, began to complain of feeling unwell on November 10. He had pains in his lower back accompanied by a high fever, and within a short while it became obvious that he had smallpox.[45] Anne moved her bed into Louis's room, "resolved to be comforted by the loss of his beauty provided his life was saved."

For the first eleven days, Louis was ill but not dangerously so; however, his condition changed on November 21, when his fever increased still further. Louis fainted and was unconscious for forty-five minutes. At about midnight on that Sunday, his life was despaired of by his doctors because the smallpox had "gone in," the pustules having been dried by the heat of the fever.

Louis was subjected to four bleedings, but this treatment, far from being helpful, merely served to debilitate him further. Within a few hours, though, the fever reduced and the smallpox came out once more. The child, "whose life was so necessary to France," began to recover. Still, he was given purges on Monday and Tuesday, at which point the illness rapidly left him and he was completely cured.

Young though he was, throughout his illness, Louis was "wholly inclined to gentleness and kindness, he spoke humanely to all who served him, said obliging and intelligent things, and was docile to all that the doctors desired of him." Louis gave his mother marks of affection, "which touched her keenly" and, having begged her to stay with him throughout the course of his infirmity, assured her that "her presence lessened his illness."

Although Anne had insisted on staying with the king, there were those who, not having had smallpox, hurriedly left court. One of those to stay away was the prince de Condé, who ignored several couriers sent by the queen urging his return from the front. Louis, his face still red and swollen, so that even his brother did not recognize him at first, "scolded those who had abandoned him." Already he had begun to take note of the faces of his courtiers, and he would remember those who absented themselves from his presence.

THREE

The Fronde

W hen it came to the education of princes, politics was considered "the true grammar,"[1] that essential ingredient
for what Louis would later describe as his *métier de roi*,
his profession as king. In this, there was no greater teacher than experience. While lengthy council meetings and endless discussions about
war or the finances were beyond his powers of understanding, let alone
concentration, Louis would attend short meetings with ministers or
join in the occasional longer session. However, as he approached his
tenth birthday, a series of events began to unfold that was to have the
most far-reaching effect on the young king. Louis was about to learn
his greatest lesson in statecraft.

The storm that was about to break over Louis's kingdom came to
be known as the Fronde, named after the catapult or sling that was

used in a child's game. It comprised a series of civil wars lasting from 1648 to 1653 and is one of the most complex events of Louis's reign.

The Fronde was the culmination of a succession of difficulties that had developed over a period of several years. In one respect, it was an expression of anger on the part of the peasantry and bourgeoisie at the ruinous levels of taxation required to support the ongoing Thirty Years' War, a situation made worse by the dishonest activities of the tax farmers and frustration over the delayed or limited payment of interest on rentes.[2] It shared some similarities with previous uprisings, such as occurred in Normandy in 1639 and more recently in the Rouergue.[3]

The Fronde was also a response to the gradual consolidation of power to the monarch, or more accurately to his first minister, to the detriment of the parlements and other courts. This process, which had begun under Richelieu, entailed the increasing use of government agents, known as intendants, who went into the provinces to do the work that was traditionally the responsibility of the local courts, and was a major step towards the establishment of an absolute monarchy. Moreover, officeholders were threatened financially by a recent rise in the number of offices created, the sale of which raised money for the treasury but devalued existing posts.

The Fronde, therefore, was also an attempt by the sovereign courts and others in positions of power to reassert the authority they had enjoyed in previous reigns; to protect themselves, the peasantry, and the bourgeoisie against increasingly crushing taxation; and, especially, to resist the advancement of absolutism, whether monarchical or ministerial.

The government inevitably saw the Fronde as a rebellion against the crown, and it is sometimes described as a dress rehearsal for the French Revolution, which would shake the country to its foundations some 150 years later. This view is not entirely accurate, as those involved in the Fronde directed their anger at Mazarin, not Louis.[4]

Although resentment had been simmering for some time, it reached a critical point in May 1648, when the *paulette* came up for renewal.

This was an annual payment in exchange for which officeholders were allowed to bequeath their offices to heirs or assignees. Seeing it as an opportunity to raise additional funds for the war, Anne and Mazarin decreed that the payment should be increased. The courts appealed to the parlement, which supported their cause.

However, the parlement went one step further and appointed thirty-two delegates to the newly established Chambre Saint-Louis. This was an assembly of representatives from each of the sovereign courts of France—the Parlement of Paris, the Cour des Aides, the Grand Conseil, and the Chambre des Comptes, which sought to reform the government and restore, as they saw it, order to the realm.[5] Defying Anne, who accused them of trying to "make a republic within a monarchy,"[6] they agreed upon a list of demands.[7] These included a version of habeas corpus, the abolition of the intendants, and the preservation of the rights and powers of officeholders. More audaciously, they demanded the right to superintend the crown's decisions on taxation, which would have made them more powerful than the king and equal to the House of Commons in England.[8]

Anne, who had sworn to preserve monarchical power and pass it on intact to Louis, refused to grant these demands. Mazarin, however, noted that the French armies were winning significant victories in the field and peace negotiations were going well. Believing that the war, the root of all their troubles, would soon be over, he advised Anne to allow parlement this one triumph. Louis watched as his mother wept with rage, but she saw the wisdom in Mazarin's words and agreed to remove the intendants, stipulating only that those serving in Picardy, Champagne, and the Lyonnais should stay. Her concession was welcomed by the Chambre Saint-Louis, but not to the extent that they suspended their sittings.

At this point, Louis's cousin, the prince de Condé,[9] the young and charismatic leader of the French forces, won a spectacular victory at Lens.[10] The battle had been crucial; the king of Spain knew that a defeated France "would fall prey to his ambition."[11] Condé recognized this too, and he urged his troops on with a stirring rallying cry, leading them to victory against heavy odds.[12] Louis, upon hearing the good news, exclaimed that parlement "would be very sorry" for it.

A few days later, Notre-Dame, decked with the captured colors of Archduke Leopold's Spanish forces, welcomed Louis and his court. They had come to hear the *Te Deum* in celebration of Condé's victory; yet, even as the hymn was being sung, three members of the parlement—Blancmesnil, Charton, and Broussel—were placed under arrest: Anne's revenge for the humiliation heaped upon her and Louis.

The most important of these men was Pierre Broussel, beloved as one of the fathers of the people. When the populace saw him being bundled into a carriage, they immediately began to riot for his release. Before long, they had blocked the roads with bricks, pieces of furniture, and chains. The infamous Day of the Barricades had dawned.

The following day, August 27, saw the situation deteriorate still further, forcing a delegation from the parlement to go to the Palais-Royal to petition for Broussel's release. Anne listened with disdain as she was urged to surrender to the will of the people. Throughout, the sound of children's laughter could be heard as Louis and his friends played outside, causing the comte d'Avaux to observe that while the young king played, he was losing his crown.[13] The comment was all the more poignant because this scene was taking place against the backdrop of civil war in England, where King Charles I was yet a prisoner.

As the negotiations continued, Anne knew she would eventually have to give way; she issued the order to free Broussel, but her price was that parlement should henceforth attend exclusively to matters of law. This was enough to cause the barricades to be removed and businesses to open again, but the peace that fell upon the city was uneasy. Night brought with it a dark rumor that the royal troops were planning to fire upon the people, and the barricades returned with astonishing swiftness. When news of this latest development reached the Palais-Royal, Philippe began to cry. It was all too much for the eight-year-old, but Louis drew his toy sword and adopted the air of a general. Putting his arms around his brother, he reassured him and tried to cheer him up. He then took Philippe to his room, tucking him safely into bed.[14]

Although Louis was aware of the troubles that had erupted in his capital, it is uncertain how much of it he understood. It was clearly a frightening time, in which the parlement threatened to seize the person of the king, while the people loathed the thought that he might leave Paris. Public anger and the resentment of the parlement were directed at Mazarin, but even Anne was afraid whenever she had to go out. Something had to be done, and it was decided that the court should retreat to Rueil[15] for a while under the plausible pretext that the Palais-Royal required a thorough cleaning.

For the first time, Louis was to be evacuated from his own capital. The plans were kept secret until the last moment when, at six in the morning of September 13, 1648, Louis, who had celebrated his tenth birthday only a week earlier, climbed into a carriage with the cardinal and a small entourage. Anne slowly made her way to the Val-de-Grâce in an attempt to show that nothing was amiss. As the king's carriage trundled towards the city gates, it encountered "some groups of rascals who shouted, 'To arms!' and attempted to pillage the carts that carried his baggage."[16] A panicked Mazarin sent a message from Louis to the queen begging her not to go to the Val-de-Grâce after all but to come straight to Rueil.

After a few days, the court moved on to Saint-Germain, from where Louis sent a declaration to parlement forbidding them to discuss anything except taxes and rentes. Yet the parlement had pressing matters to discuss; a delegation arrived at Saint-Germain, where a peace conference took place. The result was a charter of sorts, signed on October 22, in which most of the demands of the Chambre Saint-Louis were formally accepted.

At first, Anne was reluctant to sign the document because it seriously curtailed Louis's authority. She added her name to it only when Mazarin assured her that she could infringe it whenever she saw fit. Here was a valuable lesson for Louis in methods to use when dealing with his parlement. Two days after this, the Treaty of Westphalia was signed, a monumental achievement by Mazarin that ended the Thirty Years' War with the Austrian Habsburgs, but which went almost unnoticed.

The court returned to the Palais-Royal, and it was now that a schism appeared in the Fronde. Many of the bourgeois and senior members of the parlement were eager for peace, while some of the younger members continued to resist Mazarin. These divisions were exploited by the government, which adopted a policy of conciliation; however, this did nothing to stop the appearance of the *Mazarinades*. Defamatory and insulting to both Mazarin and Anne of Austria, the purpose of these pamphlets was to discredit the cardinal and further stir up opinion against him.[17] Their appearance coincided with a new threat to seize the person of the king, as well as a remonstrance against Mazarin, issued by the parlement on January 2, 1649.

There was a clear need for decisive action. Anne had no wish to "continue longer in a place where the royal authority was no longer respected, where her person was insulted daily, and where that of her minister [Mazarin] was threatened with every outrage."[18] After consulting Mazarin, Condé, and Orléans, she decided to remove Louis from Paris and "speak to its people henceforth by the mouth of cannon."[19]

January 5 marked the vigil of Epiphany. Life within the Palais-Royal went on as usual.[20] Louis sat in his mother's cabinet playing cards as the queen and her ladies looked on. As the afternoon darkened into evening, Mazarin and the princes paid court, but they left early to take supper with the maréchal de Gramont, who always gave a great feast on this day. Anne spoke to her ladies about her devotions and her plans to spend the next day at the Val-de-Grâce. The Twelfth Night cake was cut for Louis's amusement, and the bean was found in the Virgin's slice, so Anne was made the Twelfth Night queen. The ladies then shared a bottle of hippocras and retired to Anne's dressing room for supper. The talk was light—what the captain of the guards might be serving, Condé's little violin band, and they laughed at those who thought that Anne meant to leave Paris that night.

Then, just as Anne was about to undress for bed, the chief equerry, Béringhen, arrived, acting on Anne's secret orders. She told him to order the king's carriages, but, while Mme de Motteville and the other ladies suspected some plan, nobody except Anne was sure what was to happen. The queen then went to bed as usual, while the gates of the palace were closed "under orders not to open them again."

At three in the morning, Louis and Philippe were roused from their sleep and bundled into the carriages that stood at the garden gate of the Palais-Royal. Anne joined them, accompanied by the maréchal de Villeroy, Villequier, and Guitaut, captains of the royal guards, and Mme de Beauvais, Anne's chief lady-in-waiting. The carriages slowly made their way through the darkened streets, stopping at a prearranged rendezvous point to await Orléans, Condé, and members of the royal household. Mazarin's carriage drew up a few minutes later. Gradually, other members of the royal family converged, aroused at the last minute to flee the capital, so surprised by the orders that they carried no provisions with them. So much was at stake and "never was a night, without assault or warfare, more full of horror and anxiety" than the night of January 5, 1649.

The necessity for secrecy meant that no furnishings or linens had been taken to Saint-Germain in readiness for Louis's arrival. Mazarin had sent two small beds a few days earlier, one each for Louis and Anne, while he slept on a little camp bed; but the rest of the court and their households had to make do with straw, which rapidly "became so scarce at Saint-Germain that none could be bought for money."

When the people of Paris woke up to find that their king had left, all was despair and confusion. Those who could, left the city and returned to their country estates, others fled to Saint-Germain "to fulfill their duty." The duchesse de Montpensier noted that the Parisians would let nothing pass through the city gates, so Louis and Anne were deprived of every necessity.[21] They endured the hardship for several days until supplies finally came through.

The parlement saw that "visible marks of the royal vengeance were about to fall"[22] upon Paris and ordered the burghers to take up arms, while curses rained down upon Louis, Anne, Mazarin, and the princes. However, both Anne and Louis had written letters to the mayor and sheriffs of Paris, who then transmitted them to the parlement. Louis wrote:

> *Very dear and well-beloved. Being obliged with keen displeasure to leave our good city of Paris this night, in order that we be no longer exposed to the pernicious designs of the officers of our court of parliament, who, having understandings with the enemies of the State, after attacking our authority in various conjunctures and long abusing our kindness, have now conspired to seize our person, we therefore desire, by the advice of our very honored lady and mother, to tell you of our resolution, and order you, as we do hereby expressly, to employ yourselves, in all ways depending upon you, to prevent that anything shall happen in our said city to disturb its peace, or be prejudicial to our service: assuring you, as we hope, that all good burghers and inhabitants therein will continue in the duty of good and faithful subjects as they have until now, and that such will surely receive good and favorable treatment. We shall let you know within a few days the results of our resolution; meanwhile, confiding in your fidelity and your affection to our service, we shall now say nothing further or more expressly.[23]*

It is easy to forget that this confident and authoritative letter was written by an eleven-year-old. Louis made it clear that he had been aware of his imminent departure from Paris, but the event was traumatic all the same. The memory of that night—the fear of discovery, the cold, unprepared rooms at Saint-Germain, the inconvenience and the indignation of having to flee his own capital for the second time—would remain with Louis for the rest of his life. It instilled in him a dislike for Paris and led ultimately to his permanent removal to Versailles.

Of course, the court knew that friends and allies remained in Paris, officials who owed their posts to the crown or who operated under Mazarin's command. They had no quarrel with the cardinal and had no other desire than for life to return to normal. Moreover, Condé and a large force besieged Paris, although his efforts were resisted by the frondeurs, who mounted a spirited defense, and the vicomte de Turenne, who led an equally large army and threatened to storm the city and lift the siege. However, as well provisioned as they had been, the frondeurs began to run out of food, and, in the face of starvation, military failure, the threat of Spanish intrigues, and a general weariness, the Fronde began to fragment. News of the execution of Charles I in England brought home to many of the moderates the folly of continuing the uprising, and, on April 1, 1649, the Treaty of Rueil was signed. This was celebrated by a *Te Deum* and a display of fireworks, but it turned out to be nothing more than a truce. The treaty posed so much restriction on the royal authority that the court had no option but to regard it as a temporary measure.

Despite their insistence to the contrary, Anne feared that the frondeurs had wanted to dethrone Louis,[24] and she was naturally concerned about the effect the troubles would have on him. Although he had been forced to leave Paris on two occasions, the young king had at least been spared the libels of the authors of the *Mazarinades*. All that changed in the summer of 1649, when a pamphlet derided Louis and threatened him with the same fate as Charles I. Shortly afterwards, *Le Custode du Lit de la Reine* was published.[25] The title referred to the relationship between Anne and Mazarin, implying that they were lovers and, implicitly, once again raising questions about Louis's legitimacy; not for the last time would Louis's middle name, Dieudonné, be used as a weapon against him.[26] Anne's retribution was swift. Since the pamphlet was anonymous, she sued the printer, Morlot, in the court of the Châtelet, and he was sentenced to be hanged. The scaffold was duly erected in the Place de Grève, but as Morlot's tumbril approached, the crowd surged forward and beat off his escort with sticks. They then tore down the scaffold, broke the hangman's ladder, and smashed the windows of the nearby Hôtel de Ville for good measure. Morlot, under cover of the frenzy, disappeared into the mob, never to be seen again.[27]

Although tensions in Paris remained high, councillors meeting at Compiègne urged Anne to return Louis to his capital. She readily agreed in order to "let the enemies of the State see that neither she nor the king feared anything."[28]

On August 18, 1649, after more than eight months away, Louis made a magnificent entry into Paris.[29] On the plain of Saint-Denis, which was decorated with triumphal arches, Louis was met by his cheering people. The city officials knelt before him and declared their loyalty before escorting him on horseback to the Palais-Royal.[30]

On the following Saturday, Louis accompanied his mother to Notre-Dame. It was their first visit for many months and the queen's carriage was besieged by crowds of the king's subjects anxious to pay their respects, shower them with blessings and beg their forgiveness. Once inside the cathedral, Louis had to be lifted up so he could be shown to his people; delighted, they responded with shouts of "Vive le roi!"[31] Mme de Motteville was struck by the "natural impression of fidelity and love in the hearts of subjects towards their king. It is variable and defective, but it always easily returns."[32]

Then, on August 25, Louis went on horseback to the Jesuit church of Saint-Louis in the rue Saint-Antoine.[33] He "appeared at his best with his beautiful figure and wearing an admirably handsome suit," said Mme de Motteville, who described the purpose of the visit as "to awaken as much as possible the love of his subjects towards his person."[34] Louis was accompanied by the prince de Condé and his brother, the prince de Conti, while a number of seigneurs followed on behind. The people lining the streets shouted, "Vive le roi!" as the king, his hat in his hand, saluted princesses, ladies, and anyone who appeared at windows or on the specially erected scaffolding.[35] Here, at this Jesuit church, Louis gave "thanks to God, who had preserved France from the evils which had seemed to threaten her."[36]

Days later, on September 5, 1649, Louis celebrated his eleventh birthday, and the city of Paris marked the occasion with a huge fireworks display in the Place de Grève. Louis accepted an invitation to a grand ball at the Hôtel de Ville, where he danced the first *branle* with Mademoiselle, his cousin.[37] Amid all the beautiful people in their finest gowns, lace ribbons, and glittering jewels, "the good grace, the majestic bearing, and the flair of the king engaged, in all honesty, all the admiration of the company."[38] After the *branle*, Louis danced with Mme Le Feron,[39] who was followed by Laure Mancini, one of the cardinal's nieces, and several of the queen's ladies.

A sumptuous collation was served, complete with confections and excellent fruits; and while the fireworks bejewelled the sky,[40] the dancing carried on until dawn. Yet, for all the music and laughter, all was not well. Anne had ordered the whole court to attend the fête specifically "to embarrass the painted ladies, some of whom, belonging to the Fronde, displeased her."[41] More than this, she wanted "to avoid all show of fear, on the king's part, of his subjects so recently repentant."[42]

For a while a sense of calm had descended upon Paris, a feeling that life was returning to normal; but it was ephemeral. Condé, who felt he had not been sufficiently rewarded for his services to the court during the *Fronde parlementaire*, demanded redress. The immense popularity he had enjoyed following his victories at Rocroi and Lens was destroyed by his arrogance, pride, and cruelty.

Condé, supported by his brother, Conti, and their sister, the duchesse de Longueville, agitated to remove Mazarin from power and from France. The new uprising, the Fronde of the Princes, was driven by entirely selfish reasons, albeit concealed beneath a feigned concern for the interests of the people and the state. "An ill-intentioned prince of the blood is always to be dreaded," said Mme de Motteville, "his name is a great consideration among fractious minds, and he can be the cause at all times of great evils."[43] Now those fractious minds were demanding places in central government, provincial governorships, the restoration of their sinecures and honors. In short, they wanted a return to the old feudal system in which Louis would merely be the first among equals. The activities of the princes and the nobility demonstrated their political incompetence and fully justified the stance of Richelieu and Mazarin, who sought to exclude them from politics.

Most of the princes were influenced by powerful ladies: the coadjutor de Retz and the arch-intriguer, the duchesse de Chevreuse; Beaufort and the duchesse de Montbazon; Condé and the duchesse de Chatillon; Conti and Charlotte de Chevreuse, the beautiful daughter of the duchesse de Chevreuse. More dangerously, Turenne, who with Condé was one of the finest generals France had ever known, was brought into the new Fronde by his mistress, the duchesse de Longueville. In many ways, therefore, the Fronde of the Princes was as much driven by romantic intrigue as politics. Retz also engaged the services of La Rochefoucauld, who knew how to use propaganda for maximum impact.

Facing increasing hostility, Mazarin determined to continue Richelieu's work, which was to centralize power held by the king to create an absolute monarchy;[44] he would eventually be pressured into granting the princes' demands in a signed declaration, but his acquiescence would be merely a delaying tactic.

Anne, meanwhile, worried about Louis's religious instruction. She wanted to ensure that he would live up to his titles of His Most Christian Majesty and the Eldest Son of the Church, and on October 28, 1649, she wrote to the Jesuit father Florent de Montmorency, to ask him to recommend a director of conscience for the king. Their choice fell on Père Charles Paulin, who was thrilled to take on so important a post and vowed to form Louis "in all the piety worthy of so great a prince, to sow and develop in him the seeds of royal, or rather divine, virtue."[45]

Paulin would use Godeau's *Catechism royal*, in which the Catholic concept of the divine right of kings was upheld, teaching that kings

were called to priestly office. However, it failed to offer any intellectual discussion of these concepts and gave no indication of how
theologians had arrived at them. Louis, notwithstanding his divinely
appointed status, knew the practical application of these concepts but
would never fully understand their mystical origin.[46]

Within weeks, Louis was ready for his confirmation, and the *Gazette*
reported that the young king was confirmed on December 8, 1649, by
Dominique Séguier, bishop of Meaux, his first almoner. The service
took place at the chapel of Mazarin's Palais-Cardinal in the presence
of Louis's close family, including Condé, and "many other lords and
ladies of high condition."[47]

The next step was communion. For several weeks, Anne had toured
nearby churches to beg for divine favor for Louis as he prepared for
the sacrament. Unusually, the service was due to take place during the
Christmas Midnight Mass, rather than at Easter. Two reasons have been
put forward as to why Louis's first communion should be different,
the first being that Louis's piety was such that he could not wait until
Easter but was impatient to take the sacrament earlier. Alternatively,
to bring the celebration forward to Christmas would associate it with
the baptism of Clovis, an event remembered with great affection in
France and which, according to tradition, had taken place at Christmas.
Could the greatest Christian king have a finer example than that of
the first Christian king? wondered the *Gazette*.[48]

While Louis's confirmation had been a private, family affair, his first
communion would be a public occasion in which his subjects would
share. The royal children of France were, after all, "the children of
the people of Paris and of the entire nation."[49] With this in mind, the
timing of the service was changed from midnight to earlier in the day.
Moreover, it would not be held in the chapel of the Palais Cardinal
but in Louis's own parish church, Saint-Eustache.

At ten in the morning of Christmas Eve, Louis made his confession
to Père Paulin before entering his carriage, accompanied by Mazarin,
Philippe, and his governor, the maréchal de Villeroy. At the entrance

to the church, he was supported by the duc de Mercœur, Villequier, the captain of the guards, and the chief equerry, Béringhen, on one side, and the comte de Saint-Aignan, the marquis de Chapes, and Montglat on the other. Louis was received by the priests, and, carrying the cross and the holy water, he processed to the choir.

The mass was celebrated by Bishop Séguier, after which the altar was prepared for Louis's first communion.[50] The king approached "with humility and zeal," while Mazarin presented the Gospels for Louis to kiss. Séguier then offered Louis the bread before receiving the golden, lidded cup of wine from the *chef de gobelet*, which was then offered to the king.

After dining with Mazarin at the Palais Cardinal, Louis and his cortège went to hear vespers at the Jacobins of the rue Saint-Jacques before he joined his mother at the Val-de-Grâce. Louis's first communion had been a day of piety and celebration, which he had shared with his family and his people, who had lined the streets to see him, despite the Christmas Eve services that were taking place in every parish.

The first week of 1650 saw Louis performing religious duties. On New Year's Day, he attended services at Notre-Dame before going to the Maison Professe du Jesuits for vespers and a sermon by Père Guiard, Jacobin of the Grand Convent. Two days later, he was to be found at Sainte-Geneviève, where he accepted an invitation to take a collation with the canons following the office. On the fifth, he presented six consecrated loaves to his parish church of Saint-Eustache, which was decorated for the occasion with streamers bearing the king's arms.[51] Louis's acts of piety were entirely sincere. He was, and always would be, deeply religious and ever mindful of his divine appointment and his relationship with God. This would lead to much self-reflection and inner conflict in the years to come.

Of course, Louis was not only a king but also a young boy overflowing with energy. While the court was staying at Fontainebleau, Louis was getting ready for bed when he decided he would do a hundred jumps and a hundred somersaults on his bed before he climbed in to sleep. On one particularly high jump, he missed his footing as he landed, which caused him to fly off the side of the bed and bang his head on the platform. La Porte rushed to pick him up and was relieved to find that the king had only a slight injury, having been saved from the worst of the impact by landing on the carpet.[52] Needless to say, Louis was banned from turning somersaults ever again, but he loved energetic pastimes, which included playing soldiers in a specially built fort in the gardens of the Palais-Royal.[53]

In those early days of 1650, when he was not to be found in church, Louis was practising manège, or the art of horsemanship. A special course had been built in the grounds of the Palais-Cardinal, where Louis would tilt at the ring. On this particular occasion, he carried off the ring in five out of seven courses, much to the delight of everyone watching.[54]

On January 18, 1650, Anne hurried Louis into her oratory, shut the door, and made him kneel down. In the quiet of this sacred space, she explained to the king that she, Mazarin, and the duc d'Orléans had agreed to arrest Condé, who now posed a real danger to the crown. She then ordered Louis to "pray to God with her for the success of the undertaking, the end of which she awaited with much emotion and a beating heart."[55]

Condé was arrested as he arrived, so he thought, for a council meeting. At the same time, Conti and the duc de Longueville were taken into custody to prevent their attempting "by a civil war to succor the first."[56] All three were imprisoned in the donjon at Vincennes. The plan, which had been devised under conditions of the utmost secrecy, had been carried out to perfection, and it provided Louis with an indelible lesson in dissimulation. Moreover, since the princes had alienated many of their former friends and supporters in Paris, there was little chance that anyone would come to their rescue. However, they still had loyal supporters in the provinces, where they held governorships and exercised considerable power over the people. As such, Mazarin took Louis on tour of these provinces in order to ensure the support of his subjects.

As king, Louis was seen by his subjects as the guardian of their rights. A prince or a nobleman could pose a tremendous threat to these rights as they robbed, tortured, and murdered the citizenry with impunity. There was no limit to the damage they could do, both to the local economy and to the well-being of the people.[57] It was part of Louis's duty as king to ensure that his subjects were protected.

Louis's tour was, therefore, in the public interest. The *Gazette* assured its readers, who were anxious about the king's absence from Paris, that there was "no reason to be dismayed . . . it is not His Majesty's purpose to wait until trouble has risen before protecting his subjects against it, for, like a good doctor, he believes that prevention is better than cure."[58]

The first stop was Normandy, the governorship of which was held by the duc de Longueville, and which was one of the "market gardens" of France, where much of the food supplied to Paris was produced. In April, Louis journeyed into Burgundy, which was governed by Condé.

Paris, meanwhile, was left in the care of the duc d'Orléans, but his loyalty, which was never strong, was now wavering. When Mazarin compared the behavior of the Parlement and the nobility with that of the English regicides, an outraged Orléans joined the rebellion of the princes.[59]

When the uprising led by Retz joined the Fronde of the Princes,[60] Orléans was appointed leader. His first priority was to free the princes, and the first step to this goal was to secure the exile of Mazarin. The cardinal's supporters urged Anne to remove Louis to a place of safety, put herself at the head of the army, and force the submission of Orléans and the parlement. She insisted, however, that Mazarin was firmly in charge, adding for good measure that nothing would induce her to release the princes.

On February 4, Retz delivered a rousing speech in parlement, demanding the cardinal's exile. Confronted by these demands, combined with death threats, Mazarin had little choice but to comply. He left Paris on February 6,[61] leaving Anne and Louis in Paris and very alone. Anne confided to Mme de Motteville that she wished "it were always night, for though I cannot sleep the silence and the solitude please me; in the daytime I see none but those who would betray me."[62]

Within a day, a rumor spread among the populace of Paris that the queen was planning to remove Louis from the capital, and two squadrons of cavalry were stationed at strategic points in the city.[63] Orléans sent M. des Ouches, captain of his Cent-Suisses, to the Palais-Royal to make sure the king was still in residence and to ask Anne to put a stop to the rumor.[64] Anne assured Ouches that she had no intention of taking Louis away from Paris, and the proof was that both the king and Philippe were in bed, sleeping soundly. In order that the guard could "bear testimony to the duc d'Orléans," she bid him go to "see the king in his bed, being certain that the noise would not waken him." Ouches duly went to Louis's chamber and, obeying the queen's command, lifted the curtain and "watched him for some time in a deep sleep."

Anne's action persuaded Ouches that she had no desire to leave Paris, and, as he returned to his master he did his best to calm the people in the streets through which he passed, advising them to be quiet because their king was asleep. The populace, however, insisted upon seeing the king for themselves. A number of them entered the Palais-Royal "crying out that the king must be shown to them, for they wished to see him." Anne, hearing their cries, ordered the doors to be thrown open and the crowd to be conducted to Louis's bedchamber. "The rioters were enchanted at this frank treatment," said Mme de Motteville, adding:

> They stood around the king's bed, the curtains of which had been opened, and returning once more to a spirit of affection, gave him a thousand benedictions. They looked at him sleeping for a long time and could not admire him sufficiently. The sight gave them a great

respect for him; it increased their desire not to lose his presence, but they now expressed this feeling with sentiments of fidelity. Their excitement ceased, and whereas they had entered the Palais-Royal like furies, they left it full of gentleness, asking God with all their hearts to preserve their young king, whose presence had the power to charm them.[65]

Although Louis appeared to be asleep throughout this ordeal, he almost certainly was not, and the memory of this incident, more than any other, would remain with him. It would influence his decision to leave Paris for good and establish his court at Versailles, where he could control who could see him and, more importantly, who could not.

Louis was effectively a prisoner in his own capital as Orléans posted armed guards on all the gates of Paris to prevent him from leaving.[66] Meanwhile, Anne signed an order for the release of the princes;[67] a few days later, parlement registered a royal edict stating that no foreigners, not even naturalized subjects, should be allowed to become a minister. It was a direct attack on Mazarin, who, as he made his way to Germany, had received news of the king's detention. He made a detour to Le Havre and released the princes before travelling on to Schloss Bruhl, near Cologne. Here, he maintained contact with Louis and Anne through secret agents.

Louis had now been imprisoned inside his own palace for a month. To help ease the tension and introduce a sense of normality, Anne staged a ballet, in which Louis danced the part of a knight in the entourage of Cassandra. This was something of a triumph for Louis, for it was his first solo part. At another time, he played the part of the deity, Bacchante, in *Ballet des Fêtes de Bacchus*. Louis's lines looked forward to the future glory that was his as a result of his divinely granted birthright. However, when news of the events reached Mazarin, he sent a message of reproof; he felt it was important to emphasize that Louis and Philippe were depressed by being held against their will.[68]

Despite the cardinal's warnings, life did assume a sense of normality, and that summer Louis would often go to the Seine to enjoy a swim. One day, as he was driving along the Cours-la-Reine on his way back to the palace, he met Condé coming the other way. Condé, who had made a spectacular entry into Paris a few weeks earlier but had never paid Louis the courtesy of a visit, was bound by court etiquette to stop, climb out of his carriage, and salute the king. On this occasion, however, he remained in his carriage and merely bowed to Louis as he passed. It was a terrible affront to the king, and one Louis would never forget. Condé was later rebuked in parlement for his insolence, which not only upset the hierarchical order that governed all aspects of life but also brought home to him just how far his power had diminished in the capital. With nothing further to lose, as he saw it, Condé decided on civil war. His ultimate aim was to separate Navarre and Guyenne from France and rule in those regions as king in his own right.[69] There was little Louis could do to resist his cousin's ambition as yet, but he stood on the threshold of a long-awaited milestone in his life, one that would bring about a complete reversal in his affairs and those of the state: Louis was about to attain his majority.

It was eight o'clock in the morning on September 7, 1651.[70] Louis was lying in his bed in the Palais-Cardinal when the master of ceremonies came to inform him that the queen was coming to see him. She had with her Philippe, Louis's only brother, the duc d'Orléans, and many of the dukes and peers, marshals of France, and other nobles of the kingdom.[71]

Louis, upon receiving the news, sent the duc de Joyeuse, his grand chamberlain, to meet the queen at the door and escort her and her entourage to the alcove of the king's bed. Louis moved to the opening in the balustrade and received the queen, who bowed to him. He raised her up with a kiss and made a short discourse, at the end of which Philippe gave his brother "a very respectful salutation as for homage," as did Orléans and all the others in their turn. Louis then ordered Joyeuse to mount everyone on horseback, while observing strict order of rank.

The cavalcade was spectacular. It was led by the chevalier de Saint-Masgrin at the head of a company of one hundred cavaliers of the queen's light horse, and heralded by four trumpeters wearing black velvet trimmed with silver lace. The chevalier wore a coat embroidered in gold and silver and was mounted upon a white horse, caparisoned, and with ribbons in its mane and tail and a saddlecloth that matched the coat of its rider. Next came the two-hundred-strong company of the king's light horse under the command of the comte d'Olonne, and heralded by four trumpeters in blue velvet laced with gold and silver. Resplendent in his coat of gold and silver, a baldric adorned with pearls, and "hat with white plumes, dead-leaf and flame colored, with a gold cord around it," the comte rode a white horse, well caparisoned, with a red saddlecloth embroidered to match his coat. They were followed by the company of the grand provost on foot, the Cent-Suisses, and the aide of the ceremonies. The seigneurs of the court came behind them, with the governors of the towns and the lieutenant-generals of the provinces.

Six of the king's trumpeters, in blue velvet, marched next, and they were followed by six more heralds on horseback. They wore velvet caps and coats of arms of crimson velvet powdered with golden fleur-de-lis, and they were carrying the caduceus in their hands.[72] Behind them came the sieur de Saintot, master of ceremonies, whose job it was to ride back and forth keeping everyone in their place. The marquis de La Meilleraye, grand master of the artillery, followed him with the marshals of France riding two by two. All were richly dressed and riding large horses, whose trappings were "laden with gold and silver."

The comte d'Harcourt, the grand equerry of France, came next, bearing the king's sword in a blue velvet scabbard powdered with golden fleur-de-lis. His doublet was of cloth of gold and silver, and he was mounted upon a dapple-gray charger, whose crimson trappings were embroidered with gold in Spanish point, with two scarves of black taffeta for reins. He was followed by a host of pages and valets in an abundance of red, white, and blue plumes, who led the bodyguard on foot, the ushers, and the mace bearers.

It was now that the crowd got its first glimpse of the king. Among the witnesses to this spectacle was the English writer and diarist John Evelyn, who was visiting his friend Thomas Hobbes. Watching from the window, they saw Louis riding an Isabella barb, whose caparison was powdered[73] with crosses of the Order of the Holy Ghost, and fleur-de-lis, while:

> the king himself, like a young Apollo, was in a suit so covered with rich embroidery, that one could perceive nothing of the stuff under it; he went almost the whole way with his hat in his hand, saluting the ladies and acclamators, who had filled the windows with their beauty, and the air with "Vive le Roi." [74]

Evelyn added that Louis "seemed a prince of grave yet sweet countenance."

The official account noted Louis's "august countenance and gentle gravity, truly royal, and his natural civility [which] made him observable to all for the delight of the human race." The king "seemed of such tall stature that it was hard to believe he had not yet completed his fourteenth year."[75] The shouts of the crowds and the general excitement made Louis's cream-colored barb "rear and curvet, verifying the words of Plutarch, that horses never flatter kings; which gave occasion to our king to show himself one of the best riders in his kingdom."

Behind Louis were the senior members of his household, and then "the princes followed in great numbers, and the dukes and peers, without precedence of rank and in confusion, closed the cavalcade." The coach carrying the Regent Anne, Philippe, and various princesses and other ladies came next, and this was followed by the coaches of the "maids-of-honor, the ladies of the Court, and the suite of their Majesties."

The procession followed the length of the "rues Saint-Honoré, de la Ferronnerie, de Saint-Denis, past the Châtelet, by the rue de Crucifix-Saint-Jacques, the bridge Notre-Dame, the Marché-Neuf" before entering the courtyard of the Palais de la Cité from the rue Sainte-Anne.

With the cries of "Vive le roi" ringing in his ears, Louis dismounted and was received at the foot of the Sainte-Chapelle by the bishop of Bayeux and his clergy. After mass, Louis made his way to the sound of trumpets to the *grande chambre* and took his seat on the *lit de justice*. The silence that followed was broken by the calm, clear voice of the king, who announced:

> *Messieurs, I have come to my parlement to tell you that, following the law of my State, I intend to take the government myself; and I hope by the goodness of God that it will be with piety and justice. My chancellor will tell you more particularly my intentions.*

Following a short harangue by the Chancellor Séguier, Anne leaned forward in her seat to the left of the king and said:

> *Monsieur, This is the ninth year that, by the last will of the late king, my very honored lord, I have taken care of your education and the government of your State; God having, by his goodness, blessed my labor and preserved your person, which is dear and precious to me and to all your subjects. Now that the law of the kingdom calls you to government of this monarchy, I return to you, with great satisfaction, the power which was given me to govern it; and I hope that God will do you the favor to assist you with His spirit of strength and prudence, to render your reign a happy one.*

At this, Louis replied:

> *Madame, I thank you for the care you have been pleased to take of my education and of the administration of my kingdom, I beg you to continue to give me your good advice, and I desire that you shall be, after myself, the head of my council.*

Anne now rose from her seat and approached Louis in readiness to bow to him, but Louis stepped down from his *lit de justice*, "went to her, and, embracing her, kissed her; after which they returned to their seats."

Next was the turn of Philippe, who knelt before Louis, kissed his hand, and professed his fidelity. He was followed by the duc d'Orléans and the prince de Conti, and then all the other princes, chancellors, dukes and peers, the ecclesiastics, marshals of France, and the crown officers, in their turn.

Then, after a short speech by the chief president, the chancellor ordered the doors to be opened so the people could enter. They heard the sieur Guiet, clerk of the parlement, reading the edicts issued by Louis against blasphemy and duelling, and the declaration of the innocence of the prince de Condé. This declaration was surprising, given Condé's activities over the past several months; however, Louis was prepared to accept the opinions of his lawyers, and stated that "all warnings that the prince was plotting against the king whether within or without the kingdom, were not believed by His Majesty, who, on the contrary, condemned them as false and artfully invented." It was, therefore, Louis's will and pleasure that all writings on the subject that had been given to parlement and other courts should be suppressed and, if necessary, revoked and annulled as false and counterfeit, "so that in future nothing might be imputed to his cousin the Prince de Condé." Louis's gesture was one of generosity, an olive branch calculated to placate Condé and restore peace to the kingdom; yet, even as the declaration of his innocence was being read out, Condé was committing treason by amassing an army against the king and negotiating an alliance with Philip IV of Spain, whose country was still at war with France.

Returning to the Palais-Royal, Anne confided to her ladies that she saw the end of her regency "with veritable joy; if any regret mingled with this joy it was that of not placing in the hands of the king her son as absolute a sovereign authority as she wished." However, Louis's majority deprived the frondeurs of one of their main objections to the rule of Anne and Mazarin, which was that only an adult king could rule in the fullness of the royal authority. Louis was now able to issue decrees in his own right, which would confirm and support those of his mother and the cardinal. Although the parlement accepted this new state of affairs, Condé and his supporters did not, and so the civil war entered a new chapter.[76]

Condé and his Spanish allies attempted an invasion of France, but their plan was ultimately frustrated at Rethel by Turenne, who had tired of Condé's attitude and treachery. For the next few weeks Condé travelled through his governorships enlisting reinforcements, obliging Louis once again to follow in his footsteps. The king appearing before his subjects won their hearts and their loyalty, but Louis's was affected by the stress of the situation he was facing. One night, at Corbeil, he desired his brother, Philippe, to sleep in his chamber, a room that was so narrow there was space for only one person to pass through at a time. In the morning, Louis, without thinking, spat on Philippe's bed, and Philippe responded in kind. Louis, annoyed by this, spat in Philippe's face, upon which Philippe leaped onto Louis's bed and pissed over it. Louis then pissed on Philippe's bed. They then set about tugging at the curtains before challenging each other to a fight. They had to be restrained by La Porte and M. de Villeroy. Philippe was more angry than the king, but Louis was the more difficult to pacify.[77]

Everywhere he went, Louis was followed by sick and maimed soldiers begging for help, but he had no money to give them. However, the plight of the soldiers, bad though it was, diminished in the face of that of the people. Peasants in search of protection from the rebel armies that ravaged the countryside besieged the court wherever it went. Unable to put their cattle out to pasture, they brought the animals with them, only to see them die of hunger. When the cattle died, the people did too, for they had nothing to live on except the meager charity the court could afford to offer. The people had no protection from the summer heat or the chill of the night except for a few pathetic awnings, carts, and vans in the streets. "When the mothers were dead," added La Porte, "the children died after; and I saw on the bridge of Melun . . . three children lying on their dead mother, one of them still suckling her."[78]

Louis was not oblivious to the suffering of his people, but he was powerless to do anything about it. On October 8, he issued decrees against his cousin of Condé, but it would take armed conflict finally to subdue him. The tide, however, was slowly turning. Condé, who was hatching a plan to capture Louis, once again encountered Turenne at the Battle of Bléneau on April 7, 1652. The prince, soundly beaten, was forced to retreat.

Condé now turned northwards, his defeat in the provinces having motivated him to lay siege to Paris. Already he had many partisans within the city, and he found a faithful ally in Mademoiselle, who acted on behalf of her father, the duc d'Orléans. Having raised an army at Orléans, she put the town at the disposal of the prince.

By now, Condé was encamped outside Paris, having been refused entry by the city authorities. Thinking to enter through the Porte Saint-Antoine, he ordered his troops to march eastwards, while Louis and the royal army, under Turenne's command, stood to the northeast of the city monitoring events. Upon receiving intelligence of Condé's maneuver, Turenne advanced to trap the prince against the city walls, where he and his troops would be crushed.

It was July 2, 1652, one of the hottest days of the year, when the encounter between the royal forces and the rebel army took place. After several hours, an exhausted Condé went to the little house where Mademoiselle was staying. "He was in a deplorable state," observed Mademoiselle; "his face covered with dust, his hair dishevelled, his neck and shirt stained with blood."[79] Although he had not been wounded, the prince's cuirass was battered, and he carried his naked sword in his hand, having lost its scabbard. "Ah, Mademoiselle, I am in despair," he said. "I have lost all my friends. Messieurs de Nemours, de la Rochefoucault [sic], and Clinchamp, are mortally wounded." Mademoiselle reassured him that the surgeons had seen his friends and their wounds were not as bad as he feared. Although that news cheered Condé somewhat, he wept bitterly. "You must excuse the grief in which you see me," he told her. When he recovered, he supervised the organization of the baggage and then returned to his men.

Shortly after this, Mademoiselle committed the act for which she is best remembered. Going to the Bastille, which was situated just within the Porte Saint-Antoine, she ordered the cannon to be loaded and fired on the king's troops.[80] Paul Mancini, Mazarin's nephew, "young and brave, and already a man of honor, was mortally wounded; he paid with his life and his blood for the misfortune of his uncle, who seemed to be the pretext for this unjust war."[81] Mancini, who was being groomed to be his uncle's heir, had been Louis's best friend.

Mademoiselle then opened the city gates to admit Condé and what remained of his troops. A few days later, his men set fire to the Hôtel de Ville, killing several officials. Condé now became commander of the entire forces of France, while Orléans took the post of lieutenant-général of the kingdom; Broussel, whose arrest had begun the Fronde, was now *prévôt des marchands* of Paris, while the duc de Beaufort was made the governor of the city. With his people starving and the Spanish threatening his eastern border, Louis was urged once again to withdraw, this time to Lyons, but Turenne forbade it. Instead, the king went to Pontoise, where he established a parlement to rival that of Paris, which was under Condé's thumb; although Mazarin felt obliged to withdraw from France once more, it was to be a temporary measure. Condé took up arms again, but he was soundly defeated once more by Turenne at Villeneuve-le-Roi. The prince retreated to Flanders, where he placed his sword at the service of the king of Spain.

On October 21, the people of Paris crowded the streets as Louis made a spectacular entry into his capital. Riding on horseback, with his hat in the air, Louis was accompanied by Charles of England and his brother, James, duke of York, both of whom were still living in exile in France. They were followed by Prince Thomas of Carignan-Savoy, and several dukes, peers, marshals of France, and officers of the crown.[82] The Palais-Royal was filled with too many unhappy memories for Louis to want to move back in there. Instead, he took up residence in the Louvre, which had been his first home in Paris; he had decided that "private houses without moats were not suitable for him."[83]

The following day, October 22, Louis held a *lit de justice*. The divided parlements now became one again, with the direct order from the king that it was not to meddle in affairs of state. Louis also announced the exile of several of the leading frondeurs, including his cousin, Mademoiselle, whose actions at the Bastille Louis would never forget.

As Christmastime approached, the court received a visit from Retz. Recently made a cardinal, he had met Louis and the Regent Anne as they had entered the Louvre all those weeks ago, and he had offered them his congratulations. Now he returned to the Louvre to pay his respects to the king and his mother. Louis and Anne had already decided that they would arrest Retz when he came to make his obeisance, but this had proved to be their first opportunity to do so.

Retz entered the palace and made his way to the apartment of the maréchal de Villeroy before going to see the king. Louis, having been warned of the cardinal's approach, was expecting him. Coming out of the queen's apartment, where he had been waiting, he met Retz in the corridor, "employing on this occasion that judicious moderation which has since been so admirably practised by him in all his actions." With a pleasant countenance, Louis asked the cardinal if he had seen the queen. When Retz said that he had not, Louis invited him to follow; at the same time, he signalled an order to Captain Villequier to arrest Retz the moment he left Anne's apartment.[84] The Fronde finally at an end, Louis remarked that "there should be no one on stage."[85]

FOUR

"The Anointed of the Lord"

T he *Ballet de la Nuit*, composed by Isaac de Benserade, was first performed in the Petit-Bourbon, just outside the Louvre, in the presence of Queen Anne, Mazarin, and the whole court. For several weeks during the winter of 1652–53, Louis and the other dancers had practiced their steps and patiently submitted to several fittings, as the costumers had designed, sewed, and adjusted the various sumptuous outfits. Even so, as polished as the performance promised to be, it almost ended in disaster on its opening night,[1] when one of the curtains burst into flames. Undeterred, Louis kept his composure, and his calmness reassured the company and the audience.

The ballet comprised four *vielles*, or watches, each depicting a phase of the night as the hours passed between sunset and sunrise.[2] The first *vielle*, the hours of six to nine in the evening, saw the sun sink beneath the horizon as Night rode a chariot drawn by owls and escorted by four Hours of the Day, one of whom was played by Louis. Sea-nymphs were pursued by Huntresses, while Shepherds made their weary way back to their homes from the pastures. Gallants courted their Ladies, while Beggars and Vagabonds gathered by the Cour des Miracles.[3] The second *vielle* showed the hours of nine in the evening to midnight and depicted the evening entertainments, while Sport and Mirth, one of whom was played by Louis, escorted Venus, the Queen of Love. In the third *vielle*, which ranged from midnight to three in the morning, the Moon rose, her chariot accompanied by the stars. Two astrologers, Ptolemy and Zoroaster, observed the night sky, as Dwarfs came out of snail-shells, four Old Witches rode to Sabbat on broomsticks, and six Werewolves looked on. Louis was one of a group of sightseers who watched these creatures of the night. Lastly, between three in the morning and sunrise, Sleep and Silence danced across the stage, followed by a sequence of Dreams: the Bashful Lovers' Dream, the Optimist's Dream, and, finally, the king dancing the part of the Angry Man's Dream. At last the Morning Star appeared, played by Philippe, who heralded the Dawn. The final piece, the Rising Sun, was danced by Louis in a spectacular costume.

The *Ballet de la Nuit* was so successful that it was performed on another four occasions, and, in order to allow Louis's subjects to enjoy the presentation, the Petit Bourbon was opened to the public.

It was not unusual for Louis to exert himself to the point that he became ill. As he was rehearsing for the *Ballet de la Nuit*, he suffered a skin rash on his face, although the application of a balm pomade made by Vallot quickly cleared it.[4] However, following the performance of March 8, Louis was seized by a violent shivering, which lasted for an hour before giving way to a severe attack of fever. This continued through the night, much to the concern of the physicians. Again, Louis's condition was alleviated, this time with a bleeding, which was done the following morning. The next day, Louis was given an enema followed by a *bouillon purgatif pour le Roi*, a soup containing cream of tartar and senna.[5] Louis performed the ballet once again on March 16 so that his subjects could see that he had fully recovered from his illness.

However, physical exercise was not the only cause of Louis's maladies. Vallot noted that the king had overindulged in sugared drinks and was eating too many Portuguese oranges, which resulted in indigestion. Louis then went too far the other way and observed the Lenten fast too religiously, much against Vallot's advice.[6]

April saw Louis once again take to the stage, this time in *Les Noces de Pelée et de Thétis*, in which he danced alongside several young people who were to play important roles at his court. Two of these were the children of Charles I of England: James, duke of York, who would go on to become James II of England, and Henriette, who would marry Louis's brother, Philippe, while Mlle de Mortemart, the future Mme de Montespan, would go on to become Louis's most celebrated mistress.

Louis danced several parts in this ballet, including a fury and La Guerre. For La Guerre, he wore a Romanesque tunic with gold flashings and a helmet festooned with a mass of orange plumes, as he wielded a naked sword in his right hand and a lighted flambeau in his left. Louis also reprised his role of Apollo, who appears in the first entrée and shares the stage with female courtiers playing the nine Muses. Louis/Apollo relates how he endlessly runs after *la gloire* rather than Daphne, but by the third stanza he admits that, although he is a god, his fate is to run after women. Louis/Apollo must also decide which of the nine Muses is the more attractive; already the young king's senses in matters of sex are encouraged to awaken.[7] Equally important, however, was the message the ballet was intended to convey. Louis/ Apollo vanquishes a python, a symbol of the powers of darkness; in this context, it represented Louis overcoming disorder and the Fronde.

As the summer approached, preparations were underway for the most important event in the young king's life so far: his consecration, or *sacre.* The ceremony should have taken place when Louis came of age, but the troubles caused by the Fronde meant it had to be delayed. Now, in his sixteenth year, Louis made his way through the countryside and sumptuous vineyards of Champagne to the ancient city of Reims.

For almost six hundred years, the Cathedral of Notre-Dame de Reims had provided the setting for the coronation of the kings of France.[8] According to custom, the king would travel to the city in a magnificent carriage. Then, at about half a league from Reims, he would mount a horse to make his entrance. Louis broke with this tradition. He decided, instead, to enter in his mother's carriage, a fitting tribute to the lady who had fought so hard to preserve his royal authority and to make this day a reality.[9]

It was on June 4, 1654, that Louis was met at the door of Notre-Dame de Reims by the bishop of Soissons[10] and his canons, the civic officials, and the people of Reims, who thronged to catch their first glimpse of their king. Louis was escorted to the altar, where, after a short prayer was said over him, he knelt as the *Beata Dei Genitrix* was sung. He then withdrew to the archiepiscopal palace, which was to be his home for the length of his visit.[11]

The following day, Louis and his mother heard mass in the Benedictine Abbey of Reims, after which they visited the tomb of Saint Rémi. This saint had baptized Louis's predecessor, Clovis, using oil said to have been brought to earth from heaven by a dove. This tradition, which dated back to Archbishop Hincmar,[12] underpinned the French coronation ceremony, since a drop of this oil was used in the holy chrism with which all French kings were anointed.

On the eve of his coronation, Louis attended vespers at the Cathedral of Notre-Dame de Reims. After the service, he presented a silver-gilt *chef reliquaire* of Saint Rémi to the cathedral. This was a reliquary in the shape of a human head, designed to hold the skull or facial bones of a saint. Louis had it engraved with his own image on one side and a Latin inscription commemorating the event of his coronation on the other. The king then made his confession before retiring for the night.

The quiet of the archiepiscopal palace was disturbed at six in the morning, when the bishops of Beauvais and Châlons, resplendent in the full robes of their office, proceeded towards the closed doors of the king's chamber. The precentor rapped lightly with his silver staff, upon which a voice from within asked, "What do you desire?" This was the grand chamberlain, who received the answer, "The king." The grand chamberlain replied, "The king is sleeping." This ritual was repeated twice more, after which the bishop of Châlons said, "We desire Louis, the fourteenth of that name, son of the great King Louis the Thirteenth, whom God has given to be our king."

The doors now opened to admit the bishops, who stood at the foot of the richly adorned bed in which Louis lay. Louis, who pretended to be asleep, opened his eyes and crossed himself with holy water, which had been offered by the bishop of Châlons. After the bishop said a short prayer over him, Louis rose from the bed. He was wearing a shirt of white Holland cloth beneath a tunic of red satin edged in gold. These garments had openings that corresponded to the places where he would be anointed with the holy chrism. Over this simple but beautiful costume was placed a floor-length robe of cloth of silver, while a black velvet cap, garnished with a row of diamonds, a feather, and a white aigrette attached with a diamond was set on his head.

The two bishops placed themselves to the right and left of the king as they escorted him out of the palace to the door of the cathedral. The great procession was about to begin. It was led by the grand provost, who was followed by guards, drummers, trumpeters, and other musicians, all dressed in white taffeta and playing oboes, flutes, bagpipes, and sackbuts. The heralds of the various provinces of France came next, bearing staffs and clad in velvet with white stockings and tunics powdered with fleur-de-lis. These were followed by the *gentilshommes de bec-de-corbins*, named after the beak-shaped head of their halberds. The grand master of the ceremonies, in his black-hooded cloak with its silver embroidery, came next, followed by the chevaliers and officers of the Saint-Esprit. M. le Connétable, who bore the naked sword, was accompanied by two gentlemen ushers carrying the heavy silver-gilt mace.

The congregation now caught their first glimpse of Louis, who entered the cathedral with the two bishops. The Chancellor Séguier followed, wearing a crimson satin robe and *mortier* of cloth of gold. Behind him walked various members of the royal household, as well as the captain of the Scottish Guards, the comte de Noailles. Finally, there were the six *gardes de la manche* dressed in white velvet with silver embroidery.

The cathedral was a riot of color. Rich tapestries hung from the galleries, falling in three tiers that reached to the floor of the chancel, which was covered in Turkish carpets. In the center stood a chair covered in purple velvet powdered with golden fleur-de-lis, and a prie-dieu. On the high altar, upon which lay rich vestments of gold-embroidered satin, two *chef reliquaires*, of Saint Louis and Saint Rémi, caught the light of the flickering candles. Two daises, twelve feet high, stood to the right and left of the high altar and were furnished with chairs for Queen Anne and other dignitaries. From either side of the chancel, two broad staircases, carpeted with cloth of gold, led to the rood loft, the balustrade of which had been removed to allow a clear view of the throne, which stood on a raised dais beneath a purple canopy powdered with golden lilies of France.

As litanies were sung against the background of cheers coming from outside, Louis walked to the chancel and knelt on the prie-dieu, where he said a quiet but fervent prayer. The holy ampulla was now brought in by the grand prior of Saint Rémi, who entered the cathedral on a white charger magnificently caparisoned in silver, while four knights of the holy ampulla, all on horseback, held over his head a canopy of cloth of silver. The vial was set on the altar with the rest of the royal regalia.

The bishop of Soissons, assisted by the bishops of Beauvais and Châlons, approached Louis and asked him to take the oath to defend the rights of the Catholic Church. Louis, sitting and with his head covered, assented and said the oath in a firm, clear voice. The bishop now asked all present if they would accept Louis as their king. This part of the rites dated back to a time when kings were elected from among their peers. The traditional answer was "We agree," but because kingship was now a birthright, this custom had long since fallen into disuse; instead, the cathedral fell into silence as a mark of consent.

Louis was endowed with the trappings of kingship. Sandals of purple velvet were placed on his feet, over which were fastened the golden spurs. The bishop blessed the sword inside its scabbard before unsheathing it and offering it to Louis. The king kissed it and, in a prayer, dedicated it to the service of God. He then handed the sword to the constable, who held it upright as a symbol of royal power.

The bishop now took the holy ampulla and drew a drop of oil the size of a grain of wheat. He placed this on a golden paten of the chalice of Saint Rémi. Louis prostrated himself on a square of purple velvet embroidered with fleur-de-lis, which lay before the altar, as litanies were chanted and blessings of God and the saints were called down upon him. As the king knelt, his silver robe was removed in readiness for the most sacred part of the coronation ceremony, and the one after which it is named, *la sacre*, or anointing. Louis was anointed in seven places: the top of his head, the chest, between the shoulders, on the right and left shoulder, and inside each elbow.

Louis now received the vestments of his office. His silver robe was replaced, and a dalmatic, which represented the orders of deacon and subdeacon, was placed over it. On top of that he wore a great mantle of blue velvet powdered with golden fleur-de-lis, the left side of which was raised, as was that of a priest. Louis knelt once again and was anointed twice more: on the palm of each hand. He then put on gloves to protect the anointed hands as the bishop placed a ring on the fourth finger of his right hand, which symbolized the mystical marriage between Louis and France. The archbishop placed the sceptre into Louis's right hand and the hand of justice in his left hand. Finally, Louis was crowned with the great crown of

Charlemagne, which had been carried to Reims from Saint-Denis. As the crown was placed on Louis's head, the peers raised their hands towards it in a silent gesture of support.

It was time now for the enthronement. Louis was conducted up the staircase to the rood loft, where he sat on the throne in full view of his people. In procession, the dukes and peers of France kissed Louis on the cheek and paid homage.

"Vivat res in aeternum," cried the bishop, which was the signal for the doors of the cathedral to be opened so that Louis's subjects, who thronged in the square and streets outside, might see him as they shouted, "Vive le roi!" Special coins had been struck to mark the occasion, showing an image of Louis on one side and a hand holding the holy ampulla coming out of heaven on the other. These were distributed to the people.

A mass was said, during which Louis kissed the Bible. After this, he descended the staircase, still bearing the royal regalia, and went to the altar, where he handed the sceptre and the hand of justice to the awaiting officials. Louis now received four offerings: wine in a vessel of golden vermeil; a nugget of silver on a pillow fringed with gold; a nugget of gold; and a purse of red velvet embroidered in gold. The purse contained thirteen gold coins weighing five and a half pistoles each. They bore an image of Louis, crowned, and the inscription LUDOVICUS XIV FRANC. & NAVAR. REX CHRISTIANISSIMUS.[13] On the other side was an image of the town of Reims with a dove holding the holy ampulla. An inscription on the exergue read SACRATUS AC SALUTATUS REMIS 31 MAY 1654. This was the date originally set for the coronation, but it had been changed to June 7 too late for new coins to be reminted. These offerings Louis presented to the bishop of Soissons before he took up the sceptre and the hand of justice once again and returned to his throne.

According to ancient custom, the fowlers of Paris, who were installed in the upper galleries of the nave, released forty doves. The birds flew out of the windows as the *Te Deum* was sung below. Three salvoes were fired to announce that His Majesty Louis XIV had been crowned and anointed king of France.

Another mass was celebrated, after which Louis returned the regalia to the officials, while his brother, Philippe, duc d'Anjou, removed the heavy crown of Charlemagne from the king's head. Entering the oratory, which had been specially erected beside one of the pillars of the chancel, Louis made his confession and received communion of both kinds. The bread and wine had been consecrated in the magnificent golden, jewel-encrusted chalice of Saint Rémi. Following this, and taking up the regalia once more, Louis was given a lighter crown designed especially for the occasion, which was ornamented with pearls, diamonds, and other precious stones. The crown of Charlemagne was placed on a rich cushion and given to the *maréchal de l'hôpital*, who carried it before the king.

The procession that had escorted Louis into the cathedral now reformed to conduct him out. The air rang with the peal of bells and the cheers of his people as Louis made his way back to the archiepiscopal palace. Here, in a small, private ritual, Louis removed his gloves and shirt. These had been in contact with holy oil; according to ecclesiastical tradition, they could not be used for any profane purpose, and so they were burned.

A sumptuous feast now awaited Louis. Still dressed in his royal robes and his light crown, and bearing once again the sceptre and hand of justice, the king entered the Great Hall in the archiepiscopal palace and was conducted to his seat by the archbishop of Soissons. He sat at his table, which stood on a raised dais; his chair, which was surrounded by a wooden gilt balustrade, was surmounted by a canopy of cloth of silver. By his side was Philippe, who was entitled to this honor as the only brother of the king. Louis laid his royal regalia on the table, upon which also rested the great crown of Charlemagne. Now he enjoyed a feast, which consisted of five meat courses and two sweet dishes.

Only now, as he returned to his bedchamber, did Louis finally remove his coronation robes. The day had been long, with the service itself lasting five hours, and the king of France settled down to sleep as the sun set over the ancient town of Reims.

The next day, Louis dressed in cloth of silver and a black velvet cap, and mounted a white horse marvellously caparisoned in silver. Accompanied by a gorgeously dressed entourage, which included Philippe d'Anjou, Louis rode in procession to the Abbey of Saint Remi. The streets, lined with bright tapestries, were filled with the people who came out to cheer their king. Louis, waving and bowing, returned their greetings as he went.

At the church, Louis heard mass and listened to several sermons, the last of which was delivered by the bishop of Montauban. He exhorted Louis to deal severely with the Protestants in his kingdom, notwithstanding the fact that their freedom of conscience had been guaranteed them and they were protected by edict.[14] It was highly inappropriate and struck a discordant note in the otherwise harmonious and happy visit by the king.[15]

That afternoon, Louis returned to Notre-Dame de Reims, where he was invested into the Ordre du Saint-Esprit, instantly becoming grand master of the order.

Kingship conferred upon Louis a mystical union with the kingdom of France and its people. It also reinforced his relationship with God and endowed him with the power to heal. On the last day of his visit, he once again went to the Abbey de Saint Rémi, where some twenty-five hundred people, all inflicted with scrofula, awaited him in the abbey park. Louis touched each one, tracing the sign of the cross over every ravaged face with the open palm of his right hand. As he did so, he spoke the words "God heals you, the king touches you."[16] Behind him came the grand almoner, who gave each person a silver coin. Just as his coronation had lasted hours, so too did this ceremony, but Louis paused only twice to drink a glass of refreshing water. His final act was to pardon six thousand criminals, who were released from prison.

Louis's status as king had altered due to his anointing, which was understood to be the most important aspect of the ceremony in which he had just participated, and which was emphasized by the name *le sacre*. To be king meant that his subjects, high and low, saw Louis as a living God, whose anointing conferred upon him the necessary qualities to enable him to represent divine law and order in nature.[17]

Louis was the absolute ruler of eighteen million or so people, over whom he exercised complete command and the course of whose lives he could direct as he saw fit. Many, however, recognized that Louis must be guided by the teachings and ethics of Christianity. Linked to this was Louis's responsibility for the spiritual welfare of his people. It was his duty to uphold orthodoxy in spiritual affairs, and this included the appointment of prelates who would serve the church.

As ruler of all France, Louis would define the borders of his kingdom, preserve the unity of France, and win, or maintain, the loyalty of those within his kingdom who might prefer to serve their own, local feudal lords. He was also the personification of France; his achievements would be France's achievements, his misfortunes would be France's misfortunes, and his children would be, as he had been, *enfants de France*.

Louis, as the direct successor to the semidivine Roman emperors, was also understood to be semidivine. He occupied that mysterious space between mortal humanity and the Christian God, whose representative on earth he was.

Finally, Louis was the only person who could protect his subjects from oppression and injustice. This was seen during the Fronde, when injured and starving soldiers and civilians followed the court in search of comfort and relief. It would be seen again in the predawn of the Revolution, when the peasantry would flock to Versailles to beg for bread from the royal kitchens. As such, it was in the best interests of the people to support Louis in his endeavors, both peaceful and in time of war.

Guy Patin, a physician and close observer of affairs at court, expressed his "great and high hopes that something good will come from the consecration. It is said that the spirit of the king has awakened."[18] Louis himself described his *métier de roi* in much simpler terms: "The only way to reign in all hearts at once, is to be the incorruptible judge and common father to all."[19]

Two months after his coronation, Louis rejoined his army, where he witnessed two major developments in the ongoing war. The first was the siege of Stenay, seen by some as a "military consecration"[20] for Louis; this was followed by Turenne's relief of Arras. Shortly afterwards, the king returned to Paris, where he would spend the winter.

FIVE

Louis in Love

At the age of sixteen, Louis was growing out of his boyish looks and blossoming into a handsome young man. Mme de Motteville noted his "fine figure and good countenance," which "made every one admire him, and he bore in his eyes and in the whole air of his person the character of majesty which was, in virtue of his crown, essentially in him."[1]

One of the most colorful and exciting expressions of Louis's majesty was the ballet. Louis loved to dance, and, on February 4, 1655, Benserade's *Ballet des Plaisirs* was performed for the court. Louis had several costume changes as he played a shepherd, an Egyptian, and a debauched man, but the grand finale showcased his major role: the Genie de la Danse, a demigod, triumphant, charming, and glorious.

The choreography was very precise, and all the dancers took their time from the king.[2]

Among the dancers were Philippe, Louis's brother; the duke of York; Alexandre Bontemps, Louis's loyal chief *valet de chambre* and confidant; Molière, the actor and playwright who served the king variously as *tapissier du roi* and *valet de chambre*; finally there was the comte de Vivonne, brother of the future Mme de Montespan, a lady who was destined to play a major role in Louis's life in the years to come.

Among the balls and masques Louis attended was a fête hosted by Chancellor Séguier. While this was a dazzling event, others were more understated. On one occasion, Queen Anne invited Henriette-Marie of England to come and see Louis dance.[3] The evening was to be low-key, and Anne appeared *en déshabillé* to show that she was "keeping her room," accompanied only by her maids-of-honor, some of the young ladies of the court, and certain duchesses who were married to crown officers; this was in deference to the queen of England, who was still in mourning for her late husband, Charles I. The evening was intended to allow the guests to admire Louis, as well as to amuse Henriette, princess of England, who "was beginning to come out of childhood and to show that she was likely to be charming."

Although the company was small, the occasion was beautiful "and worthy of the royal persons who were present." Louis, accustomed to entertaining Mazarin's nieces, rose as soon as the music for the *branle* began and made to lead out Victoire, duchesse de Mercœur. Anne, thinking Louis had made a mistake, rose from her seat to take the duchess away, telling Louis in a low voice to dance with Henriette. The queen of England, seeing Anne's anger, ran to her and begged her not to constrain Louis, saying that the princess had injured her foot and was unable to dance. Anne replied that if the princess could not dance, then Louis would not either. Then, so as not to make a scene, the queen of England allowed Henriette to dance, although "in her soul she was very ill-pleased with the king."

This incident marked a rare lack of civility on Louis's part; the king was normally very good mannered, especially where women were concerned. Later that evening, after the guests had left, Anne soundly scolded Louis, but he answered that "he did not like little girls." Henriette was eleven at the time, and the disparity in their ages seemed greater to Louis than it did to his elders, especially as, according to Mme de Motteville, the sixteen-year-old king "seemed more like twenty." Here, she offers an interesting glimpse into the relationship between mother and son at this stage. "Before the world, the queen behaved to him in a manner both tender and respectful; but when he committed little faults she reproved him like a mother." On this occasion, Anne felt that her anger with Louis had been justified: "She had been so astonished to see him lacking in the civility he owed to the princess of England that she had not been able to restrain herself."

Anne had shown concern over Louis's relations with ladies before, and she had tackled it in a most unusual manner. One cold winter's night,[4] Louis was returning from his bath when he encountered Catherine de Beauvais, who proceeded to teach him how to perform with ladies. The incident is known only through court gossip, with the memoirist La Bruyère noting that Mme de Beauvais "was the first to assure the queen that the king, who in his youth appeared strongly indifferent to the ladies, would be, very assuredly, suited to marriage" and that he would be most suitable to father children.[5]

Mme de Beauvais was the first lady of Queen Anne's chamber and a close confidante. Born in 1615 or thereabouts, she was some twenty-three years the king's senior at the time of their encounter, but throughout his life Louis would show her great favor.[6]

What Queen Anne and La Bruyère failed to understand was that Louis was shy with girls, and this reserve showed itself as indifference. He knew Mazarin's nieces well, of course; they lived at the Louvre, and he saw them almost every day when he was in Paris. However, both his mother and the cardinal had always imposed strict guidelines, and this strengthened Louis's reticence. While the king had enjoyed friendships with the young ladies, he had never demonstrated any emotional attachment or signs of sexual desire towards any of them. However, his lesson at the hands of Mme de Beauvais appears to have opened the king's eyes to the charms of the opposite sex.

The lady Louis had led out to dance was Victoire, duchesse de Mercœur, the eldest of the Mancini sisters, and, while many expected him to be attracted to her, she being the most beautiful, he instead "attached himself" to her younger sister, Olympe.[7] At sixteen, Olympe's eyes were "full of fire." She was plump, with a beautiful complexion, pretty arms, and beautiful hands, and she wore dresses chosen to show off her assets. Louis was charmed by her, so that people "almost feared that this passion, slight as it was, might lead him to wish to do her more honor than she deserved." Anne of Austria, however, was not unduly concerned, because she believed the romance to be innocent, and she was sure of Louis's virtue, as well as that of Olympe. Even so, she was eager that none should speak of it, lest it "might lead to legitimate consequences."[8]

Anne need not have worried, for Louis's feelings were "more a sentiment which led him to amuse himself with this young girl, than a great passion."[9] For her part, Olympe had already sensed that she would never be queen. Instead, she enjoyed the privileges of being a high-ranking lady at court; she and Louis continued to be friends, and he frequently chose her for the first dance whenever they attended fêtes or masques. All the while, though, Olympe continued to dream of becoming a princess like her sister, the duchesse de Mercœur.

Although Louis "was beginning to attract to himself the eyes and hearts of his subjects," he found that though he reigned, he did not yet rule. Instead, the people looked to the cardinal for favors, for "men love and seek in the person of the king only that which will advance their personal interests,"[10] and it was Mazarin who held the reins of power. However, an incident that occurred in the spring of 1655 gave Louis the opportunity to assert his authority in a way that shocked all those who witnessed it.

That March, Louis had held a *lit de justice* at the Palais de la Cité to register edicts allowing new taxes to be raised to support the continuing war.[11] Later, however, certain members of the assembly began to complain that the edicts had been registered too quickly and they had not had time to debate them. As the clamor grew louder, news of the disquiet reached Louis and Mazarin, who were hunting together in the forest of Vincennes. Mazarin pointed out to Louis just how dangerous the situation could become, recalling as it did the overture of the Fronde. Louis understood all too well, and he took decisive action.

Louis issued an order for the parlement to meet three days later, and, when that day arrived, he left Vincennes and rode to Paris. Stopping only to visit the Sainte-Chapelle, Louis then barged into the chamber of the Palais de la Cité. He was still wearing his hunting clothes, complete with a red jacket and a gray hat, and he was accompanied by other members of the court, similarly dressed. He then sat on the *lit de justice* and spoke to the assembly:

> *Everyone knows how much trouble your meetings have stirred up in my State, and how dangerous the effects they have produced. I have learned that you pretend still to continue them, under the pretext of deliberating upon the edicts, which but lately have been read and published in my presence. I have come here expressly to forbid (at this stage, he pointed his finger at the Masters of Enquêtes) you to continue, and to you, Monsieur le Premier Président (again pointing the finger), neither to permit nor tolerate it, no matter what pressure the Masters of Enquêtes may apply to you.*

Louis had spoken. He rose and promptly left the chamber without waiting to hear what the members might have to say. After calling at the Louvre, Louis made his way back to Vincennes, where Mazarin awaited him.

Later tradition would have it that the premier président, Pomponne de Bellièvre, had started to explain to the king that the parlement was simply acting in the best interests of the state, upon which Louis replied, *"L'état c'est moi"*—'I am the state.' Alas for tradition, there is nothing to support this assertion. Moreover, Louis could not have made such a statement because he would never have thought in such terms. Rather, Louis saw himself as the servant of the state and its keystone, but he never believed himself to be the state-incarnate.[12]

The parlement was displeased with Louis's intervention, and the following day Pomponne de Bellièvre led a delegation to Vincennes, where they demanded to speak to Mazarin. They complained that Louis had behaved in "a manner so strange and so far removed from that of his predecessors and even from his own past behavior."[13] They then asked Louis's permission to reopen the negotiations surrounding the original edicts, but he firmly refused. Instead, Mazarin arranged for the maréchal de Turenne to explain to parlement that the threat posed by Condé, the ongoing war, and even the risk that a new Fronde could erupt justified the new taxes. The parlement reluctantly agreed, assisted no doubt by the promise of large financial rewards. However, it was clear to all that Louis was not a king to be trifled with. Louis's transformation largely came about as a consequence of his *sacre*. Although he had been king since he was four and a half years old, it was only once he had been anointed with the sacred oil that his kingship took on a new, more powerful aspect.

In late March 1655, Marie Du Bois, one of Louis's *valets de chambre*, returned to court after an absence of some two years. Delighted by how accomplished Louis had become, he decided to record a typical day in the life of the sixteen-year-old king.[14]

Louis's daily routine began as soon he awoke, when he recited the Office of the Holy Spirit and his chaplet. After this his preceptor, Péréfixe, came in and guided his studies, either in Scripture or the history of France. Louis now got out of bed, at which time two *valets de chambre*, one of whom was Du Bois, entered the room with a gentleman usher. Louis sat on the commode in the *chambre de l'alcôve*. He then entered the *grande chambre*,[15] where he would be met by princes and grand seigneurs who had come to attend his lever. Still wearing his dressing gown, Louis would approach them and delight them with his informal conversation.

Louis sat in a chair and washed his hands, mouth, and face. After drying himself, he would remove his nightcap, which had been tied onto his head because of the abundance of hair beneath. Going into the *ruelle*, he prayed with his almoners while everyone present knelt; no one dared stand or even make a sound during this time, or they would be escorted out of the chamber by the usher.

With prayers at an end, Louis returned to his chair, where his hair was combed and he was dressed in a simple outfit of breeches and a cambric shirt. He passed onto a grand cabinet behind his antechamber where he did his exercises, including vaulting on the horse and practicing with weapons and pikes. Coming to the alcove once again, he practiced dance steps before returning to the *grande chambre* to change clothes and eat breakfast. Louis now left his chamber, making the sign of the cross as he did every day.

Louis went to Mazarin's apartments, which were above his own, where the cardinal would instruct him in affairs of state. Sometimes this meant hearing reports from various ministers, at other times it involved more secret business.[16] These lessons would continue for an hour or an hour and a half. Upon their completion, Louis would go to say good morning to his mother before going to the Petit-Bourbon[17] to ride until his mother was ready to go to mass. Louis would accompany her to the church and then escort her back to her chambers with great deference and respect.

Returning to his own chambers, Louis changed his clothes again, dressing according to how he planned to spend the afternoon. If he wanted to go hunting, he would wear the appropriate outfit, but if he was staying indoors, he would don an unassuming costume with no embellishment. His outfit was so easy to wear that Louis would dress himself; Du Bois noted that the king had a very fine figure.

Louis would now go to dinner, often with his mother. If there were any ambassadors, he would give them an audience in the afternoons. He would listen intently as they did business, but he liked to keep them back for fifteen minutes or so afterwards to talk familiarly with them about their masters, country, and alliances, their friendships and past enemies, their houses and their kingdoms. They would return to their masters with stories about the charms of the king of France.

Free once again, Louis would sometimes go to the Cours-la-Reine, where he would exchange pleasantries with ladies and gentlemen of quality before returning to attend council. Often a play was performed in the evening, a comedy or something more serious, and Louis would receive the company with great courtesy. This would be followed by a supper, after which Louis would dance with the queen's ladies and others before settling down to play games. In one favorite game, someone would begin to tell a story, and when he or she got stuck, the story would be taken up by the next person and so on until it was finished.[18]

As midnight approached, Louis bid his mother goodnight and returned to his chamber. After saying his prayers, he went into the *grande chambre*, where those with right of entry awaited him, just as they had that morning. Louis undressed, chatting with his attendants before bidding them goodnight and retiring to the *chambre de l'alcôve*. Sitting again on the commode, he chatted with the first gentleman and others before they too left and Louis, at last, went to bed.[19]

Occasionally, Louis wished for more than lessons in statecraft and meetings with ministers and ambassadors. In the spring of 1656, he announced his desire to hold a tournament, riding at the ring in the presence of the queen and the whole court as in the days of chivalry. The course was established in the space between the Louvre and the Palais-Royal, in the gardens of which the knights mounted their horses before riding to the lists in a magnificent cavalcade, much to the delight of the people.

Of the three troops, Louis's came first, bearing colors of rose and white; the duc de Guise led the second troop, with colors of blue and white, while the duc de Candale's troop had green and white for their colors. Each wore coats fashioned in the Roman style and embroidered in gold and silver; the little caps on their heads were adorned with plumes and aigrettes. Their horses were similarly caparisoned, and men and horses were adorned with ribbons.

Fourteen pages carrying the lances and devices of the knights opened the procession, followed by six trumpeters and the king's chief equerry. All were dressed in cloth of silver with rose and white ribbons. Twelve royal pages followed, all mounted and richly dressed, laden, as were the others, with plumes and ribbons. Of the two last pages, one carried Louis's lance, the other his shield, which bore a sun and the motto *Ne piu, ne pari*—"None greater, none equal." After the pages came the brigadier, who commanded the royal troops and was richly dressed but wore no mask. Louis came next, followed by knights, all masked, richly attired and gallant. The king, however, "surpassed each one of them, as much by his fine carriage, his grace and skill, as by his quality of sovereign and master." Following Louis came Guise, whose "fine appearance . . . and romantic genius well fitted him for tournaments," and Candale, who was praised for his "fine figure and his beautiful blond head [which] received all the praises it deserved."[20] The comte de Lude won the prize, which was presented to him by the duchesse de Mercœur.

The summer saw Louis and the court travel to Compiègne, where the king could observe his armies. It was here that he received a very special visitor, Christina, the former queen of Sweden. Christina had aroused great interest by abdicating her throne "apparently from a generous disdain of a crown, and in order not to force her inclinations in favour of her nearest relation, whom her subjects desired her to marry." A controversial figure, she had abjured her religion to embrace Catholicism, renouncing "heresy in person to the pope"[21] while in Rome during a tour of Europe. She declared her desire to see France, much to the delight of Queen Anne.

Christina arrived in Paris on September 8, 1656 and lodged in the king's apartment at the Louvre. Having seen the places of interest in

Paris, she made her way to Compiègne, where she was introduced to Anne. Arrangements had been made for Christina to dine at Chantilly, and Mazarin rode out to meet her there. Two hours after dinner, Louis and Philippe arrived, disguised as private gentlemen. They entered Christina's bedchamber, where she was receiving guests, and joined the crowd.²² Mazarin, spotting them, introduced them to Christina as "two noblemen of the highest rank in France." The wile was unsuccessful, however, for Christina had seen their portraits in the Louvre; she replied that she could "well believe it, for they seemed to her born to wear crowns."²³

Louis was still shy at this stage and naïve as to the ways of the world, but he took to Christina and they became friends. Mme de Motteville made the observation that Louis recognized in Christina an aspect of his own character: "the shyness he exhibited proceeded from his self-respect and his judgment, which made him desire to be perfect in all things and to dread being found to fail in any."²⁴

Christina offered Louis some advice. Speaking of his love for Olympe, she told him he must marry her: "If I were in your place, I would marry a person I loved." This did not go down well with Queen Anne or Mazarin, "for at court they do not like those people who give their advice unasked."²⁵

Christina remained in France until late September, when she left to go to Rome; Louis and Mazarin left the following day for La Fère. The royal army under Turenne was besieging La Capelle, close to the border of the Spanish Netherlands, which caused Condé's troops to besiege Saint-Ghislain in retaliation. Turenne sent word that unless they surrendered, his attack would be merciless. Condé's commanding officer, Chamilly, saw the wisdom of obeying, and on September 27, the siege of Saint-Ghislain was lifted. La Capelle remained in French hands.

Louis, who was now camped at Guise, conducted a convoy carrying supplies to Saint-Ghislain. He entered the town as the enemy army looked on, keeping their distance. Then, with winter drawing on, the king returned to his mother, who awaited him impatiently at

Compiègne. He arrived on October 6, and two days later the court made its way back to Paris.

As 1657 dawned, the mother of Louis's friends, the Mancini sisters, died. The loss had a particularly profound effect on the duchesse de Mercœur, who was pregnant at the time. She gave birth to a son but became partially paralyzed and lost her speech. She appeared to recover, and her uncle left her bedside to attend the ballet *L'Amour Malade*, in which Louis danced, but then the duchess grew rapidly worse and died on February 8.

Later in February, Olympe, "who had had the honor of occupying the king's heart, abandoned these flattering prospects which did not wholly satisfy her"[26] and married Prince Eugène, the son of Prince Thomas of Carignan-Savoy.[27] This focused the court's attention on Olympe's younger sister, Marie.

Marie had arrived in France at her uncle's request in 1653. At first her mother had been reluctant to send her, wishing to advance her second youngest, Hortense. The reason seems to have been that Hortense was deemed much prettier, and so stood a better chance of making a good match in her new country. As for Marie, she was told to choose between going to France or remaining in Rome and conse-crating herself to God in a cloister. Her choice fell on France, much to her mother's dismay, although Mme Mancini pressed her brother the cardinal to put the girl in a convent, hoping she would never leave it. Mazarin was reluctant to do this, but, seeing that Marie was "at this time a thin, sallow-complexioned, and ungainly child" who would not make a good impression at court, he found a place for her in the Con-vent of the Visitation to see "if she would not put on a little flesh."[28]

Here Marie stayed for eighteen months before leaving to join the court, which was then at La Fère. Mazarin's motive was to marry Marie to the son of the maréchal de la Meilleraye, although the arrangement was eventually abandoned.[29] When the court returned to Paris, Marie feared she would be sent back to the convent, but Mazarin decided to keep her at court instead, and he lodged her at the Louvre with her mother. Mme Mancini, however, ill-treated her daughter, and Marie led a miserable existence, which even the delights offered by the court did little to alleviate.

When Mme Mancini became ill, Louis paid her the courtesy of visiting her most evenings. In order to reach her apartments, he had to go through Marie's room. Marie made sure to be present when the king was expected, and he made a point of stopping to talk to her. He knew she was lonely, and the sympathy he showed her and their few minutes of conversation sufficed to make her "sad and mournful days pass more quickly."[30] After the king's visit, Marie would return to her solitude "less afflicted than before."[31] Then, as Mme Mancini's condition worsened, she urged Mazarin to send Marie to a convent. She believed Marie to have a bad disposition, a view that was supported by Marie's father, an astrologer, who had foreseen that Marie would "be the cause of much evil."[32] Again Mazarin defied his sister, even though this had been her dying wish. He felt Marie and her younger sister, Hortense, should remain at court as companions for Louis.

At this point, Louis decided it was time to end hostilities with his cousin, Mlle de Montpensier, and he invited her to court, which was at Sedan. Louis was with his armies, but within a week, news arrived that the siege of Montmédy had been broken. Louis arrived at Sedan at two that afternoon, and, having ridden hard, he was covered with mud. Queen Anne, watching from a window, told Mademoiselle that she did not wish her to see the king until he had changed his dress. Louis, however, came in anyway, and "however wanting in style," Mademoiselle found him "very handsome."[33]

As he approached, Anne said, "Here is a damoiselle I must present to you, and who is very sorry for having been so naughty; but promises to be wiser in future." Louis laughed, and, after a few pleasantries, they began to speak of the siege and an adventure Louis had met on the way back.[34] Later, they all ate together as a family, and in the evening Louis danced with Mademoiselle. She noticed that Louis talked much with Marie Mancini, but since he said nothing to her about it, she asked no questions. After staying with the court for twelve days, Mademoiselle returned home.

When Olympe became comtesse de Soissons, Louis continued to visit her at her hôtel in Paris, but gradually these visits decreased. He now had other ladies to occupy his thoughts, among them Marie Mancini. However, he never forgot the advice of the ex-queen Christina, who told him he should marry where his heart lay, and there was one lady at court with whom he had fallen hopelessly in love. Her name was Mademoiselle de La Motte-Argencourt.[35]

Naturally the affair attracted the attention of the whole court, and it was reported that Louis "spoke one day to Mademoiselle de La Motte as a man in love who was no longer virtuous."[36] So stricken was the king that "he even offered, if she would love him, to resist the queen and the cardinal,"[37] that is, he would marry her against the wishes of his mother and his godfather. The lady, however, was not willing or daring enough to accept the king's proposal, and when news of it reached the queen, she scolded him, pointing out to him "in how short a time he had wandered from the paths of innocence and virtue."[38] When Mazarin found out about it, he and Queen Anne discussed the matter with Louis. Three hours later, when they emerged from behind locked doors, Louis "took no further notice of La Motte," at least according to Mademoiselle.[39] However, her account slightly abridges the story, for, as Mme de Motteville makes clear, Louis's "resolution was not formed without much pain; he groaned, he sighed, but finally he conquered."[40]

If affairs of the heart made life difficult for Louis, at least he could escape by joining his armies, now encamped at Dunkirk. Turenne, as always, led the royal forces, and this time, he was joined by some six thousand men sent by Oliver Cromwell.[41] In late May, Turenne had begun to besiege Dunkirk as the Spanish forces approached the town from the east, taking up position on the dunes. Condé saw immediately that they had failed to take account of the tides, which, as they receded, left the Spanish right flank exposed. The French, with Cromwell's Ironsides, attacked the Spanish at the center and left flank, while the French cavalry approached their right flank across the sands. The Battle of the Dunes, as it came to be known, was a major victory for the Franco-English alliance. All the while, Louis sat on the sidelines to watch, having been forbidden to approach any closer by Mazarin, who persuaded him that the life of the king was of greater value than all the armies of France. As Dunkirk capitulated, the king made a formal entrance into the town, where he received the keys. He then handed them to the English commander, Sir William Lockhart.

Louis desperately wanted to share the soldier's life with his men, and his obedience to Mazarin only went so far. Determined to ride to Mardyck, he ignored the cardinal, who pleaded with him to remain in Calais. The weather was very hot that summer, and Louis spent long days in the saddle. When he arrived at Mardyck, he found the water bad and the air corrupted from the bodies of the dead, which had lain half-buried for a year. At the end of June, he had to admit to feeling unwell and in need of rest.[42]

At first, the physicians thought Louis was simply tired; he had ridden too hard and had caught too much sun. However, it quickly became apparent that he was seriously ill. He was feverish and trembled so much it was feared he would go into convulsions. Suffering with what appears to have been typhoid fever, the king was bled eight times and purged four times with cassia and senna. Still his fever increased to the point that his physicians feared he would die. At one point Louis summoned Mazarin to his bedside and asked him to let him know when the end was near.

When news of the king's malady reached Paris, the Blessed Sacrament was exposed at every altar and prayers said in every church. At one point, Louis was given antimony, but this proved to be of no use. "To see a king die so young, gives one a great shock," said Mademoiselle. News arrived that Louis had received the last sacraments and that Queen Anne and Mazarin had left his chamber in distress. In his dispatches, Mazarin wrote of his despair at the thought of losing the best friend that he had in the world.[43]

Philippe had not seen his brother since the onset of his illness, and as Louis's condition worsened, it was considered not worth the risk to allow him to visit him now. Then, just as all seemed lost, a doctor from nearby Abbeville came to offer his services. Breaking all the rules of etiquette, he sat on the king's bed as he examined the patient, but this breach of formality was forgiven when he announced that "the young man is very ill, but he shall not die." He duly administered an emetic wine, much to the horror of Guy Patin, who believed it to be a poison. Louis began to recover, and, after a second dose of antinomy, his fever broke and he was out of danger. As soon as his health permitted, the court moved on to Compiègne and then to Paris. Everywhere he went, Louis was greeted by his joyful people, and in his own quiet way, he thanked subjects and courtiers alike for the goodwill they had shown him.

In September and October, Louis, his health fully recovered, travelled to Metz with Mazarin. The Holy Roman emperor, Ferdinand III, had died in April, and a new successor was being elected. Ferdinand had assisted the Spanish against the French, thereby violating the terms of the Treaty of Westphalia. It was generally agreed throughout Europe that the imperial crown should go to a non-Habsburg in order to curtail the power of the new emperor, whoever he might be. One of the favored candidates was the duke of Neuburg, the elector of Bavaria. Another was Louis XIV. Although Mazarin would have liked Louis to wear the imperial crown, his candidature was never taken seriously. Mazarin declared that Louis had never really coveted the crown, and he took advantage for their sojourn in Metz to educate the young king in European politics. In the end, it came to be realized that the most suitable candidate was in fact Ferdinand's son, Leopold, to whom the electors looked for future favors. Leopold was duly elected the following year, and in him Louis would find a lifelong rival.[44]

SIX

A Royal Wedding

As the hot summer of 1658 mellowed into autumn, the court once again withdrew to Fontainebleau. Among the entertainments on offer was a collation given by Philippe, which was served in the hermitage of Franchard to the accompaniment of twenty-four violins.[1] The party donned riding habits and rode out to the hermitage, except for the comtesse de Soissons, who felt unwell and travelled in a coach.

The moment they arrived, Louis decided it would be fun to scramble among the rocks, although not everyone agreed and several of the ladies remained behind with Philippe. Then, having discovered a good spot, Louis sent for the musicians and ordered the rest of the party to join him. The going was extremely hard: "I am surprised that no one was hurt," complained Mademoiselle, "for we ran great risks of having our arms and legs broken, or even our skulls fractured," and several were obliged to return to the hermitage. After supper, they returned to the château in carriages, their way lighted by flambeaux, and spent the evening watching a comedy. When that was finished, they went into the forest, where they set a fire. It got out of hand, and several trees were burned.

Most of the time was taken up with quieter pursuits of water excursions, attending plays, listening to music, or riding out in coaches to enjoy the vast grounds of the château and the huge forest beyond. One day an unexpected guest arrived: Gaston d'Orléans. Louis and his mother were playing cards when the duke was announced, and Their Majesties continued their game, barely rising from their seats. For most of Gaston's stay, Louis and Anne continued as usual, but one day they invited Gaston to accompany them. At this time Louis rarely wore a hat, and this obliged Gaston to go without his, "which very much embarrassed his Royal Highness [Gaston], who dreaded the damp air." In order to convey his discomfort, the duke placed his gloves on his head until Louis, after some time, invited him to put on his hat.[2]

Of those who had wept at the king's bedside during those dreadful days when he had lain seriously ill, perhaps the saddest was Marie Mancini. She had never forgotten the kindness Louis had shown her as her mother lay dying, and, inevitably perhaps, she fell in love with him. It was during the visit to Fontainebleau that Louis, who was still half-interested in the comtesse de Soissons, began to tire of her; or rather, as Mme de Motteville explains, "His heart grew weary of being unoccupied,"[3] and he began to notice Marie. It was the beginning of a great passion. Louis would escort her to receptions and partner her at dances, and the two of them would ride out into the forest together to escape the prying eyes of the courtiers. They both enjoyed music, and Louis, an expert player, would accompany Marie on the guitar as she sang her favorite airs.

Marie was not considered beautiful by the standards of the day, which required a pale complexion, blond hair, and blue eyes framed by dark eyebrows. Marie was blessed with an abundance of dark curls, a swarthy complexion, and brown eyes that sparkled with life, love, and not a little mischief. A cultured lady, she introduced Louis to the world of literature and painting, an area of his education that had been neglected in favor of state affairs. Louis was shy of showing his emotions, but Marie understood, and she loved him for himself, not for his crown. "There is no stronger chain to bind a noble heart," says Mme de Motteville, "than that of feeling itself beloved; and it is easy to see how, on both sides, their attachment became as strong as it was tender."[4] When the court returned to Paris, Louis did not resume his visits to the Hôtel de Soissons, spending each evening amusing Marie Mancini instead.

That autumn witnessed the arrival in Paris of a theater company led by the actor and playwright Jean-Baptiste Poquelin, better known under his stage name, Molière. His troupe had been introduced to Philippe d'Anjou by the abbé Daniel de Cosnac, the former gentleman of the chamber to the prince de Conti, who had recently entered Philippe's household. On October 24, at Philippe's request, Molière presented Corneille's *Nicomède* before Louis and the court.

Because the Louvre had no theater of its own, and the nearby Salle du Petit-Bourbon was being used by an Italian company, the performance took place upon a makeshift stage specially erected for the purpose in the Louvre's Salle des Gardes on Louis's orders. The king was very impressed, even though the play was a farce, a style of theater that had gone out of fashion. Molière followed it with a one-act comedy entitled *Le Docteur Amoureux*, which so delighted Louis that he invited Molière to establish his company in Paris. He gave the Troupe de Monsieur, as it was now called, permission to share the Salle du Petit-Bourbon with the Italian theater run by Scaramouch, each company taking it in turns to perform.[5]

Little did Louis realize that he had set upon the road to stardom one of France's greatest playwrights, but while he was enjoying the thrill of comedy theater, elsewhere more serious matters were being discussed. The subject was Louis's marriage.

Queen Anne had taken Louis's recent illness as a sign of God's displeasure. While the Lord had been merciful this time, it was clear to the queen that reconciliation must be reached between France and Spain and that the drawn-out war, so costly and destructive, must come to an end.[6]

Anne had long cherished a wish that her son should marry the Infanta Maria Teresa, the daughter of her brother, Philip IV of Spain. Until recently, King Philip refused to countenance such a match because Maria Teresa would confer to Louis her rights to the Spanish throne. Recently, however, the Spanish queen had given birth to a son, Philip Prospero, and was once more pregnant; there would be, therefore, at least two lives between Maria Teresa and the Spanish succession. Nevertheless, a Spanish match remained a desirable prospect for France, since it would seal a peace treaty between their two countries.

Despite this, Philip remained reluctant to come to the negotiating table; but no matter, Anne had a second choice: Henriette, princess of England. The princess's only fault, as far as Anne could see, was that she was not three years older, for she might have pleased Louis better had she been closer to his own age. Unfortunately, Louis did not care for Henriette, nor did Mazarin see any reason why he should influence Louis to accept her.[7]

Instead, Mazarin pressed for a match with Marguerite of Savoy. She was the daughter of Christine de France and Victor Amadeus I, and granddaughter of Henri IV, making her Louis's first cousin.[8] Initially, Savoy had been an ally of France, but for several years it had maintained strict neutrality. When Mazarin pressed Christine to support France, she said she would do so only if Louis XIV would marry her daughter, Marguerite. Mazarin, who knew that Louis could make a better match than this, could see no means by which he could satisfy Christine, but pragmatically he saw that, like the proposed Spanish marriage, this one also had its advantages: the duchy of Savoy's geographical position, sandwiched between Austria to the north and the duchies of Tuscany and Modena to the south, made it strategically important.

As such, Mazarin agreed in principle to the marriage, but he insisted that Louis should be allowed to meet Marguerite before any final decision would be reached. This was agreed, and arrangements were made to bring the king and the princess to Lyons, where the interview would take place.

Such was the protocol surrounding the events that the two courts left their respective capitals at the same time. At first, it was planned that Louis would be accompanied only by the cardinal and a gentleman-in-ordinary, while leaving Queen Anne and the rest of the court in Paris. In the event, Louis was reluctant to leave his mother behind because he "considered that her consent was necessary to his marriage." He begged her to travel with him, and she readily consented.[9]

Louis left Paris on October 25, 1658, after hearing mass at Notre-Dame. His entourage, which included Marie Mancini and Mademoiselle, was so great that everyone who saw it thought the king was making a royal progress. The weather was fine and sunny but cold, and the party travelled in coaches the first day. Louis, however, suggested that if the weather continued fine the next day, he and some of the ladies would travel on horseback. This allowed him to stay very close to Marie, talking to her "in a most gallant manner."[10]

In each town he approached, Louis received a warm and enthusiastic welcome from the people and the dignitaries. Nowhere was this more so than at Dijon, where he planned to spend a week. The Estates of Burgundy, which decided the revenue to be raised for the king's projects, was meeting, and it was hoped that Louis's presence would encourage them to be more generous than would otherwise have been the case.[11]

All the while, Louis continued his attentions to Marie, but he completely ignored her sister, the comtesse de Soissons, who was travelling with the queen, much to Louis's annoyance. Each evening he would arrange to receive a large collation, "equal to supper," in order to avoid supping with his mother. This allowed him to spend four or five pleasant hours in Marie's company, but his strategy did not go unnoticed. On one occasion, as he was enjoying his meal, the queen sent a message to him, requesting some *rissolles*,[12] as did Mademoiselle. He sent some, but there were not enough, so Anne asked for more. Louis sent word that he had enough *rissolles* for the queen and Mademoiselle but not enough for himself and his company, and "everyone believed that this was meant to apply to the comtesse de Soissons."[13] As the court left Dijon, the fine weather broke, but while the cold and the rain drove most of the ladies back to the coaches, Marie continued to ride alongside Louis all the way to Lyons.

The court reached Lyons on November 28. News arrived the next morning that the Savoyard party was expected the following Friday, December 2. On that day, Louis and Anne, with the cardinal, Philippe, and Mademoiselle, advanced to meet them, and when he heard that the duchess Christine was near, Louis took to horse to be the first to welcome her.

Anne, watching the king go, admitted that she was impatient to know what Louis would think of Princess Marguerite. She tried to feign indifference towards the marriage, but it was clear that she would have preferred Louis to marry the Infanta Maria Teresa: "I cannot but be content with what pleases the king," she said, adding, "at the same time, I think that he would better like the princess of England."[14]

Just then, Louis galloped back, looking very happy and self-satisfied. "Well, my son?" asked Anne, to which Louis replied, "She is much smaller than Madame la maréchale de Villeroy—her shape is the most graceful in the world. Her complexion . . ." Here, Louis searched for the right word ". . . is olive-colored, and it becomes her well. She has beautiful eyes, she pleases me, and I find her to my fancy."[15] Louis "had always said that his wife must be beautiful,"[16] and it seems Marguerite fulfilled his hopes.

Louis had just finished speaking when the Savoyard party approached. Anne and Duchess Christine greeted each other with a kiss before Christine presented her daughter. They then went into Anne's coach, where Louis immediately began to talk to Marguerite, and she to him, as though they had known each other all their lives This surprised Mademoiselle, who remarked that Louis was always cold with strangers and "very little disposed to be sociable."[17]

Upon reaching Lyons, Louis escorted Christine to her apartments in the archbishop's palace. Anne withdrew to her own rooms, where she was immediately joined by Mazarin, who had some news. Anne hazarded a guess: "Is it that the king, my brother, has sent to me to offer the Infanta? For that is what I least expect." "Yes, Madame," replied Mazarin, "it is that."[18]

The journey to Lyons had not been a secret; it was intended that Philip of Spain should hear of it. When he learned that Louis was contemplating another match, Philip was adamant that it "cannot be, and shall not be."[19] This had been Mazarin's intention all along, and his gamble paid off.[20] Philip IV sent Don Antonio Pimentel to treat with Mazarin.[21]

That evening, Louis and Marie were chatting as usual, when Marie asked him, "Are you not ashamed, Sire, at their wishing to give you so ugly a wife?" Whatever Louis had thought of Marguerite until that moment, he now acted very coldly towards her. He called upon her very early the next morning in order, as it was said, "that he might see her figure in an undress [en déshabillé], for it was rumored that she was hump-backed."[22] As evening fell, Louis devoted his time to Marie and addressed not a word to Marguerite.

Mazarin, meanwhile, continued his discussions with Pimentel, and at last some agreement was reached. The cardinal went to speak with Anne, who was clearly unhappy with the prospect of the Savoy match.

"Good news, madame!" Mazarin said.

"Eh, what?" Anne exclaimed, "can it be peace?"

"More than that, madame," replied Mazarin. "I bring Your Majesty both peace and the Infanta."[23]

For several days, talks between France and Savoy were suspended, but when Duchess Christine learned of Pimentel's presence, she confronted Mazarin. He told her of the proposals sent from Spain, adding that "when it comes to a question of peace, it seemed to him that it would be a crime not to listen to the proposals just made."[24] Christine understood the cardinal's position, but she asked for some promise regarding Marguerite in case Louis should not, in the end, marry the Infanta. This not unreasonable request was granted, and a paper was signed by Louis and several secretaries of state, promising that should the Spanish marriage not take place within one year, Louis would marry Marguerite.[25] Of course, everyone knew that Louis could never be held to such a promise, and by way of assuaging his feelings of guilt, Mazarin presented Marguerite with a magnificent pair of diamond earrings, other jewelry, and perfumes.[26] Louis and his court left Lyons at the end of January 1659 to find Paris in the grip of deepest winter.

Louis continued to spend most of his time at Marie's side, and not only the court but the people began to murmur about their passion. Anne was in despair; every time Louis came to see her, Marie was by his side, and she would whisper in the king's ear even as he spoke to his mother. Eventually Anne decided enough was enough, and she confronted Louis. At one time, the king would have listened to his mother, but now he was defiant, even losing his temper.[27] Anne remained firm. She was concerned only that Louis should marry the Infanta and was not prepared to allow anything to get in the way of this cherished ambition. When Pimentel came to Paris to complete his part of the negotiations, Anne received him warmly.

Once the overtures were concluded, it was time to enter into more detailed discussions of the proposed peace treaty between France and Spain; this included, of course, the terms of the marriage contract between Louis and Maria Teresa. It was agreed that this vital and delicate work, which would be conducted by Mazarin and the Spanish first minister, Don Luis de Haro, should take place on neutral territory. The tiny Ile de Faisans in the Bidassoa, the river that formed part of the border between France and Spain, was chosen as the most appropriate setting.[28] Mazarin urged Louis and Anne to follow him to Bayonne, where they could be on hand should any difficulty arise.

Mazarin, however, had not envisaged that the greatest difficulty facing him lay in Louis's love for his niece, Marie. So smitten was Louis that it was believed by some that he asked the cardinal's permission to marry her.[29] For Mademoiselle, this was "the mere rumor of the day," and she pointedly refrains from discussing it.[30] The comte de Brienne, however, wrote that Anne went so far as to consult some of the lawyers in the parlement, including his father, to find out if the Mancini match would be valid if it went ahead against her wishes. [31]

Louis's love for Marie threatened to undermine everything that Mazarin was working for. It was decided that the girl had to go away, and Brouage, south of La Rochelle on the west coast, was chosen. After some persuasion, Louis finally had to agree to the separation, and many tears were shed during their last few days together. "You weep, and yet you are the master,"[32] Marie told Louis in a scene that would later be adopted by Jean Racine.[33]

As a parting gift, Louis bought Marie a magnificent string of pearls from Henriette-Marie, who was living in reduced circumstances at Saint-Germain.[34] Marie had often admired the pearls, and as soon as Louis heard that they were for sale, he asked Mazarin to give him the seventy-eight thousand livres necessary to buy them. His delight in pleasing his lady, however, was mixed with grief at their imminent parting. The evening prior to Marie's departure, Louis, in a state of "extreme depression," went to visit his mother. Anne, seeing her son's distress, took him into her private bathroom, where he had played as a child. When he emerged an hour or so later, his eyes were swollen. The unhappy queen told Mme de Motteville, "I pity the king; he is loving and reasonable both; but I have just told him that I am certain he will one day thank me for the pain I give him, and from what I see in him I do not doubt it."[35]

The next day, June 22, Louis, "showing his grief publicly,"[36] accompanied Marie and her sisters to their carriage. Their parting was made less bitter by a promise Louis had extracted from Mazarin that he would be permitted to see Marie again on his journey south.[37] Nevertheless, as Louis closed the coach door, he whispered a few words in Marie's ear, at which she threw herself back into her seat, sobbing, "Ah! I am abandoned!"

As the carriage bearing his love drew away, Louis hurriedly took leave of his mother and rode out to Chantilly, where, it was expected, he would recover his strength. Here, Louis "found it in his reason, in his sound nature, and in a soul such as his, to which God had given the loftiness necessary to a great king."[38] From Chantilly, he went on to Fontainebleau, from where he bombarded Marie with a constant stream of letters. Mazarin, who had now joined his nieces for part of their journey, worried about the king's behavior, which was in danger of causing a scandal. It was already being talked about as far away as Flanders and Germany, and the cardinal, terrified the news would reach Madrid, wrote to Louis begging him to break off his correspondence with Marie; Louis had no intention of doing so.

The first meeting between Mazarin and Don Luis de Haro, the Spanish first minister, took place on August 13, 1659; they would not conclude until November 7, after a total of twenty-four difficult conferences. The price of peace included the restoration of the prince de Condé. Spain was keen to reward their ally, while France, not surprisingly, wanted to punish him for his treachery. In the end, France agreed to pardon Condé and to reinstate his titles and lands; his offices were also restored, with the exception of the governorship of Guyenne.[39]

Agreement was reached regarding territorial settlements, with Spain ceding several strategically important towns along France's vulnerable northeastern and eastern borders. In return, France surrendered all its conquests and promised not to support Cromwell or the king of Portugal.[40]

Then there was the question of Maria Teresa's place in the Spanish succession. Although this problem had apparently been solved by the birth of her half brother, Philip Prospero, the boy was sickly, and many did not expect him to live. Philip IV wanted his daughter to renounce her rights to the Spanish throne, a clause that was accepted by Mazarin, who nevertheless demanded an exception to certain Spanish holdings in the Low Countries.

Linked to the succession clause was the Infanta's dowry. This was set at 500 thousand écus d'or,[41] a massive sum that was to be paid in three installments, the first of which would become due upon the consummation of the marriage. The Spanish crown, however, was known to be impoverished, notwithstanding its treasures taken from the New World, and so a small word was slipped into the marriage contract—*moyennant*, which stipulated that *on condition* that the agreed sums were paid to Louis, Maria Teresa would remain "content with the dowry and would not sue for any of her other rights."[42] In other words, should the dowry not be paid, the renunciation clause would be invalidated.

As the talks were beginning, Louis and the court began the journey to the Spanish border. It was to be slow progress, with the court making several stops on the way. Blois, southwest of Fontainebleau on the Loire, was the home of Gaston d'Orléans, who served the court dinner and entertained Louis, but the visit was awkward, the food ordinary, and Louis was in a hurry to leave. The one highlight came when Louis was received by Gaston's daughters from his second marriage, one of whom, Marguerite-Louise, had once been considered as his future queen. Standing behind the Orléans ladies was a timid sixteen-year-old girl whose stepfather was attached to Gaston's household; Louise de La Vallière went unnoticed by all.

Another stop was Saint-Jean-d'Angély, to the east of Brouage, where Louis had arranged a very special rendezvous. Marie Mancini and her sisters travelled to meet the king, who had solicited from Mazarin a reluctant promise that he could speak once more to his mistress.

Louis begged Marie to forgive him for "all that she had suffered for his sake,"[43] promising to do all he could to obtain permission for her and her sisters to rejoin the court at Bordeaux. In the event, Anne replied that she would give her consent willingly provided the cardinal agreed. Marie knew that her uncle would never allow it, but Louis asked her to try to conciliate the cardinal, since doing so appeared to be the only way of ending her exile. There followed a tearful good-bye as Louis tore himself away to continue his journey.

Louis appointed the maréchal de Gramont to represent him at Madrid and officially to ask for the hand of the Infanta on his behalf. Gramont carried a letter from Louis to Maria Teresa, asking:

> *very humbly to give your consent, and to consider the matter solely as a step necessary for the welfare of our respective States, but, regarding me a little as a person keenly desirous of your friendship and esteem, to do me the favor of consulting your heart to some extent. You will find me ever ready to honor and respect you, and to show you by all my actions how solicitous I am that you shall never repent of the choice which it has pleased you to make.*[44]

January 1660 saw Louis travelling in the south of France, and it was at Aix-en-Provence that Condé returned to the court. Kneeling before Louis, he declared his extreme sadness for having, for so many years, acted in a manner disagreeable to His Majesty and how he wished to buy back with the best part of my blood, "all the trouble he had caused within and outside France." Louis forgave his cousin and promised to forget all that had passed, adding that he would keep Condé in his good graces.[45] The reconciliation with Condé and news of the death of Gaston d'Orléans the following month lifted the shadow of civil disturbances that had threatened Louis's reign.

Louis's progress took him through the Pyrenees and on to Saint-Jean-de-Luz, where he arrived on May 8, 1660. Agreements had been reached the previous November, but there were still small details to be finalized, and when they were completed, Louis and Maria Teresa were married by proxy at Fuenterrabía on June 3. All eyes were on the Infanta, whose beautiful, clear white complexion was greatly admired, as were her blue eyes. Her hair, though, was hidden beneath a *monos*, or false hair, and covered with a white cap that wrapped her head. Her dress, made of white stuff embroidered with talc[46] and worn over a *guard-infanta*,[47] was unanimously considered horrible by the French ladies. The Infanta also wore precious stones set in a great deal of gold.

The ceremony, led by the bishop of Pamplona, began with low mass, after which the proxy deed was read out aloud, upon which the bishop immediately married the couple. When the time came for the Infanta to say yes, she made a deep curtsey to her father and pronounced the word modestly. The second time she said it, though, was much louder, and with the ceremony now at an end, she knelt before her father, who kissed her tenderly and raised her with tears in his eyes.[48]

After dinner, Mme de Motteville, curious to see the new queen's own hair, asked her to show it to her. Maria Teresa was happy to oblige, and she removed her *monos* to reveal a luxurious silver blond mane.

The next day, the French court played host to the Spanish at Saint-Jean-de-Luz. Anne, now the queen mother, met her brother for the first time in forty-six years. Strict Spanish protocol got in the way of human feeling, and when Anne attempted to kiss Philip, he drew back, so that they held each other by the arms. There was no such restraint with the two queens, aunt and niece, who embraced each other tenderly, while Maria Teresa was presented with jewels, sent to her by Louis as a wedding present.[49]

The conversation between Anne and Philip opened with talk of the war, with Anne lamenting its duration. "Alas, madame, the devil made me do it," explained Philip, observing that as things stood now, they would soon have grandchildren. Anne told him she would prefer "a son for the king, rather than a wife for the prince my nephew."[50]

Mazarin, who had been talking with Don Luis de Haro, approached Anne and Philip with the news that an unknown gentleman was waiting at the door, asking to have it opened. Anne, with Philip's consent, ordered the cardinal to allow the stranger to be seen. The stranger was, of course, Louis. He was supposed to have shown himself on horseback to Maria Teresa through the windows of the room in which they sat. Instead, he had been unable to resist coming to the door in person. Anne blushed slightly at the sight of her son, but the young queen blushed even more as she watched him intently. The smiling King Philip told Anne that he had a *lindo hierno*, a handsome son-in-law. [51]

Anne wanted to ask Maria Teresa what she thought of this stranger, but King Philip told her, "It is not the time to tell it."

"And when may she tell it?" Anne inquired.

"When she has passed that door," said Philip.

Philip turned to Maria Teresa and asked in a low voice, "What does Your Majesty think about that door?"

The young queen laughed and answered, "That door seems to me very handsome and very good." [52]

As Louis withdrew, he confided to Conti and Turenne that he had been surprised by the ugliness of Maria Teresa's clothes and headdress, but when he looked at her intently, "he saw that she had much beauty, and was well assured that it would be easy for him to love her." He then went to take up position on the riverbank so he could watch his queen embark. All the way he was pressed on all sides by Spanish dignitaries, all eager to get a look at him, while his own guards mingled with their Spanish counterparts to give their blessings. As Maria Teresa's boat sailed by, Louis rode gallantly along the riverbank, hat in hand, to follow it. Three days later, on June 6, Louis and King Philip met on the Ile de Faisans to take the oath that secured peace between their two countries.

The wedding of Louis XIV and Maria Teresa took place on Wednesday, June 9. Louis wore a black costume and no jewels. [53] Maria Teresa wore her own hair, left loose and flowing. It was so abundant that the duchesse de Navailles [54] had difficulty fixing the closed crown on her head. In the end, the crown had to be held in place by ribbons tied under the queen's chin. Maria Teresa wore a sleeved bodice and petticoat skirts, dotted with little fleur-de-lis beneath royal robes powdered with golden fleur-de-lis, which fell to the ground with a very long train, rounded at the end.

The church was richly decorated, and a dais of velvet powdered with fleur-de-lis had been erected especially for the ceremony. As Louis and Maria Teresa sat under the marriage canopy, Mazarin gave them the *pax* to kiss. The service was conducted by the bishop of Bayonne. When it ended, the young queen went to rest for a while, but when she returned, she was dressed *à la Française*, and her hair, which so fascinated the French ladies, was beautifully dressed. After spending a little time alone with her aunt, Queen Anne, Marie-Thérèse, as she would henceforth be known, went with Anne and their ladies to show themselves to the people and to watch as Louis threw golden coins, which had been specially minted for the occasion, to the waiting crowds.

As darkness fell, Louis and Marie-Thérèse dined in public. The moment he finished eating, Louis indicated his desire to go to bed. Marie-Thérèse, tears shining in her eyes, turned to Anne and said, "It is too soon," but upon being told that Louis was already undressed and waiting for her, she went to her room, where she changed out of her dress. When a messenger arrived to tell her that the king awaited her, she urged her ladies to hurry: *"Presto, presto, qu'el Rey m'espera"*—"Quick, quick, the king expects me."[55] Queen Anne closed the bed curtains on the young couple, confident that the marriage would be consummated that night.

As the time came for the court to leave Saint-Jean-de-Luz and begin the long journey back to Paris, Marie-Thérèse asked Louis to grant her the favor "of allowing her to be always with him, and that he would never propose to leave her, because it would be to her the greatest pain she could receive." Louis, who was a picture of happiness, was touched by these words, and he immediately ordered the grand master of the household never to separate the queen from himself, no matter how small the house might be.[56]

The royal honeymoon was spent travelling back to Paris. The court reached Fontainebleau on July 13, and four days later, Louis and Marie-Thérèse were guests of honor at Vaux-le-Vicomte, the magnificent château of the superintendent of finances, Nicolas Foucquet.[57]Here they were treated to a sumptuous dinner before they moved on to Vincennes to prepare for Marie-Thérèse's entrance into Paris. There was a moment of sadness for Louis, who asked the cardinal's advice on some matter. Mazarin replied, "Sire, you are seeking the counsel of a man who has no longer any mind, and who raves."[58] It was his way of telling Louis that he was now seriously ill. Deeply touched, Louis withdrew to a little gallery and wept.

Arriving at Vincennes on August 26, Louis and Marie-Thérèse prepared for their entrance into Paris. The procession passed beneath an arch, which had been specially erected near the newly rebuilt Porte Saint-Antoine. Louis, wearing a costume of silver and carnation, a hat decorated with plumes and diamonds, and a sword by his side, sat on a gilded dais beside Marie-Thérèse as they received delegations from the clergy, the universities, corporations and guilds, and the four sovereign courts. They then accepted the keys to the city of Paris on a cushion and a box containing the seals of the state, after which they watched the traditional releasing of the doves.

That afternoon, their cortège took four hours to travel through the streets as it made its way to the Louvre. Anne of Austria watched from the window of the Hôtel de Beauvais in the rue Saint-Antoine with Mazarin, who was too ill to take part in the procession, Henriette de France, and Turenne.[59]

Among those who looked on were two young poets who were destined to be among the brightest lights of French literature—Jean de La Fontaine and Jean Racine—while Mme Scarron, the wife of the poet Paul Scarron, was captivated by the twenty-one-year-old king. The next day, she wrote to a friend, "I don't think anything more beautiful could be seen, and the Queen must have gone to bed last night well pleased with the husband she has chosen."

SEVEN

A New Dawn

L ouis attended the theater on September 5, 1660. It was his
twenty-second birthday, and one of the plays on the program
was *Les Précieuses Ridicules*, a witty and well-observed comedy
by Molière.

The play poked fun at salon society, which had developed in the
1620s largely under the influence of Mme de Rambouillet. The salon
provided a response to the vulgarity and violence into which the court,
then strictly a man's world, had descended; a world in which disputes
were settled by the sword, and speech was peppered with profanities.

The salon sought to promote good manners, good taste, and elegant
speech. This new refinement was articulated in polite conversation,
but especially in literature and the use of language that became

increasingly affected to the point that some, such as Molière, felt that the *exquisites* or *précieuses,* as those who frequented the salons were known, were legitimate targets for ridicule. Having attended an earlier performance of *Les Précieuses Ridicules,* the poet Gilles Ménage commented, "We admired all the absurdities which have just been so delicately and sensibly criticized; but, in the words of St. Remy to Clovis, we must now burn what we have adored and adore what we have burned."[1]

When he was in the Pyrenees the previous year, Louis was sent a copy of *Les Précieuses Ridicules* by an offended *exquisite.* This person, who preferred to remain anonymous, had expected the king to be equally affronted by the play and to ban it forthwith. Instead, Louis loved it and, even as he travelled back to Paris, he invited Molière and his company to Vincennes, where the play was performed on July 19, 1660. A month later, Louis commanded another performance, this time at the Louvre and in the presence of Philippe. By now, however, a dark cloud had descended upon the court; its cause was the rapid and steady decline of Cardinal Mazarin. When *Les Précieuses Ridicules* was performed on Louis's birthday, Louis, in deference to his godfather, stood incognito behind the cardinal's chair. As though to remove all doubt that Molière enjoyed his favor, Louis awarded the actor and playwright a grant of three thousand livres.

The king spent the autumn and winter months practising maneuvers with the musketeers, an elite regiment of which he was captain. His lessons in statecraft continued, with Louis going up to Mazarin's rooms as he always had; but entertainment was not neglected, and balls, hunting, and gambling kept the court amused throughout the slow, dismal months.

In early February 1661, Louis made plans to dance before the court, but as the workmen were making preparations in the *galerie des rois*[2] in the Louvre, a candle was accidentally knocked over, causing a fire. A few buckets of water from the Seine soon put it out, although Mademoiselle credited the Holy Sacrament, which had been sent for.[3]

Mazarin was receiving treatment for gravel, which was aggravating his gout, and he had also begun to suffer convulsions. Knowing he did not have long to live, he moved into his favorite palace at Vincennes to await the end. When Louis received a message that the cardinal desired to see him, the king wept and told the messenger that he wished Mazarin could have lived another four or five years, for then he would have left Louis "capable of governing the kingdom; but that now he should be embarrassed, not knowing whom to trust."[4] Louis's apparent lack of self-confidence would be short-lived.

By now, Louis had joined the cardinal at Vincennes, where he visited him daily. Mazarin would rally, but the good days were becoming fewer. Often, as he left the cardinal's chambers, Louis's eyes would be filled with tears.

In March, the rapidly declining cardinal was warned by his physicians that the end was approaching. Mazarin had done tremendous things for France. He had secured peace with her neighbors, guided Louis in personal matters, and given the king a thorough education in every aspect of statecraft except, significantly, finance. He had also formed a massive collection of treasures in the form of books, manuscripts, jewels, paintings, tapestries, plates, and other objets d'art, while accumulating a vast personal fortune. Mazarin was very attached to his precious possessions; one day, the young Brienne found the dying cardinal looking at his beloved paintings one final time and sighing, "I must leave all this! I'll never see these things again."[5]

Mazarin attributed much of his fortune, most of which had been amassed since his return from exile after the Fronde, to the king's largesse. Unfortunately, Louis had been unaware of his own generosity, and Mazarin had become very rich, very quickly, by diverting funds destined for the royal treasury into his own reserves.

Now, as he lay on his deathbed, his confessor warned him that he would be damned if he did not make restitution on his ill-gotten wealth.[6] Standing nearby was Jean-Baptiste Colbert, Mazarin's *intendant de la maison*[7] since 1651, who knew not only Mazarin's material worth but also how it had been acquired and where it was hidden.[8] He suggested that Mazarin should offer his fortune to Louis, not doubting that the king would refuse it or else return it immediately. This Mazarin did, and on March 3, he presented everything to Louis. In the agonizing days that followed, Mazarin considered his "poor family," who "would have no bread"; but after three days, just as the cardinal had hoped, and exactly as Colbert had predicted, Louis returned the fortune.[9] Mazarin made his will, while insisting that no inventory was to be made of his assets.

Ready now to die, Mazarin offered one last piece of advice to Louis: preserve the rights of the church; nominate to church benefices only those worthy to hold them; treat the nobility with respect and liberality; ensure judges stayed within the remit of their offices; relieve the people from the *taille*[10] and other financial burdens; and select his ministers according to their talents.[11] However, the cardinal did not advise Louis to govern alone; that decision was made by Louis himself. As he had once said, "his greatest desire was to manage his affairs for himself,"[12] and now he was more than ready.

Mazarin died just after two o'clock on the morning of March 9, 1661, at the age of fifty-nine. Louis remained with him almost to the end, but a strictly enforced tradition insisted that a king of France must never linger in the face of death, so Louis was led out of the cardinal's chamber before the end came. When he received the news that the cardinal was dead, he burst into tears, deeply mourning the loss of the man who had been his godfather, mentor, faithful minister, and close friend. The king shut himself away in his rooms, the only time in his life he would be entirely alone, and when he emerged, he was a different man. No longer the inexperienced youth who needed someone to run his affairs for him, Louis was now master, king in name and in fact. The personal reign of Louis XIV had begun.

Louis immediately summoned his first council. It was attended by two of the three ministers of state: Michel Le Tellier, the secretary for war, and Hughes de Lionne, acting secretary for foreign affairs and, for the past twenty years, Mazarin's right-hand man. The third minister, Nicolas Foucquet, *procureur-général* and superintendent of finances, was not yet aware of the cardinal's death, and even though he lived next to the château de Vincennes, he had not been called to the meeting. This first council of Louis's personal reign transacted urgent business, which included drafting the letters to be sent to foreign heads of state to inform them of Mazarin's death. The meeting lasted three hours, and before Louis left, he issued orders for a second council to meet in Paris early the following day.

At seven the next morning, March 10, Louis's former boyhood friend, Loménie de Brienne, entered the king's cabinet and announced that the chancellor, the ministers, and the council had arrived. Louis, who was already hard at work, handed Brienne an order before telling him to send the gentlemen in. All three ministers of state—Le Tellier, Lionne, and Foucquet—attended this council, as did Chancellor Séguier, the comte de Brienne, secretary of state for foreign affairs; the young Brienne, who would inherit his father's post; Phélypeaux de la Vrillière, secretary for the Pretended Reformed Religion,[13] and Henri de Guénégaud, seigneur du Plessis, secretary of state.

In a typical gesture of politeness, Louis raised his hat to his councillors before taking his seat. He then directly addressed Chancellor Séguier: "Monsieur, I have assembled you with my ministers and my secretaries of state to tell you that, up to the present, I have been willing to leave the government of my affairs to the late M. le Cardinal; it is time that I govern them myself." He ordered them to assist him when he asked for their counsel, but they were forbidden to seal any agreements except on his orders. They were to sign not even so much as a safe-conduct or a passport except on Louis's command, and they were to render account every day to the king. Turning to Foucquet, he ordered him to "make use of Colbert, whom the late M. le Cardinal had recommended to me." Louis then assured Lionne of his affection, pronouncing himself pleased with the minister's service before assigning the young Brienne to work with Lionne in the ministry of foreign affairs. Then the king added:

> *The face of the theater is changing. In the government of my State,*
> *in the management of my finances and in the foreign negotiations,*
> *I have other principles than those of the late M. le Cardinal. You*
> *know my wishes; it is for you now, messieurs, to execute them.* [14]

The meeting was at an end. Louis rose, leaving his ministers to absorb what had just happened. It was an unprecedented move. Had Louis followed tradition, the royal council would have included Anne of Austria, Philippe, Condé, Conti, and Beaufort, and members of the nobility, but Louis denied them all this privilege. The nobility, no matter how high, would have no place in Louis's new scheme of government.

That Louis had intended to rule alone came as no surprise to Michel Le Tellier; four days before Mazarin's death, Louis confided to him that he planned to abolish the *ministériat*, the office of first minister. [15] Queen Anne too was aware of Louis's decision. As she told her ladies, "Le Tellier, Foucquet, and Lionne were destined not to govern but to serve the king." [16]

Nicolas Foucquet, who had not been forewarned, was shocked and dismayed. It was widely known that he expected Louis to leave the government of the country to his council, with Foucquet stepping into Mazarin's shoes. Louis, however, was firm in his resolve to exercise what he called his *métier de roi*, his job of being king, for which his years of training under Mazarin's supervision had amply prepared him. Later, when the archbishop of Rouen, president of the Assembly of the Clergy, asked Louis to whom he should address himself now that the cardinal was dead, Louis's reply was succinct: "To me, M. l'archevêque." [17]

The France that Louis inherited was populated by some eighteen million people, half a million of whom lived in Paris. [18] However, many of the people were illiterate, while the more than one hundred regional dialects spoken in France meant that French was effectively a foreign language to many. Thanks largely to Mazarin's diplomacy and Turenne's military genius, France's borders were reasonably secure. Louis also enjoyed the loyalty of those who had previously opposed him: Turenne and Condé.

The economy gave cause for concern. During Louis's minority, the years of foreign and civil war had left farmland unable to provide food, leaving the peasantry to starve. When Louis had toured parts of the realm during the Fronde, he had witnessed the hardship faced by his people but had been powerless to help. Disorder among the civilian population had been matched by lack of discipline in the army. Without new workshops, industry came to a standstill. The Fronde had generated a flood of lawsuits, so that the only people making a living were the lawyers. Now, in 1661, national debt amounted to 143 million livres, twice the amount held in the royal treasury. With revenues for that year, 1662, and 1663 having already been spent, France was almost bankrupt.

In his memoirs, Louis wrote, "Even from childhood, the name alone of idle kings and mayors of the palace displeased me when it was pronounced in my presence."[19] Determined not to be one of those idle kings, Louis established a rigid working timetable in which he would spend two or three hours each morning and again in the afternoon working with various ministers or councillors. At other times he worked alone, taking care of various affairs as they arose. Only when work was finished for the day would he allow himself time for amusements.[20]

The king quickly identified those areas that were most in need of attention. He noted that the finances were almost entirely exhausted and even the most necessary expenses of his household and his own personal needs were either delayed or supported by credit. Meanwhile, the financiers were wealthy and had concealed their irregularities or else flaunted their insolent and audacious luxury, "as though they dreaded leaving me unaware of them."[21]

Other areas to be addressed were the church, with particular attention to be made to schism, especially Jansenism;[22] and the nobility,
chiefly those claiming nobility but who were not titled or who had
purchased their titles and were now abusing their status to tyrannize
their vassals.[23] Duelling was less of a problem because Louis enforced
already existing edicts against the practice.[24] Justice required urgent
attention, since it was required in order to reform the others. Nevertheless, Louis found it to be the greatest challenge, because offices were
filled with people without merit, judges often lacked experience and
learning, while laws governing the judiciary were routinely flouted.
The trial system was abused, and the royal council caused confusion
with contradictory decisions made in Louis's name, as though they
came from him.

Superintendent Foucquet, equally concerned about the irregularities in the finances, requested a private audience with Louis. Speaking
candidly, he declared that if there were abuses in the management of
the finances and if correct form had not been observed, it was due
to the urgent necessity of the times, namely war on two fronts as
well as the Fronde. He noted that nothing had been done except by
Mazarin's order and promised that, henceforth, there would be no
more expenditure without Louis's directive. Louis was satisfied with
Foucquet's assurances for the future; as for the past, he did not insist
upon learning the details.[25] His words were, said Foucquet, "noble and
worthy of a great king."[26]

It is often thought that the dying Mazarin had warned Louis about
Foucquet. Mme de Motteville, for instance, believed that Mazarin "had
given the King some advice, so it was said, against the Superintendent
Foucquet."[27] This is not true. The superintendent had been loyal to
the cardinal and the king during the Fronde, and his knowledge
of state affairs made him indispensable. Furthermore, Foucquet's
expertise in financial matters, which was underpinned by a powerful
client network, had been of enormous use to the cardinal and the
state. Nevertheless, Louis ordered Foucquet to record every financial

transaction in a register, complete with an abstract so Louis could see instantly the state of expenses made or impending.[28] As an added precaution, he appointed Colbert as intendant of finances; Colbert was a man in whom Louis had the greatest confidence because, as he said, of Colbert's diligence, intelligence, and integrity.[29]

Louis now turned his attention to one of the first acts of his personal reign: to establish the Académie Royale de Danse. Based in Paris, the academy would professionalize ballet. One effect of this was that the steps would become too difficult to be accomplished by the amateur dancers at court.[30] There was a political as well as artistic dimension to this approach, which would confer power upon a small group of carefully chosen individuals and provide Louis with a means of diminishing the nobility without destroying them.[31] The academy would be run by the comte de Saint-Aignan, soon to be made a duke. At the same time, Jean-Baptiste Lully was appointed superintendent of the king's music.

Louis's next priority was to attend to the late cardinal's estate. When Colbert advised Mazarin to offer his fortune to Louis, his motive was to prevent an inventory of the cardinal's fortune; for the same reason, Mazarin willed that no inventory of his assets should be made. Both men feared that an audit would reveal the true extent of the cardinal's wealth and raise questions about how he had acquired it. Colbert feared that such revelations would threaten those who had become rich in Mazarin's service, chief among whom was Colbert himself.

Mazarin and Colbert took advantage of the disordered financial system to enrich themselves at the state's expense. As superintendent of finances, it was Foucquet's job to raise funds by supervising tax collecting and by working with a network of financiers willing to lend money to the crown. He did not personally handle the cash, which went directly into the treasury, where royal treasurers disposed of it upon receiving authorization from Foucquet. Should the crown default on its loans, however, Foucquet was subject to suit.[32]

In addition to raising revenue for the crown, Foucquet was responsible for providing Mazarin with large sums of money each month.

This was supposed to finance the continuing military expenses and support the royal household,[33] the money being delivered in gold or silver coin. Mazarin spent the cash but gave no account of his outlay to Foucquet. The cardinal, therefore, was free to direct monies destined for royal or military expenses to his own use.[34]

In order to fulfill Mazarin's demands, Foucquet was often forced to borrow, usually at a rate higher than the legal rate of 5.5 percent, on his personal account. Each time he raised funds, he retained a discount, which was used to reimburse the creditor. As a lender, his own loans were refunded this way, but the method meant that the line between Foucquet's personal account and that of the state was often indistinct.

Louis, who had pointedly not been taught about state finances, was unaware of these complex processes. He did, however, insist upon an inventory of the cardinal's estate, if only to make it easier to settle the inheritance on his heirs. To accommodate Mazarin's wishes, Louis divided the cardinal's personal accounts, which he had been particularly desirous to conceal, into three parts. The first would go to the duc and duchesse de Mazarin[35] after inventory. The second would be entrusted to Colbert's safekeeping, again after inventory. The third was left in Colbert's possession and would not be inventoried. In this way, much that Mazarin wished to be hidden remained hidden.[36]

Even so, Colbert worried that he would be asked to account for the fortune he had amassed in Mazarin's service. Afraid of the consequences should Louis find out how he had come by it, he decided that a scapegoat was needed, someone who could be blamed for the disorder in the finances and would be made to pay for the crippling bankruptcy that left Louis with empty coffers and the people without food. That scapegoat was not hard to find: who better than Superintendent Foucquet?

Colbert and Foucquet came from similar backgrounds. Both of their families had emerged from the merchant classes and climbed the social ladder to public office by means of hard work and judicious marriages. However, while the Colberts rose to prominence in the provinces, the Foucquets, originally a Breton family, achieved success in Paris. Foucquet attended a more prestigious school, the Collège de Clermont in Paris.[37] His family was in royal service, and the young Foucquet's rise was facilitated by none other than Cardinal Richelieu, who employed him as an intendant. From there, he went into law, becoming *procureur-général* and, finally, superintendent of finances. Colbert studied in his native Relms before being apprenticed to a banker based in Lyons. He then went to Paris to study under a notary and an attorney before entering the ministry for war as a clerk. This brought him into the sphere of the minister for war, Michel Le Tellier, who introduced him to Mazarin.[38]

In temperament, Colbert and Foucquet were poles apart. Colbert was austere and haughty, and although he enjoyed dancing, he was otherwise unsociable. Mme de Sévigné named him "The North" because of his frosty demeanor. Foucquet too was arrogant, but he had a wide circle of friends and loved nothing better than to attend salons, write poetry, and assemble a magnificent library. He was a patron of artists, writers, and scientists, and he kept an open table. While both men worked diligently, Colbert rarely left his desk and was always to be seen with papers in his hand. Foucquet, on the other hand, often worked from home and mixed business with pleasure, which piqued Colbert.

At first, relations between the two men were friendly, but gradually Colbert came to look upon the superintendent with jealous eyes. While both men had risen to prestigious offices in the state, Foucquet held the higher position. Colbert now took every opportunity to blacken Foucquet's name, disparage his work, and arouse suspicion against him, suggesting that Foucquet's extensive building projects and his business ventures were not above board. Colbert's motive, which had become more urgent since the death of his master, was to take Foucquet's place.[39]

Colbert set about making himself indispensable to Louis. He suggested ways to reform the finances and, in a masterstroke, "found" millions of livres in cash that Mazarin had hidden in the cellars at Vincennes. His new post as intendant of finances afforded him the perfect opportunity to sow the seeds of doubt in Louis's mind about the honesty of the superintendent. Entrusted with the register of accounts, he used it to prove Foucquet's alleged dishonesty while earning Louis's confidence.

At present, however, Louis was preoccupied with weddings. The spring of 1661 saw the marriage of Marie Mancini to the Italian connétable Colonna, who was not a little surprised to find his wife was still a virgin. However, it was the marriage of Louis's brother, Philippe, that caused the most excitement at court.

Philippe's prospective bride was Henriette d'Angleterre. Born on June 16, 1644, in Exeter, Henriette was parted from her mother at only two weeks old when the queen of England took refuge in her native France. At the age of two years, Henriette joined her mother at the French court, where she lived in an apartment at the Louvre. Far from participating in court life, Henriette and her mother lived like poor refugees, and the child was often forced to stay in bed all day during the harsh winters in order to keep warm.

Following the execution of Henriette's father, Charles I, her brother became king, but Charles II was exiled from his own kingdom. At the age of eight, Henriette was sent to the convent of the Visitation at Chaillot to be educated.

Henriette's childhood was austere. Her mother was deeply religious and disapproved of many of the court entertainments, but Queen Anne took pity on the girl and brought her to court whenever she could. Henriette took part in some of the court ballets, and she witnessed Louis's coronation. Then, as though her situation had not been difficult enough, matters became still more delicate when Mazarin negotiated an alliance with Cromwell. As the daughter of a deposed and executed king, the sister of a king without a kingdom, and her native land now a republic, Henriette's stock on the marriage market crashed. With one prince after another turning her down, Louis turned to Philippe and quipped, "You will marry the Princess of England, because no one wants her." In fact, Louis feared that he would be made to marry her if his proposed match with Marie-Thérèse failed. This was the reason for his earlier rudeness toward Henriette, which was very much out of character for him. When it came to Henriette, however, the king's tactlessness knew no bounds, and he told his brother that he "need not be in so great a hurry to espouse the bones of the Innocents,"[40] a reference to the princess's almost emaciated appearance.

Then, in May 1660, Charles II was restored to the throne of England and everything changed for Henriette. No longer the poor, unwanted relative, she was now the sister of a reigning king and eminently marriageable. The negotiations for her marriage to Philippe took place at the same time that Louis's marriage was being discussed.

At first Philippe disliked Henriette. On one occasion, he showed his resentment towards her and her mother during a dispute over precedence at court. "We shall have enough to do with people who depend upon us for bread," he said, "if we permit them to go before us."[41] However, when Philippe's uncle, the duc d'Orléans died, Philippe knew that he would not inherit the Orléans appanage until he married. Suddenly the prospect of marrying Henriette did not seem so objectionable. For Philippe, therefore, the marriage was one of convenience. For Henriette too, marriage to the most eligible prince in Christendom promised to release her from her austere prison into a world of warmth and comfort, beautiful clothes, glittering entertainments, and, most importantly, freedom from her controlling mother. Louis, who felt a "natural antipathy to the English people,"[42] was nevertheless pleased with the match because it provided him with an English ally, who would protect his interests in the event of a break with Spain.[43] Moreover, his dislike of the English was "easily effaced in him by the ties of blood, which invited the princess and himself to like each other."[44] The marriage took place on March 31 at the Palais-Royal. It was a quiet ceremony with only a few guests, and, since it was Lent, there was no wedding banquet. Philippe and Henriette, whose official titles were Monsieur and Madame, withdrew to their apartments in the Tuileries. A few days later, Louis took his court to Fontainebleau, his favorite summer residence, where he would remain until December.

EIGHT
The Summer of 1661

Several weeks into his personal reign, Louis showed no sign that he was weary of the business of government. Much to the disappointment of those who wished to hold power in their own hands, Louis embraced his work with enthusiasm. He rose between eight and nine each morning, even though he usually went to bed late. Leaving Marie-Thérèse's bed, he went to his own room, where he said his prayers and dressed himself.[1] He then closed his doors so he could attend to whatever work was pressing at the time, but also to "relieve himself of the crowd."[2] At ten, Louis joined his council, where he remained until he went to mass at midday. Leaving the chapel, he would sometimes spend time with the two queens in private; at other times, he would meet his people. Louis was and would remain accessible to his subjects, granting audiences to anyone who wanted to see him and "listening patiently to such as had something to say to him." Louis nevertheless maintained a "lofty and serious air,"[3] although he was nothing but charming to the ladies. Mme de Motteville attributes this approach to the reputation acquired by his cousin, Charles II of England, and the praise he received for the way he governed his kingdom. Louis resolved to "make himself greater and more glorious than all the princes who had hitherto worn crowns."[4] Louis accepted their petitions and gave his answers on days assigned for the purpose. After dinner, he would remain with his family for a time before going to work with his ministers.

Assiduous in his application to his *métier de roi*, Louis surprised courtiers, councillors, and ministers alike, who now saw just how much he had learned while closeted with Mazarin. The king "suddenly appeared a politician in affairs of the state, a theologian in those of the Church, precise in matters of finance, speaking with justice, taking always the right side in council, [and] sensitive to the interests of private persons." Louis hated intrigue, saw through flattery, and dealt severely with "the grandees of the kingdom whom he suspected of a desire to govern him," a legacy of the Fronde. Yet no matter how much affairs of state exercised him or occupied his time, he always managed to devote some part of his day to amusements.

In the early weeks and months of his marriage, Louis was very happy with Marie-Thérèse. He thanked his mother for "having taken out of his heart Mademoiselle Mancini" and given him the Infanta, who would make him happy, "as much by her beauty as by her virtue, her compliance, and the affection" which she showed him."[5] For her part, Marie-Thérèse had been in love with Louis since childhood, saying that "not only had she loved the king, but she had even loved his portraits."[6]

Since that time, however, Louis's passion had cooled. The now pregnant[7] Marie-Thérèse was beautiful, but beauty alone was not enough to retain the king's interest, and life had become decidedly uninspiring for him. He wanted someone who would share his love of theater, dancing, riding, and cards, but the pious queen had no interest in these worldly pursuits. Instead, she "loved retirement more rather than a queen of France, who owes herself to the public, should love it."[8] While this virtue was commended by the ladies of the court, it annoyed Louis. He looked elsewhere for stimulation and found it in a most unexpected source.

Philippe and Henriette had arrived at Fontainebleau three weeks after their marriage. It soon became apparent that all was not well between them. Philippe preferred to spend time with his male favorites, and Henriette, in need of diversion, found it in Louis's company. Louis, who had once delighted in deriding Henriette, now saw her in a new light. Gone was the awkward girl with the cheap clothes and the air of a pauper. Henriette had blossomed into a beautiful woman. With her delicate "rose and jasmine" complexion, soft and brilliant eyes, red lips, and perfect teeth, she was exquisite, but Henriette possessed an enchantment that defied description: "there was something in her that made itself loved," said Mme de Motteville.[9] While Henriette was still very thin, she was graceful; she loved to dance and was an excellent rider. She loved theater as much as Louis did, and her sense of fun and adventure and her love of amusements made Henriette, rather than Marie-Thérèse, the true queen of the court.

Louis and Henriette began to spend time together. Henriette liked to swim, and she and her ladies would ride out in carriages to the Seine, returning on horseback. They were elegantly dressed, their hats a profusion of colorful plumes. Louis and the young men of the court would join them, and, after supper, they would drive to the canal, where they would walk into the night to the sound of violins.[10] At other times, Louis would take the two queens onto the canal at Fontainebleau in a gilded boat shaped like a galley. Philippe and Henriette would accompany them, and the small group would enjoy a collation served to them by Condé.[11] The duc de Beaufort also joined the court occasionally, serving at meals and riding out with Louis at the hunt.

Anne, Condé, and Beaufort were among the few older people at the otherwise youthful court: Louis and Marie-Thérèse were twenty-two, Philippe twenty, and Henriette younger still at sixteen.

Louis's attachment to Henriette began during these sultry summer days. Although it is impossible to know how innocent, or otherwise, their friendship was, their being together for so much of the time was enough to upset the young queen, awaken jealousy in Philippe, and anger in Anne and Henriette de France. At first, Anne dismissed Marie-Thérèse's fears, saying she was wrong to want to restrain Louis and that the "honorable pleasures which he sought ought not to give her pain."[12] She also tried to warn the delicate Henriette that "her late hours and her hunting parties might injure her health."[13] It was only when Louis and Henriette persisted and "went to such extremes" that Anne finally had to put her foot down. She ordered Mme de Motteville to speak to Henriette on her behalf, but her counsel fell on deaf ears.[14]

Urged, cajoled, and threatened to come to their senses, the lovers concocted a plan to convince everyone that the king was not visiting Henriette but that the object of his affection was one of the ladies of the court.[15] They identified three suitable candidates: Mlles de Pons, Chémerault, and La Vallière. In the end, their choice fell upon Louise de La Vallière, one of Henriette's maids. Louise lived in her mistress's household, which was convenient, because anyone watching Louis's movements could be persuaded that he was visiting her.

Louise was pretty, very sweet, and terribly naïve. Like many young women, she was in love with the king. When she first arrived at court, she was too afraid even to talk to him. She was certainly not the sort of lady to capture the heart of a king, especially a king who liked his ladies to be spirited, not shy and retiring. However, much to Henriette's chagrin, Louis fell deeply and passionately in love with Louise, and so began one of the most famous and charming love stories of all time.

Born at Tours on August 6, 1644, Louise-Françoise de La Baume Le Blanc de La Vallière was six years younger than the king. Her father, Laurent, was a chevalier and captain-lieutenant of the *colonel* of the

Light Cavalry. To his family name he added La Vallière, which he took from a small manor in the parish of Reugny, west of Amboise, and it is here that Louise was brought up with her elder brother, Jean-François.[16] When La Vallière died, Louise's mother, Françoise Le Provost de la Coutelaye, married Jacques de Courtarvel, marquis de Saint-Rémi, first steward to Gaston d'Orléans.[17] A playmate to Gaston's daughters from his second marriage, Louise was present at Blois when Louis called on his way to his wedding the previous year, but her shyness prevented her from coming forward to meet him.

Louise's family moved to Paris shortly afterwards, where she came to the attention of Mme de Choisy, a society lady of great wit; she once said to Louis, "Sire, if you want to become an interesting man, you must often come and talk with me," which advice Louis took, visiting the lady twice a week.[18] When Mme de Choisy wanted to establish relations with the newly wed Henriette, who was still establishing her household, she introduced Louise to the princess, who appointed her maid-of-honor.[19] So poor was Louise that her mother had to borrow the money to buy dresses suitable for her new position, but when she joined her mistress's household at the Tuileries just after the wedding, the new maid was found to be "extremely pretty, gentle, natural."[20]

Louis was attracted to Louise's beauty. Her silver-blond hair, pale complexion, and the essential dark eyebrows matched the accepted ideals of beauty, but Louise also possessed another quality that Louis could not resist: she was an accomplished equestrienne. One visitor to Paris described seeing Louise in the Tuileries gardens riding a fine Arab horse bareback and using a silk cord as a bridle.[21] In her youth, Louise injured her ankle in a riding accident, which left her with a limp, but this did not impede her riding and dancing. Louis was captivated by Louise, and the shy and deeply religious Louise fell hopelessly in love with him.

The king's attentions to Louise were meant to camouflage his friendship with Henriette; as such, it was essential that he should be seen with her, or that courtiers should notice him going to her chamber. As it was, the reverse happened. Louis openly spent time with Henriette, and his relationship with her now became a cover for his romance with Louise.

Louis danced the part of Impatience in a ballet of the same name. The role symbolized the king's desire for glory in battle and in love,[22] but few who watched guessed that their king was in the grip of a new passion. His attempt at secrecy proved the sincerity of his love for Louise,[23] but perhaps the secret was too well kept, for Louis's boyhood friend, Brienne, was straying a little too close to Mlle de La Vallière for Louis's comfort.[24]

Brienne, who had joined the court at Fontainebleau in May, had secured Louise's approval to commission Lefebvre de Venise[25] to paint her portrait. One day, Louis entered Henriette's apartments to find Brienne in the antechamber talking to Louise. The king asked what they thought they were doing, to which Brienne answered that they were discussing Louise's portrait and playing with the idea that she should be portrayed as the Madeleine. He observed that Louise's face possessed "something of the air of Greek statues, it very much pleases me." At this, Louise blushed and Louis passed by without uttering a word. Brienne immediately realized he had made a mistake. Deciding to brazen it out, he asked Louise if she was still interested in being painted as the Madeleine, but Louis, who had overheard, said, "No, she must be painted as Diana; she is too young to be painted as a penitent." There followed a sleepless night for Brienne, who rose in the early hours to attend council. Louis, however, was waiting for him, and he took Brienne aside into a private room and closed the door before asking him outright, "Do you love her, Brienne?"

"Who, Sire?" Brienne pretended to wonder, "Mlle de La Vallière?"

"Yes," said Louis, "it is her of whom I speak."

Brienne assured the king that he was not in love with Louise, although he admitted that he was attracted to her and that if he had not been married, he would have offered her his services.

"Ah," sighed Louis, "you love her. Why do you lie?"

Brienne replied that he had never lied to the king, adding that he could love Louise, but not enough. "Indeed," he sighed in his turn, "she pleases you more than me and you love her."

Louis replied, "Whether I do or do not love her, leave her portrait alone and you will please me."

In the end, Louise was painted as Diana, with Actaeon lurking in the background. Looking upon the pastoral scene, Brienne observed, "And this poor Actaeon was me, an innocent prank that the King played on me."

The pastoral theme continued on the stage when, in July, Louis performed in Lully's *Ballet des Saisons*. He took the part of Ceres, the goddess of the corn, which symbolized his power to look after his people as the goddess looks after nature, especially agriculture.[26] He appeared again as Springtime, with Louise dancing the part of a nymph. The ballet was so well received that it was performed five times.

Louis had, at this time, a favorite named the duc de Saint-Aignan, an older man who knew how to keep a confidence. He was one of the few who were aware of Louis's love for Louise, and when he lent them his room one day in late July, Louise became Louis's mistress in the fullest sense.[27]

No matter how he tried, it was very difficult for Louis to keep anything private, and the affair soon came to the attention of his mother. Anne was distressed by her son's new passion, but she listened to her advisors, who suggested she use more moderation than she had over the king's affair with Henriette. Anne had a ready weapon: Louis was the Most Christian King, and he always endeavored to live up to the title. It was well known that he would tolerate no vice, and that he disliked the debauched, the blasphemous, and the impious.[28] Anne played on these virtues as she reminded her son what he owed to God and his country, adding that there were those who would use his attachment to Louise to "form intrigues about him which would some day be to his injury."[29] She urged him to hide his affair from Marie-Thérèse for fear that grief might endanger the child she was carrying. Louis agreed, and the secret of his affair was preserved.

For Louis, the first summer of his personal reign was the nearest thing to paradise he had ever known. He was free to rule alone and in his own way; he had a child on the way, which he hoped would be a boy; he was surrounded by the beauty of nature; and he was in love. There was one cloud on the horizon, however, and it heralded a storm that would threaten the peace of the French church: Jansenism.

Based on the teachings of Cornelius Jansen, bishop of Ypres, Jansenism taught that everything in the universe happened by divine will, and human lives and history were directed and controlled by the omnipotent God. Salvation, moreover, came through divine grace, similar to the Calvinist doctrine of predestination. The earliest and most important proponent of divine omnipotence, grace, and predestination was the 5th-century bishop Augustine of Hippo. Rendered into simple terms, some people were preselected for salvation, while others were condemned to unavoidable damnation.

Jansen's teachings contradicted the doctrine of human free will, the efficacy of divine grace, and the idea that humankind could be saved from eternal damnation by right worship and the performance of good works, which was espoused by Catholicism. At this period, the most important Catholic sect was the Society of Jesus, or the Jesuits.[30] When Jansen's book, the *Augustinus*, was published posthumously in 1641, it was immediately criticized by Jesuit scholars. However, the *Augustinus* was not universally censured, and the abbé de Saint-Cyran, Jansen's friend and collaborator, embraced his friend's teachings.

Saint-Cyran was the confessor and spiritual director to the nuns of the convent of Port Royal, the abbess of which was Mère Angélique, and the convent became a center for Jansenist teaching. Two years after the publication of Jansen's work, Mère Angélique's brother, the theologian Antoine Arnauld, wrote the treatise *On Frequent Communion*, which promoted fear of God, as a polemic against the Jesuits.[31]

The doctors of the Sorbonne also denounced Jansen's theses, and the university syndic, Nicolas Cornet, appealed to Pope Innocent X to issue a bull condemning the Five Propositions supposedly contained in the *Augustinus*. The bull appeared in 1653, and the whole of the French clergy was required to sign assent to it. Although Arnauld conceded that the Five Propositions mentioned in the bull contravened church doctrine, and were therefore heretical, he denied that they appeared in the *Augustinus*. The net began to tighten when schools run by Port Royal were investigated, and in January 1655, the duc de Liancourt was refused absolution until he removed his daughter from one of its schools and dismissed two members of his household who were thought to be Jansenists.[32]

The following year, in January 1656, the mathematician, philosopher, and writer Blaise Pascal published the first of his *Lettres Provinciales* attacking the Jesuits. That October, the new pope, Alexander VII, issued a bull, *Ad sacrum beati Petri sedem*, in which he insisted, contrary to Arnauld's assertions, that the Five Propositions were indeed to be found in the *Augustinus*.[33]

The Assembly of the Clergy issued a formulary accepting Alexander's bull and required all clerics to sign it. This step was controversial from the beginning, and Louis was obliged to hold a *lit de justice* in order to force its registration. While most clerics agreed to sign the formulary, the Port Royal community argued over the finer points. Influenced by Arnauld's distinction between church law and fact, they agreed that the pope could rule on doctrine but he could not rule against what was a matter of fact; that is, they agreed with the pope that the Five Propositions were heretical, but they denied that they were present in Jansen's work. At this point, other considerations intervened, and the issue of the formulary was set aside, at least for a time.

Louis became personally involved in the Jansenist controversy during the first months of his personal rule in 1661 when an Assembly of the Clergy brought the formulary back to the fore. Arnauld had been forced into hiding during the controversy of the formulary, and in June, his friends issued a compromise in the form of a *Summons to Sign the*

Formulary. This allowed the distinction between law and fact to stand, and many of the nuns of Port Royal felt able to sign it. Louis, however, was dissatisfied with this solution, and the royal court ordered those who had signed the *Summons* to retract.[34]

The king's dislike of Port Royal and Jansenism was influenced by two concerns. The first was political in that Port Royal, while it had remained neutral during the Fronde, was associated with people such as the duchesse de Chevreuse and the duchesse de Longueville, both of whom had been prominent figures during the uprising. This alone would have aroused Louis's suspicions, but they were reinforced by theological interests: Louis, who had been tutored by Jesuits, shared the same religious views as his confessor, the Jesuit Father Annat. Since the Jesuits thought Jansenism to be analogous to Calvinism, they regarded its doctrines as heretical, even though Calvinist teachings closely reflected those of Augustine. Louis had a great deal of respect for Father Annat, whom he saw as right-minded, disinterested, and not given to intrigue.[35]

Louis was also worried about the strong sense of community that existed at Port Royal, which made it seem to him like a shadowy sect whose influence reached the court, the government through Arnauld de Pomponne, and even the judiciary.[36] The convent was potentially too powerful and disruptive for Louis to leave it alone. As he wrote in his memoirs, "I applied myself to destroy Jansenism and to disperse the community where this spirit of novelty was taking form, well intended perhaps, but which did not know or did not wish to know the dangerous consequences that it could have."[37]

A further attempt to uphold the distinction between law and fact prompted Louis to impose a new formulary, which required all clergy to sign to the facts of the case. As July drew to a close, the Port Royal community lodged an appeal on technical grounds, which brought them much-needed respite.

⚜

For Louis's minister, Superintendent Foucquet, the summer of 1661 held little pleasure. Since his implacable enemy, Colbert, had taken up a post in finances, Foucquet had lived in fear. He was right to be afraid. Every evening, Colbert visited the king, portfolio in hand, and told him anything he liked about the disarray in the treasury while placing all the blame on the superintendent. Louis, who knew nothing about running the finances, believed everything Colbert said. Moreover, Colbert had engaged an ally, his former patron, Michel Le Tellier, minister for war. Together, they persuaded Louis that Foucquet, despite his promises to the contrary, was using the disorder of the finances to mask the fact that he was stealing from the king.

Louis was alarmed and angered, but there was worse to come. Colbert had assigned his cousin, Jean-Charles Colbert du Terron, governor of Brouage, to spy on Foucquet's activities in Brittany, including his island marquisate of Belle-Isle-en-Mer. Terron observed Foucquet's shipyards, warehouses, armed garrisons, and his fleet with its flagship, *l'Écureuil*,[38] but he misinterpreted what he saw. Foucquet had long been engaged in overseas trade as well as privateering, for which defense measures were necessary. As to his ships, he wanted France to have a fleet to rival those of the great seafaring nations of England and Holland.

Colbert, who saw none of this firsthand, explained Foucquet's maritime enterprises in the most menacing terms to Louis. He told the king that Foucquet was planning a new Fronde and that his Breton strongholds and garrisons, complete with his Breton clientele, were intended to support this uprising. This evoked terrible memories of the Fronde, while the thought that a nobleman as independent, powerful, and well-connected as Foucquet was free to follow his own ambition persuaded Louis that he must act against him. That Foucquet had been one of his most loyal allies during the uprising now meant little to Louis. Should any man look for advancement, let him find it in loyal service to the king.

Louis's estimation of Foucquet as it is written in his memoirs betrays how far he had been persuaded by Colbert at that point. Later, when he came to edit the work, Louis left this part almost entirely intact, showing that he continued to believe in the superintendent's culpability.[39] "The sight of the vast establishments that this man had planned," he wrote, "and the insolent acquisitions he had made, could only convince me of the profligacy of his ambition; and the general calamity of all my people relentlessly urged my justice against him."

Louis acknowledged that his earlier decision to keep Foucquet in his post would be seen as strange by many, given that he knew about the superintendent's "thieving." However, the king had recognized Foucquet's intelligence and was aware of his deep knowledge of internal affairs of state. This encouraged Louis to imagine that, provided Foucquet acknowledged his past faults and promised to make amends, he could be of great service.[40] Now, he said, he realized his mistake. Rather than becoming wiser and profiting from Louis's benevolence, Foucquet, he thought, merely became more skillful in his dishonesty: "for he could not prevent himself from continuing his excessive expenditure, fortifying strongholds, adorning his palaces, forming cabals, and purchasing under the names of his friends important offices at my expense, in the hope of soon making himself the sovereign arbiter of the State."

Initially, Louis had considered simply excluding Foucquet from affairs of state, "but having since then considered that, given his restless disposition, he would not be able to support this change of fortune without trying something new," he thought it best to arrest Foucquet. This decision was finalized on May 4, but Louis postponed issuing the order until the autumn. The delay allowed the unsuspecting Foucquet time to collect that year's taxes, since Louis required a fund of 4 million livres to cover such expenses as might arise.

For the time being, Louis continued to retain Foucquet in office, assigning him certain sensitive missions, chief among which were providing aid to enemies of Spain and assisting in the negotiations for the marriage of Charles II of England to the Portuguese Infanta,

Catherine of Braganza. His success in these missions heightened Foucquet's hopes of succeeding Mazarin. In reality, Louis was playing the game he had played on the Cardinal de Retz, to lull his victim into a false sense of security until he was ready to strike.

Louis knew that if his plan to ruin Foucquet was to work, he had to remove two major obstacles. The first was Foucquet's post as *procureur-général*, which carried certain immunities and made him justiciable to parlement, where several of the judges were his relatives and many more were his friends. Louis did not trust parlement to view Foucquet's case objectively and feared they would not find against him. To avoid this difficulty, Colbert suggested that Foucquet might be persuaded to sell his post, especially if he thought it would be replaced by a higher one. Louis embraced this idea, hinting to Foucquet that he could become first minister or chancellor in the event of Séguier's death, a post he was known to want. Louis even held out the hope that Foucquet might be received into the Ordre du Saint-Esprit, a great honor.[41]

When Foucquet announced his intention to sell his office of *procureur-général*, his friends urged him not to do so. One, Mme d'Huxelles, warned him that a cabal was being formed, with men such as Turenne, Condé, and Lamoignon[42] joining Colbert's campaign against him. Were he to sell his office, he would place himself in grave danger. Foucquet, however, placed his faith in the king. He sold his post to a friend, Achille de Harlay, receiving 1,400,000 livres for it. Of this, he used 400,000 to compensate his brother, Basile, who held the survivance of the post. The rest he gave to Louis as a cash sum.

The second obstacle was a little trickier. For some time Foucquet had been a favorite of Anne of Austria, whose pension he paid and to whom he gave money for her various charities; moreover, the queen liked him personally. Louis, who was still to some extent under his mother's influence, did not want to anger her, but in order to proceed against Foucquet he needed his mother's compliance.[43] A solution to the dilemma presented itself at the end of June, when Anne's old friend, the duchesse de Chevreuse, came to Fontainebleau for a few days. She had recently remarried, her new husband being the marquis de Laigues. For reasons that are not clear, Laigues hated Foucquet and wished to do him harm. In this, the marquis exercised a great sway over his wife, who, in her turn, exerted her influence over Anne. When Anne travelled to the duchess's home at Dampierre, Foucquet's ruin was sealed.

Foucquet now committed a gross error. Having learned about Anne of Austria's meeting at Dampierre, he confronted her, wanting to know why she had met with his enemies. Anne, affronted by such insolence, gave him short shrift; any feelings of friendship she had towards him were now gone. Mme d'Huxelles wrote to tell him that the queen-mother had forbidden her confessor, a friend of Foucquet's, to speak to him; she then told him to burn the letter after he had read it, adding ominously, "Be more careful of your security than you have been."[44] Once again, Foucquet refused to heed the warning; he believed that Queen Anne would never abandon him.[45]

At this stage, Louis's affair with Louise was still a closely guarded secret. There was, however, one means by which the secrets of Louis's heart could be penetrated, and it was linked to his religious devotion. Louis, now an adulterer, had begun to neglect these duties. This had been brought to Foucquet's attention by Anne's confessor prior to her interdiction. From the same source, Foucquet had also learned that the reason for Louis's uncharacteristic behavior was his involvement with Mlle de La Vallière. This information was confirmed by Foucquet's mistress, Catherine de Menneville, one of Anne's ladies.

Foucquet's normally sharp intelligence and ability to read any situation had been critically disturbed by worry about his work, fear of the cabal against him, and the ravages of a tertian illness that had affected him, more or less seriously, for several weeks. Seeing the potential of recruiting Louise as an ally, much as he had done with other members of the court, he decided to approach her. The story goes that he used a go-between to offer the young lady 20 thousand pistoles, a huge sum of money for anyone, let alone someone who had grown up in relative poverty. Louise, however, was incensed by what she saw as an affront to her honor, saying that not even 200 thousand livres would be enough to make her take a false step. The anonymous go-between felt sure that Louise would report Foucquet to Louis, and urged the superintendent to "get the start" on her by telling the king that Louise had approached him and asked for the money. Foucquet was too much of a gentleman even to consider following this piece of advice.[46] He did, however, compound his faux pas when he encountered Louise a short while later. As he began to praise the merits of the king to her, Louise completely misinterpreted the superintendent's intentions. That evening, she went to Louis and told him everything that had happened, and Louis, like Louise, saw only insolence and sinister designs behind Foucquet's actions.

Louis had several reasons for wanting to destroy Foucquet: he thought the superintendent was stealing from him, he was concerned about Foucquet's activities in Brittany, and he was angry that Foucquet had dared to approach Louise. There were, however, other factors to consider: he resented Foucquet's wealth, feeling sure he had not come by it honestly. He was irritated by Foucquet personally—by his warm and genial character, his baroque lavish lifestyle, and impeccable aesthetic tastes. There was, however, something more deeply disturbing. Since Mazarin's death, Louis had felt that he had never been taken seriously as he embarked upon his personal reign. Several people expected him to grow tired of governing and give it up in favor of the pleasures of youth. Primary among these was Foucquet. Louis felt the need to exert himself and show that he was resolute.

Everything was now in place; it only required Louis to set the time and the place. Given that Foucquet's family heartlands, his business interests, and a large section of his clientele were based in Brittany, Louis announced a meeting of the Estates [47] of that province, to be held at Nantes. This would be the pretext for a royal progress to Brittany, during which Foucquet would be arrested. At first, Louis settled on August 15, but he later postponed his journey, setting the day when his plan would come to fruition on September 5, his twenty-third birthday.

NINE

At Vaux-le-Vicomte

T he sun shone brightly that afternoon as Louis and his court set out from Fontainebleau. It was three o'clock on August 17, and the long cortège made its way slowly along the dusty roads that led to Vaux-le-Vicomte. The château, built by Superintendent Foucquet over a period of five years, had only just been completed. To celebrate, Foucquet had invited the king and the court to a very special party, and Louis had graciously accepted.

Louis was accompanied by his mother, Philippe and Henriette, Condé, Conti, their sister, the duchesse de Longueville, and her husband, as well as the ducs de Beaufort and Guise. Queen Marie-Thérèse was now six months pregnant, and, feeling unable to face the journey, she remained behind at Fontainebleau.[1]

At six o'clock, carriages carrying the king, the court and their household, guards and musketeers—some six thousand people in all—thundered along the tree-lined approach before turning sharply right to enter through the great iron gates. Foucquet, his wife, and a group of friends, including Jean de La Fontaine, stood on the steps of the château awaiting them. It was to be a magical evening, and Foucquet had organized several surprises, which he hoped would delight the king. As the carriages drew to a halt, the superintendent stepped forward to welcome Louis to Vaux.

After a short rest to recover from the lengthy journey, Louis allowed his host to show him the château. The decoration was so recently completed that the smell of paint still hung in the air, but Louis could appreciate the beauty of Le Brun's artistry. He admired also the exquisite tapestries manufactured by the factory Foucquet had established at nearby Maincy. Louis was then presented with a portrait of himself. Commissioned by Foucquet and painted in secret by Charles Le Brun, the portrait was an image of royal power. The king, wearing the robes and holding the insignia of royalty, sat on the *lit de justice*. At the base of the portrait, among the trophies of painting and the arts, were burning weapons, an image of Love restraining Rebellion and a small portrait of Henri IV.[2] Foucquet envisaged Louis as the bringer of peace and a patron and muse of the arts, all the while hinting that Louis should perhaps appoint him as his superintendent-chancellor, as his grandfather had done with Sully.[3]

Louis now took a tour of the gardens, the court following on behind. As a courtesy to Queen Anne, Foucquet had arranged for her to make the tour in a carriage. "Vaux will never be as beautiful as it was that evening," writes La Fontaine, who had already fallen under the château's magical spell.[4] The spectacular fountain called the Bassin de la Gerbe, the Crown Fountain, and Animal Fountain vied for attention, while the water from a hundred jets reached thirty-six feet into the air. Louis was filled with admiration for their beauty, but even more so for the machinery that powered them. The Bassin de la Gerbe in particular caught his attention, for it was as wide as a man and twenty feet high, with the water gushing out with such force that it had to be considered one of the most beautiful fountains in Europe.

The king turned to see the château nestling in its vast grounds, with its orange trees, fountains, and flower gardens. Woodlands stretched out on either side as beautiful ladies walked the pathways, with "courtiers bedecked with ribbons and plumes making the most beautiful sight that can be imagined."[5]

With the sun now beginning to set, the court returned to the château, where a medley of dishes prepared by Foucquet's steward, Vatel, was served. As twenty-four violins played softly in the background, the eighty tables and thirty or so buffets groaned under the weight of fine dishes, which included pheasant, ortolan, quail, young partridge, bisque, ragout, and a wide selection of wines, while Foucquet and his wife did the honors of their house. One hundred and twenty serviettes were called into service, as well as five hundred silver plates, thirty-six dozen trays, and a complete service of vermeil.[6]

After supper, the party returned to the garden, following the avenue of fir trees, at the end of which a stage had been erected. When everyone had taken their seats, Molière appeared, still wearing his ordinary clothes. He announced apologetically that he had no troupe with him and there could be no show unless help arrived. He appealed to Louis for permission to begin, at which the king nodded his assent. Suddenly, a large rock[7] turned into a seashell, from which emerged a naiad, played by Molière's partner, Madeleine Béjart. In Louis's name she commanded the trees and statues to come to life before she exited the stage to make way for dancing fauns, satyrs, and gods.[8] There followed a play in three acts, Les Fâcheux, commissioned by Foucquet and written by Molière, with a prologue by Paul Pellison. This was a new kind of entertainment, the comedy-ballet, born of necessity, for Molière was given only two weeks to conceive, write, learn, and rehearse the play.

The plot of Les Fâcheux is very light: a young man making his way to a tryst with his lover is stopped at every step by several people who insist upon telling him the excruciating details of their various exploits. These are the 'bores' of the title, and sharp-eyed members of the audience would have recognized many of them as being based upon people at the court.[9]

As Louis stood up at the end of the play, the horizon exploded as rockets screamed high into the darkened sky and fell back to earth in cascades of fiery shapes in the form of names, initials, and fleur-de-lis. On the canal floated a huge whale, from the belly of which a host of firecrackers and rockets crackled and shot out, so that the very water appeared to be on fire. The sound of trumpets and drums competed with the noise of the fireworks, lending the scene the air of a "furious battle." The château blazed with the light of countless lanterns and candles.

Louis thought he had seen all the pleasures his superintendent had to offer, and he signalled for his carriage for the return journey to Fontainebleau. Suddenly, the lantern on top of the dome was streaming with thousands of rockets, which tore into the sky and fell to earth in a shower of fiery stars. In a final act of magnanimity, Foucquet offered Vaux-le-Vicomte as a gift to the king.[10]

That evening had been the most spectacular event that anyone could remember. Throughout the festivities, Louis had been gracious, giving no indication of his feelings of contempt towards Foucquet. However, according to Choisy,[11] Foucquet had received a note from his friend, Mme du Plessis-Bellière, warning him that he was to be arrested during the party but that Queen Anne had delayed the order. This was also the understanding of Brienne, who said that the Queen Mother prevented Louis from acting against Foucquet, saying "Ah! my son, that action will do you little honor: this poor man is ruining himself to give you good cheer and you would have him arrested prisoner in his house!"[12] The idea that Louis would do such a thing is not impossible, but it is doubtful, because he had already decided when and where Foucquet would be arrested, and his decision had been taken with a view to engendering maximum impact.

On the other hand, there could be some truth in Choisy's assertion that Foucquet, despite the apparent success of the fête, had finally begun to suspect that he would be ruined. He had been warned by his close friend, Gourville, that Louis was offended by the magnificence of Vaux. Of course, Louis had visited the château before. He, his mother, and brother had been guests at an informal evening hosted by Foucquet in the summer of 1659. He had returned the following year, when he and Marie-Thérèse stopped there on their way to Paris after their marriage. At those times, the château had been far from complete. Now, in the summer of 1661, there was still much work to do, but Le Brun had drawn up plans for the decorative scheme for the ceiling of the oval salon, and Foucquet showed these to the king. Le Brun's original design featured the Foucquet squirrel as a new star in the firmament, supported by Saturn and framed by Mars and Jupiter. Below, Apollo, representing Foucquet, sits in his summer palace surrounded by the gods of Olympus and gazing up into the heavens. Louis saw this cheeky squirrel everywhere he looked, along with Foucquet's motto, *Quo non ascendet?* 'Whither will he not climb?'[13]

Louis, who had danced the part of Apollo several times, was astonished and angered by Foucquet's apparent insolence. As they made their way back to Fontainebleau, the king supposedly said to his mother, "Ah, madame, will we not make all those people disgorge?"[14] Mme de La Fayette was probably closest to the truth when she said that Louis was astonished by Vaux and Foucquet noticed that he was, although both men maintained their composure.[15]

Louis returned to Fontainebleau, where, on August 25, he suppressed the *ordonnance de comptant*, a secret expenses account.[16] This was approved by Chancellor Séguier, but Foucquet saw it as an erosion of some of his powers, and he could not prevent himself from exclaiming, "I am, therefore, no longer anything?"[17] He immediately recovered himself, adding that other ways would be found to cover this kind of expense, and Louis agreed.

That evening, Molière gave a special performance of *Les Fâcheux* at Fontainebleau before the king and the whole court. This time there was an additional character. Louis had enjoyed the play so much when he saw it at Vaux that he suggested to Molière that he might include a character based upon his own master of the wardrobe, the marquis de Soyecourt, who went on to become the master of the hunt. Far from being offended at being numbered among the 'bores,' Soyecourt was enthusiastic, even assisting Molière with hunting terminology so that he could get the characterization right.[18] He was depicted as Dorante, an excruciatingly boring man, who insisted upon telling the hapless lover his exploits while chasing a buck.[19]

At last the time came for Louis to depart for Nantes, and he set off on August 29. The best way to travel to the Breton town was to ride to Orléans and take a leisurely boat down the Loire, but Louis was too impatient to sit for days on a boat; he preferred to ride all the way. Having arrived at Orléans, he lit a candle at Notre-Dame de Cléry before going on to Blois, where he spent the night. The next day he travelled in stages as far as Angers, where he accepted a carriage offered by the bishop, Monseigneur Henri Arnauld. Arriving at Ancenis, he slept at La Croix de Lorraine, where he was joined by several military personnel.[20] Louis was expected to stop for dinner at the Château de Clermont, but he decided to press on for Nantes, where he arrived four hours earlier than anticipated.

With Nantes awash with early autumn rain, Louis decided to dispense with the usual protocol and entered the magnificent Château des Ducs de Bretagne by carriage. A meal was prepared for him, after which he held an audience with various civil and ecclesiastical dignitaries. He then met members of the Chambre des Comptes[21] before going onto the château's ramparts to inspect the cannon, but Louis's mind was elsewhere. Particularly keen to see the minutiae of the plans for the arrest of Foucquet, he met Colbert and Le Tellier, who had spent the last few days formulating the final details.[22] Their plan, which left nothing to chance, specified who Foucquet's jailer would be, the châteaux where he would be held on the journey back to Paris; it even arranged for him to be served bouillon for shock following his arrest. The time had been set for the afternoon so that the matter need not be hurried, but when Louis looked over the plan, several changes were made. The most important of these was that the arrest should take place in the morning as Foucquet was leaving the council meeting. The plans were so secret that Louis posted musketeers outside his room, which was accessed by a small corridor. No one was allowed to enter unless Louis was warned first by the sound of a silver bell.

Foucquet had arrived in Nantes shortly before Louis and was installed with his wife at the Hôtel de Rougé, a house belonging to Mme du Plessis-Bellière situated at the far side of the town. He was still unwell, and Louis, who feared he might try to escape, kept track of the stages of Foucquet's illness.[23] He sent for Brienne, who, upon entering the king's chamber, just had time to see papers strewn over a table before Louis drew a green taffeta cloth across them.[24] Brienne was ordered to go to Foucquet's lodgings to see how he was, but he encountered the superintendent on the road, making his way towards the château; he was well enough to come out and pay his respects to the king.[25]

Louis needed a reliable man to execute the order of arrest, and he chose Charles de Batz Castelmore, sieur d'Artagnan,[26] captain-lieutenant of the first company of musketeers. On Thursday, September 1, a messenger arrived at d'Artagnan's lodgings to find him in bed with a fever, but Louis was suspicious and ordered that he must come whatever state he was in. It was only when the musketeer arrived at the château that Louis saw that his illness was genuine. He told d'Artagnan that he had selected him for an important commission, and that he should return in two or three days' time. Louis also told him to take care of his health.[27]

Although Louis had summoned the Estates of Brittany as the pretext for his visit to Nantes, Louis attended only one meeting. Foucquet, on the other hand, attended several, and, by the time they had come to an end, he had managed to secure a grant of three million écus for Louis, an achievement the king met with indifference.[28]

Louis was impatient.[29] Over the next few days, he sent people to d'Artagnan on various pretexts until, at midday on Sunday, September 4, the musketeer finally arrived at the château. The king led him into his room, closing the door himself, and told him that what he was about to hear must remain secret. He then declared that "being dissatisfied with M. Foucquet, he had resolved to arrest him." He gave d'Artagnan a packet of papers containing his orders before sending him to Le Tellier.[30]

To arrest a man as important as the superintendent of finances was no insignificant commission, and as d'Artagnan entered Le Tellier's chamber, he felt faint and asked for a drink of wine. Once revived, d'Artagnan opened the packet Louis had given him and found an order for Foucquet's arrest, a letter containing the route he had to take, and other orders concerning Foucquet's route to prison. Another letter sent a brigadier of six musketeers to Ancenis, where they would receive further orders, which were to arrest the royal couriers along the route to Paris to prevent news of the arrest from leaking out.[31] Other documents, written by Le Tellier, were addressed to the governors of various places where Foucquet was to be held.

The next day, September 5, was Louis's twenty-third birthday, and this was the day that his plan to arrest Foucquet would finally be executed. To cover his designs, he organized a hunting party, which justified the presence of the musketeers and light horse. A meeting of the royal council had been scheduled for that morning, and d'Artagnan and his men were already mounted and waiting for it to end. As the other council members left, Louis detained Foucquet on the pretext that he had some papers to give him. Louis pretended to rummage about on the desk in search of these documents, all the while glancing through the window. When he saw d'Artagnan waiting in the courtyard of the château, he let Foucquet go.

D'Artagnan's orders required him to arrest Foucquet only when he exited the château grounds so as not to encroach on the prerogative of the captain of the guard, whose job it was to protect the royal residences. The musketeers, spotting Le Tellier, asked him if this order still stood, to which the minister replied that it did. As Foucquet descended the stairs to the courtyard, he was besieged by petitioners who asked him for money or pushed requests into his hand, and he disappeared into the crowd before d'Artagnan could reach him. As d'Artagnan ran out of the château precincts with several musketeers, he sent his adjutant to inform Louis what had happened. Foucquet was spotted in a sedan chair heading towards the Place de la Cathédrale. D'Artagnan raced up to him and stopped the chair, saying he had something to tell him. Foucquet asked if it could wait until he arrived back at his lodgings, but d'Artagnan told him that it could not. Foucquet stepped out of the chair and raised his hat, and at that moment, d'Artagnan told him he had been ordered by the king to arrest him. Foucquet asked to see the order, saying that he believed himself to be in higher favor with the king than anyone in the kingdom. As he read the order for his arrest, Foucquet's face reflected his state of shock, and when he handed the paper back to d'Artagnan, he asked him to execute his orders without creating a scandal.[32] Brienne was sent to tell the king that his orders had been successfully carried out. As he approached the château, he saw a carriage enclosed in iron trellises and surrounded by musketeers; inside was d'Artagnan with Foucquet sitting quietly beside him.[33]

As he later wrote to his mother,[34] Louis was very pleased with the success of the plan and proud of the people who had obeyed his orders so efficiently. He sent officials to place seals on each of Foucquet's properties as well as those of his friends. Foucquet's family was scattered to various parts of France, and musketeers were sent to Belle-Isle in case the superintendent had arranged armed resistance on the island. Louis's precautions to prevent messengers leaking news of Foucquet's arrest were not entirely successful. La Forêt, Foucquet's *valet de chambre*, managed to slip through the cordon and gave the news to his master's friends and associates, many of whom would be arrested or would manage to flee. At the same time, Colbert began his campaign to win over two of Foucquet's most powerful allies in

Brittany, Neuchèze and Duquesne, and to gain control of the superin-tendent's sea ports and ships. These were necessary steps in his attempt to restructure the royal navy, a project that was close to his heart, if not to Louis's.[35]

As he announced the news of Foucquet's arrest, Louis noticed the clear distress of Lionne, one of the fallen superintendent's closest friends. Louis reassured the minister, saying, "You were his friend, but I am content with your services."[36] Louis, who months earlier had expressed his intention to rule without a first minister, had made his point; yet, while he thought he had achieved a coup d'état, in reality he had helped to perpetrate one of the most serious miscarriages of justice ever to taint his reign.

TEN

The Sun King

W hile Louis had already announced his intention to rule alone, he did not feel that he had achieved this aim until he was able to take full control of the finances. This, for him, was the most important consequence of removing Fouquet, because, he said, "What I believed I had done on that occasion that was most worthy of being observed and the most advantageous for my people, was the suppression of the office of superintendent; or rather, to take charge of it myself."[1] Although the task before him was formidable, Louis embraced it with enthusiasm, because, as he wrote, "I have always considered the satisfaction that is to be found in doing one's duty as the sweetest pleasure in the world."[2]

Louis was eager to establish a new system for managing the finances. Colbert had recently been appointed to the high council of ministers with the title of intendant of finances, and he conceived and drafted a set of regulations for the creation of a new *conseil royal*.[3] This would be presided over by the king, who would oversee and sign everything concerning the collecting of taxes and state expenditure. Below the king would be three ministers, among them Colbert. The council would meet three times each week, on Tuesdays, Thursdays, and Saturdays.

The tax farms were re-contracted, the posts purchased by auction, with the whole process being supervised by Louis. Together with the requirement that the value of the contracts was payable on a monthly basis, this reform saved some 5 million livres per year in interest on loans and provided for the most urgent state expenses.[4] At the same time, commission on the direct taxes was reduced, which allowed Louis to reduce the *taille*, the tax burden on the peasantry.[5]

Louis then established a Chamber of Justice, which would compel those who had grown wealthy to the detriment of the state to contribute heavily to its expenses. The chamber also examined all the contracts pertaining to the king's debts. These were found to be so extensive that to repay them would lead to the ruin of his subjects unless Louis continued to use the inefficient ways that had prevailed for so long, and which would yield relatively little in return. For this reason, Louis liquidated his debts as well as debts owed to him. Because these "discussions were delicate, and that most of those concerned had a lot of influence and many relatives in the ordinary courts of justice," Louis felt it necessary to form a new court to be run by the most distinguished people taken from other courts.[6]

Among those to benefit from Louis's financial reforms were the poor at the Salpêrière in Paris. The king was adamant that everyone in the realm, even the most unfortunate, should have enough to eat, whether by work or through state assistance.[7]

As well as the finances, industry was also to be reformed, with Louis issuing orders to import workers from Holland, Flanders, Germany, Italy, Scandinavia, England, Spain, and Russia. These workers brought various skills, such as weaving, cloth-making, leather-working, glass-making, and steel-working. There were goldsmiths, tar-makers, and stocking-makers, all living on generous subsidies. While some were resented by local laborers, most settled in France, made money, expanded their businesses, and employed French workers.[8]

Louis desired that France should be self-sufficient, all the country's needs to be catered for without resorting to the import of foreign goods. Items that were brought in were subject to heavy taxes. In order to limit the number of expensive English horses coming into France, Louis ordered the establishment of studs in Normandy, Poitou, Berry, and Languedoc. Colbert took over the factory established by Foucquet for the manufacture of tapestries and converted it into the now famous Gobelins.

It was while Louis was occupied with these matters that news arrived of a serious diplomatic incident that had just occurred in London. Despite the signing of the treaty of the Pyrenees and the apparent peace between France and Spain, the ambassadors of these two countries continued a kind of cold war, which had spilled into an argument over rank and precedence. While attending a ceremony in England, the servants of the Spanish ambassador, the baron de Vatteville, attacked the cortège of Louis's ambassador, the comte d'Estrades, with the encouragement of the local populace. The comte's horses were killed and his servants were injured in the scuffle, preventing d'Estrades from taking his rightful place in the ceremony.

Louis, upon hearing about the quarrel, took matters into his own hands. The Spanish ambassador in Paris was banished and all communication with Spain was forbidden. Louis's ambassador in Madrid was also recalled.[9] Louis then urged Charles II of England, "who had no other interest in this dispute than to prevent any sort of disturbance or agitation in his capital city," to punish the offenders.[10]

This incident caused one of the few arguments between Louis and Marie-Thérèse. The queen, who was even more withdrawn than usual due to her pregnancy, raged at Louis and even took her father's side against him. Stung to the quick, Louis threatened to have his revenge against his father-in-law and was even prepared to go to war, carrying out "to the last extreme a resentment as just as this one," where he would "acquire honor" in placing himself at the head of his armies.[11]

Luckily, Philip IV of Spain was anxious to make reparation and recognize the supremacy of France. Meanwhile, Philip's ambassadors visited Louis in his great office at the Louvre, where the papal nuncio, the ambassadors, residents, and envoys at the Court, as well as the important peoples of his state were assembled. There, having presented Louis with his credentials, the Spanish ambassador extraordinary[12] told Louis that Philip of Spain had been equally displeased and surprised by the events in London. He had recalled the baron de Vatteville and dismissed him from office in order to satisfy Louis and to show him how much resentment his actions had caused. He added that Philip had ordered his ambassadors in England and elsewhere not to compete with Louis's ambassadors and ministers in any public ceremonies that they might attend. Louis was himself very pleased to hear this declaration and professed that, "It obliged me to continue to live on good terms" with Philip.[13]

As though disputes of rank and position among the ambassadors were not enough, Louis also took the Venetians to task for referring to France and Spain as being *delle due corone*, of two crowns; Louis felt that this implied equality and put a stop to it.[14]

While Louis was still basking in the glow of these diplomatic victories, an event occurred that crowned everything he had achieved so far. Marie-Thérèse's pains began, and for the next twelve hours she endured the discomfort and indignity of going through her labor in a stifling room filled with those who claimed their right to witness the royal birth. Louis had gone to confession at five o'clock that morning, receiving communion while pleading for divine protection for the queen. He went to her chamber immediately afterwards, and remained by her side throughout her labor.

The queen "was very ill at her delivery and in peril of her life," writes Mme de Motteville, adding that she was in great pain, which distressed Louis, who was "so keenly touched with sorrow that he left no room for doubt that the love he felt for her was deeper in his heart than that for others."[15] As her pains continued, Marie-Thérèse cried out, "I don't want to give birth, I want to die," but then, just as midday approached, she gave birth to their first child; it was a boy, a new dauphin. The ecstatic king forgot his dignity for a moment and flung open the windows of the queen's chamber to shout to the crowds waiting in the courtyard below, "The queen has given birth to a boy!"

Jean Loret announced the birth, which took place at Fontainebleau on November 1, in his *Muze historique*. He described the child as "a living masterpiece, admirably well made."[16] The new dauphin was immediately given over to the care of his governess, Julie de Montausier, who had been especially selected by Louis. As the king would write to his son, his subjects rejoiced at his birth, showing their "natural affection for their princes," from whom they expected much.[17]

One of the expectations a prince was required to fulfill was to ensure his people were properly fed. While he had begun to implement measures to look after the poor, Louis now faced an even more urgent problem. The oppressive heat of the summer had been broken by violent thunderstorms that damaged crops and brought the threat of famine. Acting once again on Colbert's advice, Louis dealt with the crisis by adopting what can only be described as socialist policies. He obliged those provinces that had produced a surplus to assist the others. He also required private individuals to open their stores and to display their wares at a fair price. He issued orders to import as much wheat as possible by sea, which was paid for from the royal treasury. The wheat was distributed free to the lower classes of the largest cities, while the rest was sold at a modest price to those who could afford to pay for it. Any profits made went immediately to relieve the poor. To those in the countryside, where it was more difficult to send the wheat, Louis sent money instead. In this way, wrote Louis, he appeared to all his subjects "like a true father of a family, who provides for his household and shares equally food to his children and to his servants."[18]

Despite what Mme de Motteville believed, Louis's thoughts remained very much with Louise. He had seen her on September 9 as soon as he arrived back from Nantes. Their reunion, however, was to be short-lived, for Henriette was eager to return home to Saint-Cloud. No matter; Louis took the opportunity to ride to Vincennes, where he made a survey of the château before moving on to inspect the works at the Louvre. He then arrived at Saint-Cloud, where he dined with Philippe and Henriette, with Louise in attendance, before arriving back at Fontainebleau in the early evening. Henriette returned to Fontainebleau shortly afterwards, and Louis, when he was not occupied with the business of government, was able to ride with Louise in the woods and at the hunt, and favor her with a stolen dance at the ball.

As winter approached, it was time to return to Paris. Henriette was among the first to leave Fontainebleau, making her way to the Tuileries, and Louise de La Vallière shared her mistress's carriage. Just as they were leaving, Louise's friend, the intriguing Mlle de Montalais,[19] threw a packet of letters from Henriette's lover, the comte de Guiche,[20] into the coach. Montalais was acting as a go-between for Henriette and Guiche, and their surreptitious activities almost proved disastrous for Louise, who became unwittingly involved in the intrigue between the two lovers.

Louis suspected that something was going on, and he asked Louise what she knew. Louise, however, did not want to betray her friend, so she said nothing. Louis became angry, but still Louise refused to say anything. Louis stormed out, leaving Louise in despair, but she had one consolation: they had often said that should they ever argue, they would not go to sleep without writing to each other. On this occasion, however, Louis sent no word, and the tearful Louise left the Tuileries at dawn and walked all the way to Chaillot, where she knocked at the door of an obscure little convent. The nuns would not let her enter, and Louise was forced instead to stay in the outer parlor, where she sank to the floor, weeping bitterly.[21]

Later that morning, Louis knew nothing about his mistress's plight. He received an ambassador from Spain, Don Christobal de Gaviria, who was taking his leave of the French court. Amid the diplomatic niceties, Louis became aware of whispering among the courtiers that Louise had fled to a convent.

Louis rushed to the Tuileries to find out what was going on, but Henriette knew no more than he did. Montalais, with a sense of guilt because she felt responsible for what had happened, told Louis that Louise had run away in despair. Louis had some idea of where he might find his mistress. Hurrying to Chaillot, his face muffled in a gray cloak, he found her still lying on the floor of the convent, heartbroken. As they sat together alone, Louise spilled out all that she had hidden from him. This, however, did not win her the king's forgiveness; he told her only that she must return and ordered a carriage to take her home.

Louise's troubles were still not at an end, for Philippe refused to allow her back into his wife's household. Louis decided to appeal to Henriette, and, entering the Tuileries by a private door, he found his sister-in-law in a small room. Louis kept his head down: he did not wish her to see him, as he had been crying and his eyes were red and swollen. He implored Henriette to take Louise back, but she proved stubborn. Louis tried another avenue: he told her everything he knew about her liaison with Guiche. Now, Henriette could be spiteful, and Louis was taking a huge risk in provoking her, but his gamble paid off. Seeing how smitten he was, Henriette's heart softened and she relented. She agreed not only to allow Louise to return to her duties but she also promised to end her affair with Guiche.

For her part, Louise was anxious to regain the king's confidence, but this would not be an easy task. "He could not come to terms with the fact that she was capable of concealing anything from him, and she could not bear that he was displeased with her, so that she was off her head for some time."[22] The problem lay in jealousy on Louis's part. If Louise could hide her mistress's affair, perhaps she could hide other things too. He had heard a story that Louise had been courted in the past by a neighbor, the young son of Jacques de Bragelongne, and now his head spun with wild imaginings. Fearing that she still loved the young man, he summoned Montalais and, with all the inquietude of a man in love, questioned her several times about the supposed affair. Montalais was able to put the king's mind at rest. Louise had no interest in any of her past admirers, she assured him; "she thought only of being loved by the king and loving him."[23]

Louis was reassured, but it would not be long before his mistress was dragged into another intrigue. As the king's favorite, Louise held a very powerful position at court, yet her modesty and disinterestedness would not allow her to take advantage of it. This caused no end of annoyance to those around her, who viewed her as a means of access to the king. It was not long before a plot was hatched by the comtesse de Soissons, Louis's former favorite, and the marquis de Vardes, an attractive widower with no other thoughts in his head than intrigue and mischief. Together they devised a plan to alert the as yet unaware queen of the king's attachment to Mlle de La Vallière. This, they reasoned, would arouse the queen's jealousy and secure Louise's dismissal from court.

Their plan was to write an anonymous letter to Marie-Thérèse, supposedly from Spain, warning her of the king's affection for Louise. Vardes composed the text, but as Marie-Thérèse could not yet read French very well, they looked for someone who could translate it into Spanish. As it happened, the comte de Guiche was known to be familiar with the language, and this worked out very well. Vardes was aware that Louise had spurned Guiche's advances while the court was still at Fontainebleau during the summer, and he took advantage of this by telling the comte that Louise was trying to ruin him in the eyes of the king. The resentful Guiche readily agreed to join the plot, and he translated the letter into Spanish for them.

The letter was placed into an old Spanish envelope the comtesse had found in her mistress's room. It was now passed through a chain of hands: a guard passed it to one of the queen's maids, who handed it to Doña Molina, first lady of the queen's bedchamber. Doña Molina was suspicious of the manner in which the letter had arrived. Normally, royal letters were delivered by ambassadors, while those that arrived by post were handed to the king by a functionary; they were never delivered by servants. Moreover, the letter had been folded incorrectly, and Doña Molina's instinct told her to hand the letter to Louis, who, upon reading it, flew into a rage. He demanded to know if Marie-Thérèse had read it, and Doña Molina assured him that she had not. Louis said nothing more, but he began making inquiries into who was behind the letter. He even approached Vardes, whom he knew to be a "man of confidence and whom he trusted," but Vardes threw suspicion on Mlle de Montpensier, "whose mind is so restless," and the duchesse de Navailles, the head of the queen's household, "who now stood in the king's mind as a crazy reformer of the human species." That lady's close friendship with Mme de Motteville caused him to suspect her of having written the letter. "But he suspended his judgment on this for a time," she wrote, "and his anger did not break forth upon any one. In the end, we shall see him punish, justly, the authors of this poor trick."[24]

While Louis could control most things, even the ladies of the court, there was one area where his power was strictly limited. This was in matters of religion. The Catholic Church held absolute sway, even over the most absolute of monarchs. Louis, who had been brought up to be a good son of the church, knew well that God had set him above all others and, by the same token, he was answerable only to God. This was a source of great inner conflict, for the church condemned his relationship with Louise, but Louis would make his confession to Père Annat, and the sincerity with which he spoke and his promise to amend his ways ensured his absolution. At times, however, Louis would encounter preachers who could afford to be less indulgent and forgiving than his usual confessor. Such a preacher came to the Louvre to deliver a series of Lenten sermons. His name was Jacques-Bénigne Bossuet.

Bossuet was a doctor of theology at the Faculty of Paris. He was both learned and eloquent, two qualities Louis admired. In the first of his sermons, Bossuet spoke on "evil living" and urged Louis to listen to the small voice of his conscience; were he to do so, "the Divine Word will rush in, as with a scourge, breaking every idol, casting down every altar where the creature is adored." He reminded Louis, absolute monarch though he was, that there was another kingdom above his earthly one, where "sovereigns would meet on equal terms with their subjects, who would have been changed into their companions by Heavenly Insight."[25]

Bossuet warned Louis that "there is a God in Heaven who avenges the sins of the people," but he avenged those of kings even more. "It is He who wills me to speak as I do," Bossuet thundered, "and if Your Majesty will hear Him, He will whisper to your inmost heart those things which men dare not say to you." Then, as though to drive the point home, he added that "our Sovereigns would justly anger the Living God if, surrounded by His benefits as they are, they should seek to taste those earthly joys which He expressly forbids them."[26]

Bossuet appealed to Louis's deep piety in an attempt to separate him from Louise, but he had words for her too. Louise, whose piety and devotion were every bit as deep and sincere as Louis's—the lady whom Louis had considered too young to be depicted as a penitent—listened as the preacher spoke of the fall of the Magdalen and how she was saved by repentance: "Magdalen's heart is broken, her face is suffused with shame, her mind is bent upon the true vision of her state, upon the profound realization of her danger. She is so utterly wretched that she hurries to the Physician with all her heart in her eyes; her sense of shame flings her humbly at His feet; knowledge of her danger keeps her still afraid, even after He has spoken to her; she hardly knows which to ponder most—her hope of future resistance to temptation or the joy of having been so blissfully, so mercifully, forgiven."[27] These powerful words would echo in her innermost being and haunt Louise throughout her life at court.

Louis, however, had other matters to consider. He had planned a ceremony to celebrate the birth of the dauphin the previous November, and in June he took part in the *courses de bagues*, a grand carousel on the square between the Tuileries and the Louvre.[28] It comprised tilting at the ring, with Louis and all the court and their households dressing in spectacular costumes. In order to allow the maximum number of people to see the ceremony, Louis ordered all the participants to assemble at the Arsenal and to ride from there to the arena.

There was significant religious symbolism here. The carousel[29] emulated the path of the stars, homage to the God of Light by his daughter, Circe. While Louis had portrayed Circe in a previous ballet, this time he was to be identified as the God of Light. His costume was that of a Roman emperor, his helmet adorned with tall orange and red plumes. His shield bore the image of the sun and the inscription UT VIDI VICI, 'As I saw I conquered.'

Philippe, as the king of Persia, followed next, the moon on his shield illustrating the inscription UNO SOLI MINOR, 'The sun alone is greater than me.' Behind Philippe came Condé as king of the Turks. His shield bore a crescent and the words CRESCIT UT ASPICITUR. The meaning was clear: "As the crescent grows larger and brighter according to how the sun looks upon it, so the Prince who takes it for his Device wishes it to be understood that, taking from the King all his grandeur and glory and all his *éclat*, he recognizes that his glory grows in proportion to the favorable regards that he receives from His Majesty."[30] Condé, the former frondeur, knew his only chance for glory came with service to the king. Louise appeared too, but in a small, undistinguished role.

The carousel was initially meant to be a light entertainment, but, as Louis noted, "It grew into quite a great and magnificent spectacle, be it by the number of drills, or by the novelty of the costumes or by the variety of the devices."[31] Louis was very fond of spectacular entertainments, and he was always eager to participate. He considered them to belong not so much to the king as to the court and his subjects, and they formed part of his policy of being open and approachable to all the people.[32]

It was then that Louis formally adopted his own personal device, "which I have kept ever since," he writes, "and which you see in so many places," a symbol that should "represent the duties of a prince and inspire me always to fulfill them."[33] The symbol he chose was the image of the sun, which,

> *according to the rules of art is the most noble of all, and which by virtue of its uniqueness, by the brilliance that surrounds it, by the light that it imparts to the other stars that make up a kind of court; by its equal and just sharing of that same light to the various regions of the world; by the good it does in all places, endlessly producing on all sides life, joy and activity; by its relentless movement, while it appears nevertheless always still; by that constant and invariable course, from which it never deviates or turns away, is assuredly the most vibrant and the most beautiful image of a great monarch.*[34]

To this device was added the motto *Nec pluribus impar*, 'Not unequal to many,' which suggests Louis's capacity to "rule other empires, as the sun lights other worlds equally exposed to its rays."[35]

Louis had vanquished his enemies at home and placed himself in a position to dominate those abroad; he had a queen who had secured his throne by giving him a dauphin. The day of the Sun King had dawned.

ELEVEN

Le Château de Cartes

A t the dawn of 1662, Louis was already beginning to mark out those he deemed worthy of receiving his favor. He created sixty knights of the Ordre du Saint-Esprit, the ceremony taking place as it always did in the church of the Augustins.[1] He also selected sixty courtiers who would have the right to join him on all the journeys he took for pleasure without first asking permission. These privileged people, among them Louise, were allocated a kind of uniform consisting of a jacket of blue watered silk embroidered with gold and silver, which was similar to the king's own.[2]

Louis liked to walk with Queen Marie-Thérèse during the winter months, and he accompanied her two or three times to Saint-Germain. This picture of apparent domestic bliss, however, was soon overshadowed by another intrigue as sharp-eyed courtiers observed that Louis had taken an interest in another lady, Anne-Lucie de La Motte-Houdancourt.

The driving force behind this affair was, once again, the mischievous comtesse de Soissons, who, frustrated in her first attempt to replace Louise de La Vallière with a new lady, had decided to try once again. La Motte-Houdancourt, one of the queen's ladies, was not considered the most radiant beauty at court, although it was said that she managed to attract lovers away from the exquisite Catherine de Menneville.[3] Mme de Soissons introduced her to Louis during one of his retreats to Saint-Germain rather than at Paris, because that way she hoped to escape the watchful eye of the duchesse de Navailles.

As he had done with Henriette d'Angleterre and Louise de La Vallière, Louis found that he had a rival as he began to court La Motte-Houdancourt. Unlike Guiche and Brienne, however, the self-important chevalier de Gramont felt that a lady so favored by the king must be fully deserving of his own attention, and he began to court her too. When his rival refused to step aside, Louis coolly exiled him.[4]

As it was, Louis quickly encountered an even more formidable foe than the insolent chevalier. The duchesse de Navailles, who was justly proud of her reputation for propriety, heard disturbing rumors of the king's new passion. One story that was circulating among the ladies of the court had it that Louis had been seen speaking to La Motte-Houdancourt through her chamber window. Another tale went further, insisting that the king had actually entered the lady's chamber and had offered her a pair of diamond earrings. The story went that La Motte-Houdancourt had thrown the earrings back in Louis's face, exclaiming, "I care neither for you nor your pendants, unless you will give up La Vallière."[5]

The indignant duchesse de Navailles took matters into her own hands. On a recent visit to Paris with the queen mother, she had visited a casuist, M. Joly, who advised her to "do her duty and resist the king, even if it should bring her disgrace."[6] When the duchesse found out that Louis and some of his companions had been seen scurrying along the roof and making their way towards the ladies' chamber, she knew exactly what to do. She arranged to seal the doors and windows with iron bars, after which she went to bed satisfied with her day's work. The following morning, however, she awoke to find the bars torn away and scattered about the courtyard below. At dinner, Louis could not resist having a little joke with the duchesse de Navailles: "It must be ghosts," he told her, "for the door was shut, and your guards saw no one come in."[7]

Marie-Thérèse had already guessed that Louis was having an affair with Louise de La Vallière, although she kept her knowledge to herself. Her conjecture was confirmed during an interview with the comtesse de Soissons, who had accompanied her to the Carmelite convent on the rue de Bouloy. The two ladies were visiting Anne of Austria, who was staying at the convent to convalesce after a recent illness. Marie-Thérèse nevertheless harbored hopes that she had been wrong in her assumption until Soissons told her the truth, and "the certainty of which caused her to shed many tears."[8] There was worse to come, because at the same time she found out about La Motte-Houdancourt. Upon her return to the Louvre, the inconsolable queen poured out her heart to Doña Molina, the only person she felt she could trust.

Now that the relatively open secret about Louise was officially out, Louis no longer concealed his liaison. Instead of telling the queen that he had just come from visiting Henriette, he openly admitted that he had been seeing Louise.[9] It was said that Marie-Thérèse hated La Motte-Houdancourt even more than she did Louise, "for she would rather have witnessed his making open love to the former than allow him to pay the least attention to the latter."[10]

As it was, those in the know understood perfectly that Louis had only pretended to take notice of La Motte-Houdancourt in order to hide his passion for Louise.[11] Confirmation of this came when La Motte-Houdancourt sent Louis a letter. Warned by Queen Anne that the letter would urge him to abandon Louise, Louis read it and found that his mother had spoken the truth. Moreover, it bore all the hallmarks of having been dictated to La Motte-Houdancourt by Mme de Soissons. Louis burned the letter, "and from that moment La Motte ceased to exist for him."[12]

Shortly after this diversion, Louis became a father for the second time when Marie-Thérèse gave birth to a daughter on November 18, 1662. The king immediately sent out couriers to carry the good news to all the courts of Europe, while foreign kings, dukes, and princelings rushed their ambassadors to France with their congratulations. However, even as the first of them arrived, it was too late. The little princess, Anne-Elisabeth de France, had died on December 30. The poor child barely made an impact on the world; and, as the custom in France and Spain dictated, she was scarcely mourned by the court because she was less than seven years old.[13]

As 1663 dawned, Louis found himself surrounded by men who wanted to use his grandeur and opulence for their own ends and women whose hearts were agitated by his many fine qualities. A prince, however, can offer only "limited favor, and can only love imperfectly," so that "these desires and these benefits, which bear their poison with them, often fill with bitterness those who, in the vanity of their thoughts and desires, seek only their own satisfaction." Yet, enclosed though he was on all sides by ambitious courtiers, Louis was happy. His kingdom was at peace; his enemies, at home and abroad, were subdued, while his armies were prepared to fight; his world was filled with pleasure, but "he was a Christian; and that one word enclosed all that in the future he had to fear."[14]

The apparent serenity of Louis's life was seriously tested soon afterwards, when his mother became ill at Eastertime 1663. At first she tried to make light of it, but she quickly succumbed to a tertian fever accompanied by drowsiness, a feeling of oppression, and headaches. Louis was naturally anxious, while Philippe's heart was gripped with fear. The whole court was in a state of sadness.[15]

One day, the ninth of her illness, Anne was bled once again, but she had lost so much blood by repeated bleedings that she fainted. As she fell, Philippe slipped beneath her so she would fall on him and not hurt herself. Marie-Thérèse gave way to her fear and ran into the bathroom where Louis was. She cried that the queen mother "was lost, that her mother was dead."[16] Louis, "who in all the queen mother's illnesses, and especially this one, showed the feelings of a son who was full of affection," ran back into his mother's room and helped to lift her back into bed. As Anne recovered from her faint, Louis brought the still-weeping queen back to her bedside, where "they remained, very uneasy at her state."

As Anne's condition worsened, she had a long, private interview with Louis, after which she asked her confessor to visit her every day. As the days went by, her fever became double tertian. Louis kept vigil by her bed and even ordered a mattress to be brought and laid on the floor at the foot of her bed, where "sometimes he threw himself down all dressed upon it." One night, Mme de Motteville watched the king's face as he slept:

I admired the tenderness of his heart combined with so many great qualities not usually to be found with kindliness; and in spite of my sadness and anxiety I recalled, as I looked at him, those heroes that romance depicts lying in a wood or on the sea-shore; and passing on from those futile thoughts to others more solid and more suited to the then state of things, I could not help wishing for him all the blessings of heaven in time and in eternity.[17]

Louis helped to change his mother's bed and "served her better and more adroitly than any of her women." Then, after nearly eight weeks had passed, the king begged her to take an emetic, which the doctors had prescribed, but which she had persisted in refusing. After Louis's pleading and the reassurance of her confessor, Anne finally took the emetic and was completely cured.

One evening, as Anne of Austria played host to Louis and the rest of her family in her chamber, the conversation turned to women's jealousy. Marie-Thérèse asked Henriette if she would be jealous if Philippe gave her cause to be. Henriette said she would not, because "in truth it was useless to be so,"[18] adding that "the sensitiveness of women only hardened the heart of husbands, and what ought to be agreeable to them as a mark of affection, displeased and importuned them." Louis then asked Mme de Béthune if she had ever been jealous of her husband, but the lady said she had not. At this point Marie-Thérèse laughed and rose to go to supper, saying as she did so that Mme de Béthune "seemed the silliest person in the company; and for her part she could not say as much." This removed any remaining doubt in Louis's mind that the queen knew about his affair with Louise and that her silence had been "more the result of discretion and the fear of displeasing him than of ignorance."

During this time, Louis's physician, Vallot, monitored the king closely and came to the conclusion that he was suffering from "dull, sick headaches, with an inclination to dizziness; some heart trouble, weakness, and depression." His opinion was that Louis hunted too much and that he "did not have all the sleep he needed." Louis reluctantly agreed to get more sleep, and, even more reluctantly, he submitted to the various treatments the good doctor inflicted on him. The potions, bleedings, and purges, however, were sweetened by a concoction specifically invented for him, which consisted of peony heads, red roses, prepared pearls, and refined spirit of vitriol.[19] Despite Vallot's attentions, Louis recovered from these ailments.

Possibly one of the things that kept Louis awake at night was his concern over extending the terms of the Concordat of Bologna[20] to the new provinces of Artois, Roussillon, and the Three Bishoprics.[21] Pope Alexander VII, however, declared that Louis should not have the right to appoint his own bishops and abbots. Louis was on the point of accepting this decision when reports of a new diplomatic incident arrived.[22]

It was understood that Alexander VII did not have much longer to live, and Louis had sent his first gentleman of the bedchamber, the duc de Créqui, to Rome as ambassador extraordinary. His primary mission was to see what he could do to secure the appointment of a pope sympathetic to France in the imminently expected conclave. In the meantime, Créqui was to assure Alexander of Louis's veneration for his person and the fervor of his opposition to the heretical Jansenists and Huguenots. More delicately, Créqui was to skate over the issue of France's attitude towards the League of Christian Princes against the Turks. Although Louis was adamant not to join the league, he was eager not to let the pope know this.[23]

Créqui arrived at the Palazzo Farnese in Rome on June 2, 1662 to find that relations between the French guards and the pope's Corsican guards were less than cordial. It was only a matter of time before violence broke out between them, and this occurred on August 20, when the Corsicans beset the French at the barracks close to the palace. The ensuing argument quickly escalated into a scuffle; the French brandished their swords and the Corsicans fired their arquebuses seemingly aimlessly as they cried, "Kill them, they are French!"

As this was going on, Créqui returned home from a visit to the prince Borghese. He managed to get safely inside the Palazzo Farnese, but when he and his wife went out onto the balcony, they were showered by a hail of bullets, one of which came so close to the duke that it swept his hair. As the brawl escalated, several people in the street were killed or wounded, and the diplomatic immunity of France was seriously compromised.

When news of the incident reached Louis, he demanded an immediate apology from Alexander, only to be rebuffed. The pope's nephew, Cardinal Flavio Chigi, stepped in to offer his services, saying he would call upon Créqui if he could be assured he would be treated with courtesy. Créqui took exception to this and pointed out that he was a gentleman and therefore incapable of acting indecorously. Chigi, authorized by the pope to convey an apology, arrived at the Palazzo

Farnese five days later. The angry duke, however, found the apology unsatisfactory, since it merely excused the behavior of the Corsican guards by explaining that they could not be overmastered. Little attempt was made to punish the offenders; rather, they were allowed to leave Rome if they chose. Some thirty-two guards did so choose, leaving the French to surmise that the papal court secretly supported their actions.

When Louis wrote to Alexander, his anger was barely concealed. In his letter, which was dated August 30, 1662, he notified the pope that as a result of the violent incident, he was withdrawing his ambassador from Rome so that "his person and our dignity would no longer remain exposed to such outrage which, until now, there have been no examples even among the barbarians." He wanted to know if the pope approved of the incident at the barracks and if he planned to give Louis "reparation proportionate to the greatness of the offense which not only violated, but shamefully overturned the right of the people." Louis, however, did not demand anything of the pope, who had, he wrote, "for so long made a habit of refusing us everything, and has shown up to now such aversion to anything regarding our person and our crown that we believe it best to defer to his own discretion his resolutions upon which we will be guided."[24]

As Louis waited for his dispute with the pope to be resolved, he turned his thoughts to his own reign and how he might document its history. One of the ways he would do so was by minting commemorative medals, and in February 1663, he ordered Colbert to establish a new institution, the Académie des Inscriptions. Otherwise known as the Petit Académie because it initially had only four members, its purpose was to record the history of Louis XIV's reign in inscriptions, mottoes, and medals commemorating various military victories and other special events. It would also organize and record royal festivities, as well as oversee court ballets and operas. One of the original four members was Louis Douvrier, who had created Louis's Sun King medal.[25]

Another means of documenting the glory and achievements of Louis's reign was in tapestry. In June 1662, Colbert had purchased the Gobelins manufactory, and three weeks later, on June 20, Louis had ordered all the looms, tools, tapestries, and materials to be transferred there from the workshop established by Foucquet at Maincy.[26] Foucquet had employed some 209 people, among whom were nineteen Flemish tapestry-weavers, who worked under Le Brun's supervision as they transformed his cartoons into magnificent works of art.[27] Several of the tapestries that were sent to the Gobelins had been specially designed for Foucquet, but these were easily adapted for the king's use by replacing Foucquet's squirrel device with Louis's monogram.[28] Now, on March 8, 1663, Charles Le Brun was formally appointed director of the Gobelins, a position he would hold until 1667, when he was made director of the royal manufactures of the crown furniture, established at the Gobelins.[29] With these new establishments firmly under control, Louis decided it was time to visit Versailles.

Louis was still dauphin when he first saw Versailles. His father's hunting lodge was known affectionately as the *château de cartes* because the red of the brick, the white stone, and the black slate roof reminded onlookers of the colorful backs of playing cards. Louis XIII had acquired the nearby village and other properties, including the hamlet of Trianon, from the Gondi family, and it would be on this land that his son would build the famous park.[30]

As a child, Louis had made the occasional hunting excursion,[31] but other than that, he had shown no particular interest in the little hunting lodge. It was not until he was twenty-three that he set about transforming it into the beautiful palace that would glorify his reign. He did so for two main reasons: he wanted a place to which he could escape with Louise, and he was anxious to eradicate all memory of the magnificent fête presented by Foucquet. The spectacular at Vaux-le-Vicomte aroused jealousy in the young king, who was affronted by Foucquet's power, wealth, and excellent taste, but it also stimulated within him a sense of rivalry, and his desire was not to emulate the superintendent's achievements but to surpass them. Another reason would emerge more gradually: Versailles was to become the new seat of government in France; but more than that, it was to be a gilded cage in which Louis could hold, tame, and control his relatives and courtiers. It would be populated by the nobility, who would be so afraid of losing his favor that they would allow themselves to become dependent on him for everything.

Not everyone thought Versailles was a suitable place to build a magnificent château. If Saint-Simon, admittedly writing at a later date, is to be believed, the area was most unsuitable. Versailles, he wrote, was "the most thankless of places; without view, without woods, without water, without soil, for all is either sand or bog, and consequently with an air that cannot be pure."[32]

Louis, however, could see its potential, and renovation work had begun almost immediately after Foucquet's arrest. He employed the people who had created Vaux-le-Vicomte for the ex-superintendent: Louis Le Vau, the architect; André Le Nôtre, who designed the gardens; and Charles Le Brun, the interior designer and painter. Over the next two years, some of the apartments were repaired, and two painters, Charles Errard and Noël Coypel, were given the job of decorating them. A special apartment was prepared for the dauphin, while the buildings surrounding the forecourt were demolished to make way for larger ones.[33]

Now, in March 1663, Louis began transporting more than a thousand seedling orange trees from Vaux-le-Vicomte to Versailles. These were placed in the Orangery, a new structure built of brick and stone to the south of the château. While the new building work was expensive, the cost of moving the earth was even more so.[34] Over the next two years alone, Louis would spend more than 500 thousand écus, much to the alarm of Colbert, whose task it was to raise the money. Although the companies Colbert had inaugurated or supervised, and the enterprises and workers he had encouraged, were doing good business, he was still concerned about the revenues raised, and resented spending such vast sums on Versailles. He warned the king that if he wanted to see where the money had been spent at the château, he would have difficulty in finding it. He reproached Louis, as far as he dared, for neglecting the Louvre, which he thought more worthy of the king's attention, and urged him to divert the funds there instead.[35]

Colbert, however, was wrong to suggest that Louis was neglecting the Louvre, as work was still continuing on renovations begun by his grandfather, Henri IV. This work, which was referred to as the "Grand Design," had been taken over by Mazarin, although his preoccupation with the Thirty Years' War and the Fronde had prevented him from devoting as much time to it as he would have liked. When Louis returned to Paris after the Fronde, the renovation of the Louvre resumed with the enlargement of the Petite Gallery and the improvement of its links with the rest of the building. Since that time, while the restoration work had slowed considerably, it had not stopped, and Charles Le Brun was already in the process of decorating the Galerie d'Apollon. Louis, therefore, continued to devote much time and attention to the Louvre. At the same time, however, he had no intention of abandoning his favorite project, and instead of going to Fontainebleau that summer, he announced that he would take the court to Versailles. Then something happened that threatened to frustrate this plan.

That May, Marie-Thérèse suffered an attack of measles, and perhaps inevitably, Louis began to feel unwell soon afterwards. Vallot recommended bleeding, to which Louis submitted with his customary resignation, while a purging later that day seem to do the trick. Louis felt very well and was impatient to travel to Versailles, despite the protests of the hapless physician. Once there, he went for a walk, but it was not long before he began to feel unwell again, and the following day, the measles showed itself.[36]

Louis was ill for several days. In the grip of fever, he muttered about Louise, although he did not want to see her for fear of infecting her.[37] Throughout their romance, Louise had maintained her policy never to ask the king for anything, but simply to return love for love. Although Louis gave her small trinkets as love tokens, Louise received very little from him. She owned no expensive jewelry, her only dresses were those her meager wages paid for, and she continued to live in one small garret room. Louis now sought to give her family greater social standing by elevating her brother's military prospects.

Jean-François de La Baum La Blanc had been a lieutenant to the king at Château Amboise since 1659, although there is nothing to suggest that he and Louis actually knew each other. In 1663, he was made a cornet in the dauphin's Company of Light Horse.[38] This regiment was, in fact, the "foundation of an Army-Corps," the standard of which bore a dolphin playing in a rough sea and the motto *Pericula Ludus*, 'Danger is my pleasure.' Later the same year, Louis achieved the young man's marriage to a Breton heiress, Gabrielle Glé de la Cotardais. She was due to inherit 40 thousand livres, and La Vallière had been courting her for six months. The marriage contract was signed on June 11 by Louis, Marie-Thérèse, Philippe, Henriette, Condé, his son, Enghien, as well as the eighteen-month-old dauphin, who traced an *L* and a *D* in a baby hand.[39] The wedding, which took place the next day at the Church of the Assumption, was witnessed by the highest in the land, including sixty members of the aristocracy.

Louis, however, was also occupied with other, more weighty matters to do with territory and the security of France. In October of the previous year, he had bought the strategically important towns of Dunkirk and Mardyck from Charles II, including "all the cannons and munitions of war that were in them." He paid 5 million livres for them, payable in installments; but Charles was so short of money that he struck a bargain with Louis, offering them to his cousin for a substantial discount if Louis would settle the balance immediately. Louis readily agreed "so that this important place cost the king but little money and showed his opulence and adroitness." At the same time, it demonstrated "the weakness of the king of England in having abandoned for so small a sum a place which put him in a position to enter Flanders or France, and so help France or Spain as he might see fit." The comte d'Estrades, Louis's ambassador in London who had been employed in the negotiations, said that "the English people murmured loudly" at this transaction.[40]

Also the previous year, Charles IV of Lorraine had signed the Treaty of Montmartre, in which he would cede the town of Marsal to France as a pledge to his agreement to revert the duchies of Lorraine and Bar to the French. Now, in July 1663, news arrived that Charles was reinforcing his garrison in the town before the French troops could take possession of it. Louis immediately ordered a siege and made preparations to join his army.

Even as Louis was getting ready to leave, he gave special thought to Louise's welfare, and for a very special reason. She was four months pregnant with their first child. While Louis usually confided his more delicate affairs to his gentleman of the bedchamber, Saint-Aignan, this time he turned to Colbert to help him make arrangements for when the child was born. Colbert, as severe and serious as he ever was, did in fact have a tender side to his character, although he usually concealed it very well. He had already demonstrated his reliability and his devotion to Louis on many occasions, and his wife hailed from the same region as Louise, making him a good choice for such a delicate assignment.

Louis attended services for the feast of Saint-Louis, which fell on August 25, before he departed for Châlons. Five days later, he arrived at Metz, where he reviewed the troops of the maréchal de La Ferté-Senneterre. The maréchal was preparing to set out to reinforce the siege, but as it turned out, the mere threat of more troops was enough to frighten Charles into giving up. He met Louis at Metz on September 3 and signed a new agreement. Marsal was now in the hands of the French without a shot being fired.[41]

Upon his return from Marsal, Louis turned his attention once more to Louise. He removed her from her cramped and drafty room and installed her in the Palais Brion, which he had bought and furnished. This was a small, one-story palace built in the grounds of the Palais-Royal,[42] and Louise lived there in a very retired manner, never going out, and always dressed in a loose-fitting robe. When she received guests for card parties, she kept to her bed all the while. As her time neared, Colbert found her a maid, the demoiselle du Plessis, who brought supplies for the baby. He then arranged for the baby to be placed initially into the care of two of his own servants, Beauchamp and his wife, who lived nearby.

In the middle of September 1663, Louis took the two queens, Philippe, Henriette, and the whole court to Versailles for a week. The queen mother's apartments had been decorated in Chinese silver and filigree gold and filled with her favorite jasmine plants. Louis's rooms also were "not only superbly, but even gallantly furnished and decorated with everything that can be agreeable to the sight and the sense of smell."[43]

On this occasion, the apartments appointed to the courtiers were furnished, and food, firewood, and candles were provided for everyone, "which has never been convenient in royal houses."[44] Previously, those who stayed with the king had to provide for themselves, although their visits rarely lasted for more than three months at a time. Louis intended to change all that, and his purpose was to make his courtiers mindful of their subjection to, and dependence upon, him. He wanted them to become used to the delights of life at court, with endless fêtes, ballets, plays, and hunts, so that they would never think that there might be a life away from him.

Louis treated the court to a series of lavish entertainments, which took place over the entire eight days of their stay. There were ballets, balls, plays, singing and music of all kinds, walks, and hunting. Among the plays was a new one by Molière, *l'Impromptu*, which had been written, learned, and rehearsed in eight days. Almost immediately, it was printed out and published under the title *l'Impromptu de Versailles*.[45] However, the visit was not entirely dominated by pleasure. Louis had already established Versailles as a place of work. Every Monday, people would bring their petitions to the château, where a large table had been set up in one of the guardrooms. The petitions were received by the marquis de Louvois,[46] who presented them at the end of each week to the council. They were then sent on to the relevant secretary of state, who would deal with the issues or requests contained within the petitions. After a week, the secretaries would present a report to Louis, who would pronounce his decision, which was either nothing would be done; he agreed with the petitioner; or he would consider the matter further, a verdict that could result in a positive or a negative judgment.[47]

Louis was with Louise when her labor pains began, but he could not remain with her for the birth. Instead, he made a show of normality by going out hunting. At three thirty in the morning of Wednesday, December 19, Louise gave birth to a boy. Both mother and child were well and the baby was found to be strong. Louise, however, was allowed to keep her child for less than three hours before he was whisked away by the midwife, M. Boucher.[48] He carried the baby to M. and Mme Beauchamp, who waited near the Hôtel Bouillon to receive him. Later that day, the baby was taken to the church of Saint-Leu-Saint-Gilles in the rue Saint-Denis, where, on the orders of the king, he was named Charles, son of M. de Lincour and demoiselle Elisabeth du Beux. The Beauchamps stood as godparents under the names Gury Focard and Clémence Pré.[49]

Despite his delight at having become the father of a second son, albeit an illegitimate one, that winter brought Louis the unhappy news of the deaths of two princesses. The first was his aunt, the duchesse de Savoy, who was followed several days later by his cousin, the younger duchesse de Savoy. Earlier that year, Louis's prospective bride, Marguerite de Savoy, who had become duchesse de Parma, had died at the age of only twenty-seven. Did Louis, as Mme de Motteville[50] wonders, "consider from this how fragile is the grandeur of the great of this earth"?

TWELVE

The Pleasures of the Enchanted Isle

I n the spring of 1664, Louis again took the court to Versailles. The old *château de cartes* still stood; Louis had threatened that if the builders attempted to demolish it, he would simply order it to be rebuilt brick by brick. Nevertheless, the new work was very much in evidence. The buildings surrounding the château had now been joined by a royal ménagerie, where exotic animals roaming in open spaces could be viewed from apartments specifically designed and decorated for recreation and dining.[1] A kitchen had also been built, which occupied a separate building to the northeast of the château, while the terraced eastern approach was lined with trees.

Work in the surrounding land had also progressed, and the château was now enveloped on three sides by parterres, all of which extended to the park. The one to the north already had waterworks installed; that to the south, next to the Orangery, featured flowerbeds filled with plants of various kinds. The parterre to the west, which was planted with lawns, extended to the *allée royale*, otherwise known as the Tapis Vert. Beyond the park were natural woodlands through which hunting parties entered the park on the western side. It was here in this green space that Louis treated more than six hundred people to one of "the finest fêtes in the world."[2] Mme de Motteville believed that Louis planned *Les Plaisirs de l'Île Enchanté*, a weeklong series of entertainments, to "efface the memory of past illnesses," and this was probably true to some extent. There were other reasons, though. Louis was anxious to eradicate all memory of the magnificent fête given by Foucquet almost three years earlier. On a more romantic note, he wished to use the occasion as a tribute to the two queens, although everyone knew that the real recipient of that honor was Louise de la Vallière.[3]

While Saint-Aignan managed every aspect of the fête, all was arranged according to Louis's strict orders. The king planned it "in the manner in which he did everything," wrote Bussy-Rabutin, "that is to say, the most gallant and the most magnificent way that can be imagined."[4] There was a sense of excitement in the air—this was, after all, the first official court entertainment to be held at Versailles. Even nature conspired to help make the festivities the best they could be, and the heavy rains of the past few days stopped, allowing the sun to reign over clear blue skies.

The main feature, and the theme, of *Les Plaisirs de l'Île Enchanté* was Ariosto's *Orlando furioso*,[5] which was to be played out over three days on stages set against the backdrop of the *allée royale*. The scenes were illuminated by the light of white wax flambeaux and four thousand candles, which stood up bravely to the summer breezes.[6] The action followed the adventures of Roger and his chevaliers, beginning with their capture by the sorceress Alcine, and ending with the marriage of the heroic Roger and the fair Angélique.

Louis played the part of Roger. He appeared on a magnificent horse, its harness the color of fire, shining with gold and silver and studded with precious stones. He carried weapons in the style of the ancient Greeks, and his armor was made of plates of silver over which he wore a richly embroidered cloak that shimmered with gold and diamonds. His helmet was covered with flame-colored feathers.[7]

At the end of the first day, the duc de Guise, the marquis de Soye-court, and the marquis de La Vallière, Louise's brother, competed in a tournament. La Vallière, who played the part of Zerbin, was the eventual victor; his prize was a sword of honor encrusted with diamonds, which he received from the hands of the queen mother.

The court then went to supper. Everyone ate to the sound of music, which had been composed for the occasion, while dancers dressed as the twelve signs of the zodiac and the four seasons performed a ballet. The dishes were carried in a procession choreographed and supervised by Molière. The servers were dressed as harvesters and grape-pickers, while men dressed in frosted costumes, their furs and dance steps representing coldness and weakness, carried bowls filled with artificial ice and snow.[8]

On the second day, Louis, still in the character of Roger, offered the two queens a comedy in six acts by Molière, *La Princess d'Elide*, which was appropriately set in Spain. As night fell, Roger and his chevaliers held tournaments on the orders of Alcine, whose palace was just visible beyond the waters of the Bassin des Cygnes, today's Bassin d'Apollon.[9]

The opening scene of day three took place at the palace of Alcine. Heaven had granted Roger and the chevaliers their freedom from Alcine's charms. Troubled by this turn of events, the sorceress crossed the lake on a sea monster with two of her nymphs to praise the queen mother. A ballet set to Lully's music followed, after which Roger and the chevaliers were released from their enchantment. Islands in the lake suddenly burst into life, and the air filled with the sounds of violins, trumpets, and timpani, the musicians all in rich apparel. Alcine, still riding her sea monster, and her two nymphs once again addressed the queen mother as Heaven, Earth, and Sea burst in an explosion of fire, which destroyed Alcine's palace and brought the three-day *Orlando furioso* to a spectacular end.[10]

Les Plaisirs de l'Ile Enchanté continued on Saturday, May 10, with a *course de têtes*, a kind of tilt in which the rider wields his lance to spear the heads of a series of mannequins, which were suspended along the course at a certain height. Louis was the victor on this occasion. The following evening featured a performance of *Les Fâcheux*, Molière's comedy-ballet, which had received its début at Vaux-le-Vicomte. Molière, as always, played several of the characters, while the music was primarily by Beauchamp, with contributions from Lully.

Much of Monday was taken up by a special event, which Louis had arranged as a surprise. Some days before, he had written to Colbert about an idea that would cost money, but would "give pleasure to many here—and especially the two Queens." The king's idea was to hold a lottery, which he thought should cost no more than 3 thousand pistoles, which, "if well laid out," ought to buy lots of jewels. He instructed Colbert not to buy clothes as prizes, nor did he want anyone else to know about the lottery, because "that way, it will be all the easier for you to get things at a moderate price." The main prize should be worth five hundred pistoles, but Colbert could use his discretion in buying the others. This was Louis's way of appeasing his thrifty minister.[11] Louis then drew up a list of winners, which included the names of Louise and her sister-in-law. It was the strongest hint yet of Louise's presence in the king's life.

A joust followed, in which Saint-Aignan and the marquis de Soyecourt competed for honors. That evening, Louis presented a new play by Molière, entitled *Tartuffe; ou l'Imposteur*, which proved to be a highly controversial work. Artistically, the work was acclaimed by those who appreciated good theater and Moliere's not always subtle humor, but the controversy lay with its subject matter.

The word *tartuffe* meant 'hypocrite,' and the play satirized the many at court who mistook ostentatious display for serious devotion in religious matters. Molière was not being cruel or cynical; rather, he was urging people to laugh at themselves, not to take themselves too seriously. However, some saw the play as an attack on true religion and were deeply affronted by it. Among them was Anne of Austria, who took the matter personally. She thought that Louis was using *Tartuffe* to make fun of her piety. Mother and son quarrelled, and Anne quickly found support from the Sorbonne, the prince de Conti, and President Lamoignon of the Parlement of Paris.

Lamoignon's involvement was particularly important because he was a member of a secretive and very influential masonic organization called the Compagnie du Saint-Sacrement. The compagnie had known about *Tartuffe* since at least the previous April, when, at a secret meeting, they had agreed to work for the play's suppression. How they had learned about it is not certain, but their advance knowledge demonstrated their wide infiltration into all sections of society.[12] On April 30, Molière had travelled to Versailles, where he had read his work to Louis. The king had enjoyed it so much that he had immediately placed it on the program for the fête, where it made its début on May 12.

Anne and her supporters brought *Tartuffe* to the attention of Péréfixe, Louis's former tutor, who was now archbishop of Paris. Péréfixe had a private word with Louis, and although he very much admired the play, the king reluctantly agreed to ban all public performances of it. The *Gazette* praised Louis, who was "enlightened in all things," for banning a play that was "injurious to religion and likely to exercise a harmful influence."[13]

The curé of Saint-Barthélemy, Pierre Roullé, went further, saying that Louis's decision to ban *Tartuffe* was a "heroic act worthy of his greatness of heart and respect for God and the church."[14] So angry was Roullé that he thought Molière ought to be "burned at the stake as a foretaste of the fires of hell in expiation of a crime which is treason against heaven and calculated to ruin the Catholic religion."[15]

Molière had anticipated a hostile reaction to *Tartuffe* and had written his own defense into the text of act 1, scene 4:

Devotion, like courage, has its pretenders; and in the same way that the truly brave are not those who make the most noise where honor leads them, so the real and truly pious men whose example we ought to follow, are not those who affect such grimaces. What! will you make no distinction between hypocrisy and true religion? Will you call them both by the same name, and render the same homage to the mask as to the face? Will you put on the same level falsehood and sincerity, and confound appearance with reality? Will you esteem the shadow as much as the substance, and false coin as much as good?[16]

When he read Roullé's letter, he was so afraid that he appealed to the king for protection. Louis, who thought that Roullé was taking things too far, scolded the curé. Even so, he felt the need to clarify his own position towards *Tartuffe* in the official protocol to the fête at Versailles:

This evening His Majesty had a comedy entitled Tartuffe *performed which the Sieur de Molière had written against the hypocrites. Although His Majesty found it extremely diverting, he felt that there was so great a resemblance between those whom a sincere devotion put in the way of heaven and those whom a vain ostentation of good works did not prevent from achieving bad ones, that in his extreme care for matters pertaining to religion he could not permit this resemblance between vice and virtue, which might be mistaken one for the other; and although he did not doubt the good intentions of the author, he prohibited the public performance of the play and deprived himself of this pleasure in order that it should not be abused by others who might be less capable of a just discrimination.*[17]

Despite the pleading of Molière, who stood to lose income because of the ban, Louis stood firm. He announced that there would be no further public performances of *Tartuffe*, but his interdiction did not extend to private performances. The idea of presenting a banned play proved very appealing, and several people invited Molière to read or perform it in their homes. The most prestigious private performance took place in July at the home of the duc and duchesse d'Orléans. The following year, Louis would take over as Molière's official patron, with the new Troupe du Roy receiving an annual allowance of 6 thousand livres.[18]

The visit to Versailles had been a great success, despite the differences of opinion over *Tartuffe*. Not only had Louis entertained his court in grand style but he had also established Versailles as a place of work; council meetings and other business continued to take place amid the festivities. The court had not long been back in Paris, however, when a most unpleasant incident occurred.

It had always been the custom that out of respect for the two queens, the ladies of the court would not attend on any of the king's mistresses. This rule was broken by Mme de Brancas, the wife of the queen mother's *chevalier d'honneur*, who accompanied Louise on some of her excursions.[19] This upset Anne of Austria, who reprimanded Mme de Brancas. In her turn, Mme de Brancas complained to Louis, adding that the comtesse de Flex and the duchesse de Navailles had turned the queen mother against her. Louis took Mme de Brancas at her word and was angry that she had been badly treated. This caused much ill feeling between Louis and his mother.

As to the duchesse de Navailles, she had incurred Louis's wrath over the La Motte-Houdancourt affair, so he was already ill disposed towards her and her husband. This new incident hardened his heart still further, although he took no further action, at least for now. Shortly afterwards, he took the court to Fontainebleau, where he intended to spend part of the summer.

It was while the court was at Fontainebleau that Louis played host to Cardinal Chigi. He was sent by Pope Alexander to attempt to smooth relations between Louis and the Vatican, which had deteriorated markedly since the incident with the Corsican guards. When Louis seized the papal state of Avignon in 1663, Alexander realized that the king would have no hesitation in going to war. The pope backed down on that occasion, and on February 12, 1664, the Treaty of Pisa was signed.

The *Gazette*[20] noted that Alexander made reparation proportionate to the insult offered to Louis, whose glory was such that one could not injure him without being obliged to make full atonement. In this case, the full atonement demanded by Louis required the Italians to build a pyramid opposite the Corsican barracks where the incident had occurred in commemoration of the event. The pyramid would bear a detailed inscription describing exactly what had taken place. Now Cardinal Chigi had come to France with a full apology from the pope, but there was a problem: Chigi had envisaged a magnificent reception in Paris, complete with a parade through the streets and a public welcome from the king. When he learned that Louis was at Fontainebleau, the cardinal was outraged. He felt it was beneath his dignity to be received in the king's country palace and wrote to ask Louis if he could be welcomed in Paris instead. Louis refused. Chigi would meet Louis at Fontainebleau or not at all. As it was, Louis received the papal envoy in his bedroom, where Chigi read aloud the pope's letter of apology. With the formalities out of the way, Louis introduced Chigi to his master of the revels for the occasion. This was Molière, and Louis treated the cardinal with a special performance of *Tartuffe*. It had long been the maxim in the government of France to look upon the pope "as a sacred but overreaching person, whose feet one must kiss, but whose hands one must sometimes bind,"[21] and nobody demonstrated this more effectively than Louis XIV. As the first son of the church, Louis was obliged to obey the Holy Father in spiritual affairs, but he was not subordinate to him politically.[22]

Louis had not long triumphed over the papal nuncio when he was dragged into a domestic incident, this time involving the duc and duchesse de Navailles. The duc was in command of the light horse, and upon his arrival at Fontainebleau, he requisitioned quarters for his regiment. When Louis told him he must pay for them himself, Navailles remarked, "Your Majesty's servants are very unfortunate to be treated in this way."[23] As so often on occasions such as this, Louis did not answer, but it was clear to all who witnessed the scene that he was angry. Retribution came heavily and swiftly when Louis ordered the duc de Navailles to resign his position of governor of Havre-de-Grâce and give up his lieutenancy of the light horse, while the duchesse was dismissed from her post as lady-of-honor. Louis gave them 900 thousand livres as compensation for their loss of income, but in fact their office and income had been worth much more. The duchesse de Navailles was replaced by Julie, duchesse de Montausier, who had been serving as governess of the children of France.

Louis's vengeance deeply wounded Marie-Thérèse, for she was fond of Mme de Navailles. The tearful queen spoke to Louis in a bid to make him change his mind, but he refused to listen to reason. As Mme de Navailles left the court, the queen embraced her and assured her that she would never forget her.

Anne of Austria, whom the faithful Mme de Motteville said seldom shed tears, also wept for the duc and duchesse de Navailles, for they were good people and did not deserve such treatment. The queen mother tried to intervene with Louis on their behalf, but he would have none of it. For some time, Louis had been slipping away from his mother's influence, and now she was beginning to see all too clearly how far.

The coldness between the king and his mother had not yet thawed when they had another confrontation; this time it concerned religious affairs and an allegedly broken promise, and it almost broke up their relationship for good.[24] The abbé de Prière wanted to transform his order and had placed his plans before the royal council. Anne of Austria took an interest in the reforms the abbé wanted to implement, and Louis apparently promised her that she would be pleased with his decision when it came. As he awaited the king's verdict, the abbé became ill and asked Louis to postpone making a decision until after he had recovered. When Louis made his pronouncement anyway, his mother was appalled. Not only did she think he was wrong to do so but she also thought his decision was not the one he had promised her. To make matters worse, Louis defended himself before the comtesse de Soissons and others, saying that his mother "had not told the truth, or something to that effect, which did not seem respectful to her."

Anne was deeply hurt by Louis's words, which, when taken together with their earlier argument, further saddened and distressed her. As the chill silence between them deepened, she made up her mind to withdraw from the court and retire to the Val-de-Grâce. Le Tellier and others tried to reconcile the two, but all their attempts failed. "These two royal persons were both angry, and neither could resolve to speak to the other."

One day when Louis was in his mother's apartments, Philippe and Henriette withdrew to allow them the privacy to resolve their differences, but Louis, "after standing for some time looking out of the window, made a low bow to the queen mother and went away without saying a word." Anne went to find Philippe and said, "You see how he treats me!" Philippe led her away onto a terrace so she could avoid the eyes of the courtiers and there she wept, saying to Doña Molina, "Do you think we spoke together, the king and I, in the cabinet? I assure you no; we came out in the same state in which we went in."

The queen mother was so upset by Louis's behavior that she decided not to take supper with her family that evening. As Louis made his way to her apartments, he met Marie-Thérèse coming the other way and asked her why she was returning before supper. Marie-Thérèse answered that the queen mother had sent her away because she could not eat. Louis, now pale and confused, went to take his supper with the queen, but it was clear that he was troubled. His conscience was pricking him over the way he was treating his mother, but he still could not bring himself to reconcile with her.

Anne was at prayer in her oratory the next day when Doña Molina came in. When she saw the queen mother in tears, she discreetly turned to leave, but Anne bid her stay and kneel down beside her. Doña Molina asked Anne what was the matter, but all Anne managed to say was, "*Ay, Molina, estos hijos!*" "Ah, Molina, these children!"

Later that day, as Anne was making her devotions, her confessor ordered her to speak to Louis first "and to listen no longer to her vexation or her sorrow." Although she feared that Louis might heap further humiliations upon her, Anne resolved to talk to him and to "sacrifice her feelings to God."

For his part, Louis continued to be distressed at the discord between himself and his mother, and he made his way to her chamber with the intention of reaching rapprochement with her. However, as soon as he stepped through the door, Anne, who was resolved to speak first, poured out everything she had intended to say to him. Louis replied in a manner "both affectionate and submissive," and, kneeling before her, he begged her forgiveness and wept for having "failed in his duty towards her." He told her that he had not slept all night; he said that Le Tellier had told him of her desire to retire to the Val-de-Grâce; he begged her earnestly not to leave the court and asked her to promise him that she would never leave him.

Now that Louis had realized the error of his ways, Anne felt emboldened to tell him a few things she believed he ought to hear. She began by telling him that he was "too intoxicated with his own greatness" and that he "set no limits to either his desires or his vengeance." She pointed out the "peril in which he stood as regarded his salvation," and she "said all she could to bring him back to his own self, and to oblige him to at least desire to break the chains that bound him to sin."

Louis's tearful reply was sincere. He knew he had done wrong and said that "he felt at times the pain and shame of it." He admitted that although he had tried to "restrain himself from offending God, and from giving way to his passions," he had failed, because they "had now become stronger than his reason; that he could no longer resist their violence, nor did he even feel the desire to do so." He returned to the subject of the ladies of quality attending on Louise de La Vallière but said that "as she had desired it, it must be done, and he begged his mother not to oppose it."

Anne was satisfied that Louis at least knew he had done wrong, for it showed her that God had not entirely abandoned him, but she urged Louis not to displease God any more than he had done. Mother and son spoke about the dismissal of the duc and duchesse de Navailles and about the things Mme de Brancas had said. In the end, they resolved their differences and were reunited. This whole chapter of troubles inspired Mme de Motteville to make an observation about Louis:

> The things that I have just told will show that the king had great contradictions within him; that his virtues were mingled with much that opposed them; and that, bearing in himself the common nature of human frailty, he was not always virtuous nor always just. Nevertheless, I cannot avoid saying that, to my mind, there was strength in the acknowledgment he made of his weakness, and much Christian humility in blaming himself for his injustices. [25]

She added that no man who would be placed in the ranks of heroes "should be exempt from faults"; for it was true that Louis had a dark side, and it was about to make its devastating appearance.

THIRTEEN

The Dark Side of the Sun

I t was eight o'clock in the evening when Louis took to his horse and rode through the October darkness towards Paris. He was going to see his mother. She had gone the day before to visit the Carmelites, but she had taken ill and had been obliged to spend the night at the Val-de-Grâce. Louis was anxious, and his desire to see her was born of the great affection in which he held her, but his worries were happily misplaced, for Anne recovered enough to be able to return to Vincennes a short while later.[1]

Anne kept to her room for a time, and one day when Louis came to visit her, he brought Louise with him. Anne received the young woman in what was a major victory for Louis, for it implied that

Anne had accepted the royal mistress and implicitly approved of her. Louis and Louise played cards with Philippe and Henriette, but if the king was happy with the situation, Marie-Thérèse absolutely was not. The queen, who was pregnant at the time, was also keeping to her rooms that night, and when she heard about what was going on in the queen mother's chambers, she became very distressed. She commanded Mme de Motteville, who was attending her, to speak to Anne about it.

As Mme de Motteville made her way to her mistress's apartments, she encountered Mme de Montausier, who seemed very pleased that Louise had been received. "Do you see, Madame," she said, "what an admirable action the queen mother has done in being willing to receive La Vallière? That is the action of a very clever woman and a politician. But, she is so weak that we can scarcely hope she will sustain her action as she ought." Mme de Motteville was astonished by these words, and she hurried on without making an answer. When she found Anne in her oratory, one look told her that all was not well and that the queen mother had only pretended, for the king's sake, to accept Louise. Mme de Motteville went to Paris to spend the night. She felt she had failed in her duty to bring comfort to the queen, and instead "trusted in the prudence of the queen mother", whom she knew "too well to doubt that she would employ it fully."[2]

Louis's love for the arts was such that he wanted to reward those whose work he adored. He ordered Colbert to draw up a list of savants and men of letters, both French and foreign, who were to receive a royal grant. The first list, which appeared in 1662, is lost, but the lists from 1664 to 1683 survive and include the illustrious names of Molière, Pierre and Thomas Corneille, Jean Racine, and Charles Perrault. They each received a silk purse containing gold coins every year from the king. The value of these gifts varied, with Molière and Corneille receiving a thousand livres each. Racine received six hundred, while Perrault was given fifteen hundred.[3]

There was one very important omission from the list: Jean de la Fontaine, who had found himself out of favor for writing in defense of his former patron, Nicolas Foucquet. He had composed the famous *Élégie*,[4] a poem brimming over with sadness, sentiment, and regret at Foucquet's fate:

> *Fill the air with your plaints in your grottos deep,*
> *Weep, Nymphs of Vaux—and swell your streams,*
> *And let o'erflowing Anqueil[5] ravage the treasures*
> *With which Flora's glances have adorned your banks.*
> *No one shall blame your innocent tears,*
> *So may you freely yield to your urgent grief;*
> *All men look to you for that sympathetic act:*
> *The Fates content: misfortune has smitten Orontes.*[6]

Later in the poem, La Fontaine urges the Nymphs to appeal to Louis to show clemency for Foucquet:

> *Ye, whose home he made so fine,*
> *Nymphs, who owe to him your fairest charms,*
> *If along your banks Louis should stray,*
> *Try to soften him, to relax his angry mood;*
> *He loves his people; he is just; he is wise;*
> *Make him aspire to be termed clement;*
> *For clemency makes monarchs equal with the gods.*
> *Let him study magnanimous Henri's[7] life*
> *Who, able to revenge himself, desired it not.*
> *Inspire in Louis equal mercy;*
> *No victory so fine as that o'er one's own heart*
> *Orontes now does clemency deserve*
> *What though he yielded to promptings of unchecked power,*
> *His hard fate is punishment sufficient,*
> *And to be unfortunate is to be innocent.*

However, despite the tears of the poor Nymphs, it would soon become clear that Louis was in no mood to be merciful.

Upon Foucquet's arrest in September 1661, seals were placed on all his properties and his papers were seized. These papers were carefully scrutinized, and it was quickly found that many among them praised the superintendent's work or justified his actions. Among these were letters sent to Foucquet by Mazarin, all of which were quietly withdrawn. Over the course of the process, false or redacted documents would be inserted among genuine ones in order to enhance the apparent guilt of the accused. Other letters, many of which were compromising, had allegedly been sent to Foucquet by certain ladies at the court. Louis ordered them to be suppressed, but several of them found their way into the public domain in order to blacken Foucquet's name and destroy whatever sympathy he might have enjoyed among courtiers.

One document, however, proved even more explosive. This was a paper that would become known to history as the *Projet de Saint-Mandé*, an elaborate plan detailing the measures Foucquet, his friends, and business partners should take in the event of his arrest by the unpredictable Mazarin. Foucquet had written it at a particularly difficult period in his relationship with the cardinal, and he had revisited it several times as changes in his circumstances arose. Read in an unfavorable light, and when taken together with Foucquet's activities in Brittany,[8] the *Projet* could be interpreted as proof that Foucquet intended to commit high treason.

All the while, Foucquet had languished in the grim donjon of Vincennes, a mere stone's throw from his home at Saint-Mandé. During his first week of captivity, he wrote two letters to Michel Le Tellier, although it was clear that both were intended for the king. In the first, he wrote as a sick man afraid of death, begging for medical and spiritual assistance.[9] Whether or not this one was answered is not known. The second letter, which was very long, was not the work of a frail and frightened man but that of an accused minister expressing indignation at his treatment, pointing out his past services, and appealing to Louis's "goodness and his clemency, which are truly royal virtues . . . and for justice,[10] which, if it is there to punish faults, it is also there to reward service." He could not understand how matters had turned out as they had, but he would have been prepared to give up his post as superintendent if the king had asked him to. As it was, he asked Louis to change his imprisonment into exile, for he owned a dreary cottage in a remote corner of Brittany, where he could retire and live as a private person under the supervision of La Meilleraye.[11] He closed by begging Le Tellier to find time to read the letter in full to Louis, and appealing to the king for "the same mercy that he would desire God to show him one day."[12]

Foucquet did not receive the grace that he asked for. Louis ordered Le Tellier to write to d'Artagnan[13] that Foucquet's letters were too long, that His Majesty did not have time to read them. Five days later, he dictated another letter forbidding Foucquet to write any more letters without the express order of the king.[14]

The former superintendent had little idea of what was going on beyond the walls of his cell. He had no contact with his family apart from a few letters that he was allowed to exchange with his wife. These were passed through the hands of Michel Le Tellier, who ensured that they contained nothing but essential family business.

Louis's dilemma was to try Foucquet without subjecting the state finances to inquiry; to do so would not be in the best interests of the state, and it would alienate many prominent families in France and abroad.[15] As such, Louis thought that a small panel of masters of requests presided over by Chancellor Séguier would be appropriate.[16] This was not an unusual approach in such cases, and the process would be swiftly and satisfactorily accomplished.

Colbert, however, urged Louis to try the former superintendent against the setting of a dramatic show trial, as befitting the circumstances of his arrest. For this, it would be necessary to establish a *Chambre de justice*.[17] Colbert's motive was simple: it allowed for the reformation of the finances by highlighting alleged abuses in the system over a period of several years. In this case, the former superintendent would be tried not only for irregularities that occurred during his tenure but also for financial crimes going back to 1635; that is, sixteen years before he took office. Colbert's hostility towards Foucquet was useful to Louis, whose wish to bring the former superintendent down was driven by his need to enhance royal power, to crush once and for all any chance that the Fronde may rise again,[18] and to rid his kingdom of a man who was more magnificent than himself. Louis agreed to Colbert's proposal.

The judges and officials were duly appointed. Colbert was careful to choose men who were known to be unsympathetic towards Foucquet, but whom he trusted to find the verdict and recommend the sentence required by the king. This process took several weeks, and the *Chambre* held its first sitting on December 3, 1661. Chancellor Séguier, who distinguished himself by his hostility towards the defendant, led the *Chambre*; the premier président of the Parlement of Paris, Guillaume de Lamoignon, was appointed presiding magistrate. The second president was François-Theodore de Nesmond, and Denis Talon, one of Foucquet's fiercest enemies, took the post of *procureur-général* for the *Chambre*. Lamoignon, who had ties with Foucquet and was suspected of being sympathetic towards him, was replaced midway through the process by Séguier.[19] The *Chambre* was tasked to establish Foucquet's guilt without also putting Mazarin on trial or incriminating Colbert and others.

Two members of the *Chambre*, Pierre Poncet and Jacques Renard, interrogated Foucquet in his cell at Vincennes. They were accompanied by the *greffier*, or clerk of the court, Joseph Foucault, who noted down Foucquet's every word. They assailed Foucquet with leading questions and used legal though unethical means to place him under as much pressure as possible.

Thus far, Foucquet had been denied access to his papers and was forbidden to see the notes on his case. He was also denied counsel.

However, his sharp intelligence and thorough knowledge of the legal system told him much of what he needed to know about the case that was being built against him. This insight allowed him to mount a brilliant defense. Recognizing that Colbert and his clients were behind the attack on him, Foucquet implicated his former friend and colleague, whose financial activities were equally suspect. He also humiliated the *Chambre*, whose case was encumbered by weak accusations and its own partiality.

The charges Foucquet was to face fell into two categories: financial crimes and high treason. On the financial side, he was accused of making false loans to the state; agreeing to private advances of funds to the state; making use of state revenues for his own, private purposes; creating false identities in order to speculate in tax farming.[20]

None of these charges could be proven, and the only evidence that apparently supported them lay in Foucquet's apparent wealth, of which the château Vaux-le-Vicomte was the most obvious example. In his defense, Foucquet pointed out that his debts far exceeded his assets, and he insisted that the *Chambre* should audit his accounts. This was not done.[21] In fact, the charge of peculation and other finance-related crimes against Foucquet were not as sharply defined as Colbert asserted. Certainly, Foucquet's accounts were in serious disarray, but that was the case with financiers in general.

The charge of high treason was based upon the plan found at Foucquet's house at Saint-Mandé. Certainly, if it had been read by anyone determined to ruin Foucquet, they would find their ammunition in this document. On the other hand, Foucquet had made no attempt to implement any of the measures described in it, nor had he told anyone about the plan.[22] The charge of high treason, though unsustainable, would become one of the highlights of the trial.

In October 1662, the *Chambre* appointed two *rapporteurs*, or court reporters, whose responsibility was to sum up the prosecution's case and, where appropriate, offer their recommendations for sentencing. The *rapporteurs* selected for Foucquet's trial were Jacques Le Cormier de

Sainte-Hélène and Olivier Lefèvre d'Ormesson. Acting on the advice of their lawyers, Foucquet's wife and mother immediately challenged the appointment of these two men due to their association with Colbert. In view of this, Lamoignon advised Louis to recuse the two men. The conscientious premier président was anxious that due process should be observed, and he feared for the integrity of the *Chambre*. Louis, following the counsel of Colbert, Le Tellier, and others, insisted that Sainte-Hélène and Ormesson should take up their posts, stating that the Mmes Foucquet were afraid of the "known integrity of these magistrates, and that fear is one more reason to appoint them."[23] The suspicions of the Foucquet ladies would prove to be justified in Sainte-Hélène's case. However, Ormesson's reputation for probity and integrity would show itself to be well earned.

At the end of August 1664, the *Chambre* discovered that some of the original documents pertaining to the case had been tampered with. One of their members, Louis Berryer, was blamed for having omitted some lines from one of the witness statements, and the resulting uproar held the process back by some four weeks. The reputation of the *Chambre*, however, had been dented.[24] Notwithstanding this, the trial of Nicolas Foucquet finally opened on November 14, 1664, at the Arsenal in Paris, more than three years after his arrest. The proceedings at the court, which would sit for most days until December 4, were interrupted after only two days when the queen became dangerously ill.

Marie-Thérèse, who was pregnant with her third child, had been feeling unwell for some time. A month earlier, Louis had announced that he would take the court to Versailles, but Marie-Thérèse, fearing the long journey might cause her to miscarry, did not want to go. Louis, however, did not want to leave her behind, so he designed a special chair that would allow her to make the journey. The contraption was a kind of portable bed, and when the queen tried it, she found it to be very comfortable.[25] Upon her return, she came down with a tertian fever and violent pains in her legs. On November 4, she gave birth prematurely to a daughter, Marie-Anne de France, who was given the title la Petite Madame.[26] The following day, the queen had convulsions, and her life was despaired of. Louis, weeping with grief, was very attentive, but the queen's life was in the hands of God. The king, as though to purchase divine favor for Marie-Thérèse, distributed money to the poor and ordered the release of some prisoners, all the while bargaining with God to save the queen. He confided to the maréchal de Villeroy that while Marie-Thérèse was in labor, "although it would be the greatest misfortune in the world for him to lose a child, he could be consoled for that, provided God did him the favor to preserve the queen's life, and also that his child could [live long enough to] be baptized."[27]

It was about this time[28] that Sebastiano Locatelli, an Italian abbot and visitor to the court, took the opportunity to watch Louis as he went to mass at Saint-Germain-l'Auxerrois and later wrote a description of the king. Louis wore a suit of black velvet with a large floral [jacquard-type] design, with the insignia of the Saint-Esprit on his cloak. He carried a short cane in his hand and wore a small hat decorated with a rose of diamonds on one side. Locatelli noted that Condé and other dukes and peers were better dressed than the king, but Louis, probably influenced by his mother, preferred to dress plainly for church. Louis's dark blond hair was still long and luxurious, his forehead was high, and his eyes were "more blue than dark." His nose was aquiline, and his mouth and chin were "very beautiful." The king's figure was plump, and his skin was "more olive than white"; he was also rather tall, while his shoulders were slightly bowed, which "indicated well that vigor that is apparent in all his actions."[29]

As Marie-Thérèse received the last rites, Louis was inconsolable. "It is the most magnificent and the saddest things in the world to see the king and all the court, with the candles and a thousand torches, going to ask for the sacrament and escort it back," said Mme de Sévigné. It had not been without difficulty to make the queen receive it, and Louis was required to warn her of the gravity of her condition. Aware of the queen's illness, Mme Foucquet the Elder offered a remedy of her own recipe to Anne of Austria, a plaster that, when applied, reduced the queen's fever. An hour later, she was on the road to recovery.[30]

While Marie-Thérèse lay on what everyone thought to be her deathbed, she made a special request to Louis: to arrange a marriage for Louise de La Vallière. Louis was taken aback by such a surprising appeal. He did not want to promise, but he also did not want to refuse his wife's dying wish, so he compromised by assuring her that he would not oppose it, but that they might look for a suitable husband for Louise together.

The story goes that every eligible man at court and beyond refused Louise's hand, but in fact Louise was the one who refused to take a husband.[31] If she were to marry, it would be as a bride of Christ. When Marie-Thérèse recovered, Louis broke the promise he had made to her. If there had been talk of marriage, he said, it was only because he knew Louise would never hear of it.

It was time, Louis thought, to have a little fun, to lift the somber mood that had descended upon the court during the past few weeks. He had recently taken up writing verses, his poesy guided by Saint-Aignan and Dangeau.[32] One day he wrote a little madrigal, although he was not very pleased with it, and he decided to ask the elderly maréchal de Gramont to read it to see if he had "ever seen one so irrelevant." He went on to explain that "because it is known that I have lately taken a liking to poems, people bring me all sorts of them."[33]

The maréchal, having read the madrigal, told Louis, "Sire, Your Majesty judges divinely everything; it is true that this is the silliest and most ridiculous madrigal that I have ever read."

The king laughed at this and replied, "Is it not true that whoever wrote this is indeed a fop?"

"Sire, there is no other name for him."

"Oh, good," said Louis, "I am delighted that you have spoken so plainly; it is I who wrote it."

"Ah, Sire, what treachery!" cried Gramont. "Will Your Majesty give it back to me; I read it too quickly."

"No, M. le maréchal," replied the king. "The first impressions are always the most natural."

While Louis laughed at his little joke, others found it the "cruelest thing one could do to an old courtier." Louis, however, was in excellent spirits: he had been successful in keeping his beloved Louise all to himself, and his queen had been restored to him. However, those who thought that Mme Foucquet's intervention in the queen's crisis might help to alleviate her son's plight were sadly mistaken. The trial was quickly resumed until December 9, when, for the next eight days, the *rapporteurs* presented their summing up, offered their verdicts, and recommended the sentence each thought Foucquet should receive.

Ormesson was the first to address the court. He found Foucquet guilty of certain financial irregularities but insisted that these must be judged in context. Foucquet, he noted, had taken his orders directly from Mazarin, an Italian unfamiliar with the French financial system. He pointed out that because actual proof of the former superintendent's guilt was incomplete, Foucquet could be found guilty only of negligence and misappropriation of public funds, for which he should receive the lesser sentence of banishment and the confiscation of his assets by the crown, except for 5 thousand livres to be donated to charity.[34]

Sainte-Hélène now stood to give his verdict, which was that Foucquet was guilty of embezzlement, malfeasance during his tenure as superintendent, and high treason. Proof of treason lay in the *Projet de Saint-Mandé*, which Sainte-Hélène had interpreted as a plot to kill the king. Regicide, he pointed out, required the death penalty, but in view of Foucquet's noble birth, he should not be hanged but beheaded within the Bastille, while his possessions should be forfeited to the crown.

For the next four days, each of the judges registered their votes and presented the grounds upon which they reached their judgments. On December 20, the final verdict was announced: nine judges had agreed with Sainte-Hélène and found for death; the other thirteen had been persuaded by Ormesson's arguments and found Foucquet guilty of financial misdemeanors with a sentence of banishment for life beyond the borders of the kingdom.[35]

This sentence, harsh though it was, brought comfort to Foucquet's friends and supporters; however, one of these, Mme de Sévigné, could not shake off a feeling of unease. She had been following the trial and writing a running commentary to a friend. After listing the verdicts reached by the various members of the *Chambre*, she wrote:

> *This is where we are, which is a state so advantageous that our joy is not unmixed; for you know that M. Colbert is so angry, that we expect something atrocious and unjust that will throw us back into despair. Were it not for that, my poor, Monsieur, we would have the joy of seeing our friend, unhappy though he may be, at least with his life saved, which is a great thing.*[36]

Her instincts were correct: not only was Colbert furious but Louis was also displeased with the final verdict and sentencing. He had expected Foucquet to be executed if found guilty[37] and had warned his mother not to appeal for clemency should Foucquet be sentenced to death.[38] When the verdict became known, he told Louise that Foucquet would die for all he would do to help him.[39]

On the other hand, Louis had urged Colbert not to "break his head over it. Why? Because Ormesson does not want to hang Fouquet, is it necessary that I should hang him?"[40] The king would not order Foucquet's execution, but he refused to accept the sentence of banishment. Louis reasoned that Foucquet knew so much of the secret affairs of state that it would be unwise to allow him to live freely abroad.[41] However, the faults that marred the trial—the irregularities in the inventories of Foucquet's papers; the hostility towards the defendant throughout; the forged and redacted documents; and the damage caused to the finances of everyone concerned—rendered the imposition of the death penalty unacceptable.[42] Instead, Louis changed the sentence to life imprisonment. Under normal circumstances, a man would be allowed to have the company of his wife in prison,[43] and certainly Mme Foucquet wanted to join her husband, but Louis ruled this out. Foucquet would be held in solitary confinement amid the grim isolation of the citadel of Pignerol, a remote French outpost in the Italian Alps.[44]

Such was the penalty for those whom Louis thought overshadowed him with their magnificence, their learning, and their impeccable taste in all things that spoke of the glory of France. In ruining Foucquet, Louis broke the recent tradition of rule by first minister and, with it, the threat of a new Fronde; and Foucquet's terrible fate served as a dire warning to any who entertained ambitious thoughts.

The plight of the fallen superintendent had won him much sympathy. People who would gleefully have strangled him with their bare hands three years earlier now came out to cheer their support and wish him well as his fortified carriage rolled out of Paris on that cruel late-December day.

Henceforth, the minutiae of Foucquet's life would be closely monitored and controlled by the king. Foucquet would live in a cell comprising three small rooms, including a garderobe. Even among prisoners, rank was preserved, so Foucquet ate food similar to that he had enjoyed as a free man. He had a cruet set, fine tableware, and linen; his clothes were washed by washerwomen, and his suits were changed with the seasons; he had a comfortable bed with a canopy, mats on the floor and tapestries on the walls; two valets served him and looked after his every need. However, those valets were under instructions to spy upon him and report to the jailer, Saint-Mars, everything Foucquet said or did. Reports were sent back to Paris and read to Louis. Foucquet was denied writing materials and was allowed to read only one book at a time, the titles restricted to religious works and a history of France. He spoke to no one other than his valets and his jailer. Although he was allowed to hear mass, it was said in another room, and he could confess only four times a year. Foucquet's life had been spared, but his imprisonment would be a kind of living death.[45]

As far as Mme de Sévigné was concerned, Louis was not to blame for the terrible treatment Foucquet had suffered; instead, she attributed it to Colbert and his creatures. In doing so, she failed to acknowledge that Louis had it in his power to pardon Foucquet, or at least to reduce his sentence in some way. In increasing that sentence—which, as far as is known, was unique in the history of the French monarchy—Louis did not break the law, but his decision was both unfair and unethical, and it left an indelible blemish upon his *gloire*.

FOURTEEN

Mars and Athena

The year 1666 did not open happily for Louis. Only a few weeks previously, on September 17, his father-in-law and uncle, Philip IV of Spain, died. The queen was particularly affected, and Louis and his court went into mourning.

At about the same time, Anne of Austria, who had been ill for some time, began to decline. She had noticed the first signs of the illness that was to kill her at the time of the *Plaisirs de l'Ile Enchanté*, the series of entertainments given by Louis at Versailles during that glorious summer of 1664. For some time, she had experienced pain in her breast, though she neglected it at first, with the result that when the cancer showed itself, there was little that could be done. Now that 1665 was drawing to a close, both Louis and Philippe sensed that their mother's troubles would not end happily. That year they spent a gloomy Christmas until, partly against their better judgment, they looked for a means to brighten this darkest of winters. The opportunity arose with the necessity to entertain certain foreign visitors, whom Louis wished to dazzle with the grandeur of his court. Philippe hosted a great supper followed by a magnificent ball, which provided a much-needed diversion from the cares and worries that beset the entire court. Marie-Thérèse, who did not attend, made a suit for Louis to wear for the occasion. Because he was still in mourning for the king of Spain, the suit was of violet, but it was "so covered with great pearls and diamonds that it was marvelous to behold."[1]

The next day, any thoughts of further diversions were put aside when Queen Anne's condition took a turn for the worse. She had a violent fever, with a strong chill, after which erysipelas appeared, a side effect of her cancer. At this point, she was urged to dismiss her usual doctor and use the services of a Milanese physician who had helped another woman with the same condition. Anne at first showed no inclination to do so; instead, she seemed resigned to her suffering, which she accepted as the will of God. It was not until Louis coaxed her that she consented to see the Milanese. Unfortunately, in the opinion of Mme de Motteville, this physician's remedies had "no other effect than to hasten her death."[2]

Over the next few days, the queen mother's condition grew worse, and her pain was so severe that it made her cry. She endured it with great fortitude, telling one of her ladies, "I am not weeping; these tears that you see coming out of my eyes, it is pain that forces them out, for you know I am no weeper."[3]

On Tuesday, January 19, Anne's doctors advised Louis to make his mother consider taking the Holy Viaticum. When the archbishop of Auch, to whom Anne "had entrusted the care of the most important matter of her life, which was to help her end it,"[4] repeated the advice given her by the king, she showed fear for the first time and, at last, consented. As Louis watched his mother receive the final sacrament, he said in a low voice, "Look at the queen my mother; never did I see her more beautiful."[5]

It was time now for Anne to take her leave of her four children: Louis and Philippe, Marie-Thérèse and Henriette. They "threw themselves on their knees beside her bed and kissed her hands and wept,"[6] but Anne's thoughts were now with God. As Louis stood before her, tears streaming down his face, Anne turned her gaze upon him and looked at him fixedly. Speaking "with the majesty of a queen and the authority of a mother," she uttered these mysterious words: "Do what I told you. I tell it to you again, with the Holy Sacrament on my lips." Louis, his eyes filled with tears, bowed his head and assured her that he would not fail. "To this hour," wrote Mme de Motteville, "we are ignorant of what it was."[7]

The end came on Wednesday, January 20, between four and five in the morning. Philippe, overwhelmed with grief, withdrew to his house at Saint-Cloud and could not face returning to the Louvre even to hear the reading of his mother's will. Louis attended to these matters as early as it was possible to do so, and the late queen's will was read by Le Tellier in the presence of the king and Anne's ladies. When at last he went to bed, he spent the whole night weeping.

The following morning, his eyes still heavy and red, Louis spoke of his mother to the duchesse de Montausier, saying that

> he had the consolation of thinking that he had never disobeyed her in anything of consequence; and, continuing to speak of her noble qualities, he added, that the queen his mother was not only a great queen, but that she deserved to be put in the rank of the greatest kings.[8]

Mme de Motteville described his words as "a eulogy that was indeed worthy of her for whom it was made, and worthy, too, of him who made it."[9]

As Louis wrote in his memoirs,[10] "[I] knew better than anyone the vigor with which this princess had maintained my dignity when I was unable to defend it myself." Louis, of course, is speaking of her actions during the Fronde. "It was impossible," he continued, "that a son attached by the bonds of nature could see her die without extreme sadness."

He spoke about their daily life together, and how the respects he had always paid her were more than "the obligations one does out of propriety," but that he lived under the same roof, shared the same table with her, and diligently visited her several times a day, despite the pressures of his work, all of which was done not for reasons of state but as a "mark of the pleasure that I took in her company."[11]

Louis could not bear to remain at the Louvre, where his mother had died. He immediately withdrew, first to Versailles, where he found some much-needed privacy, and then on to Saint-Germain. Here he began to perform the duties the tragedy of losing his mother had imposed upon him. He wrote letters informing the princes of Europe, a duty that "cost me more than can be imagined, and particularly the letters that I wrote to the Emperor, and to the kings of Spain and to the king of England," to whom propriety obliged him to write in his own hand.[12]

Louis then ordered the executors of his mother's will to carry out her last wishes punctually. There was, however, one exception. Anne had asked for no ceremony, but Louis needed an outlet for his grief, and he ordered the same etiquette that she had decreed for his father's funeral to be applied to hers.[13] In accordance with royal protocol, Louis did not attend his mother's funeral; instead, he withdrew again to the solitude of Versailles.[14]

Louis had asked for no letters of condolence from private individuals; he accepted only official ones. When the marquis de La Vallière, Louise's brother, committed a monumental breach of etiquette by sending commiserations to the king, he received an appropriate reply. "What I have suffered in losing the queen, madam my mother," Louis wrote, "surpasses all the efforts of your imagination; and to respond to you in one word, know that only the hand that has brought me such a severe blow is able to soften it."[15]

The marquis was really no more than a "vehicle for liberalities not openly to be shown to Louise."[16] Even so, Louis was in no mood to indulge him, for while Louise had been present at a mass said for Anne of Austria, it would soon become clear that her star was fading.

The death of his mother left Louis bereft, but it also brought a freedom he had never known. If the loss of Mazarin had allowed Louis to assume fully the mantle of kingship, the loss of Anne of Austria lifted all restrictions to his behavior. Their recent arguments had inspired caution in the king, who was careful to conceal his passion for Louise. Now he no longer feared bringing her to court but instead flaunted her openly. This brought with it a consequence he did not expect, for the need for secrecy turned out to have been the spice that flavored their relationship, the possibility of discovery and further admonishment adding to the excitement. It began to dawn on Louis that he was no longer in love with Louise, although he kept her by his side. That March, he rode in excellent spirits to Mouchy to review his troops, [17] but Louise, who travelled alongside him, was not the only one to notice his coldness towards her. Within weeks, the prince de Condé was speculating that "His Majesty is soon going to make Mlle de La Vallière a Duchess." The classic "golden handshake" offered to every mistress was to elevate her to the status of duchesse, complete with lands and revenues to allow her to maintain her dignity. Condé, as it turned out, was correct.

By letters patent issued in May 1667,[18] Louis conferred honors upon Louise, who received the estate of Vaujours[19] and the barony of Saint-Christophe in Anjou, both of which were rich in revenues and tenures. With these properties, Louis gave Louise the title he felt was most worthy of someone of her noble and ancient lineage, that of duchesse de La Vallière. At the same time, he affirmed that his daughter by Louise, Marie-Anne de Blois,[20] would inherit her mother's titles and estates and pass them on to her own legitimate children, male and female.

There was, however, a clause of reversion, which stated that should Marie-Anne predecease her mother without legitimate issue, the properties belonging to the duchy would go to Louise, but only on condition that she could not dispose of it and that after her death all would revert to the crown. Louis then declared Marie-Anne "legitimate and capable of all civil honors and effects."[21]

Louis had long been concerned that throughout their relationship, Louise had asked for nothing but his love; even now she owned very few possessions except some pieces of jewelry. Now Louise was a duchess, while Marie-Anne acquired the right to be called La Vallière.[22] Louis wrote, "[I] believed I was right to ensure to this child the honors of her birth, and to give the mother an establishment suitable to the affection that I had for her for six years,"[23] yet to all who had eyes to see, these honors represented a parting gift to Louise. This was confirmed when Louis sent her to Fontainebleau shortly afterwards, there to await further instructions.

Condé attributed Louise's good fortune to the affection with which she was held at court, where "she does no harm, and tries to do all the good she can," and perhaps this had something to do with it. On the other hand, Louis's munificence could have been inspired by thoughts of his own mortality, for at the time he was preparing to go to war and had not "resolved to go to the army to remain distant from peril".[24]

Racine dedicated his tragedy *Alexandre le Grand* to Louis:

> I do not content myself with placing at the head of my work the name of Alexander, I add also that of Your Majesty, that is to say, that I bring together all that is the greatest with which the present century and the centuries past can furnish us.

Racine, who compares Louis to Alexander, one of the king's heroes, continues: "It is not extraordinary to see a young man win battles, to see him set on fire all over the world," adding that history "is full of young conquerors, and we know with what passion Your Majesty has sought opportunities to distinguish himself at an age when Alexander was still crying for the victories of his father." Yet Louis, "who, at Alexander's age, had the command of Augustus; who, almost without venturing from the center of his kingdom, had spread his light to the end of the world," is placed far above the great Macedonian general. Now, as the summer of 1667 approached, Louis's plans to emulate the great Alexander were coming to fruition.

The cause of Louis's reflections was the accession to the Spanish throne by Carlos II, son of the late Philip IV, after the death of Philip Prospero. The new king was disabled physically and mentally, and was widely expected to die without an heir. Such an event, which was thought to be imminent, would provide Louis the opportunity to address concerns about the security of his borders.

It had long been Louis's ambition to extend the eastern borders of France as far as the Rhine by absorbing Lorraine and conquering Franche-Comté. The frontier was also vulnerable to the northeast, and Mazarin's earlier attempts to provide a barrier to protect Paris from a sudden attack had been unsuccessful. With no lasting peace between France and Spain, Louis planned to push the French frontier to the river Scheldt, which ran through the Spanish Netherlands.[25]

As matters stood, there were two options Louis could take. The first was to negotiate the possible partition of the Spanish Netherlands with Emperor Leopold, who was about to marry Margarita Teresa, the half sister of Queen Marie-Thérèse.[26] Such an arrangement would satisfy both the king and the emperor, both of whom would acquire territory in right of their respective wives. Emperor Leopold was hampered at home by the League of the Rhine and occupied on his eastern frontier by Turkish attempts to seize the whole of Hungary.[27]

The other option was for Louis to claim compensation for the 500 thousand écus owed to him as his wife's dowry, and which remained almost wholly unpaid.[28] While Marie-Thérèse's right of succession had been annulled by the Act of Renunciation, this had been agreed in exchange for the dowry. Since much of the dowry remained outstanding, Louis reasoned, the Act of Renunciation could not be upheld.

In order to support his argument for compensation, Louis could appeal to a little-known law, the *Jus Devolutionis*, or Law of Devolution. This stipulated that where a man married more than once, the inheritance would devolve upon the children of the first marriage and not the second. Marie-Thérèse, as the eldest child of the late Philip IV, had a valid claim to her father's royal estate, a claim that Louis, as her husband, could exploit. Unfortunately for Louis, the Law of Devolution was observed in only a few locations: Brabant, Malines, Namur, and Hainaut; even here, it applied only to private property, not political rights such as matters of succession to the crown.[29]

As April 1667 drew to a close, a peace conference was held at Breda in the Spanish Netherlands, attended by France, England, Holland, Sweden, and Denmark. As the talks dragged on, Louis felt threatened by rapprochement between England and the Dutch Republic, but he was not without resources. His legal advisors had produced a pamphlet, *A Treatise upon the Right of the Most Christian Queen to Various States in the Spanish Monarchy*, which explained Louis's duties: as a king to fight injustice, as a husband to oppose the usurpation of his wife's property, and as a father to preserve his son's patrimony.[30]

Summaries of the *Treatise* were sent to the Dutch States General and to the queen regent, Mariana of Spain. The Dutch were so alarmed that they attempted a coup against England, with their renowned commander, Ruyter, managing to sail up the Thames as far as Gravesend before menacing towns along the Medway. For her part, the regent Mariana refused to accede to Louis's demands, but she reckoned without the military might available to the Sun King.

While Louis's navy was still relatively weak,[31] his army had recovered from the ravages of the Fronde. No longer disorderly and disloyal, the French army, although small in comparison to its size in later years, was well trained, disciplined, and, more importantly, had been kept in a state of preparedness for war. Moreover, Louis took personal interest in his troops, and for the past fifteen months he had spent a total of twenty-two days inspecting his regiments. Thanks to the reforms implemented by Colbert, Louis now had the money to carry out his military plans, and he was ready to launch his assault on Flanders.

Louis left Saint-Germain on May 16, arriving at Amiens on the twentieth. Here, he spent the next four days reviewing his troops before heading for Compiègne the next day. The king's troops were under the command of Turenne, although Louis took personal charge of certain operations. In several cases, French troops vastly outnumbered the Spanish, and as the sieges got underway, many towns capitulated within days. As town after town fell, Louis received the surrender and made a formal entry, although it is true to say that resistance was often token, so Louis had little in the way of victory to celebrate.

On June 22, Louis conducted the siege of Tournai, with the town surrendering on the twenty-fifth, and its castle the next day. July 6 saw the fall of Douai, which capitulated after a five-day siege, with Louis making a discreet entrance on the seventh. Two weeks later, he and Marie-Thérèse made their formal entry, where the *Te Deum* was sung along with the celebrations. Louis took Alost on August 8, and at the end of the month, Lille fell after a monthlong siege.

Throughout, Louis did not shy away from danger but often placed himself within range of enemy cannon. He shared the victories and the hardships with his men, and never failed to stay overnight in the camp with them, despite the rain and the fact that he suffered from toothache for more than a fortnight.[32] The king's direct approach and personal interest in his armies should come as no surprise: he confided to "a person he esteemed," that if he ever made war, he "would go to it in person." His anonymous confidant answered that it would be a great imprudence, even a fault in a king to risk his life in such a way, noting that France had once suffered from the imprudence of François I. Louis replied, "Imprudent if you please; but all the same, that imprudence put [François] in the rank of the greatest kings."[33] At Lille, however, his troops refused to allow him to join them in the trenches, warning that it was too dangerous. Louis reluctantly agreed, with the stipulation, "Since you want me to take care of myself for your sakes, I also want you to look after yourselves for mine."[34]

Louis wore buff, lost a little weight, and caught the sun during the campaign. He continued to take care of his appearance, having his hair curled, taking a long time to dress, and spending half an hour in front of his mirror each day curling his mustache and arranging it with wax. This preening did not go for nothing, however; at intervals, Louis sent for Marie-Thérèse, who hastened with her ladies to Compiègne, where she would meet the king as he returned from the front to celebrate his latest victories.

The first such occasion took place on June 9. As Marie-Thérèse set out, the almost forgotten Louise, left alone at Versailles, decided to break etiquette and journey out to join the court. Riding in her new ducal carriage, she caught up with the queen's party at La Fère, where it had stopped for the night. When she turned up unannounced in the queen's dressing room, Marie-Thérèse made it clear that she was unwelcome.[35] The queen issued orders to the officers of her escort to allow no one to leave before her the next morning, so that she would be the first to reach the king. However, as the court approached the rendezvous point at Avesnes, Louis was spotted awaiting his queen on the rising ground. At that point, Louise's carriage suddenly raced across the fields before anything could be done to stop her.[36] Louis's greeting was icy, and as the court settled at Avesnes, he paid Louise only the most formal of visits.

Louise, having broken the most rigid royal protocols by approaching Louis in advance of the queen, now compounded her error by upsetting Louis's strictly laid-out social arrangements by not joining the court for supper that evening.[37] As to Louis, his sharp-eyed cousin of Montpensier had noticed that he had other matters on his mind than the unhappy Louise,[38] for among those who watched the proceedings with interest was Mme de Montespan, better known as Athénaïs.

Born into a proud but impoverished aristocratic family that could trace its ancestry back to 1094, Françoise de Rochechoart de

Mortemart, marquise de Montespan, had made her social début in 1660, when she entered the court under the name Mlle de Tonnay-Charrante.[39] Her mother, a member of Anne of Austria's household, had assisted Athénaïs in gaining an appointment as maid of honor to Marie-Thérèse. Athénaïs made one of her earliest court appearances at the age of twenty in Benserade's *Hercule amoureux*, in which Louis danced the parts of Mars and the Sun.

Athénaïs was cultured, intellectual, a lover of music, dance, and literature. Attracted to salon society, she became a regular at the salon of the maréchal d'Albret, and it was here that she changed her name from Françoise to the more classical-sounding Athénaïs, naming herself after Athena, the Greek goddess of wisdom, virginity, and victory. The salon also introduced her to a new friend, Mme Scarron, the widow of the poet Paul Scarron.

Athénaïs married Louis-Henri de Pardaillan de Gondrin, marquis de Montespan, whose family was as impoverished and aristocratic as her own, on February 6, 1663.[40] The wedding took place at the church of Saint-Sulpice in Paris, and the couple set up home in the rue Tarenne in the district of Saint-Germain-des-Prés.[41]

Athénaïs continued in her position at court, and two weeks after her marriage, she took part in a new ballet at the Louvre, dancing alongside Louise de La Vallière. However, Athénaïs's life was not entirely carefree: her husband was the nephew of the staunchly Jansenist archbishop of Sens, and so was unwelcome at court. If the family was to gain any social advancement, Athénaïs would have to be the one to work for it. Moreover, their financial problems were worsened by the marquis's love of gambling, which caused him to amass debts at an alarming rate. Seeing that he was unable to make his way at court, Montespan left to join the army. This was no great blow to Athénaïs however, as the first few months of their living together had brought her to the realization that she was no longer in love with him; indeed, she felt that he was beneath her. As things would turn out, Montespan's debts would increase still further as the result of his need to purchase his uniform, equipment, and weapons, as well as to finance his gambling habit, which he could not give up.

Athénaïs had become pregnant almost straightaway, and she gave birth to her first child, Marie-Christine, who was baptized at Saint-Sulpice on November 17. With her pregnancy came the forfeiture of her post as maid of honor, so Athénaïs now found herself in need of employment. She applied to become a lady-in-waiting to the queen, and it appears that she secured the post thanks to the intervention of Philippe, who was a close friend of Athénaïs's sister, Madame de Thianges. Despite the coldness between Athénaïs and her husband, she managed to become pregnant again and, on November 5, 1664, gave birth to a son, Louis-Antoine, marquis d'Antin.

Quite when Athénaïs de Montespan caught Louis's attention cannot precisely be known. Mademoiselle thought that Louis had taken her as a mistress during the Flanders campaign in 1667. When Louise had been discovered in the queen's dressing room, Mesdames de Bade and Montausier voiced their commiserations with Marie-Thérèse. Mme de Montespan interrupted them, exclaiming perhaps a little too loudly, "Heaven defend me from being mistress to the King; but, were such a misfortune to befall me, I should certainly not have the effrontery to appear before the Queen."[42]

One night, Mme de Montespan asked Mademoiselle to hold her cards for her while she remained in her chamber. This was near the king's own rooms, and it was noticed that a sentinel who was usually posted on the stairs between the two apartments had been removed and placed below to prevent anyone ascending. Louis spent almost the entire day in his chamber with the door locked. For her part, Mme de Montespan failed to appear at the queen's card table, and she did not accompany her on her promenades as she usually would.[43]

Mademoiselle was not the only one to notice. Marie-Thérèse received an anonymous letter informing her that the king was in love with Mme de Montespan. The queen could not believe it, and the news seemed even less credible when she was told that Mme de Montausier was conducting the intrigue and that Louis had spent almost the whole time they were at Compiègne in La Montespan's chamber. Sensing that someone was trying to cause trouble between the queen and her ladies, it was agreed that the letter must have been written by Mme d'Armagnac.[44] Marie-Thérèse sent the letter to Louis, and to show that she "entirely discredited the accusation, the Queen treated Madame de Montespan with even greater consideration."[45] The queen was right to be cautious, for no one could tell at this stage whether the king's liaison with Mme de Montespan would be nothing more than a dalliance, and had not Louis, who was now twenty-nine, promised Marie-Thérèse that he would settle down at the age of thirty?

FIFTEEN
The Triple Alliance

Louis's sudden and decisive victories in the Spanish Netherlands frightened the English and the Dutch into a truce. Meeting at Breda, the two former enemies agreed to a rapprochement, and when they were joined by Sweden in May 1668, the Triple Alliance of The Hague was formed. The new alliance wasted no time in threatening France with war if Louis refused to relinquish the conquests he had acquired during the Devolution War.[1] Louis, however, had anticipated this threat, and even before the alliance had formed, he was deep into his counterstroke. He had ordered his ambassador to Venice, de Grémonville, to negotiate a secret partition treaty with Emperor Leopold.

While Grémonville's talks were still ongoing, Louis pressed ahead with his plans to seize Franche-Comté. Condé was appointed general for this campaign, and he arrived at Dijon in December 1667 to begin his preparations. When Louis arrived in the province on February 7, 1668, Besançon had already surrendered without a shot having been fired. At Dôle, which capitulated after a four-day siege, Louis and his general attended a *Te Deum* to celebrate the victory before moving on to Gray. With the fall of that town on February 19, Louis made his way back to Paris.

Within days of Louis's return, peace talks began. The capture of Franche-Comté gave Louis a valuable bargaining chip, allowing him to conclude a favorable peace. The Dutch acted as mediators, Jan de Witt, grand pensionary of the United Provinces, being inclined to satisfy the French in the face of Spanish intransigence. At Saint-Germain, Louis advocated peace, against the advice of Louvois, Turenne, and Condé, who desired to continue the war.[2]

The preliminary peace accords were signed on April 15, and the treaty ratified at Aix-la-Chapelle on May 2 after a series of intense negotiations.[3] Under the terms of this treaty, Louis returned most of the towns he had conquered in the recent Devolution War to Spain, but the twelve towns he retained left the Spanish Netherlands exposed to further attack. These were fortified by Vauban to form part of a protective *ceinture de fer*, or 'iron belt.' Louis had no real interest in extending his borders to natural boundaries but to those he could best defend.

Louis was now in a position of strength, not least because several German states and princes left the League of the Rhine, causing it to collapse. This greatly concerned the Dutch, while the English feared French expansionism.[4] Meanwhile, Louis's partition treaty with Leopold had been signed.[5] His seizure of Franche-Comté had been intended to force Spain to recognize the provisions of the partition treaty; once Spain did so, the province was returned to them.[6]

Louis's invasion and seizure of the Franche-Comté had interrupted a carnival that he was planning for the entertainment of the court. He made up for the disappointment now by offering a fête at Versailles. Here, new developments in the gardens had seen the construction of a labyrinth. This was intended to be used for the instruction and amusement of the dauphin,[7] and each fountain, complete with basin and shells, illustrated one of Aesop's fables. The leaden animals were depicted in their environments and painted in natural colors. The work coincided with the publication of the six first books of La Fontaine's *Fables*, one of the texts used by Bossuet as he taught the dauphin.[8]

The fête took place over several days during the third week of July. Its theme was the celebration of nature under the command of the king, and it was every bit as sumptuous as the court had now come to expect. There were fireworks, music, and endless suppers. Louis was accompanied at the table by Louise and her sister-in-law, the marquise de La Vallière; Athénaïs had to make do with sitting among the queen's ladies, but this was a calculated strategy on Louis's part, for he could watch her every move, her every expression from a safe distance.

Louis still loved Louise, but he was no longer in love with her, a subtle distinction. Seeing that she was no longer the object of his passion, she dared to confront him.[9] Louis hated scandal, and he responded coldly, saying that he was "too sincere to deceive her any longer; but that, nevertheless, he had not ceased to feel for herself a very sincere affection." He believed that she had every reason to be satisfied with all that he was doing for her, adding that "she was too intelligent not to be aware that a King of his type did not like to be under any kind of constraint." Her tears failed to move him; indeed, he told her that if she wished "to retain his affection, she must ask nothing from him that he did not give of his own free will." Instead, she should "continue to live with Mme de Montespan as she has hitherto done." Louis threatened to "take other steps" if Louise showed any hostility towards Athénaïs, but the truth was that he needed Louise to remain at court, no matter how unhappy she might be. As Bussy-Rabutin put it, Louis "needed a pretext for madame de Montespan."[10] This was, therefore, Louise's primary function now. Louis kept her at court in order to conceal his relationship with Athénaïs, much as Louise had been intended to conceal Louis's relationship with Henriette. Louise also acted as an unwilling decoy in order to discourage Athénaïs's husband from causing trouble.

Naturally, dancing formed part of the entertainments, and Louis danced in the ballet *Triumph of Bacchus*. Another highlight was Molière's *Georges Dandin, or the Astonished Husband*, set to music by Lully and presented as a drama-ballet. This told the story of a country gentleman who had married above his station and who was astonished when his wife betrayed him with another man. Initially, the cuckolded husband threatened to drown himself in a fountain, but he settled instead to drink away his sorrows.

The theme of Molière's play coincided rather neatly with the experience of another betrayed husband, albeit one of higher birth. This was the marquis de Montespan, Athénaïs's husband, and as luck would have it, the marquis selected that moment to launch an attack on Louis.

Montespan was already blazing his way through Parisian society, slandering the king to anyone who would listen. Now he cornered Mademoiselle and showed her the text of a harangue he intended to read out to Louis. Here, Louis was likened to David, who seduced Bathsheba; the harangue also warned the king of the divine retribution that would surely rain down upon him, and it ended with the demand that Athénaïs be returned to him. The bemused Mademoiselle told him he must be mad to even contemplate reading the harangue to Louis. She added that no one would believe that he had written it himself, but would instead attribute it to the archbishop of Sens, Montespan's uncle, who had no love for Athénaïs.[11]

The following day, Mademoiselle went to Saint-Germain, where she took Athénaïs for a private walk. She warned Athénaïs that she had seen her husband and that he was as mad as ever, adding that she had told him to keep his mouth shut or he would end up in prison. Athénaïs's reply was a show of bravado that concealed the fear she felt. Just then, a messenger came to say that Montespan had come to the palace and had managed to get inside the duchesse de Montausier's apartment. He had learned that the duc de Montausier had been appointed governor to the dauphin and guessed that the appointment had been an expression of Louis's gratitude for the role the duchess had played in the early stages of his affair with Athenais. Now Montespan accused the duchess of abetting the affair, and his abusive manner had reduced the elderly lady to tears. "He said the most insulting things to me," she sobbed. "I thanked God that there were only women here; if there had been any men, he would have been thrown out of the window."[12]

As outraged as Louis was, there was little he could do about Montespan's *gasconnades*,[13] even if they did disturb the peace of the court. A man was perfectly within his rights to yell at, rape, or otherwise abuse his wife. Eventually, though, Louis was forced to act, and on September 22, he issued a *lettre de cachet*[14] ordering Montespan's imprisonment in the For-l'Eveque "for having criticized unfavorably the King's selection of M. de Montausier."[15] After several days, Montespan was released on condition that he would trouble his wife no more, but instead would withdraw to his father's estates in Guyenne, there to remain until Louis granted him permission to leave. As he kicked his heels in the country, Montespan's anger lost much of its fire, although he expressed his displeasure in other ways. As though a widower, he wore mourning and forced the couple's children to do the same, and even held a mock funeral for his wife. Visiting a nearby church, he announced that the side door was too small to allow his cuckold's horns to go through, so he insisted upon entering through the main door instead. Naturally his exploits reached Paris, where they became a source of amused gossip.[16] "Now that he has buried you," Louis told Athénaïs, "it is to be hoped that he will let you rest in peace."[17]

In the meantime, as September drew to a close, Louis took the court to Chambord.[18] This magnificent but aging château on the banks of the Loire was well known to Louise, who had spent part of her childhood there. Here she reproached Louis for his love for Athénaïs in the subtlest of ways. She knew of a couplet that had been etched into a windowpane by François I: *Souvent femme varie; mal habit qui s'y fie,* 'Woman is often fickle; foolish the man who trusts her.'

When Louise pointed this out to Louis as an allusion to his own inconsistency, he ordered it to be removed.[19] He had more important matters to occupy him than an aggrieved mistress, for Athénaïs had discovered that she was pregnant with their first child. In order to conceal her condition, she had designed a new style of dress, a *robe battant*, known ironically as *l'Innocent*. It was a loose-fitting, flowing gown of chiffon, which was immediately adopted by all the most fashionable ladies.[20]

Such subterfuge was necessary because the marquis de Montespan had the legal right to claim as his own any child his wife had with the king. Later, a charming, if partly apocryphal, story emerged surrounding the birth of this child. As he had done with Louise, Louis took a house for Athénaïs in which she prepared to give birth to her child. As her time drew near, Louis arranged for an accoucheur, a M. Clément, to attend her. Clément was admitted to the house and taken to a darkened room to find a masked woman lying on the bed and a young man obscured behind the bed curtains. Clément voiced his thoughts that the couple must be attempting to conceal a scandal, but he was told to be quiet and get on with his job. Clément said that he was hungry and asked for something to eat, upon which the man went out and prepared him some bread and jam. Clément then asked for some wine, upon which the young man told him to have patience before duly fetching a glass. Just as the accoucheur was about to request another drink, the lady on the bed began to moan, at which Clément began to attend her. The young man hid himself once again behind the curtains, but he held the lady's hand and stroked her hair throughout her labor, always asking when it would be over. After an hour or so the child was born. So secret was the birth that its sex was unconfirmed, although it is generally believed to have been a girl, and that she was named Louise-Françoise. The child was spirited away by one of Athénaïs's maids, Mlle Descœillets, and her secret life ended after only three years.[21]

It was about this time that a long-standing dispute with the Jansenists at Port Royal was resolved. Four years previously, Hardouin de Péréfixe, Louis's former tutor, reopened the controversy of the formulary by requiring the French clergy as a whole to sign it. He went to Port Royal to force the nuns to comply, but his visit achieved nothing. A subsequent attempt was no more successful than the first, and in his anger, he abused the abbess, Mère de Ligny. A week later, he returned, and when twelve of the nuns still refused to sign the formulary, he sent them to other convents. He then imposed a nun from the convent of the Visitation to watch over those who remained at Port Royal. In the end, Péréfixe managed to obtain only seven signatures on the formulary.[22]

In an effort to bring the revolt to a close, Louis asked for and obtained a bull from Alexander VII, the *Regiminus Apostolici*. Péréfixe took this to Port Royal for the nuns to sign, but those who had refused to place their names on the earlier bull also refused to sign this one. Four of those who had signed the previous one now joined their sisters in rebellion.

As Péréfixe's persecution of the Port Royal community continued, Louis imposed the *Regiminus Apostolici* on his kingdom as a whole. It was to be signed by all clerics, including secular, as well as women in religious orders, who were also required to acknowledge the presence of the Five Propositions. This was resisted by several prominent bishops, but Pope Alexander died before he could order the removal of the rebels.

Pope Alexander had dealt heavily with a matter that could, with tact, have been diffused relatively easily. However, when he died in 1667, he was succeeded by the more judicious and diplomatic Clement IX. In March 1668, Clement granted Louis the *régale*, or regalian rights, which he had long desired to exercise over the Three Bishoprics. The *régale* allowed Louis to stand in for a deceased bishop and to benefit from the revenues pertaining to the see. It also allowed him to nominate to all non-parochial benefices. The following month, Clement extended the grant to Roussillon, Artois, and the newly acquired regions in Flanders.[23] That autumn, negotiations concerning the acceptance of statements of obedience took place, which led to a compromise, known as the *Pax Clementia*. Louis was happy to accept this, provided it did not interfere with his regalian rights, and peace in the Gallican Church was restored.

To mark the event, Louis ordered a new medal, which was struck the following year. It bore the inscription RESTITUTA ECCLESIAE GALLICANAE CONCORDIA, 'Concord re-established in the Gallican Church,' and was accompanied by a commentary:

Among the theologians of France there were such bitter disputes on matters of grace that their animosity was already causing a great scandal, and that it was feared that things might go still farther. The King acted together with the Pope to suppress these seeds of division. The Holy Father addressed several letters to the prelates of the kingdom, and His Majesty published edicts which restored the Gallican Church to its former tranquillity. This is the subject of this medal. On an altar we see the open Bible, and on this Bible are placed the keys of Saint Peter and the sceptre with the hand of justice, which mark the cooperation of ecclesiastical power and royal authority. The radiant dove symbolizes the Holy Spirit who presided over this act.[24]

It would soon become apparent, however, that the peace that had descended upon religious affairs in France was, in fact, little more than a cease-fire, for a new battle was about to be fought. Louis's suspicions regarding the Jansenists had never diminished. He viewed their teachings as being too close to Calvinism, and he would continue to see them as a threat to the unity of his kingdom. For now, though, he decided to leave them in peace, for he wanted to focus upon his plans to subdue another section of society—the nobility.

During the years 1661–2, Louis had appointed eight prelates and sixty-three knights of the Ordre du Saint-Esprit. It was the first time such promotions had taken place since 1633. Louis knew that "no reward costs our people less, and none touches the noble heart more than these distinctions of rank, which are almost the first motive of all human actions, but above all the most noble and the most grand."[25]

By January 1665, Louis had regulated the ordre de Saint-Michel, restricting membership to one hundred persons, including those he chose to retain from the previous membership. Louis had then, in July of the following year, decreed that all who would claim admittance to the order would be obliged to produce their titles of nobility before specially designated intendants. Eligibility was further restricted to Catholics, except for foreigners, and candidates had to provide considerable service in the military over a period of at least ten years.[26]

These measures formed part of Louis's policy to regulate and subjugate the nobility. He sought the establishment of a useful aristocracy, one that would devote their services to the state rather than their own interests, thereby allowing Louis the assurance that there would be no renewal of the Fronde or any similar uprising. The process had begun with senior judges in 1661 and continued with the *Recherche de la noblesse*, or investigation into titles of nobility. No family was exempt, and in December 1668, Mme de Sévigné wrote that her family had been required to prove their nobility in their ancestral Brittany, where "those who have the most have taken pleasure in making use of this occasion to display their merchandise."[27]

Aside from establishing the authenticity of the letters of nobility, the intendants were also required to ensure that claimants lived a gentlemanly existence. This meant that their ancestors had not worked in crafts or trades or had been otherwise employed in positions demeaning to people of their status.[28] These inspections were more than an inconvenience or an opportunity to show off, for if people could not prove their nobility or if they presented false proofs, their names would be written onto the tax register, making them liable to the same tax burdens as members of the third estate.[29] In addition, they would be forced to pay a fine as punishment for assuming a title to which they had no right. There was, however, a system of appeal, and this course would be followed by many who wished, for financial reasons or out of self-esteem or family pride, to retain their noble status.[30]

As first gentleman of the realm, Louis required an aristocracy who would serve in his armies and in his own household. While he could create new nobles for political purposes, the promise of ennoblement was a crucial factor in ensuring a regular supply of soldiers and sailors.[31] One of the best ways to achieve promotion to the second estate was to excel in the army, and, as it happened, the opportunity for many men to do just that was soon to present itself.

The Dutch had frequently been useful allies of France, but they had incurred Louis's displeasure for several reasons. They were republicans; their success in commerce had brought prosperity and strength, which made them difficult to undermine; and they had rejected Catholicism. In 1648, they had signed the Treaty of Münster with Spain, which had frustrated Mazarin and prevented the annexation or partition of the Spanish Netherlands. More recently, they had formed the Triple Alliance with England and Sweden.[32] Louis, who resented any form of opposition, had come to view the Dutch with implacable hatred, and he desired nothing so much as to crush them completely.

The king was encouraged in this ambition by Colbert, who took exception to Dutch mercantile supremacy. Since 1667, he had been engaged in a trade war through tariffs, but even the peaceable Colbert had come to view war as the only means to gain ascendancy over his rivals in commerce. Louvois, associate secretary for war and always spoiling for a fight, was happy to pursue any aggressive policy Louis might suggest.[33] Turenne, newly converted to Catholicism, belligerent and incautious, was eager to lead the charge against the Protestant Dutch.

For four years, Louis's diplomatists had roamed the rest of Europe seeking support for an attack on the United Provinces. In Sweden, the ruling aristocracy found that support for France would be well rewarded. In England, the efforts of French diplomacy fell on very fertile ground indeed. Charles II of England had always been fascinated by Louis, who ruled France as absolute monarch, while Charles was tied to a parliament with which he was becoming increasingly disillusioned. He had never been an enthusiastic member of the Triple Alliance, and he was eager to establish closer links with France,[34] but how to fulfill this aspiration? The answer came from a source as charming as it was unexpected.

Henriette, duchesse d'Orléans, had never forgotten her English roots, and she was always desirous to protect the interests of the country of her birth. She was the only one of Charles I's children to be brought up a Catholic, and her faith, which had sustained her through many difficult times, was deep, sincere, and strong. It had been her desire to bring her beloved brother into what she believed to be the true faith, not least because she knew he also secretly cherished a desire to convert to Catholicism. Henriette devised a plan by which Louis could have English support for his war, while Charles could fulfill his ambitions, both religious and political.

Henriette approached Louis with the warning that the growing hostility of those jealous of French power could lead to his becoming isolated in Europe. She suggested that a way to overcome this would be to cultivate the friendship of Charles. Louis liked the idea and ordered his ambassador, the marquis de Ruvigny, to make overtures to the English king. For his part, Charles expressed his willingness to forge a treaty with Louis as "between gentleman and gentleman."[35]

The negotiations were directed by Louis and known only to a handful of carefully selected confidants. For several months, Henriette and Charles exchanged letters, using cyphers to ensure that the content of their correspondence would remain secret should any of it be intercepted. Eventually, the project reached the stage where Louis thought that Henriette should travel to England to conclude a treaty with Charles in person.

The prospect of seeing Charles after so many years delighted the duchess, but her excitement rapidly turned to disappointment when Philippe forbade her to go on the grounds that Henriette was pregnant.

Even Louis did not possess the authority to override his brother's marital rights, so the plans to send Henriette to England were postponed.

Shortly after he had begun work on Versailles, Louis had razed the small hamlet of Trianon and developed its surrounding land to expand the park. Here, at a distance from the château and screened by trees, he had built a palace in miniature, Trianon. The exterior walls were lined with blue-and-white delft tiles, and the color scheme was carried inside by white stucco ornamented with azure. The palace was built in an enchanting and exotic fusion of classical and oriental styles.[36]

Louis used Trianon as a private love nest, where he and Athénaïs would go to escape the court. The salon was used for formal entertaining; the wonderful meals the couple enjoyed together were prepared in the pavilions that flanked the main building. Louis and Athénaïs would then withdraw to the *chambre des amours*, the bedroom. Decorated in cool white, silver, and blue, with a luxurious mirrored bed trimmed with gold and silver, the bedroom was the showpiece of Trianon. Here, Louis and Athénaïs would make love as the heady scent of jasmine, tuberose, and orange blossom wafted in through the open windows.

Soon, Athénaïs wanted a bigger, better house than Trianon. She wanted a château that would reflect her status and which was built and decorated to her own tastes. The young architect, Jules Hardouin-Mansart, who had taken over the development of Versailles upon the death of Louis Le Vau, was chosen to design it for her. The new château was to be built upon land close to Versailles, and Athénaïs was involved in every stage of its creation. Like Versailles, the château was oriented east to west, and featured a gallery 210 feet in length by 25 feet wide. It boasted a chapel, an orangery, and, of course, magnificent parklands designed by Le Nôtre.[37]

By the spring of 1670, new arrangements for Henriette's voyage to England were far advanced. Due to the necessary secrecy that surrounded the negotiation and the treaty that was the expected result, it was imperative that no one should know the true reason for Henriette's journey. Philippe, however, seeing his wife closeted with Louis, became insanely jealous and in a fit of pique announced once again that she was not allowed to leave. Louis urged him to compassion. Henriette had not seen her brother for almost ten years, he reasoned. At this, Philippe softened; in that case she could travel to England and he would accompany her. To allow such a scenario would be to court disaster. Philippe was anything but discreet, and his presence would threaten everything they had achieved so far. In the end, Louis was firm. Henriette would make the journey alone. Philippe at last acquiesced on the condition that his wife spend no more than three days in England and travel no deeper into the country than Dover for the duration of her stay. The conditions were far from ideal, but they were the best on offer, and Louis, Henriette, and Charles would simply have to abide by Philippe's wishes.

In May, Henriette set sail after a difficult journey to the coast. Upon her arrival, she was greeted warmly and enthusiastically by her brother. It was soon clear, however, that the finishing touches to the treaty would take longer to settle than originally expected. Henriette sent a message to Louis, asking him to arrange for her to stay longer than the allotted three days,[38] which Louis, if not Philippe, was pleased to grant.

The Treaty of Dover was finally signed on June 1, 1670. Under its terms, Louis would pay Charles the sum of 2 million livres within six months, which would allow him to declare his conversion to Catholicism at a time he thought best. Charles would declare war on Holland when Louis was ready, and Louis would pay Charles 3 million livres a year for the duration of the war. Of the fruits of the war, Charles would receive the Zeeland Islands, and he would assist Louis in making good any new claims that might accrue to him for the Spanish throne. However, Charles was not obliged to do anything that would infringe on the Triple Alliance.[39]

Louis had planned to meet Henriette at Beauvais as she made her return journey, but Philippe, still filled with indignation, refused to travel out to welcome her back, which meant that no one else was allowed to. However, she did receive a rapturous welcome from the king at Versailles. He celebrated her diplomatic success with the gift of 6 thousand pistoles. Henriette was "looking very pretty and happy,"[40] although she was somewhat tired from her long journey. Louis, more sensitive to Henriette's needs than her husband, insisted that she stay the night at Versailles, but Philippe would not hear of it. He wanted to return immediately to Saint-Germain.

A few days later, Henriette and Philippe went on to Saint-Cloud, and it was here, after taking a drink of chicory water, that Henriette suddenly became very ill. The news arrived at Versailles, and Louis ordered his physician, M. Vallot, to go to Saint-Cloud to attend the duchess. No sooner had Vallot left than another courier arrived bearing a distressing message from Henriette to the queen: "If the Queen wished to see her still alive she humbly entreated she would make haste; for that if she delayed coming she would see her no more."[41]

Despite feeling unwell himself, Louis, accompanied by the queen, Louise, Athénaïs, and Mademoiselle, immediately set out for Saint-Cloud. On the way, they met Vallot coming the other way. The physician assured them that "it was nothing but *une colique*, and that Madame's illness would be neither long nor dangerous."[42] His prediction, however, would turn out to be only partly true.

The royal party arrived at Saint-Cloud to find Henriette lying on a little bed, dishabille and in obvious pain. "She had all the appearance of a dying person," noted Mademoiselle,[43] and when Henriette said, "You see to what state I am reduced," everyone, including Louis, burst into tears.

It was obvious, despite Vallot's optimism, that Henriette was not going to survive this illness; and one by one her shocked and grieving guests took their leave of her. Louis spoke a few words to her in a low voice. Henriette then called out for an emetic, only to be told by her doctors that it would be useless. They still thought her condition was caused by colic and that she would recover after nine or ten hours at the most. Louis, however, tried to reason with them, but when they still refused to administer the requested medicine, he could barely hide his anger: "Surely, you will not allow a woman to die without giving assistance!"[44] The fact was, however, that none of Henriette's attendants believed she was going to die; yet the curé of Saint-Cloud, who had come to offer spiritual comfort, told Mademoiselle that he was waiting for their departure so that he could hear the duchess's last confession. Louis now embraced the woman who had once been his lover and for whom he had always retained a special affection, "and bade her farewell; and she spoke to him in the most affectionate manner."[45] The king then withdrew, taking the royal party with him.

Henriette died at three in the morning of June 30, and Louis was told three hours later. He took the news badly, and his grief at Henriette's death was profound. When the queen and Mademoiselle came to accompany him to mass, they found him still in his *robe de chambre*. "I dare not show myself before my cousin," he said. "He shed tears for the loss of Madame," wrote Mademoiselle, "and after mass he spoke to me of her death."[46]

The following morning, Louis and Marie-Thérèse drove out to Saint-Cloud, "where they alighted to sprinkle the body of Madame with holy water."[47] At the beginning of her final illness, Henriette thought she had been poisoned, and as the rumors persisted, Louis ordered a postmortem in order to establish the truth. Court physicians, "several able surgeons," and the English ambassador, Ralph Montagu, attended as the body was opened. No signs of poison were found, and the cause of death was unanimously agreed to have been "an overflow of bile," or, as it was explained to Montagu, "the Princess had died of colic, or *cholera morbus*."[48] Henriette's heart was sent to the Val-de-Grâce and placed next to that of Anne of Austria. Her funeral was held at Saint-Denis, although strict royal etiquette forbade Louis and Philippe to take part.

SIXTEEN

Marriages and Intrigues

C ousin, here is an unexpected alliance for you, should you like to form it?" Louis made this offer to Mademoiselle within hours of the death of Henriette, and her response was nothing less than Louis would have expected: "You are the master," she told him. "I can have no other will but yours."[1]

As it happened, Mademoiselle's response reflected her own feelings. She did not wish to marry Philippe, although her reluctance was no reflection on her cousin. While they were friends, she was adamant that she would never marry the newly widowed prince, declaring herself "indifferent to all the advantages and honor of the connection," for Philippe "was much younger than myself, and . . . I was not of a sufficient submissive spirit to allow of our being happy together."[2]

It was true that Mademoiselle was almost thirteen years older than Philippe, but that did not seem to worry either of them. Indeed, Philippe declared himself "ardently desirous" to marry her and wished to sign the contract straightaway so that the wedding could take place as soon as possible. He saw the proposed marriage as an excellent opportunity, and he explained his well-developed plans to Louis. He would marry Mademoiselle, he said, but they would have no children because of her age. Her immense fortune would, therefore, go to his eldest daughter, who would in her turn marry the dauphin and, in due course, become queen of France. When Louis told Mademoiselle this, she replied, "I suppose this article would form part of the contract, though it seems to me that the son of Your Majesty is hardly one that need look to a wife for a fortune."[3]

Louis had not taken his brother's design seriously and had told him not to count on it. The king, if not Philippe, had more eligible ladies in mind for the dauphin than his niece. At present, he was seriously considering marrying his son to one of the daughters of Ferdinand Maria, elector of Bavaria.

Philippe was, of course, still in mourning for Henriette, and the court, which continued to miss her sparkling personality, remained in a somber mood. Louis decided that a ball would be the best way to lift everyone's spirits, and he arranged an especially lavish occasion to be held on Shrove Tuesday before the austerities of Lent began. To his chagrin, even this happy announcement failed to enliven his courtiers; such was his disappointment that he almost postponed the ball. In the end, it did go ahead, but when Louis stepped onto the dance floor, he did so without either Louise or Athénaïs on his arm, while Philippe naturally stayed away.

As she sat in her darkening apartments, a depressed Louise brooded upon her situation. She knew full well where Louis would go after the ball finished, and the thought of him spending the night hours in Athénaïs's warm embrace was more than she could bear. She threw off her glittering court gown and put on the dull gray dress she had worn before her career as king's mistress had begun. Then, at six in the morning of the day that ashes were imposed upon Christians as a sign of repentance, Louise slipped away from court without a word to anyone. Only in a letter that she left for Louis did she give any indication that she had gone to the convent of Sainte-Marie de Chaillot, which she reached just as the day was dawning.[4]

When news of Louise's flight reached Louis, his reaction was initially one of indifference. He had planned to take the court to Versailles that morning, and he departed as expected, sharing his carriage with Athénaïs and Mademoiselle. His first inclination was to grant Louise the freedom she seemed so ardently to desire, but then he thought better of it. Louise had not outlived her usefulness at court, and the king realized that he was not prepared to let her go.[5]

The first time Louise fled, Louis ran after her himself, weeping with her on the cold floor of the convent as he urged her to return to him; this time, he sent the comte de Lauzun to retrieve her, but he was unable to coax the distraught lady out of her retreat. M. de Bellefonds had no better luck, so Louis ordered the no-nonsense Colbert to bring her out, granting him permission to use the royal authority if necessary. Louise's escape had lasted a total of twelve hours before she was back at Louis's side. Louis, whose love for Louise had never fully diminished, wept, as did Athénaïs, but for entirely different reasons.

As for Philippe, he was still in want of a wife, and one of his friends, Anne de Gonzague de Clèves, princess Palatine, thought she knew the perfect match for him. She had several nieces, one of whom was the eighteen-year-old Elisabeth-Charlotte, daughter of Karl Ludwig von der Pfalz.[6]

Elisabeth-Charlotte, or Liselotte as she was known to those close to her, was born in Heidelberg on May 27, 1652 to a family of little importance. She was relatively poor and, by almost universal consensus, was not considered to be beautiful. As far as her dowry was concerned, her family could provide only a modest one at best. It would comprise jewelry, plate, and some money, all of which would amount to a total of 10,400 livres.[7] Karl Ludwig promised to pay a further 64 thousand livres, although in the end this would not be paid.

Liselotte was unpretentious and possessed both a sparkling personality and a quick wit. Young, she promised to provide her husband with more children, perhaps even a brood of much-needed sons. As matters stood, Louis had two sons, although the youngest would die in July 1671, leaving only the dauphin. Philippe was the father of two daughters, but he had no sons. As usual with dynastic marriages, Liselotte was required to renounce her claims of inheritance, forfeiting all her lands and goods within Bavaria.[8] She was also required to convert to Catholicism.

Philippe and Liselotte were married by proxy on November 16, 1671, shortly after which she began her journey towards her new home. Grieved at leaving her father, she admitted that she "cried all night from Strasbourg to Chalons."[9] Here, the marriage was formalized with a nuptial blessing and mass on November 21. Liselotte's first impressions of her husband were good. "Monsieur is the best man in the world, and we get on very well together," she wrote to her aunt, the Electress Sophia of Hanover. "None of his portraits are in the least like him."[10]

Liselotte was not the only lady to be preoccupied with marriage. The reason why Mademoiselle did not want to marry Philippe, eligible catch though he was, was that she was in love with another man. The object of her affections was none other than the comte de Lauzun. Several years younger than Mademoiselle, short and ugly, fair and stocky, and as ill-favored as he was depraved, the term *insolent* seems to have been coined especially for him.

Antoine-Nompar de Caumont, comte de Lauzun, had arrived at court as a young Gascon of little wealth and fewer prospects. Lauzun was the third surviving son of Gabriel-Nompar de Caumont, comte de Lauzun, and Charlotte de Caumont, the daughter of Henry Nompar de Caumont, duc de La Force.[11] Upon his arrival at court, he was still known as the marquis de Puyguilhem, and he took the title comte de Lauzun upon the death of his father when it was refused by his elder brother.[12] Lauzun was taken under the wing of his father's first cousin, the maréchal de Gramont, who introduced him at court. Louis was quite taken by him, and it is true to say that there was never a dull moment in his company. In time, the marquis became the closest any man ever did to being the king's favorite, which was surprising, given the comte's behavior.

As far back as April 1666, just after the queen's near miss with death, Henriette had taken advantage of Louise's pregnancy to promote her friend, Catherine de Gramont, princess de Monaco, as king's mistress. For several months, Louis was infatuated by Catherine, although this did not go down well with her jealous cousin, Lauzun. He wanted to have his revenge, but he could not take out his anger on the king, whose person was sacred, so he punished Mme de Monaco instead. It was during the festivities at Versailles,[13] and the ladies were sitting on the floor, where it was cooler. Lauzun came in and flirted awhile, but then he pressed his heel into the princess's open palm, performed a neat pirouette, and promptly left the room.[14] Only the lady's self-command prevented her from crying out.

Lauzun's mischief then took a different turn. He knew that Louis usually went to bed with his mistress in the afternoon, and that he was expecting to receive Mme de Monaco at a certain hour. The marquis waited until Louis posted the key to his office outside the door, stole it, and threw it down the privy. He then hid himself in the garderobe to await the afternoon's delights. Sure enough, the lady arrived, swathed in a cloak and escorted by Bontemps.[15] Surprised to find no key, Bontemps gently scratched[16] on the door and asked Louis to open. Louis, puzzled, told him the key was outside as always. The valet searched, but the key was nowhere to be found. Louis, meanwhile, frantically tugged at the door in a bid to force it to open, but to no avail, and the tryst had to be postponed until another day.

Shortly after this, Lauzun and Mme de Monaco had a blazing row, upon which she ran to Louis for to defend her. Louis summoned Lauzun and ordered him to explain himself. Lauzun lost his temper and seized his sword, which he snapped in two, saying that he would not use it again in the service of a master who broke his word at the bidding of a whore.[17] At this, Louis opened the window and flung out his cane with the words that he would have "regretted having struck a gentleman."

In 1670, when Louis set out to inspect his new conquests in the Low Countries, he took the court with him to share in his triumphs. Lauzun, who was given the command of the expedition, acquitted himself admirably, especially in his care for the ladies. It was his gallantry and undoubted charm that seemed to have attracted him to Mademoiselle, and she soon fell hopelessly in love with him. He brought out the giddy schoolgirl in her, and she managed to persuade herself that he was just as amorous of her as she was of him. A fling, however, would not do. Mademoiselle, at forty-three, was not getting any younger, and she wanted to settle down to a life of married bliss; she, therefore, took it into her head that she and Lauzun would marry.

For his part, Lauzun showed every sign that he loved the besotted lady, while not daring to believe that he could be so lucky. "Which of two epithets suits me the best," he wondered, "whether I am wise or foolish?" He went on, "Rather than that you should divert yourself by giving a truthful answer, perhaps it will be better that you should not reply at all." That way, he could "carry away the remembrance of a vision" which will make him "at one time the happiest of men, and at another . . . overwhelmed with grief."[18]

Mademoiselle certainly dazzled Lauzun, but it was not her beauty that attracted him. He had his sights firmly set upon her fortune, her vast estates, and her beautiful houses. More appealing even than these assets, wonderful though they were, was her close proximity to the king. "I have no pleasure in anything which does not enable me to be of service to the King,"[19] he assured her, and in this he was perfectly sincere.

As always, nothing could be done without Louis's consent. Mademoiselle spoke to him about her desire to marry Lauzun, but Louis had only warnings for her. "Think well of this affair before you carry it further," he urged her, "for it is not one of those which should be lightly entered on." He added that he could neither advise nor forbid her to proceed in the affair, but begged her to think carefully before she went through with the marriage. He then warned her to keep the matter secret until it had been resolved, for he had heard rumors concerning the proposed marriage, and "Monsieur de Lauzun has his enemies; therefore, take your measure accordingly."[20]

Lauzun's enemies were powerful indeed. Philippe thought Lauzun was not good enough to marry a cousin of the king.[21] Louvois did not approve because Lauzun was an ally of Colbert, Louvois's enemy. Queen Marie-Thérèse thought it better if Mademoiselle did not marry at all but instead kept her money for her son, the duc d'Anjou. She spoke against the marriage to Louis, but this only angered the king, and the two had an argument which left the queen in tears.[22]

In spite of all the opposition against it, formal permission for the marriage came several days later, when the couple presented their supplication to the king at parlement. The duc de Montausier, who had represented them, gave Mademoiselle the news she had been longing to hear: "The thing is settled," he said, but he added a word of caution: "I advise you to delay no longer: if you take my advice, you will marry tonight."[23]

It was whispered at court that Mademoiselle was claiming that Louis had advised her to marry Lauzun.[24] When Louis asked her about it, she denied it and the king believed her. Nevertheless, there were dark forces at work, and Mademoiselle was warned once again not to delay the wedding. Colbert, one of the few who supported the marriage, offered to help with the contract, an easy task, since Mademoiselle intended to make over to Lauzun everything she owned.[25] The couple chose to hold their wedding at Conflans, a house not too far away, so that Lauzun could be back in time to attend upon the king.

The following day, Lauzun's sister, Mme de Nogent, arrived with news that the contract was not yet completed; it would be necessary to postpone the wedding until the following day.[26] The next day, however, was a Friday, and the superstitious Mademoiselle refused to be married on a Friday. Still, somewhat belatedly, the couple began to sense the need for urgency. Speaking alone later that day, they decided to drive to Charenton,[27] where they would make their confessions and be married there after mass.

At eight the following morning, a messenger arrived from the king. Louis wished to speak to his cousin immediately. The situation was ominous, and Mademoiselle "set out in the greatest agitation."[28] As she entered the king's chamber, Mademoiselle was struck by Louis's sad expression, and his words confirmed her worst fears. "I am wretched at what I have to say to you," he began, "but it is reported, and believed, in the world, that you are sacrificed to make the fortune of Monsieur de Lauzun. This would prejudice me in foreign countries. I therefore cannot permit the affair to be concluded."[29]

Mademoiselle threw herself at Louis's feet and cried, "I entreat you to kill me rather than prevent my marrying Monsieur de Lauzun!" Louis fell to his knees and embraced his cousin, mixing his tears with hers as he said, "Why did you give me time to consider of the matter? You ought to have permitted no delay." Her reply was withering. "Helas, Sire! Your Majesty had never broken your word to anybody in the world; how could I believe that you would begin with myself and Monsieur de Lauzun?"[30] The truth was that the couple should have heeded the warnings of their friends and married as soon as Louis had given his consent. The delay had allowed Lauzun's enemies to persuade the king to change his mind.

Such was Lauzun's devotion to Louis that he quickly recovered from his disappointment. He even reproached his grieving former fiancée for staying away from court, saying that she "did wrong in remaining so long away from the King."[31] If Mademoiselle is to be believed, this was simply a show of bravado on his part, and in his heart, he was as unhappy as she. If so, he rapidly recovered, and by the autumn of 1671, his thoughts were focused upon other matters.

In October of that year, the duc de Mazarin resigned his post as grand master of the artillery.[32] Lauzun eagerly wished to replace him, and after much persuasion, Louis finally promised the post to him on condition he keep it secret until the formal announcement could be made. Although Lauzun agreed to this, he nevertheless broke his promise, and word of the appointment reached Louvois. The minister could not countenance the idea of Lauzun, arrogant, capricious, and a close friend of Colbert's, occupying such a position, and he spoke to Louis about it. When Louis learned that Lauzun had broken his word, he was furious. He assured Louvois that nothing had yet been settled.

When, after some time, Louis made no announcement of his new appointment, Lauzun at first became puzzled and then suspicious. He approached Louis, only to be dismissed. It was not yet time, Louis told him. Lauzun feared that the king had changed his mind and poured out his troubles to Athénaïs, who promised to speak to Louis on his behalf.

As the days went by, Lauzun still heard nothing, and he grew impatient. Still not realizing the reason for his disappointment, he decided upon a course "so rash that it would be unbelievable had it not been vouched for by the entire Court of the day."[33] Expecting Louis to visit Athénaïs that afternoon, he hid under her bed with the connivance of one of her maids. Louis duly arrived, and, after the couple had made love, they began to talk. Lauzun now learned the truth: his careless talk had prevented his appointment, and Louis was angry that he had not kept the secret. Moreover, far from representing his case to Louis as she had promised, Athénaïs spoke against Lauzun, rendering him a great disservice.

After a while, the lovers parted. Louis returned to his apartments, while Athénaïs prepared for the rehearsal of a court ballet. Lauzun slipped out of her chamber but lingered by the door until she came out; meeting her in the corridor, he gallantly offered to escort her to the room where the rehearsal was to be held. He began to chat to her, eventually asking her if she had managed to speak to the king as she had promised. She assured him that she had, adding that she had spoken very favorably about him. Lauzun listened eagerly until she finished before he suddenly turned on her, calling her a liar, a trollop, a whore, and a piece of dog filth. He then repeated word for word everything that had passed between her and the king. The poor lady was so shocked that it was all she could do to stagger into the rehearsal room, where, to the great concern of all, she promptly fainted away. That evening, Athénaïs recounted her conversation with Lauzun to Louis, although both were at a loss as to how he could have known what had been said. It simply did not occur to either of them that he could have been so bold as to hide in the room and listen to their every word.

Thus far, Louis had been more than tolerant of Lauzun's insolence, but enough was enough. Within days the comte was arrested under a *lettre de cachet* and escorted by d'Artagnan and his musketeers to Pignerol, where he arrived on December 12, 1671. He would spend the next ten years of his life wondering what he had done to upset Louis, while making Saint-Mars's life a misery by refusing to eat, setting his chamber on fire, and attempting to tunnel his way to freedom.

SEVENTEEN
The Dutch War

The spring of 1671 was pleasant and serene, giving no indication of the storms that were about to break over Europe.
In April, Louis was at Versailles, where he spent his time
overseeing the building of "the most beautiful fountains ever seen."[1]
On the twenty-third, he and his court attended a lavish party hosted
by the prince de Condé at his château at Chantilly. This spectacular
three-day event was nevertheless to be marked by a tragedy that would
be long remembered. The king arrived on Wednesday evening and
enjoyed a collation served in an area carpeted by jonquils before going
on a deer hunt. The course was lined with lanterns, but the beauty of
the fireworks, which cost 16 thousand francs, was blotted out by the

brilliance of the moon. The hunt over, Louis ate supper and played games before retiring to bed.

The following day, as the court sat down to eat, the sheer number of guests meant that there was not quite enough meat to go around and people at two of the tables had to go without. This greatly upset Vatel, whose reputation as *maître d'hôtel* was well deserved. Condé tried to reassure him that all was well and that "nothing was so beautiful as the King's supper."[2] Still, Vatel, who had not slept for several days, would not be comforted.

At four o'clock the following morning, Vatel waited anxiously for the expected delivery of fish. When one solitary cart arrived, he asked the driver if that was all. The driver thought he was referring to his catch only and replied, "Oui, Monsieur." When, after a while, no further carts arrived, Vatel's despair deepened. He told his friend Gourville that he would not survive this indignity. He went to his room, placed his sword against the door, and ran himself through three times before falling down dead. Shortly afterwards, the first of several fish carts trundled into view, coming from all directions.[3] Upon hearing the news of Vatel's suicide, Louis told Condé that he had "put off coming to Chantilly for five years because he understood the expense of the trouble." He added that Monsieur le prince did not have to provide more than two laden tables.[4] Vatel's duties were taken over by Gourville, and the party continued with collations, suppers, walks, games, and hunting. "All was perfumed with jonquils; all was charming," declared Mme de Sévigné;[5] yet, amid all the amusements, Louis's mind was focused upon war.

Ever since he was a little boy, Louis had been passionately engrossed in everything military. He delighted in inspections, troop movements, victory parades, and lavish displays. He loved nothing more than to spend time with his army out in the field enjoying the thrills, the discomforts, and the dangers of life as a soldier. There was glory in it too. Following the recent Devolution War, the city of Paris celebrated the king's victories by awarding him the epithet "the Great." The title first appeared on a medal struck in 1671, which showed the king in armor, a large plume adorning his helmet and his hair falling in waves around his shoulders. The inscription read LUDOVICUS MAGNUS, Louis the Great.[6]

Now, thanks to Colbert's fiscal reforms and the efforts of the war minister, Michel Le Tellier, and his son, the marquis de Louvois, Louis had a large and powerful force at his command. Five years earlier, at the time of the Devolution War, the army could boast no more than 72,000 men. Now, on the eve of the Dutch War, their numbers had increased to 120,000. In civilian life, the nobility had been forced to bend to Louis's will. Now the military was to follow suit. A hierarchy of ranks was introduced, most of which had to be attained by merit rather than purchase.[7]

Training programs were implemented and discipline was tightened, with men being drilled by the infamous inspector-general of infantry, Jean Martinet, who invented marching in step and other regimes. The wearing of uniforms, which once identified troops serving the armies of individual noblemen, became more widespread and applied to all regiments and units. Louvois applied stricter rules to the nobility, who were now disciplined for absenteeism and fraud.[8]

Munitions factories were established, although weapons were still not advanced at this point. The matchlock musket was still in use, as were pikes, at least until 1687, when Vauban made them obsolete with the invention of the ring bayonet.[9] Army magazines sprang up, allowing a greater concentration of troops, who no longer had to forage and pillage for provisions, and allowed winter campaigns. Increasingly, Louis personally directed campaigns, taking advice from Jules-Louis Bolé de Chamblay, the equivalent of his chief of staff. The two greatest generals of the age, Turenne and Condé, kept each other in check.[10]

Le Tellier's reforms in the army were matched in the navy by Colbert. Upon taking office in 1661, Colbert had found the navy in a state of neglect, a situation that was not helped by Louis's lack of interest. However, the money available to the king as a result of Colbert's economic strategies allowed funds to be diverted to building France's sea power. By 1677, Louis would have a fleet comprising 116 men-of-war, 83 other ships, and a strong Mediterranean fleet—the largest navy in Europe.[11]

To man this fleet, Colbert organized a system of conscription in preference to the press-gang system favored in England. He founded the Inscription Maritime, which required all sailors to serve in the navy for six months every three years. Ports were renovated, with Toulon, Brest, and Rochefort becoming major bases. Vauban, meanwhile, strengthened the defenses at Ath, Oudenarde, Charleroi, and Dunkirk. When Louis left Chantilly, he made his way to Dunkirk, where he stayed for some time with his troops, who were arriving at the rate of some nine thousand each day.[12] As he continued his preparations to wage war on the Dutch, Louis was in command of superior forces, the largest seen so far in France; and they were now amassing on the Dutch border.

By mid-December 1671, the Dutch were so concerned about Louis's intentions that they sent their ambassador, Peter de Groot, with a letter for the king. In this letter, which was summarized by Saint-Maurice,[13] the Dutch wrote that they had been assured that the "great armament" that Louis was making was in order to wage war on them. They found this difficult to believe because they had never lacked respect for him, nor had they done anything against his interests. They had even refused to listen to suggestions that they should attack him. They had, rather, punctiliously carried out all the latest treaties made with his crown "and, therefore, feeling their consciences to be clear, they could not imagine that he had anything against them; that, if they had done him any disservice, or if without knowing it, they had failed him in any respect, if His Majesty would have the goodness to let them know, they were ready to give him all befitting satisfaction."

Louis made arrangements to receive de Groot but then put him off, preferring to play his cards very close to his chest. In the end, he did give the ambassador an audience, but this was merely to warn him that he intended to increase his armament by land and sea, and, having done so, he would use it in a manner appropriate to his dignity. He added that he owed no explanations to anyone.[14] Shortly afterwards, he sent Louvois to the electorate of Cologne to negotiate the support of the elector and the bishop of Münster, and to arrange the supply of provisions for the French troops.[15]

On April 27, Louis was attended at his *lever* as usual. After mass, he entered his carriage, which was drawn by six horses, and drove alone towards the duc d'Estrées's home at Nanteuil before going on to Villers-Cotterets, where he rendezvoused with his brother and a large company. He had not even said good-bye to the queen or dauphin, so sudden was his departure.[16] By May 5, he was at Charleroi, where he reviewed his troops as they arrived at the town. He was especially impressed by the Royal Piémont, which was "very fine."[17] The armies marched in good order and were well paid. Again, Louis took personal direction of all matters concerning the military, taking everything in his stride and not uttering a word of annoyance. He ordered marches, established the camps, marked out the guard stations, all of which he visited in person; he worked harder than any of his officers and even ate on the march.[18] Louis always had a map of the area in his hand, and he would consult his officers, but the final decisions and orders were his own.[19]

Nothing seemed "so important to the reputation of my troops" as to begin a campaign with some brilliant feat of arms, Louis wrote to Louvois from his camp near Neuss on May 31. To this end, he had arranged to lay siege to four places at once, which, for the sake of his *gloire*, he would personally direct. The four places he chose were Wesel, the troops to be commanded by Condé; Büderich, the siege of which was to be led by Turenne; Orsoi, under Philippe's command; while the siege of Rheinberg would be directed by Louis personally. The town was close enough for him to monitor the other sieges.[20] Again, his bravery in the face of danger was not in doubt.

At the dawn of June 6, three of these towns had been taken, and only Rheinberg held out. Louis summoned the governor and told him that if he was obliged to open the trench and fire the cannon, he would hang him and put his entire garrison to the sword. The governor surrendered, upon which Louis allowed him and his men to retreat to Maastricht, taking with them provisions for the whole garrison and with their dignity intact.[21]

Emmerich and Rees were the next to fall, and it was at Rees that Turenne suggested Louis cross the Rhine between Schenck and Arnhem in order to be in the best position to penetrate into the interior of the United Provinces. The river was very wide, but the dry summer had left it relatively shallow, and it was fordable in several places.[22] Calming their nerves with a little brandy, the troops prepared to cross. The cavalry went first, swimming the horses across, but they did not get very far before the Dutch caught sight of them, waded into the water, and began attacking with swords. Guiche, who tried to contain the threat, witnessed the "most pitiable sight in the world: more than thirty officers or horsemen drowned or drowning, and Revel at their head; the Rhine filled with men, horses, flags, helmets and other similar things"; for gunfire from the enemy right had caused some of the horses to panic, and it was all the French could do to save themselves and their horses.[23] The success of the French offensive now hanging in the balance, Louis issued orders to fire the cannon, which forced the Dutch into retreat and allowed the men to build a bridge of light boats to assist the others to cross. When he reached the other bank, Louis publicly embraced Guiche; he would later write to the comte's father that what had happened that day was memorable in so many ways, "but I assure you, that among those that touched me the most, I can award the distinction that the comte de Guich has deserved."[24] So proud was Louis of the crossing of the Rhine that the event would be commemorated on the main bas-relief of the Porte Saint-Denis.

Louis now seemed unstoppable as he took the forts on the IJssel without encountering any significant resistance. Utrecht, abandoned by the Dutch, was his for the taking, and he obliged on June 23.

Amsterdam lay only two days away, separated by flat country, which lay below sea level. The Dutch had claimed the land from the North Sea and defended it with sand dunes and dykes. Windmills fed water into storage systems from which it flowed into rivers at low tide, where the cycle began again.[25] It was a simple matter to interrupt the cycle, and this is exactly what the Dutch now did. Within five days Amsterdam became an island surrounded by sea water. Louis could only look on as the waters lapped at his feet.

Meanwhile, on the English coast at Sole Bay, the Dutch had surprised a joint naval force of French and English ships, and although the outcome of the subsequent sea battle was indecisive, the Dutch had caused sufficient damage to the enemy to prevent their attempting any further action.[26]

Louis, threatened by the rising waters, began pillaging small towns and attacking isolated enemy forces wherever he found them. This naturally terrorized the civilian population, but it also ignited a bitter and lasting hatred of the French.

While this was going on, Holland was torn by revolution. The grand pensionary, Jan de Witt, was deposed and murdered, and William of Orange was proclaimed stadtholder, captain, and admiral-general. He was only twenty-two, a staunch Calvinist, short, anaemic, and asthmatic, yet Orange would come to personify his country's hatred for Louis and the French.

The Dutch now approached France to discuss peace. Their ambassador, Peter de Groot, was received by Louvois and Pomponne, and he offered them the following terms. Louis would receive Maastricht and the Rhine towns, as well as 600 thousand francs to offset the costs of the war. Louvois, however, was scornful, so the Dutch increased their concessions, adding all the towns held by Holland beyond the seven provinces, and increasing the sum offered to 10 million francs. This was a significant offer, for it would have provided Louis with a barrier extending from the Meuse to the Scheldt, which separated the United Provinces from the Spanish Netherlands. In time, the Spanish

Netherlands would have been subjugated, and Louis would be in a strong position to wreak his vengeance on the Dutch.

While Pomponne was eager to accept these terms, Louvois advised Louis to demand still more. He pressed for the frontier to be withdrawn as far as the Wahal, with all the fortified towns on the river to be handed over to Louis or to be dismantled. In addition, all edicts that were unfavorable to French commerce were to be revoked, while a treaty of commerce with Holland that favored the French West and the East India Companies would be concluded. France also demanded the payment of an indemnity of 10,500,000 francs, with an embassy to be sent to France every year to present Louis with a gold medal bearing a motto of thanks for his having "left to the United Provinces the independence which the Kings, his predecessors, had enabled her to acquire."[27]

It was widely expected in France that the Dutch would acquiesce, for, as Mme de Sévigné wrote, "nothing could resist the forces and the conduct of His Majesty."[28] Louis put it another way: "daily progress of my army puts me in a position to impose any conditions I please on the States, but I wish to listen to the promptings of my own generosity so far as is consistent with authority and the just rights of victory."[29] As to posterity, Louis said that

> it may believe if it chooses in my reasons for so acting, and can at its pleasure ascribe my refusal to my ambition and the desire for vengeance for the injuries I had sustained from the Dutch. I shall not justify myself. Ambition and glory are always pardonable in a prince, and particularly in a prince so young and so well treated by fortune as I was.[30]

For his part, de Groot let it be known that he "would sooner die than accept such terms from France."[31] The war was set to continue, but with much of Holland flooded, Louis had little choice but to return to France, and he was back in Saint-Germain by early August. In December, Spain, Holland, the emperor Leopold, and the elector of Brandenburg formed a league against France. Louis's Dutch War was now a European conflict. As 1672 came to an end, the duc de Luxembourg, at the head of ten thousand men, took advantage of the freezing conditions to launch a "lightning war." He left Utrecht for Amsterdam, burning houses and ships as he went; however, a sudden thaw obliged him to draw back until the beginning of January.[32]

In late February 1673, Louis was once again at Versailles. One cold day, he received an unexpected visitor, Armande Béjart, the wife of Molière. She was in a state of angry despair and had come to appeal to Louis for help as she fought to secure a Christian burial for her husband.

Molière had been suffering from tuberculosis for quite some time, and although he felt his condition to be worsening, he insisted that the fourth performance of his play *Le Malade Imaginaire* should go on as planned. Against the advice of his friends, he was on stage as expected at 4:00 P.M. on February 17, waiting for the curtain to rise. Towards the end of the play, Molière was seized by a sudden convulsion. It was noticed by the audience, so Molière disguised it with a forced laugh, and he managed to finish the play. Upon returning to his dressing room, his protégé, Michel Baron, was alarmed by how unwell Molière looked, and he wrapped the actor's frozen hands in a muff before calling for the sedan chair to carry him back to his home in the rue de Richelieu.

Baron remained with Molière all the way home, where he immediately put him to bed. He asked if Molière would like some of the soup that Armande always had at hand, but Molière could not face it and asked for a small piece of Parmesan cheese and a little bread instead. He called for Armande to bring him a pillow stuffed with an herb that would help him to sleep, but moments later, he coughed violently and spat blood into a bowl. Seeing this, Baron cried out in alarm, but Molière reassured him: it was not the first time this had happened, and previous times had been worse. Nevertheless, he sent the young man to seek Armande.

As it happened, two sisters of charity, the members of whose community often visited Paris during Lent to beg for alms, were staying at Molière's house. They made him comfortable, while he "expressed to them the sentiments of a good Christian and all the resignation which he owed to God."[33] Shortly afterwards, Baron returned with Armande to find Molière dead.

Upon hearing the story, Louis was shocked and saddened, for he genuinely loved and admired Molière, one of the finest playwrights of the age. More distressing than this sad story, however, was that Molière had died without benefit of clergy.

The church in Paris had long excommunicated actors and refused to allow them a Christian burial unless they renounced their profession. Armande explained to Louis how her husband had sent to the nearby church of Saint-Eustache for a priest, but two of them had refused to come, while a third, having been awoken from his sleep, arrived too late. Armande then turned to the archbishop of Paris, Harlay de Champvallon,[34] who referred her petition to one of his officers. Since then, a further four days passed and Molière remained unburied. In desperation, Armande now approached Louis for help. She knew Louis had supported Molière in the past and had even taken his side during the controversy over *Tartuffe*. Louis promised the unhappy widow that he would do all he could. However, he had always been reluctant to offend the church, and he was anxious to avoid a public outcry. He sent Armande back to the archbishop, insisting that his must be the final word. At the same time, he sent a message to Harlay de Champvallon ordering him to "so arrange matters as to avoid any demonstration or scandal."[35] As a result, the archbishop agreed to give Molière a Christian burial, but only on condition that it was "conducted without ceremony or advertisement."[36]

In the end, Molière was buried in the cemetery of Saint-Eustache at night, but it was no quiet affair. A crowd, friends or protestors, it cannot be said which, descended upon the house in the rue de Richelieu, after which the funeral cortège moved slowly towards the cemetery, where Molière was finally laid to rest by the light of a hundred torches.

With the coming of spring, Louis's thoughts returned to war, and on May 1, he left once again for the front. He focused his efforts on capturing Maastricht. This large fortified town was of strategic importance, since it guarded the route to France across the Meuse. Moreover, Maastricht was used by William of Orange and Emperor Leopold as their center of communications.

Now Louis's siege of Maastricht gave Vauban the opportunity to try out a new siege technique he had learned while observing the Turks at Candia.[37] The usual method was to dig a straight, narrow trench towards the walls of the city to be besieged and then mine the walls or launch an assault. The disadvantage was that it left little room for maneuvering and exposed the diggers to enemy fire. Vauban's method was to construct a series of concentric trenches joined by a short perpendicular trench until the town walls were reached. It was a slow process, but the diggers were better protected, it allowed the troops freer movement, and the high parapets offered greater cover.[38]

After thirteen days, the third parallel was completed and the troops moved in. Maastricht was ready to fall. Many men were killed or injured on both sides in the ensuing assault, among them d'Artagnan.[39] A week later, on July 1, the governor of Maastricht, Jacques de Fariaux, surrendered.

Now in French hands, Maastricht required fortification. A despairing Colbert, worried as always by the cost, protested that he would have difficulty finding the required 20 million livres. In the end, he was forced to resort to "extraordinary means"; that is, he now understood the difficulties faced by Foucquet as he raised funds for wars, and he was obliged to adopt the former superintendent's methods. Now Colbert sold offices, alienated royal domains, and introduced new taxes. Colbert's incompetence in raising the necessary funds in due time did not please Louis.[40]

Despite the emperor's support of William of Orange, Louis's campaign had been largely successful. The only significant loss so far had been Naarden: when Luxembourg was unable to prevent Orange from capturing it, he was ordered to withdraw.[41] This, however, was about to change. The commander of the Austrian army, Raimondo Montecuccoli, was making his way towards Bonn, where he expected to rendezvous with William of Orange. Louis sent an urgent message to his commander at Utrecht, the duc de Luxembourg, ordering him to prevent Montecuccoli from crossing the Rhine. Unfortunately, Luxembourg was unable to reach the Austrians in time, and the joint forces of Montecuccoli and Orange besieged Bonn, which surrendered on November 12.[42] What Louis had most feared now became a reality. The German states formed an alliance, and they joined the war on Orange's side.[43]

In February 1674, the Congress of Cologne attempted to find acceptable peace terms, while England signed a separate peace treaty with Holland. A few weeks later, Louis's allies, the bishop of Münster and the elector of Cologne, deserted him. At the diet of Ratisbon, on May 28, Leopold declared war on France. The whole of Europe, it seemed, was turning against Louis.[44] However, with the fall of Besançon and Dôle, Franche-Comté once more fell to Louis.[45] Four medals were struck to commemorate these victories.[46] On July 9, the king was back at Fontainebleau.

As though the war were not enough to contend with, Louis was aware of rumors that Louise de La Vallière was making plans to leave the court for good. The lady who served to hide Louis's relationship with Athénaïs desperately wanted to take the veil, but she had not yet confided her intentions to the king. Nevertheless, he had heard enough to be alarmed. He had long been concerned that the marquis de Montespan might reclaim his wife and her children by Louis, dragging them away from court against their will and his.

Louis decided to act. One option was to legitimate Athénaïs's children, as he had done with Louise's; but the fact that Athénaïs was a married woman complicated matters considerably. There was, however, a way past even this complication. Louis looked to the example of his grandfather, Henri IV. Henri had legitimated César de Vendôme and Antoine de Moret, both of whom had been born to married women.[47] The old king had simply declared, "We knew that the marriage was null and unconsummated, as is proved by the decree of separation and nullity of the said marriage which ensued."[48] Unfortunately, the Montespan marriage had been consummated, and the couple had two children to prove it, so annulment was not an option in this case. Meanwhile, when Athénaïs gave birth to a daughter on June 1, 1673, this further increased the pressure on Louis to find a solution. The answer he came up with was to use subterfuge.

On December 18, Athénaïs's little girl was baptized Louise-Françoise, an interesting choice of name. While the certificate gave the name of the child, it omitted that of her mother. The godfather was Louis-Auguste, the future duc du Maine, Louis's three-year-old son by Athénaïs, but no family name was entered on the certificate. The godmother was Louise-Françoise de La Vallière, who, once again, proved herself so useful that it is easy to see why Louis did not want to let her go.

Two days later, the parlement registered the deeds of legitimation. They carried this short preamble: "Louis, by the Grace of God, etc. The natural love that we bear Our children, and many other sentiments, oblige Us to recognize Louis-Auguste, Louis-César and Louise-Françoise."[49] The identity of the mother had been concealed beneath the phrase "many other reasons" to frustrate any attempt by the marquis de Montespan from claiming these children of the royal blood as his own.

Louise had given her name to Athénaïs's child, but if she thought that Louis would show his gratitude by allowing her to take the veil, she was mistaken. As long as Athénaïs's husband presented a threat, Louise's presence at court was essential.

Several years previously, the marquis de Montespan had made an attempt to secure a formal separation from Athénaïs, only to find himself accused of injuring his wife, of cruelty, and dissipating a fortune he had never had.[50] Now Louis decided to appeal to Montespan, and his moment could not have been more propitious. For some time, Montespan's mother had been unwell. He had been allowed to return from his exile in order to comfort her in her final weeks and settle her affairs, including his inheritance. The marquis came to Paris, but there was to be no repetition of the scandalous behavior, despite the fears of Louis and Athénaïs. In mourning and subdued, he was resigned to his fate and agreed to all that Louis and Athénaïs asked of him.[51] Montespan was ordered to repay Athénaïs the 64 thousand livres of her dowry that he had already received, as well as 4 thousand livres each year in alimony. More importantly, at least from Louis's perspective, he was served with a formal petition forbidding him to come near Athénaïs.[52]

With Athénaïs formally separated[53] from her husband, there was no reason to keep Louise at court, yet Louis still required one more service of her. He had planned a series of festivities to be held at Saint-Germain, and he intended them to be magnificent. He had given up dancing some three years before, but he once more took to the floor for this special occasion. Beginning on January 12, 1674, the court was treated to a sparkling round of plays, operas, and balls, but one of the highlights was the début of Marie-Anne, Mlle de Blois, Louis's eight-year-old daughter by Louise. The little girl had been practicing her steps for weeks and now here she was, a beautiful doll in her first ball gown of black velvet glittering with diamonds. She was escorted onto the dance floor by the young prince de Roche-Aymon, who was not much older than his partner. Three days later, Mlle de Blois was pronounced the *chef-d'œuvre* among the young people of the court, while January 24 saw her final appearance, for this occasion at least. The sight of her daughter's triumph moved Louise deeply. "I admit that I was delighted to see her looking as pretty as she was," she said, "at the same time, I have my scruples. I love her, but she will not hold me back for one moment."[54]

The time had finally come. Louise had spent several weeks putting her affairs in order as she prepared to leave the world. Louis could do no more to stop her. He wept as the woman he had once loved so passionately bade him farewell. Louise, fearing her resolve would weaken, or that the king's love for her might reawaken, simply bowed and withdrew.

Another who feared that the old flame would rekindle in Louis's heart was Athénaïs. Bored and a little disconcerted by her rival's leave-taking, she was impatient for the former favorite to leave.[55] Still, she grabbed Louise and whisked her off to the apartments they had once shared and treated her to her last supper at court.[56]

The next day, Louise attended the king's mass, oblivious to the tears that streamed down Louis's face. An hour later, she sat in her carriage as courtiers milled around her. She had changed into a sumptuous gown for her final journey before her cloistered life began, and it was remarked that she had never looked more beautiful. At the age of twenty-nine, the duchesse de La Vallière, who had been so burdened with guilt for the sin of having loved the king, left Fontainebleau, her face lit up with the sweetest smile. Going to a living death, she had never been happier or more content. [57]

Louis's emotions ran deep, and he expressed them freely, but such displays were quickly over. He had other matters on his mind. The Dutch war, now a pan-European conflict, was still ongoing. In August 1674, the prince de Condé achieved a victory at Seneffe, where 107 enemy colors were captured, but Condé chose this moment to retire, and he returned to his château of Chantilly. With the death of the maréchal de Turenne, who was stuck down by a stray cannonball as Salzbach, Louis had lost two of his finest generals. On the king's orders, Turenne was buried with honors at Saint-Denis, to rest among Louis's Bourbon ancestors.

Louis's pursuit of *gloire* was costing more than valuable lives. His people were facing increasing hardship. In July 1675, Bossuet wrote to inform Louis of the miserable state of the people, which was caused by the behavior of soldiers billeted in the provinces, as well as the increased taxation that the people simply could not afford to pay. Bossuet implored Louis to find some remedy.[58]

For now, however, Louis did nothing. In 1676, he appointed Vauban to establish a secure frontier in the east. Vauban identified the towns of Condé and Bouchain as good places to begin what he called the *pré carré*, or 'duelling area.' Beyond these lay the strategically important Valenciennes and Cambrai.

ABOVE: *Louis XIV, King of France and Navarre* by Charles Le Brun, 1661. *Courtesy of Wikipedia.* RIGHT: *Louis XIII, the father of Louis XIV* by Philippe de Champagne, 1655. *Courtesy of Wikipedia.*

ABOVE LEFT: *Anne of Austria, mother of Louis XIV and regent* by Peter Paul Rubens, c. 1620s. *Courtesy of Wikipedia.*

ABOVE RIGHT: *Portrait of Philippe of Orléans, Duke of Orléans (1640–1701)* by Antoine Mathieu, c. 1660s. *Courtesy of Wikipedia.*

RIGHT: *Cardinal Jules Mazarin, Louis's godfather and mentor* by Pierre Mignard, 1658. *Courtesy of Wikipedia.*

ABOVE LEFT: *Marie-Thérèse* by Jean Nocret, c. 1660. *Courtesy of Wikipedia.* ABOVE RIGHT: *Louise de La Vallière* by Jean Nocret, 1661. *Courtesy of Wikipedia.* BELOW: La Fête Les Plaisirs de l'Ile Enchantée. *Courtesy of gallica.bnf.fr / Bibliotheque nationale de France.*

Athénaïs de Montespan, artist unknown. *Courtesy of Wikipedia.*

RIGHT: Madame de Maintenon, Louis's second wife. *Courtesy of Wikipedia.* BELOW: Louis XIV in 1673, at the height of his power and glory, after Lefebvre. *Courtesy of Wikipedia.*

RIGHT: *Louis XIV* by Hyacinthe Rigaud, 1701, which shows the damage caused to Louis's face by the dental surgery. *Courtesy of Wikipedia.* BELOW: *Louis XIV and His Family,* attributed to Nicolas de Largillière, c. 1710. *Courtesy of Wikipedia.*

ABOVE: Aerial view of the Palace of Versailles, France. *Photo © ToucanWings/Wikimedia Commons.*
BELOW: Galerie des Glaces (Hall of Mirrors) in the Palace of Versailles, Versailles, France. *Photo © Myrabella / Wikimedia Commons.*

Château Marly-le-roi by Pierre-Denis Martin, 1724. *Photo © RMN-Grand Palais (Château de Versailles) / Gérard Blot.w*

Leaving Bouchain to his brother, Louis was now positioned at Heurtebise, close to Valenciennes, as Orange began his descent on the French camp. The maréchal de Lorges was ready to meet them without hesitation, but Louis held back. His way had always been to consult a military council, and that is what he did now. The consensus was not to attack, and Louis followed this advice, but he would always regret missing an encounter that could have shortened the war considerably.[59] While Louis could only stand by and watch the advance of the Dutch, Philippe had better luck at Cassell, from which Orange was forced to flee so quickly that he left behind his gold plate and some very useful maps of all the strongholds in Europe.[60]

By this time, peace talks had already opened at Nijmegen. Louis had all but ignored them, but now he began to pay them proper attention. His change of heart was due in part to the great financial burden the war imposed upon his people. There was already unrest in some provinces; that revolt was taking place in Brittany and Bordeaux, both "difficult" provinces, was almost inevitable. What was worse, the chevalier de Rohan had made overtures to the governor of the Spanish Netherlands concerning an armed invasion of Brittany by the prince of Orange. When the plot was uncovered, Rohan and his fellow conspirators were executed for treason.

At Nijmegen, peace negotiations continued, and it was here at the forum of peace rather than the theater of war that Louis "appeared the master of Europe." As La Fare explained, the king could choose between enslaving Europe or granting it peace.[61] That he chose peace was Louis's masterstroke.

To secure the peace, Louis offered Ghent, recently captured with Ypres by France, to Charles of England. In the end, he managed to extend part of his frontier to the Rhine and formally acquired Franche-Comté, Cambrai, and Valenciennes, although Ghent, Courtrai, and Charleroi were restored to Spain. While the emperor gave Louis Breisach and Freiburg, the king broke the links connecting the Habsburg's possessions between Milan and Luxemburg.[62]

The treaty of Nijmegen, however, brought more than peace. Louis had imposed his conditions

> with the arrogance of a conqueror; nevertheless they were not so outrageous as to render his enemies desperate and force them to reunite against him in a final conflict: he often spoke to Europe as a master, but at the same time acted as a statesman. [63]

Indeed, as La Fare wrote, "We had never dreamt of taking Holland, but to chastise her: a bad idea, for we impressed fear and hatred in the hearts of men who, in their own interests, were our natural allies." Moreover, France had caused the Dutch to throw themselves under the influence of a leader who had made them warlike and a republic, transforming a state that could never have been a danger to them into one of their most potent enemies, "without whom all the others would not be capable of resisting us." [64]

The ink on the treaty of Nijmegen was barely dry when Orange graphically demonstrated his scorn for it. He attacked the maréchal de Luxembourg, who had broken off the siege of Mons the moment he heard of the peace. A long and bloody battle ensued, "which cost the lives of two thousand French and as many of the enemy." Louis was now

> at the height of his greatness. Victorious since he had begun to reign, having besieged no place which he had not taken, superior in every way to his united enemies, for six years the terror of Europe and at last her arbiter and peacemaker, he now added Franche-Comté, Dunkirk, and one-half of Flanders to his possessions; moreover, and he might well count this the greatest of his advantages, he was the king of a nation happy in itself and the model of all others. [65]

Time would tell how long this situation would last.

EIGHTEEN

Les Femmes

When, in July 1675, Louis returned from the war, one of his first thoughts was to visit Mme de Montespan, but it was clear to close observers that something had changed. Just as he had in the time of Louise de La Vallière, Bishop Bossuet had warned Louis to give up his mistress for the salvation of his soul. Bossuet had chosen his moment well, for it was Easter, when the king would receive the sacraments in a public ceremony, but only if he was truly repentant and only if the church would grant him absolution for his sins.

According to Primi Visconti, Louis had let Athénaïs go to Paris, resolved that she would never set foot in Versailles again.[1] Clearly Louis had listened to the bishop, but in the end he proved incapable of being parted from Athénaïs for very long, and she maintained her apartments at Versailles after all.

Yet even though Louis was seeing Athénaïs once again, courtiers were uncertain whether or not he loved her as he had done. While there were those, such as Mme de Richelieu, the queen's lady-in-waiting, who thought that they were no longer lovers, others, such as Primi Visconti, thought relations had resumed as usual.[2] Louis was dining at Athénaïs's house at Clagny when news of the death of Turenne arrived, a disaster the devout attributed to the resumption of sin.[3] The following day, Louis created eight new maréchaux, one of whom was Athénaïs's brother, Vivonne, which inspired the quip that "seven had been made maréchaux by the sword and one by the scabbard."[4] Mme de Sévigné thought that the attachment between Louis and Athénaïs was "still extreme," although she remained uncertain whether they were still lovers, for behind Athénaïs's apparent triumph lay an inner sadness.[5]

The cause of Athénaïs's "inner sadness" was not hard to find, for Louis had not remained faithful to her. From the early 1670s onwards, he had taken a succession of minor or casual mistresses, one of whom was Athénaïs's own lady-in-waiting, Mlle Desœillets.

Claude de Vin Desœillets was the daughter of a successful actress, but rather than follow her mother onto the boards, she decided to try her luck at court. With the help of the duc de Mortemart, who had also protected her mother, Mlle Desœillets entered Athénaïs's household in about 1668. Athénaïs favored taking plain women into her service, and Mlle Desœillets was no exception. Nevertheless, she did not go unnoticed by Louis. According to Primi Visconti,[6] Mlle Desœillets gave out that Louis had "commerce" with her at various times and even boasted that she had children by him. It is known that Louis had a daughter by Mlle Desœillets, who was given the name Louise de la Maisonblanche and brought up by foster parents. Although he did not acknowledge his daughter, Louis did not forget her; once she was of age, he married her to the marquise de la Queue, who received the post of captain of the guards and a suitable sum of money.[7]

248

Louis often found himself alone with Mlle Desœillets when her mistress was busy or unwell, but was she content to be just a casual lover? It has been hinted that she harbored hopes to replace Athénaïs to become Louis's *maîtresse déclarée* and had, in fact, caught his attention long enough for her to believe her hopes might be fulfilled; but then Louis changed his mind and Mlle Desœillets was discarded. Whether or not this was true cannot be said for certain, but that Athénaïs did not dismiss her suggests that she was unaware of the close liaison between Louis and Mlle Desœillets, or that she did not regard her servant as a threat.[8] Mlle Desœillets would remain in Athénaïs's service for another two years.

If Louis's feelings for Athénaïs had mellowed, she remained very important to him. Newly returned from the war in July 1676, he was spending time with Marie-Thérèse and the dauphin when he learned that Athénaïs was at Clagny, having just returned from taking the water cure at Bourbon. Louis promptly abandoned his disappointed son and weeping queen to spend a long time with her.[9] By the following month, Athénaïs was pregnant.

Now that it was obvious that Athénaïs was once again in the king's favor, some courtiers decided to cultivate her friendship. One day, her dressmaker arrived carrying a dress she had ordered.[10] When he showed it to her, however, the bodice had entirely the wrong measurements, and the resultant cries and complaints made the poor man tremble with fear. "Madame," he said, "as time is pressing, see if this other dress would suit you instead." Athénaïs agreed, upon which he produced another gown. It was a magnificent creation of "gold upon gold, embroidered with gold, edged with gold, and on top of that a crinkled gold woven with gold mixed with a certain gold, which made the most divine fabric that can ever be imagined," enthused Mme de Sévigné. "It was the fairies who made this work in secret," she continued; "no living soul knew anything about it." At that point, Louis arrived. "Madame, it is made for you," he told her; but who had given it? "Langlée," offered Louis, referring to Monsieur de Langlée, a quarterrmaster in the royal army and a celebrated arbiter of fashion. A while later, Athénaïs's friend and gambling partner, the marquis de Dangeau, offered her some animals for her ménagerie at Clagny. It was filled, so said Mme de Sévigné, with "the most passionate turtle doves, the fattest pigs, the fullest cows, the curliest sheep and the goosiest geese."[11]

Athénaïs was being wooed by courtiers, but it was not long before Louis turned his attention to another lady. Her name was Anne de Rohan-Chabot, princesse de Soubise. A beautiful woman of twenty-eight, with a good figure and strawberry blond hair, she maintained her delicate beauty with a diet of white meats, fish, salads, and fruit. Her name had been linked with the king's as long ago as November 1668.[12] She was glimpsed in his company again a year later, and though her family rejoiced at the thought of the rewards they might expect, no one was ever sure just what favors, if any, she granted Louis. Now, here she was again, seven years later, and observers still could not agree to what extent she was the royal mistress.[13] Saint-Maurice commented that Louis "looks favorably upon madame de Soubise,"[14] while Ezéchiel Spanheim thought she was too devoted to her husband and too virtuous to succumb to the king's advances.[15] Saint-Simon[16] believed that their relationship had been consummated, and that Bontemps would take her through back passages to Louis's bedroom. This account, however, is based upon an unconfirmed account by the maréchal de Rochefort. If the relationship was sexual, the prince de Soubise did not appear to object; rather, he saw it as an opportunity to advance the family's fortune.[17]

One person who was most certainly not happy about Louis's liaison, sexual or otherwise, with Mme de Soubise was Athénaïs. Noticing that Mme de Soubise wore emerald earrings on certain days, she placed her under surveillance only to discover that those days coincided with the absence from court of the prince de Soubise, at which times the princesse would dine with the king.[18] Mme de Sévigné noticed signs of jealousy in Mme de Montespan on these occasions,[19] but Athénaïs had nothing to fear, as Mme de Soubise merely wanted to serve her family's interests. She had arranged to have her husband sent away from court so she could be free to pursue the king. Her plans worked, but only insofar as Louis surrendered to her charms. He offered to increase her pension, but he refused to appoint her to a court position, and, as Mme de Sévigné remarked, the princesse de Soubise was "too well advised to raise the standard of such perfidy with so little prospect of enjoying it for long; she would be precisely exposed to the wrath of Mme de Montespan."[20]

Clearly, Mme de Soubise was never a serious contender for Louis's affections; but, as Mme de Sévigné shrewdly observed, she had "opened the way to infidelity and served only as a thoroughfare for other women who were younger and more tempting."[21] Mme de Sévigné's words proved prophetic. Although Louis remained friendly with the princesse de Soubise, his infatuation with her rapidly faded;[22] however, with Athénaïs once again pregnant, Louis looked elsewhere for consolation, and his eye fell upon another court beauty, Marie-Élisabeth, dame de Ludres.

A lay-canoness in the convent of Poussay in the mountains of the Vosges, Marie-Élisabeth was a petite and pretty twenty-year-old with the figure of a Greek goddess and beautiful eyes of Atlantic blue.[23] Many noticed the resemblance between her and Athénaïs; except while Athénaïs was blond, Marie-Élisabeth had glorious red hair. She also spoke with a strong northern accent, which Louis found enchanting.[24]

At the age of fifteen, Marie-Élisabeth had been engaged to the duc de Lorraine, who was then in his sixties. Accounts differ as to how the engagement ended, with some asserting that she became his mistress only to be dismissed when he tired of her. Other accounts maintain that he agreed to marry her but was dissuaded by his family and his current mistress, who persuaded Marie-Élisabeth's family to take her away.[25] Whatever the truth, Marie-Élisabeth entered the court in the service of Henriette d'Orléans before transferring to the queen's household upon the death of her mistress.[26]

Shortly after this, all the queen's maids of honor were dismissed and replaced by respectable married ladies-in-waiting. This was said to have been on the queen's orders, but many believed that the jealous Athénaïs was behind the move.[27] Marie-Élisabeth survived the cull and was invited by Liselotte to join her household. Almost six years later, in early 1677, the beautiful redhead caught the king's eye.

It was not long before Marie-Élisabeth announced that she was pregnant with Louis's child, which caused her stock to rise considerably. When high-ranking ladies of the court stood when she entered the room, the queen knew the king had a new love. Her indifference to the situation was revealed when she announced that it was Mme de Montespan's business. Conversely, Athénaïs would fix withering looks upon the king's new fancy, and exchanges between the two women always ended with them insulting each other.[28] Meanwhile, Athénaïs persuaded Louis that Marie-Élisabeth's body was covered with scurf, the result of a poison which her mother had given her when she was twelve to make her ugly and so discourage the attentions of the duc de Lorraine.[29]

When, in February, Louis returned to the front, Marie-Élisabeth moved into the country home of a wealthy financier. Athénaïs also withdrew to the country, where she gave birth to a daughter, Françoise-Marie, on May 4. At the end of that month, Louis returned from the army to find Athénaïs more beautiful than ever, and those who had anticipated her dismissal saw how wrong they had been. As it happened, Louis had begun to be annoyed with Marie-Élisabeth, who openly flaunted her status and adopted an unattractive air of superiority. Moreover, it turned out that she had not been pregnant after all. When she fell from grace, few showed any sympathy for her, and Mme de Sévigné, who visited the court that summer, witnessed Mme de Montespan in all her glory: "Oh, my daughter! What triumph at Versailles! What redoubled pride! What solid establishment!" She compared Athénaïs with Diane de Poitiers, the mistress of Henri II, who retained the full power and influence of her beauty even into old age.[30]

Marie-Élisabeth de Ludres nonetheless maintained her position at court and Louis would give her a kind word from time to time, but this simply reignited Athénaïs's anger, who took out her fury on her vanquished rival. Marie-Élisabeth refused Louis's offer of a pension, but if she hoped he would revive their relationship, she was to be disappointed. A few months later, she finally gave up and left the court to enter a convent, the Dames de Sainte-Marie, in Paris. When she sought Philippe's permission to leave, he consulted Louis, who asked, "Is she not there already?"[31] He had not entirely forgotten her, however, and three years later he again offered her a pension. This time she accepted, taking the money with her as she retired to a cloistered life in Nancy.[32]

By this time, Louis's passion for Athénaïs had cooled markedly, and she lived every day with the fear that a new lady might take her place in his heart. Under the strain of such insecurity, Athénaïs's dark jealousy and stormy temper knew no bounds, and she exploded every time Louis so much as looked at another lady.[33]

So afraid was Athénaïs of losing the king's love that she insisted on travelling with him when he returned to the front. Pregnant once again and having gained a lot of weight, she endured the long and arduous journey and harsh conditions only to become ill with a tertian fever.[34] It was said that things were not good between them, and that Athénaïs was merely "an old habit that His Majesty could not break off."[35]

Athénaïs went to the country to give birth to a son, the future comte de Toulouse, who was born on June 6, 1678. Louis welcomed her back at court, much to the surprise of many who thought she was gone for good. By now Athénaïs had lost her figure and Louis was more irritated than enchanted by her.[36] She would have lengthy massages with aromatic oils, which annoyed Louis even more. He was allergic to perfume, and her heavy scent made him so sick that he was reluctant to share his carriage with her.[37]

As Louis's relations with Athénaïs sunk ever further, something happened to offer him much-needed distraction, as well as the opportunity to strengthen the security of the state and boost his power still further in Europe. Carlos II, the sickly king of Spain whose imminent death had been expected for the past eighteen years, had grown into a cruel, ugly, and unkempt man. It remained uncertain whether or not he would be capable of fathering a child, but this did not prevent his announcing his intention to marry, and Louis promptly sent a portrait of his seventeen-year-old niece, Marie-Louise d'Orléans, to Carlos.[38]

Marie-Louise was beautiful, with dark, almond-shaped eyes set in an exquisite face framed by an abundance of black curly hair. She had all the delicacy of her late mother, Henriette, and the dusky coloring inherited from her father, Philippe, and his Médicis ancestors. When Carlos saw her portrait, he fell in love with her and wasted no time in opening negotiations for her hand. In January 1679, he offered his formal proposal, which Louis accepted.[39] That summer, Louis announced the marriage to the court, when Liselotte noted that they were "overwhelmed with visitors, because the whole of France is coming to congratulate us in the betrothal of" Marie-Louise.[40]

Everyone, it seems, was happy with the match—everyone, that is, except Marie-Louise. Liselotte, who knew firsthand the difficulties involved in moving to a strange country, sympathized, but Marie-Louise had long set her heart upon marrying the dauphin, as had her father.[41] The highest aspiration of any princess of France was, after all, to become queen of France. Sadly, this was not to be; Louis considered his niece too valuable an asset to be kept hidden away in France. Her marriage to Carlos was crucial for France because it offered a solution to the perennial problem of the Spanish succession. Marie-Louise, so Louis hoped, would produce a son and heir who could be educated to favor France. Failing that, and the prospect was admittedly a remote one, she could arrange the transfer of the Spanish crown to a Bourbon prince following Carlos's death.[42]

The political and dynastic implications of her marriage did nothing to comfort Marie-Louise. As she wept, Louis tried to reassure her, saying. "I make you Queen of Spain: what could I do more, even for my daughter?" "Ah, Sire," she replied, "but how much more you might do for your *niece*."[43] Later, when she had completed her round of farewell visits, Marie-Louise was still not reconciled to her fate. Frantically she flung herself at Louis's feet as he was going to mass. "Don't make me go," she pleaded, but Louis would not be moved. He smiled and told her, "Madame, it would be a fine thing if the Most Catholic Queen prevented the Most Christian King from going to mass."[44] Then, as he sent her away, Louis bade her a firm "Farewell. For ever. It would be your greatest misfortune to see France again."[45] Indeed it would, for a queen would be repudiated if she failed to provide heirs. Louis's sense of duty was so strong that he thought it was shared by all members of his family; he expected them to sacrifice their personal happiness for the sake of France, and this included his young niece.

Of course, Marie-Louise married Carlos, but her life was not a happy one. Aside from the strict court protocols that regimented and restricted every area of her life, she would have no children. Liselotte thought she understood the reasons: "It is not the Queen of Spain's fault that she has no children," she wrote, "but the King's."[46] There was another reason for her misery, however. The duke of Pastranne took it upon himself to cause trouble for her. He never had a good word to say about her, and he spread malicious gossip in Spanish so she could not fully understand him. "There was not a woman in France worth anything, be she whom she might," he said, "but that he found some extremely willing."[47] This slur naturally reached France, where it caused great indignation.

While life was looking very bleak for Marie-Louise, another princess was already making her way to a new life in France. As he was dining in the queen's apartments one evening, Louis seemed lost in thought. He was studying a portrait of a lady, which he then attached to a tapestry and announced, "Here is the princess of Bavaria."[48] The diners maintained a tactful silence, for the face they looked upon could not be considered beautiful.

Marie-Anne Christine Victoire of Wittelsbach, princess of Bavaria, was the daughter of Christine de France, duchesse de Savoy, and

Louis had selected her as a suitable bride for the dauphin as a means of securing the alliance between France and Bavaria. Louis had already shown the portrait to his son, asking him "whether he could endure to take unto himself an ugly wife." The dauphin's reply was admirable. "He wasn't in the least bit in the world worried about it, and that he would be quite content if his wife was intelligent and virtuous, however uncomely she might be." [49] This reply sealed Louis's decision to select Marie-Anne as his son's bride, and when the dauphin saw the portrait, he pronounced himself very pleased with it. Louis agreed with the dauphin's sentiments: "Although not handsome," he said, "she is not displeasing; and is a person of much worth." [50] Still, he intended to test her sense of humor: "If she has any wit," he said, "I shall speedily begin to tease her about her ugliness." [51]

The dauphin and dauphine were married by proxy at Munich, and as his new daughter-in-law made her way into France, the impatient Louis hurried off in his coach so he could meet her before anyone else. Driving back with her, he introduced her firstly to the queen. He then attended her *coucher*, the ceremony in which she prepared for bed, along with the rest of the court and watched with satisfaction as Marie-Thérèse presented her with her chemise. At the table, the dauphine, who was as yet unaccustomed to French ways, could not understand why everyone ate together. "They will eat all and leave me nothing," she said, much to Louis's amusement. [52] Liselotte knew exactly how she felt, for she had experienced the culture clash firsthand. "If she were not going to be so great a queen," she wrote, "I should pity her for having to go to a country about which she knows nothing at all." [53]

As it was, Marie-Anne had both wit and intelligence in abundance. A linguist, she spoke French and Italian as well as her native German, and she had almost mastered Latin. She would not share all of her husband's interests, though, for she disliked hunting and gambling. She excelled in engaging and delightful conversation, which immediately endeared her to Louis, as did her religious devotion, a subject that was becoming increasingly important to Louis.

Louis, meanwhile, continued his clashes with Athénaïs, but he found solace in the charms of a new beauty at court. Her name was Marie-Angélique de Scorailles, but she was known as Mlle de Fontanges, and she had been a member of Liselotte's household since October 1678. Aged seventeen, she was strikingly beautiful, with her gray eyes and blond hair that was tinted with red, but she was no intellectual. Choisy declared her "beautiful as an angel and stupid as a basket."[54] Liselotte agreed, noting that she was a "stupid little thing,"[55] although she did concede that she was also "good hearted and as beautiful as an angel."[56] She added that, while Louis loved her, her love for him was "only after the fashion of a heroine of romance, because she was dreadfully sentimental."[57]

Ironically, Louis had been introduced to Mlle de Fontanges by Athénaïs herself. She was growing concerned about the attention the king was paying to another lady, the widow Scarron, who had been appointed as governess to her children by Louis. While Mlle de Fontanges was beautiful, Athénaïs knew that this was not enough to hold Louis's interest for long, and she did not see the much younger lady as a threat.[58] Louis, however, was enchanted. By March it was believed that he would make a conquest of Mlle de Fontanges, if he had not done so already; for, as Bussy-Rabutin put it, "kings who desire do not sigh for long."[59]

For a while, Athénaïs was unaware of just how far Louis would take his latest fancy. He used her preoccupation with gambling to slip away to the Palais-Royal for secret trysts with his new mistress. In time, however, Athénaïs realized her error, and Louis and she had a blazing quarrel. He was tired of her temper, her jealousy, and her excessive gaming, which he found distasteful at a time when his people were overburdened with taxation. It was believed that Louis used the approaching Eastertide, always a time when his conscience was pricked, as a pretext to send Athénaïs away from court.[60]

Mademoiselle, however, noted that Louis had looked "extremely afflicted" by Athénaïs's departure, suggesting he had sent her away against his inclination. As it was, he declined to take the sacraments that Easter; instead he shut himself away and saw few people. When he later went to the queen's apartments, "he had his eyes red, as though he had been weeping," while Athénaïs's retreat provoked much opinion at court.[61] Mademoiselle saw her as she was visiting her children in Paris, and she asked her if she intended to return to Versailles, but Athénaïs only laughed. As it was, Athénaïs, who had left for Paris on March 15, returned after a few days, only to leave again. This pattern of behavior continued for several weeks until Louis hit upon the perfect solution.

The usual golden handshake for a discarded mistress was to make her a duchess, allowing her to live comfortably on the revenues of her new estates. In Athénaïs's case, Louis could not elevate her without also making her husband a duke. He decided instead to grant her a favor she had long coveted but which he had always denied her. He appointed her superintendent of the queen's household. This post came with a good stipend and granted Athénaïs the rank of honorary duchess with the right to sit on a tabouret in the queen's presence.[62] The present incumbent, Mme de Soissons, who had held the post since 1660, was pensioned off with a payment of 200 thousand écus.[63] Athénaïs's faith deepened; she became increasingly involved in charitable works, and there is no reason to believe that her devotion was anything but sincere.[64]

Bussy-Rabutin notes that Athénaïs spoke often with a priest, Père César, and it was even rumored that she might return to her husband, an eventuality that Père de La Chaise was working to bring about. She visited her children often, but whenever Louis saw her, it was always in the presence of Philippe.[65]

In the summer of 1679, it was believed that Mlle de Fontanges was pregnant with Louis's child, although this proved not to be the case.[66] Still, Louis remained passionately in love with her; he was enchanted by her little quirks and faux pas. Out hunting one day, she swept into a low-hanging branch, which pulled off her hat and sent her hair tumbling about her shoulders. She nonchalantly swept it up into a knot on the top of her head and tied it with a ribbon. Louis loved the new "style," and of course the ladies of the court began to wear their hair *à la Fontanges*.[67] On another occasion, she entered a ballroom and, looking neither left nor right, made straight for Louis without even noticing the queen, an incident that gave the king much amusement.[68]

While the new affair invoked the fury of Athénaïs, few people knew much about it, for Louis took pleasure in the mystery.[69] "Never have the king's amours been conducted more secretly than those of mademoiselle de Fontanges," wrote Bussy-Rabutin.[70] Try as they might, courtiers were not even certain where the new mistress was lodged; in fact, as Primi Visconti had discerned, a suite of rooms had been especially prepared for her above the king's rooms at Saint-Germain.[71]

When Louis went to mass on New Year's Day 1680, Mlle de Fontanges also attended, displaying her status as *maîtresse déclarée* by wearing a dress that was made of the same material as Louis's coat, trimmed with a blue ribbon to match his sash.[72] However, she was absent from the next court event, the wedding of Mlle de Blois, Louis's daughter by Louise de La Vallière. It later emerged that she had been pregnant but had miscarried. A few weeks later, however, she had recovered sufficiently to accompany Louis and the whole court as they went to meet the new dauphine. Mlle de Fontanges travelled like a duchess in a beautiful new carriage drawn by eight horses: two more than Athénaïs ever had.[73]

When the end came, it came swiftly. At Easter, significantly, Louis made Mlle de Fontanges a duchess with a pension of 80 thousand livres before sending her away to the Abbey de Maubuisson, which Louis had presented to her sister. Although Athénaïs was angry that her rival had been elevated to a position she could never enjoy, others correctly saw the move as an indication that Louis was tiring of his latest mistress. She really had nothing to keep the king's interest alive, no conversation, no wit; she had only her stunning good looks, but even they had begun to fade following her miscarriage, from which she never fully recovered. Mme de Sévigné noted how she remained at Maubuisson, weak with fever and suffering a considerable loss of blood, she had even begun to swell: "her beautiful face is a little bloated."[74] She was, as Mme de Sévigné put it, "wounded in the service" of the king.[75] As Louis sent the prior Trimont de Cabrières[76] to treat Mlle de Fontanges, Athénaïs's fall from grace was almost complete: "The king does not look at her," announced Bussy-Rabutin, "and you may believe that the courtiers follow this example."[77]

Behind the scenes, however, Louis was under pressure to repudiate Mlle de Fontages. The pope had ordered his confessor, Père de La Chaise, to resign if she was to return to court.[78] Louis ignored the threat, and an apparently cured Mlle de Fontanges returned to court a few weeks later. Louis rushed to be with her, and their relationship resumed as before. Unfortunately, her condition deteriorated once more, and by the beginning of July, Louis's passion had cooled to the point of indifference. Within two weeks, she was back with her sister, who had transferred to Chelles. She continued to travel in the style her rank afforded her, and she had everything she could want except her health and the king's love.

It was now, just after Easter, when Louis paid court to a new and mysterious lady, Olympe de Piennes de Brouilly. A rich heiress, she was only nineteen or twenty years old, and very beautiful. When she danced at a recent carnival ballet, she captured the hearts of all the courtiers, including the aged duc de la Ferté, who even abandoned gluttony and drinking for her; but the duke was married, and Olympe could take her pick when it came to lovers.

One day, Mlle de Piennes came to Saint-Cloud with her two younger sisters and her aunt. They had come on the pretext of visiting Françoise, Mme Scarron, but the true purpose of their visit was a secret tryst between Olympe and the king, who had arrived on the pretext of visiting his brother. Françoise, who was fond of the young lady, had prepared a sumptuous meal for her guests. As they sat down to eat,

Louis suddenly appeared, looking stern and pretending to wonder what they were doing there, while the court played along with the game. Louis then threw off his frown and took Mlle de Piennes to a window, where he could speak privately with her. That spring and early summer, the two enjoyed a brief affair, with one of Louis's servants driving to Paris each morning to bring her to Versailles and returning her to her home each evening.[79]

At the beginning of September, Mlle de Fontanges expressed fears that she had been poisoned. Although she returned to court, she kept to her room, rarely visited by the king, and there she remained until the following March. With her health steadily worsening, she withdrew to the convent of Port Royal. Louis would inquire after her progress three times a week, but by now it was obvious to all that she had not much longer to live. Louis granted her an honor unique among his mistresses: he visited her as she lay on her deathbed. Looking into the once beautiful face of this woman, who was still only twenty years old, the tears coursed down his face. She died shortly after he left, and Louis paid for annual services in her memory.[80]

That Mlle de Fontanges believed herself to have been the victim of poison was disturbing, and people spoke about it in whispered tones throughout the court. Louis tried to prevent a postmortem, but Mlle de Fontanges's family insisted that an examination be held. As it turned out, the doctors who carried out the postmortem found that she had died of natural causes; accounts vary, but some disease of the lungs was indicated, possibly tuberculosis or cancer, and her condition was worsened by her constant loss of blood following her miscarriage.[81] Louis, however, was right to be wary. Mademoiselle de Fontanges had died at the height of the *Affaire des Poisons*, which had haunted Paris for some years.[82]

NINETEEN
The Affair of the Poisons

I t all started in 1666, when Antoine Dreux d'Aubray, civil lieutenant of the city of Paris, died. He was followed to his grave
four years later by his sons, Antoine and François, who died
within three months of each other. They had been the victims of
Dreux d'Aubray's daughter, Marie-Madeleine de Gobelin, marquise
de Brinvilliers,[1] who managed to evade justice for several years before
being arrested, tried, and hanged in 1676. Then there was the agonizing death, in the summer of 1670, of Henriette, duchesse d'Orléans,
who believed to the end that she had been poisoned.[2] However, it was
upon the arrest of Catherine Montvoisin, known as la Voisin, that the
Affaire des Poisons can truly be said to have begun.

La Voisin was a diviner who specialized in palmistry, astrology, and physiognomy; she also sold perfumes and cures for various minor ailments, no doubt made from the many plants she collected. She also carried out abortions. Primi Visconti, himself a celebrated diviner,[3] said that la Voisin was visited by most of the ladies of Paris.[4] Some consulted her to see what the future held for them, others to acquire potions to clear a complexion or to obtain powders to make a man fall in love with them. La Voisin also helped ladies who fell pregnant with an unwanted baby, or who wished to rid themselves of an undesired husband.

La Voisin became wealthy on the proceeds of her craft and lived a comfortable life, but her husband was a drunken brute who routinely abused her. She spoke often of her desire to get rid of him, and while her friends advised her simply to murder him, she knew that option would not be so easy. The main obstacle to this course of action was her husband's friendship with the public executioner. He had promised Montvoisin that if he were to die unexpectedly, he would order a postmortem.[5]

Apparently a devout Christian, la Voisin believed her powers had come from God, and she rejoiced that the souls of the fetuses she had aborted were saved by baptism. When two of her former associates were arrested and interrogated by Gabriel-Nicolas de La Reynie, chief of the Paris police, they gave him enough information to allow him to draw up a list of some four hundred names, among them that of la Voisin. She was arrested on March 12, 1679, as she left mass, and she joined the growing number of diviners and witches to be imprisoned at the château de Vincennes, on the eastern outskirts of Paris.

Louis appointed a special commission to try those arrested in the poisons affair. He did this for several good reasons, one of which was to relieve the regular courts, which were already pressed by other cases. Louis expected, or feared, that certain unsavory details would emerge during the trials, and it was easier to contain them if the investigations were confined to a special commission. Similarly, there was the fear that persons from the highest stratum of society might be implicated in the affair, and Louis wished their involvement to be kept secret.[6] Lastly, a specially appointed commission would be less vulnerable to pressure from interested parties, and so would better be able to maintain its objectivity.[7] It would sit in the Paris Arsenal, from which it took its name—the Chambre de l'Arsenal—although it soon came to be known as the Chambre Ardente, or 'Burning Chamber,' for it sat in a chamber hung with black cloth and lit with torches. The usual sentence for poisonings and witchcraft was death by burning.

The Chambre Ardente would be presided over by La Reynie,[8] who, with Colbert,[9] countersigned the establishing letters patent on April 7, 1679. Three days later, its first sessions were held. Over the next two years, the Chambre would interrogate 442 people, of whom 367 would go on to be arrested. Of these arrests, 218 would be sustained. Thirty-six prisoners would be condemned to death, and some would be tortured[10] prior to execution; two prisoners would die of natural causes while in prison; five would be condemned to the galleys; twenty-three would be exiled. Lastly, at least one prisoner would commit suicide, or attempt to, while in prison. Many of the guilty, however, had powerful accomplices in high places, and their cases would never come to trial.[11]

On more than one occasion, Louis felt the need to interfere in the process. He warned the comtesse de Soissons, her friend, the marquise d'Alluye, and several other high-ranking courtiers that their names had been mentioned by prisoners at Vincennes. This gave them time to leave Paris, and some went abroad until the panic died down, while others went into hiding in obscure parts of France. Then several prisoners named someone very close to the king indeed—Athénaïs de Montespan.

Athénaïs was mentioned in connection with an old case, which involved la Voisin and two of her accomplices, a sorcerer known as Lesage, the 'Wise One,' and François Mariette, a young priest of the Church of Saint-Séverin who was also a sorcerer. They testified that from the year 1667, Athénaïs was in the hands of la Voisin, whom she had consulted for help to make Louis fall in love with her.[12] Shortly after this, following a disagreement over money, Lesage and Mariette parted from la Voisin, and Athénaïs turned to them instead. Under interrogation, they alleged that Athénaïs had taken part in a ritual during which Mariette, wearing his stole and using holy water, had read the gospel of the Kings while Lesage burned incense. Athénaïs recited a spell written for her by the two men. According to Lesage, Athénaïs also wanted to bring about the death of Louise de La Vallière, but Mariette refuted this, saying she merely wanted Louise to be sent away from court.

On another occasion, a special mass was performed for Athénaïs. She brought two pigeons' hearts to a chapel at Saint-Séverin, and the two hearts were passed beneath the chalice during the ritual. Lesage asserted that a consecrated wafer was also used in the rite, but this was again denied by Mariette.

Following this mass, another two or three were enacted in the same chapel. One of these was said by Lesage to have included a spell that used the bones of a dead man, the purpose of which was to cause the death of Louise de La Vallière. Mariette denied this once again, insisting that Athénaïs's purpose had been to secure Louise's dismissal from court.

When they were arrested in 1668, Mariette was sentenced to banishment for nine years, while Lesage was sent to the galleys. His sentence was commuted in 1674, which, coincidentally or otherwise, was the same year that Louise left court for good. Athénaïs's involvement had been overlooked at the time, only to be reopened during the poisons affair.

Lesage and Mariette were not the only ones to claim to have assisted Athénaïs. A sorcerer named Françoise Filastre asked Bellier, a diviner, to carry something to a lady of the court. Bellier refused, believing that she would be hanged if caught. Her fears suggest that this was to have been a love potion to be given to Louis, or possibly poison to be administered to Mlle de Fontanges.[13] La Filastre denied these allegations, insisting she had only wanted to know Athénaïs so she could use their acquaintance to earn 10 thousand écus. However, a Norman peasant, Philippe Galet, confessed to having supplied la Filastre with love potions, made with bread and cantharides, which were handed to Mme de Montespan.[14] This, Galet recalled, took place in 1675, which coincided rather neatly with the time Louis became ill with an attack of the vapors and headaches. The vapors was a relatively new condition, which became very fashionable at court once Louis was diagnosed with it. It produced some alarming symptoms, including depression, an increase in the watery humors, fever, inflamed eyes and face, a bitter taste in the mouth, and weakness in the legs.[15]

Much of this information had come from the testimony of Marie Marguerite Montvoisin, the daughter of la Voisin, who had been arrested on January 20, 1680. Suicidally depressed and very afraid, she had said little until after the execution of her mother on February 22, either in an attempt to protect her mother, or out of fear of what she thought her mother might do to her if she said anything about her activities. Louis, who was spending the summer inspecting the fortifications on his newly established borders, was kept informed of all the proceedings of the Chambre Ardente, and on August 2, 1680, he wrote to La Reynie:

> *Having seen the declaration made on the 12th of last month by Marguerite Monvoisin, prisoner at my castle of Vincennes, I write you this letter to inform you of my intention that you should devote all possible care to elucidate the facts contained in the said declaration—that you should take care to have written down in separate reports the examinations, confrontations, and everything concerning the inquiry that may be made of the said declaration, and that meanwhile you defer reporting to my royal Chamber sitting at the Arsenal the depositions of Romani and Bertrand.*[16]

Louis was right to be concerned, for a sinister pattern was forming. Marguerite Montvoisin's evidence suggested that whenever Athénaïs feared she was losing Louis's love, she would turn to la Voisin and others for help. She would obtain love powders, which she would then give to Louis, slipping them into his food or drink without his knowledge,[17] but an even more shocking revelation was to come.

Mlle Montvoisin spoke of a certain Abbé Étienne Guibourg, an elderly priest who worked in the slums of Saint-Denis. His speciality was to perform black masses. Whenever a woman came to him for help, he would use her naked body as his altar. Mlle Montvoisin described how the woman would lie down on a mattress, which was supported by two chairs placed close together. Her head, supported by a cushion, would rest on another chair, which was placed slightly lower than the other two, while her legs would hang over the edge of the mattress. A serviette would then be placed on the woman's body, upon which would be arranged a cross and a chalice. Mlle Montvoisin noted that about three years earlier, that is, in 1677 or early 1678, Mme de Montespan had participated in one of Guibourg's black masses, arriving at six in the evening and leaving at midnight. La Voisin then told her that in order to ensure the ritual worked, she ought to participate a further two or three times, but when Athénaïs protested that she did not have the time, la Voisin volunteered to participate in her stead.

It was further alleged that if Athénaïs could not retain Louis's love by these means, she was prepared to take an even more sinister course: she sought to bring about the death of her rival, Mlle de Fontanges, by means of poison-impregnated fabric or gloves.[18]

There is no doubt that Athénaïs visited fortune-tellers before she became Louis's mistress. It was a common practice among the ladies of the court. It is also probably true that she tried to retain Louis's love by slipping him love powders when she felt the need to do so. This, however, was the extent of her commerce with la Voisin and her accomplices. Athénaïs could not have been guilty of the other, terrible crimes of which she had been accused, for several reasons: her piety, which was every bit as deep and sincere as that of Louise de La Vallière, would not permit her to participate in such sacrilegious activities. She loved Louis, who was the father of all but two of her children, upon whom she relied for support and position, and whom she had every reason not to harm. Moreover, prisoners facing death would frequently implicate important people in the hope that the subsequent investigation would buy them more time. Athénaïs would have found it difficult indeed to go anywhere at all, let alone the sleazy slums of Saint-Denis, without several people knowing about it. Following her altercation with Lauzun several years earlier, Athénaïs had become paranoid about her personal safety.[19] She had requested, and received, a bodyguard, who accompanied her everywhere she went.[20] Lastly, la Voisin and Guibourg believed that the lady they had met and carried out black masses for was Athénaïs, but they never saw her face and they could not be sure. Then there is Mlle Montvoisin's assertion that apart from the times that her mother gave powders to Mme de Montespan, la Voisin had only ever had direct dealings with Mlle Desœillets, Athénaïs's personal maid and formerly one of Louis's casual lovers. Mlle Montvoisin identified this lady by her brown hair, but Athénaïs was blond.[21] As to the accusation that Athénaïs had attempted to murder Mlle de Fontanges, once again, Athénaïs's alleged involvement with her death is far from certain, while Mlle Desœillets's part was never fully explained.

Mlle Desœillets, it emerged, had participated in black masses said by Abbé Guibourg. On one occasion, she attended with a foreigner, an English milord who was said to be her lover. She met Guibourg at la Voisin's house, where the ritual was performed using her menstrual blood, the Englishman's semen, some powders, the blood of a bat, and the blood of a child whose throat had been cut.[22] This was then mixed with flour to stiffen the compound. Guibourg then said mass, which he began at the canon, during which he said a conjuration including the name of the king.

The object was to produce a charm or spell against Louis, and it was done on behalf of Desœillets and the English milord. Desœillets spoke with such passion as she made complaints against Louis that the Englishman had to calm her down.

The pair claimed that they put the compound onto Louis's clothes when he passed by, which Desœillets said was easy to do since she spent her time at court. This compound was designed to make Louis die of a languishing illness.[23] With the help of the marquis de Louvois,[24] who was Athénaïs's enemy, Mlle Desœillets managed to escape prosecution for her crimes, which in ordinary circumstances would have earned her the death penalty. Since that time, she had left court and was living comfortably, dividing her time between her house on the rue Montmartre in Paris and her Château de Suisnes in the country.[25]

The Desœillets murder plot was not the only one to be uncovered during the *Affaire des Poisons*. Another conspiracy involved several men who wanted to avenge the ex-superintendent Foucquet, or to liberate him from prison, which necessitated Louis's murder. Of the conspirators, all but two were executed. One died under torture before his case could go to trial, and another was acquitted. He was Roger de Pardaillon de Gondrin, marquis de Termes, a cousin by marriage to Athénaïs, whom Louis went on to employ as a valet of the bedchamber.[26]

Throughout the entire poisons affair, Louis asked to be kept informed of the interrogations and proceedings, but he maintained a dignified silence regarding the murder plots against him. He also remained silent about Mme de Montespan's possible involvement with the plots, as well as her alleged participation in black masses and child sacrifice; she would never be in his favor again, however, and he would move her out of her apartments, which were close to his, and install her in the specially renovated *appartement des bains*, or bath chamber. Even so, his order to La Reynie to continue the reports regarding her on separate sheets of paper testifies to his concern for her and for his own dignity; indeed, he would destroy these records in 1709, two years after Athénaïs's death, burning them with his own hands.[27] Meanwhile, it took some time before Colbert could persuade Louis of Athénaïs's innocence. She had, after all, been his abiding passion for some twelve years, and by her he had fathered seven children. He allowed her to remain at court, but she would never enjoy the favor he had shown her previously, and he did not resume sexual relations with her. Then again, Louis's personal life was about to take an entirely new course.

TWENTY

Mme de Maintenon

I n 1680, Louis was in his forty-second year. He had secured his borders, brought peace to his kingdom, and made himself the master of Europe. He now had time to address some of France's needs, and he began with his capital. Already, he had authorized new paving stones to be laid in the streets of Paris. This achievement was marked by a medal, struck in 1669, which showed a lady standing upon a new pavement, and bearing the legend URBS NOVO LAPIDE STRATA, 'The city of Paris newly paved.'[1] Another, struck the following year, commemorated the embellishment and enlargement of the city. However, Paris had long been menaced by crime perpetrated by professional mendicants.

Some years earlier, the Compagnie du Saint-Sacrement had founded the Hôpital Général, the edict for its establishment being sealed by Louis on April 27, 1656. Spread across five houses—la Salpêtrière, Bicêtre, la Pitié, Scipion, and Chaillot[2]—its purpose was to provide lodgings and work for the vagabonds and beggars whose growing numbers and aggressive tactics caused such a problem in Paris. The beggars would congregate in an area known as the Cour des Miracles in the north of the city. They would simulate wounds and debilitating illness and go out into the streets to extract money out of sympathetic passersby. Upon returning to their own district at night, they would remove their painted-on scabs and deformities—hence the name Cour des Miracles—only to begin the process again the following morning.

Now, several years later, the problem persisted. Louis was obliged to order La Reynie to raid the Cour des Miracles and arrest as many "vagabonds and Bohemians" as he could find. Some were imprisoned, while others were sent to the Hôpital Général. Here, the inmates were forced to do endless hours of hard labor every day, except when they attended compulsory services at the chapel. Those who escaped from the Hôpital Général were sent to an even harsher life in the galleys.[3]

Louis's apparent success in freeing the streets of Paris of mendicants emboldened him to act against France's Gypsy population. Often confused with wanderers and vagrants, Gypsies, or "Bohemians," were persecuted throughout Europe. In July 1682, Louis countersigned a plan drawn up by Colbert to force bailiffs, seneschals, and their lieutenants to arrest gypsy men so they could be sent to the galleys, even if they had not committed a crime. The women, on the other hand, were to have their heads shaved, and, if they refused to give up their lifestyle, they could be beaten and exiled.[4] As with most of Colbert's actions, however, his prime motive was to provide labor for his projects, in this case the galleys.

Louis's recent victories in the Dutch War and Vauban's *ceinture de fer* had rendered the defensive fortifications of Paris obsolete, and work was begun to dismantle them. This released resources that could be used elsewhere, and Louis directed them towards beautifying the city and beginning new and exciting building projects.

One of these projects, a joint collaboration between Louis and Colbert, saw the resumption of work on the Louvre. In 1661, when Louis had taken personal power, Henri IV's Grand Design was some fifty years old and no longer looked quite so impressive. Fresh plans were needed. Colbert invited architects from all over France and Italy to submit ideas for the next phase, a new wing. Initial interest was shown in the designs sent by Gian Lorenzo Bernini, but these were ultimately rejected on the grounds that they took no account of comfort, convenience, and security,[5] although the architect was commissioned to produce a magnificent bust of the Sun King, which was justifiably well received.

In the end, the commission to construct the new wing was awarded to a group of French architects, artists, and theorists, including Louis Le Vau, Charles Le Brun, Charles Perrault, and François d'Orbay. Le Vau also renovated the Tuileries for Louis to use while the Louvre was uninhabitable. However, these works slowed considerably as Louis increasingly turned his attention to Versailles.

Louis lent his support to Colbert's ambition to build an observatory in Paris. Work had begun in 1667 to designs by Claude Perrault.[6] Its four walls were oriented towards the cardinal points of the compass, the southern wall lying along Paris's latitude, while the median plan bisected the Paris meridian, which was calculated in 1667. Many great achievements took place at the observatory: the true dimensions of the solar system would be measured here, and Cassini would discover the rings and satellites of Saturn in the 1670s. Picard, Roberval, and La Hire would be able to present Louis with the first general map of his kingdom. Picard was also a member of the team that measured the size of the earth.[7]

The next project was entirely Louis's own. This was the building of the Hôtel royal des Invalides.[8] Louis was concerned about the care available to soldiers who had been disabled in his wars, and as early as 1670 he announced his intention to build a hostel, financed by monastic revenues, where they could live out the rest of their lives in comfort. The foundation deed for Les Invalides was signed four years later. Now officers and soldiers who had previously been reduced to begging in the streets to survive, or who otherwise would have taken refuge in a monastery, would have a place to live. This hospice would cater for all the worldly needs of its residents, and its administration would be overseen by the minister for war, in this case the marquis de Louvois. There was also a church run by the Lazarists, members of the Congregation of the Mission, which had been founded by Vincent de Paul in 1625 and which was dedicated to preaching to the poor and, by extension, catering for their needs.

At Les Invalides, personal hygiene was paramount; fresh water, bread, meat, and wine were provided, as were latrines complete with seats. The infirmary was run by the Filles de la Charité and accommodated three hundred men, each in his own bed. It was staffed by a doctor, a surgeon, and an apothecary, each of whom had his own team of assistants. A rudimentary system of occupational therapy was also available. In return for the privilege of living at Les Invalides, residents were required to observe strict discipline. While the men were allowed to do small jobs to earn some money, begging was absolutely forbidden and punishable by expulsion. Blasphemy was an even worse crime, and could earn a man a spell in prison.

If Versailles reflects Louis at his most glorious, Les Invalides shows him at his most philanthropic. The king was, in fact, entering a quieter, gentler phase in his life. After the horrors of *l'Affaire des Poisons*, he found comfort in the company of a new lady at court; or rather, he began to see a lady who had been at court for some while in a new light.

Françoise, marquise de Maintenon, was the granddaughter of the poet and Huguenot soldier Théodore Agrippa d'Aubigné. The close friend of Henri de Navarre, the future Henri IV of France and Louis's grandfather, d'Aubigné had fought in the wars of religion that rocked the previous century. Her father, Constant d'Aubigné, was a wastrel who squandered his money and his time on gambling, drinking, and whoring. Having married against his father's wishes, he killed a man in a duel, although this went unpunished. When he abducted a girl to whom his friend had taken a fancy, he received the death penalty. He saved his life by joining the army, but the army he chose was a Huguenot one, which happened to be in open rebellion against the regent, Queen Marie de Médicis. Not for the last time, Constant then switched loyalties and allied himself with Catholic extremists. This led to his being disowned by his horrified father, who branded him a bastard.

Constant discovered his young wife with her lover and murdered them both. This being a crime of passion he again escaped punishment, but his betrayal of the Huguenots at the siege of La Rochelle resulted in his imprisonment at Bordeaux. Here he met Jeanne de Cardilhac, the sixteen-year-old daughter of the prison governor. Stories differ as to what happened next, with some suggesting that he seduced the girl and was forced to marry her, while others insist that they fell in love. Whatever the case, the couple married in December 27, 1627. His prison sentence was quashed, and the penurious Constant made a living as a professional gambler before turning his talents to coining. The couple moved to Niort, a hundred miles north of Bordeaux, where their first child, a son named Constant after his father, was born.

Constant now joined the cause of Gaston d'Orléans, Louis's rebellious uncle, whom he served by recruiting men to the prince's mercenary army. When Gaston's rebellion failed, Constant was once more captured. Held in a succession of prisons, he fathered another son, Charles, and in 1635, a daughter, named Françoise after her godfather, François de La Rochefoucauld. The children's aunt, Madame de Villette, had already taken in the two boys, and now she offered a home to Françoise. Here, the three children were brought up as Huguenots.

Jeanne d'Aubigné went to Paris, where she lived in poverty as she tried to salvage whatever she could of her husband's property.

Françoise, who was nicknamed Bignette, was reunited with her mother at the age of seven or eight, but the cold and distant Jeanne showed her no affection and the child cried for her aunt Villette. Jeanne did not wish her daughter to be raised as a Huguenot, and she forced her to learn the Catholic catechism and attend mass, but she had not reckoned on the girl's strong will. Françoise had to be dragged to the church, and, once inside, she promptly turned her back to the altar. For this she received a sound beating, which she accepted with the remark that "it was a glorious thing to suffer in the cause of religion."[9]

Constant d'Aubigné, meanwhile, was deeply in debt. Out of sheer desperation, he accepted the offer of a post as governor of the Caribbean island of Marie-Galante.[10] Upon approaching Martinique, Françoise was so ill that her family thought she was dead. As they prepared to bury her at sea, her mother, acting on an irresistible impulse, rushed forward to check her pulse once more. She felt a feeble beat and cried, "My daughter is not dead!" Years later, Françoise would be reminded of her lucky escape when, under different circumstances, the bishop of Metz would tell her, "Madame, people are not brought back from that point for nothing."[11]

The d'Aubignés remained in the West Indies for some eighteen months before returning to France. Françoise's brother, Charles, was employed as a page in the home of Madame de Neuillant, a distant relative, and now the lady approached Anne of Austria on Françoise's behalf. She persuaded Anne that a good Catholic girl ought not to be exposed to Calvinist influences. Anne agreed, and Mme de Neuillant was granted the guardianship of Françoise.

Now Françoise spent her days with Mme de Neuillant's daughter, Angélique, and a cousin, Bérénice de Baudean, dressed in peasant clothes and clogs. The three girls were put to work in the farmyard with masks over their noses to protect their delicate skin from the sun. Here, they took care of flocks of turkeys and geese, and forked out hay for the carriage horses, while learning by heart verses from a book.[12] After a while, however, Mme de Neuillant came to realize that the road upon which she had set the young Françoise was not the one she had described to Anne of Austria. Particularly, Françoise was not receiving the promised religious instruction. There was only one remedy, and this was to send the girl to a convent, and the Ursuline convent at Niort was selected.[13]

Here, Françoise became attached to one of the nuns, Mother Celeste. For her sake she would delve into her studies, assist the younger girls with their studies, and even iron their undergarments so that they would look clean and presentable in class. Try as they might, though, the nuns could not make Françoise embrace Catholicism. In the end, they were forced to concede defeat and return her to her mother.

As it was, Jeanne d'Aubigné was still embroiled in lawsuits and had no time for her daughter, who was not yet thirteen. Instead, she sent her to another Ursuline convent, this time in the Faubourg Saint-Jacques in Paris. Life now became very hard for Françoise, who was treated harshly by the nuns. The girl wrote an impassioned plea to her aunt Villette, begging her "to take me away from these people, among whom my life is worse than death. Ah! madame and aunt, you cannot imagine the hell that this so-called house of God is to me."[14] The nuns intercepted the letter, upon which they learned of the despair they had inflicted on the thirteen-year-old. From that point on they treated her with greater kindness. Significantly, she was no longer forced to attend mass or observe feast days. Now that she did not waste her energy fighting such undesired obligations, Françoise began to take an interest in them. During a debate between a Huguenot minister and a Catholic priest, she was impressed by the priest, particularly his knowledge and interpretation of the Bible. Her own familiarity with Scripture was very advanced for one so young, and it was at this point that her interest in Catholicism was awakened. Françoise, however, took time to consider the matter thoroughly before she finally converted; and when she did so, it was only after she had been assured that her aunt Villette would not be condemned for being a Huguenot.[15]

Françoise left the convent to live with her mother in a small room on the rue de Tournelles in Paris. She was rescued from a dull life as a seamstress, working alongside her sullen and unloving mother, when a gentleman who frequented a nearby salon asked Jeanne for information about Martinique, for he was considering travelling there for his health. Jeanne did not wish to receive him in their tiny house, so she went to his rooms, taking Françoise with her. This, then, was how Françoise made the acquaintance of Paul Scarron, the man who was to be her husband.

Paul Scarron was a burlesque poet with a keen mind and even sharper wit. He had contracted rheumatoid arthritis in his youth, which had left him deformed and partially paralyzed but had done nothing to diminish his kind disposition. He noticed the young woman, whose shabby dress was too short, and who looked thoroughly miserable among the fashionable ladies who graced his salon. He immediately offered Françoise a sum of money to help alleviate her obvious poverty, but her refusal was so haughty that it had the opposite effect to the one she had intended, for Scarron took an even greater interest in her. Shortly after this, however, Jeanne returned to Niort, taking Françoise with her. Jeanne's unhappy and difficult life was coming to its end, and she died at Niort, leaving Françoise with no other choice than to return to the care of Mme de Neuillant.

About a year later, Mme de Neuillant arranged for Françoise to be married to Paul Scarron, much to the horror of her friends, who were outraged that the fifteen-year-old should be sacrificed to the middle-aged cripple. Scarron, too, was sensitive to the situation, and he offered Françoise the choice of becoming his wife and nurse, to provide him comfort and care in his old age, or to receive enough money from him to serve as a dowry and allow her to enter a convent of her own choosing. Françoise, although pious and interested in religion, had felt no calling as a nun, and so she chose to be his wife.[16]

Although her husband's physical disabilities ensured that their marriage would never be consummated, Françoise was very happy as Mme

Scarron. It was at his home that she learned many of the skills that would serve her well later in life: learning Latin, Italian, and Spanish, writing to dictation, and the art of being a caring companion to an invalid. This, however, did not mean that she had no life beyond the domestic. She was beautiful, intelligent, and an excellent conversationalist, and the Scarron home was a magnet for the Parisian intellectual elite. So prized was Françoise by Paris society that she was invited to join Henriette of England, the princess Palatine, Cardinal Mazarin, and several ladies of the court on the balcony of the Hôtel d'Aumont to watch as Louis XIV and Marie-Thérèse made their entry into Paris following their marriage. Impressed by Louis, she wrote to a friend, "The Queen must have gone to bed, last night, tolerably well pleased with the husband of her choice."[17] A few weeks after this, Françoise was widowed.

Among the friends Françoise had made at the salons was Athénaïs de Montespan. Athénaïs had already borne Louis a child, the mysterious daughter whose life began and ended in secret. As her reign as favorite continued, it was inevitable that more children would be born to the couple. Over the next two years, she and Marie-Thérèse would present Louis with four sons. Athénaïs, as favorite, would not have time to devote to her children, and they could not live with her at court. She needed someone to take care of them, and she turned to Françoise for help.

Françoise was known for her discretion; she lived away from court and was reliable. She was the perfect choice for governess to a brood of royal children. Before she accepted, she consulted her spiritual advisor, Abbé Gobelin.[18] On his advice she told Athénaïs that if Louis ordered her to take up the post, she would do so. Louis did order her, and he installed his children in a house on the rue des Tournelles in the Marais district.

Françoise's time was not devoted exclusively to Athénaïs's illegitimate children. There was also Toscan, an illegitimate son of her brother, Charles, and Louise, the two-year-old daughter of her friend

Bonne, marquise d'Heudicourt. Marthe-Marguerite,[19] the daughter of Françoise's cousin, Philippe, would eventually join her other charges. As the number of children increased, the need for a larger home became pressing, and Louis purchased a rambling house on the rue Vaugirard.

The need for privacy remained paramount, and Françoise went to a great deal of trouble to prevent others from finding out what was going on behind the high walls that enclosed the house.[20] One visitor to the rue Vaugirard, who arrived under conditions of the utmost secrecy, was Louis, but he came as a father, not as a king, for tragedy had recently touched his life. Three of his legitimate children had died within months of each other. Philippe, who had not yet reached his third birthday; Louis-François, his third son, who was barely four months old; and a daughter, Marie-Thérèse, who had died at the age of five. Stricken by sorrow, Louis found consolation in visiting his two sons in Françoise's care. There was Louis-Auguste, a curly-haired cherub, and Louis-César, not yet a toddler, delightful children who raised his spirits, stirred his heart, and awakened in him a strong paternal sentiment.

Inevitably, Louis encountered Françoise during these visits, but he did not take to her at all. He found this woman, who always dressed modestly[21] in black, prudish, too controlled, and over-intelligent; when speaking of her to Athénaïs, he referred to her as "your learned lady."[22] When Françoise fell victim to a mischief perpetrated by Bonne, her best friend, Louis was unsympathetic. Bonne had written letters to her lover in which she had given away the secret of Françoise's occupation. Françoise's loyalty was such that she refused to believe her friend capable of such wickedness unless she saw the letters for herself. Athénaïs arranged for her to come to court, where she was presented to Louis, who sternly showed her the letters. Françoise had no choice but to break off all contact with Bonne.

Françoise continued to do her duty, to look after the children and do her best to preserve what little secrecy remained, while Louis continued to visit the large house on the rue Vaugirard to see his sons. He was growing closer to them, especially Louis-Auguste, who quickly became his favorite. He was struck by how tenderly Mme Scarron cared for them, as though she had been their loving mother. Gradually, he began to see her in a new light, and his initial aversion turned to admiration. "She knows well how to love," he said; "it would be a pleasure to be loved by her."[23]

Life changed markedly for Françoise when Louis legitimized his children in 1673. Louis-Auguste became duc du Maine, and Louis-César was made comte de Vexin. Françoise was retained as their governess, and the little ménage left the rue Vaugirard and moved into Saint-Germain, where Françoise became an official member of Athénaïs's household. Here, she was greeted with great excitement by her friends, especially Mme de Sévigné. "Mme Scarron sups here every night," she enthused. "It is a pleasure to hear her discuss [any subject]. She dresses in a modest but sumptuous way. She is delightful, beautiful, pleasant, and always quite at her ease."[24] For her part, Françoise received this honor with her customary insouciance, insisting that she would not allow it to go to her head.

One thing particularly concerned Françoise, however, and that was money. Louis had not yet paid her for her services, so she approached him about it. She explained that she wanted the money to buy a small property so she could have somewhere to live in retirement. Louis awarded her a pension of 200 thousand livres,[25] as well as an additional sum of 100 thousand francs. This, combined with 40 thousand francs of her own savings, allowed her to buy the château of Maintenon, which sat in a large estate to the west of Versailles.[26] The property brought with it the title of marquise and gave Françoise the name by which she is best known, Mme de Maintenon.[27]

Françoise clashed repeatedly with Athénaïs over the care of the children. Both the duc du Maine and the comte de Vexin were delicate, which Françoise managed by ensuring they followed a wholesome diet, but Athénaïs insisted upon feeding them unhealthy foods and otherwise interfering in their upbringing. Françoise's distress worsened when the duc du Maine contracted a feverish illness, which left him with one leg shorter than the other. She wanted desperately to continue to care for the boys, but doing so merely increased her love for them, so that shutting herself up with them gave her "a thousand causes for grief and pain."[28] She felt she would die of unhappiness: "There is nothing so silly as to love to excess a child that is not my own," she confided to the Abbé Gobelin.[29]

One day, Louis wished to assess for himself the little duc du Maine's progress. He dismissed his attendants and talked alone with the boy for some time, and the child responded with grace, openness, and respect. When Louis allowed his attendants to return, he told them how delighted he was with his son, adding that he now understood Françoise's influence. He had finally deduced the fine qualities of the "learned lady."[30]

It was Louis's custom to write little notes to Athénaïs when he could not see her. On one occasion she was entertaining guests in her rooms, and Louis asked Françoise to answer a note on Athénaïs's behalf. He could not help but notice the difference between the attitudes of the two women, and from that moment on he preferred to receive notes from Françoise and talk to her at every opportunity. Naturally, this aroused Athénaïs's jealousy. Louis had taken casual mistresses before, of course, but few of them had threatened to replace Athénaïs in the king's affections. This time, it was different. Athénaïs knew she had a rival, and she tried to get rid of her by making an attempt to marry her off to the duc de Villars-Brancas, "a disagreeable and very beggarly man," whom Françoise had not the slightest intention of marrying.[31]

It was about this time that Louis presented Françoise with 100 thousand francs, a significant sum of money, a small portion of which she gave to various convents. In September, he awarded her a thirty-year monopoly on the manufacture of ovens and furnace hearths used in the baking and dyeing trades. The following month, he gave her a total of 200 thousand francs. By the beginning of November 1674, he had taken Françoise as his mistress, but she was little more than just another conquest in a string of conquests, at least at first.[32] As time went by, Louis became increasingly fond of her, while she saw it as her Christian duty to save his soul. For some time, she had hoped that he would leave Athénaïs and return to the queen. "You know what need I have for prayers," she wrote to Abbé Gobelin; "I ask yours again, and that you will pray and get prayers for the King, who is on the edge of a great precipice."[33] The crisis that had occasioned this plea was Louis's affair with Mlle de Fontanges.

Louis was touched that Françoise took such an interest in him and that she was so concerned for his welfare. One day, when Mlle de Fontanges was being difficult and was threatening to create a scandal, he asked Françoise to have a quiet word with his fractious mistress. Françoise took the opportunity to try to persuade the new young favorite, "by every possible argument, but with great respect and judgment," to break with the king.[34] Mlle de Fontanges paid her the courtesy of hearing her out, but Françoise was asking too much. At length, the young beauty interrupted her. "But, madame," she cried, "you advise me to throw off a passion, as one speaks of throwing off a costume."[35] Needless to say, she maintained her place in Louis's heart.

The arrival at court of the new dauphine, Marie-Anne, solved a dilemma that been exercising Louis for some time. The elder of the children that Athénaïs had borne him had left Françoise's care and were now being taught by male tutors, while the younger ones were being cared for by a new governess on the rue Vaugirard. This left Françoise without an official position and there was no reason for her to remain at court. Louis, however, was reluctant to let her go. Now the perfect solution presented itself: he would appoint her second lady-in-waiting to the new dauphine.[36]

Louis was thrilled to be thrown into Françoise's company once again. With Mlle de Fontanges increasingly unwell following her miscarriage and Athénaïs becoming more fractious by the day, Louis sought refuge with Françoise, and by January 1680 they were lovers once again.[37] "No one, without exception, is more agreeable to the king than Madame de Maintenon," noted Bussy-Rabutin.[38] Mme de Sévigné agreed: "They speak in whispers, calling Madame de Maintenon, Madame de Maintenant; 'Madame *Now*,' who 'spends each evening between eight and ten with Louis, escorted to and from his apartments by M. de Chamarante, in front of the whole world.'"[39]

There was, however, some mystery as to the true nature of their relationship, as detailed by Primi Visconti, who wrote that Louis "spent most of his time with Madame de Maintenon, to the detriment of Madame de Montespan and Mademoiselle de Fontanges, and although she was old, nobody knew what to think about it. Some people believed her to be the King's confidante, others regarded her as a go-between, or a clever woman of whom he made use to write his *Mémoires*."[40] One thing Mme de Sévigné was sure of, however, was that "Mme de Maintenon showed the King an entirely new world, previously unknown to him; the enjoyment of friendship and conversation without constraint, without petty quarrels, and Louis found it charming."[41]

Louis's long conversations with Françoise awakened in him the realization that he should abandon his irreligious life. His devotion, which had always been deep and genuine, but which had languished under a bushel for so many years, began to emerge once again. He took instruction from Père Bourdaloue, Bossuet, and others, and paid close attention to their sermons. Françoise placed much of the blame for Louis's straying onto the queen. As she wrote to the Abbé Gobelin, "If the Queen had a director like you, there would be no good that one might not hope from the union of the royal family." Instead, the queen's spiritual director "leads her by ways (to my mind) fitter for a Carmelite nun than a queen."[42]

Françoise used her influence with Louis to persuade him to go back to the queen. Her gentle words, as well as his belated return to a Christian life, led to a reconciliation that delighted Marie-Thérèse. She had never been happier. She told everyone that Mme de

JOSEPHINE WILKINSON

Maintenon had been raised up by God to be her friend and support, and she attributed the restoration of Louis's friendship wholly to her good offices.[43] Yet, however pleased she was to receive Louis's undivided attention once more, her happiness was tinged with sadness, even fear, for she remained in awe of the king. Particularly, Marie-Thérèse, who had never fully mastered the French language, feared that she would be unable to hold her side in conversation with him. On one occasion, as she sat waiting to visit him in his apartments, she turned to Françoise and explained that she did not wish to be alone with the king, and asked if she would accompany her. Françoise obliged, but as they approached the door to Louis's chamber, she shoved the trembling queen inside[44] and shut the door on her.

Louis, the First Son of the Church and the Most Christian King, had embraced, albeit belatedly, the commandment Thou shalt not commit adultery. His devotion, however, stopped short of his allowing outside interference in the Gallican Church. Already he had been at odds with the pope over the issue of the *régale*, a conflict that had rumbled on for several years.[45] In 1673 and again in 1675, he had extended the *régale* to the whole of France, a move that was ignored by the then pope, Clement X. Two Augustinian bishops in the south, Pavillon, bishop of Alet, and Caulet, bishop of Pamiers, also refused to accept the extension of the king's regalian rights, going as far as to excommunicate clerics whom Louis had appointed. Another who opposed this measure was Innocent XI.[46]

With the dispute still unresolved, the Assembly of the Clergy assured the king of their continued attachment to him, which they declared to be so strong that nothing could tear them asunder. Their stance was tested shortly thereafter, following the death of one of the pope's staunchest supporters against Louis, the bishop of Pamiers, and the subsequent excommunication of the *vicar-général* appointed by the archbishop of Toulouse. This sequence of events brought Louis into a renewed conflict with the pope, and he needed all the support he could muster.[47]

284

The clergy rose to the occasion, and in March 1682, the Assemblée Générale drew up a set of four articles.[48] The first asserted that royal power was not subject to church control, the church could not depose princes, nor could it release their subjects from their oath of fidelity to their sovereign. The second affirmed the superiority of the Ecumenical Council over the pope. The third acknowledged the pope as the head of the church, but his authority was constrained by its laws and he was obliged to respect the privilege of national churches. The fourth accepted the pope's supremacy in areas of church doctrine, but it agreed that he was not infallible and his judgments were subject to reform until they received the consent of the church.

Innocent XI, who had succeeded Clement X in 1676, showed these articles the contempt he felt they deserved, and the following year he ordered all the bishops who had signed them to send him a written apology expressing their sorrow and anger about their publication.[49] The Four Articles, however, were not drafted by Louis but were produced by Bishop Bossuet working in collaboration with Archbishop Le Tellier of Reims. They took the matter of Louis's dispute over the *régale* to an extreme even Louis would not have wished. Nevertheless, the saber had been brandished and the supremacy of the Gallican Church had been asserted, but Louis's next foray into religious affairs would be even more far-reaching, and the consequences for France would be devastating. Before that, however, Louis would experience the happiness of seeing one of his most cherished dreams come to fruition.

TWENTY-ONE

Versailles

The Versailles of Louis XIV had begun as a dream. In the springtime of his youth, he had planned the château and its sprawling gardens as an expression of his love for Louise de La Vallière. Now the dream had become a reality. The château lay before him, a magnificent symbol of his power and glory. Beyond it, the gardens stretched out as far as the eye could see. It was late spring. The flowers were blooming, and the trees had taken on their mantles of green. The air was pleasantly warm, and a cooling breeze gently swept across the empty courtyard.

Louis had arrived amid great ceremony, but it was not Louise at his side; it was the queen, Marie-Thérèse. Philippe and Liselotte followed, and ranged behind them were the princes of the blood, courtiers, ministers, and an army of servants. All eyes gazed at Louis's creation, overawed by its grandeur. All were familiar with Versailles; they had been there countless times, passed endless days and nights in lavish entertainments, but this time it was different. This was no ordinary visit. As the wide, golden central gate slowly opened, Louis and Marie-Thérèse advanced into the courtyard, while the rest of the family and the court made their way through the smaller gates on either side. From now on, Versailles was to be Louis's home, the seat of the royal family and the center of government. It was May 6, 1682, and the Sun King had taken possession of his new palace.

Versailles, or what there was of it, scarcely merited such a stately entrance. Many of the buildings were obscured by scaffolding. Work had barely begun on the north wing, although the south wing was habitable. The western façade was completed, but the space within was a clutter of scaffolding and tables covered with drawings, brushes, and paint. The smell of fresh paint and gilding was overpowering, while the chambers, corridors, and staircases were filled with masons;[1] the sound of their constant hammering could disturb the serenity of even the most forbearing of people. In the gardens too there was still much work to be done, but there were splendors, hints of the marvels to come. The walls and ceiling of the Grand Staircase, which would become known as the *escalier des ambassadeurs* because Louis would greet foreign ambassadors here, were decorated with images from antiquity, especially chosen to portray Louis in all his glory.

Louis was impatient to see his dream fulfilled, and for this reason he moved the court into the château in a bid to expedite the work. For those with eyes to see and the vision to imagine, however, Versailles was essentially realized; it stood on the threshold of being.

The ladies and gentlemen of the court made the best of a difficult situation. It was not pleasant to live in what was effectively a building site, but it was a court after all and they were courtiers. The ladies wore brightly colored dresses in silk or brocade over white chemises, which fell from the shoulders to reveal a pure décolleté adorned with jewels. Pearls were still popular, worn as necklaces and decorating the hair. In the summer, the ladies carried fans of lace, while furred muffs kept their hands warm in wintertime. The gentlemen followed Louis's example and wore long brocade coats, left open to show off an elaborately embroidered waistcoat or a pure white shirt of silk or lawn beneath. A flourish of ribbons, now back in vogue, fastened cravats, ornamented one shoulder, and adorned sword hilts, lace cuffs, and feathered hats. Shoes were square-toed with high red heels and decorated with large bows. Perruques were routinely worn now, framing the face and flowing in luxurious curls to the waist. The courtiers experimented with color, and perruques of all shades were seen, though Louis favored black.

The court had barely settled into Versailles when the king's happiness was crowned with a new addition to the royal family. The dauphine, who was seven months pregnant when she moved to her new home, felt her first contractions at the beginning of August, but she had told only the queen. Now, two days later, there was no chance of concealing the fact that her baby was on its way. Louis had already appointed an accoucheur, the same Clément who had delivered the duc du Maine, and he trusted him completely.

As Versailles bustled with excited ministers, ambassadors, foreign leaders, secretaries, servants, and subjects, only Louis remained calm enough to go to bed that night.[2] Nevertheless, even he had to be alerted to the imminent birth, and at five the following morning, some brave soul was sent to rouse him. The king asked if his presence was needed immediately, and upon being assured that it was not, he calmly went to mass before making his way to his daughter-in-law's chamber. Inside, the crowds pressed on all sides, and Louis was obliged to push his way in. He fed the dauphine chicken broth with his own hand, all the while offering words of comfort and encouragement. Marie-Thérèse, who also attended, sent orders for the relics of Sainte-Marguerite to be exposed in the chamber, a privilege usually reserved for the accouchements of the queens of France.

The dauphine's pains continued into the next day, when a birthing chair was brought in readiness, but with still no sign of the baby, Louis left to go to dinner. He returned to the dauphine's chamber and remained with her throughout the night. However, the dawn brought with it no change, and Marie-Anne began to despair. She told Louis that it was unfortunate for her to have known so good a prince, and to have had so good a father and so good a husband, to leave them so soon."[3] Louis tenderly replied that "he would be content if she had a girl, provided she suffered less and that she was soon delivered."[4]

The anxious faces burst into smiles when, at last, the cry of the newborn baby was heard. Louis had prearranged a special code with Clément: he would ask if the child was a boy or a girl, upon which Clément would reply "I do not know" for a girl, or "I do not know yet" for a boy. When the moment they had all been waiting for arrived, Louis duly asked the sex of the child. Clément replied that he did not know yet, but his tone and the glint in his eye gave the game away. Louis wanted to be the first to announce the birth of his grandson, the first of a new generation of Bourbon princes. He turned to the waiting crowd and told them that a new duc de Bourgogne had been born. He then left the chamber and began to make his way through the throng of courtiers, who threw themselves at his feet, kissed his hands, and even tried to embrace him. With a son and a grandson, the Bourbon line was doubly secure.[5]

Marie-Thérèse had also found happiness at last, although for her it was tinged with loneliness. She shared the court's love of gambling and joined courtiers at the various tables in the salons. Her favorite game was *hombre*, although she was not very good at it and she frequently lost. After a few games, she would withdraw to her room, where she would shut herself up with a few favored ladies and pray silently at her small altar. Her inability to master the French language and her lack of wit were insurmountable barriers to her ever being able to form a court of her own, as Louis had encouraged her to do when they were first married. The king spent his days with his ministers, courtiers, and his mistresses, yet he would always return to the queen's bed every night no matter how late the hour, though he came out of duty, not love, and Marie-Thérèse, who had seen six of her seven children die, had little but her rigid Spanish Catholicism to console her.[6]

In May 1683, Louis, the queen, the dauphine, Philippe, and Liselotte, followed by a large entourage, travelled to Franche-Comté and Alsace to inspect the fortifications. It was a long journey, and upon their return to Versailles, it was obvious that the queen was not well. She had developed an abscess under her left arm, which the physicians treated by bleeding her. Naturally, the only effect this had was to weaken the queen still further. Louis was the first to realize that she was not going to recover. He rushed to the chapel and ordered the altar candles and the sacred heart to be taken to her bedroom. Here, the queen received the last sacraments "with exemplary resignation,"[7] while Louis followed the sad ceremony with great devotion. Marie-Thérèse died on July 30 after only four days of illness. Louis tearfully noted, "This is the first grief she has ever caused me,"[8] but Liselotte, who had loved the queen and was deeply distressed by her death, had much more to say. "Her death is entirely due to the ignorance of the doctors, who killed her as surely as if they had pierced her heart with a sword,"[9] she wrote. In another letter, she related a tragic comment uttered by the queen: "Marie-Thérèse said on her deathbed that in all her life since she became Queen she had had only one really happy day."[10]

Françoise, who had attended Marie-Thérèse throughout her short illness, turned to withdraw to her own apartments. However, the duc de La Rochefoucauld stopped her and drew her attention to the grieving king: "This is not the time to leave him, Madame," he said. "In the state he is in now, he really wants you."[11] Louis, despite the almost offhand words he had spoken following the death of his wife and queen, was affected by her loss, but his grief was short-lived. Nevertheless, he could never bear to remain in a place where someone close to him had died, so, as he had done following the deaths of Mazarin and his mother, he made arrangements to leave Versailles for a while. This was the first sadness to be associated with his glittering château, but it would not be the last. He then travelled to Saint-Cloud, where he spent a few days before moving on to Fontainebleau, which would be his home for much of the rest of the summer.

The sorrow was not yet over for Louis, however. Colbert was finally succumbing to the pressures of working for so demanding a master. For almost a quarter of a century, the minister had served Louis well. Apart from reforming the fiscal system, he had also improved the postal service and the roads, and he was the driving force behind the Canal du Midi, a remarkable civil engineering project that linked France's Atlantic coast with the Mediterranean. He regulated manufacturing and commerce,[12] and renovated France's navy. Now, overburdened, his initial enthusiasm and love for his office had gone; the pleasant, open demeanor he showed his colleagues gave way to depression and irascibility. He constantly fretted about finding Louis the increasing amounts of money he needed for Versailles, military earthworks, and other buildings projects. He worried about the deepening poverty of Louis's subjects, for which he would carry the blame.[13] Louis, it seemed, could never be satisfied. Even as he toured his latest fortifications or conducted sieges, he was always thinking about his beloved Versailles; his most recent tour was no exception, and he wrote to Colbert ordering him to hurry the work because he might have to shorten his journey by a few days.[14]

Colbert, however, was now seriously ill, and it was left to his son, the marquis de Seignelay, to organize the queen's obsequies and take care of her debts. Seignelay kept the king informed of his father's progress, while Louis sent sympathetic letters in which he expressed the hope that God would not take from the world he who was so necessary to the welfare of the state. He spoke of his friendship for his minister,[15] but in truth, their relationship had never been anything more than master and servant. Louis certainly respected Colbert, even though the minister did not always agree with royal policy, and when Colbert died on September 6, 1683, Louis sent a letter of sincere condolence to his widow. She had lost a husband who was dear to her, he wrote, while he had lost a minister with whom he was fully satisfied.[16]

Colbert had achieved much during his lifetime in Louis's service. Following the arrest of Foucquet at the very start of Louis's personal reign, he had seized and developed the overseas trade Foucquet had initiated. He fostered commerce by encouraging shipbuilding and imposing taxes on foreign ships entering French ports. Colbert both hated and admired the Dutch, and he adopted many of their business practices as he organized overseas companies, but his heavy-handed approach and insistence upon directing affairs from Paris antagonized local officials, especially in Marseilles, who preferred to carry on their businesses as they saw fit. As a result, the most successful companies were those that traded privately.

The most productive of Colbert's enterprises was the East India Company, which he founded in 1664 and which would outlast the reign of Louis XIV. The Levant Company, founded five years later, lacked investment and clashed with the Chamber of Commerce of Marseilles, which traded with Turkey with greater success.

Offshore, the French population of the West Indies was growing, but Colbert interfered with trade in a bid to rival the Dutch, and his approach merely annoyed the settlers and proved detrimental to their businesses. The situation was better in Canada, however. Still known as New France at this stage, it was administered as any other French province was, with a governor and an intendant. Further south, Père Jacques Marquette and a fur trader named Louis Joliet discovered the Mississippi in 1669–70. Shortly afterwards, La Salle[17] opened up the Mississippi basin as far as the Gulf of Mexico. He sailed the river to its mouth and named it "Colbert" in recognition of the assistance he had received from the minister. Three years later, the region would be named La Louisiane in honor of Louis XIV, who nevertheless showed little interest in France's overseas enterprise.[18]

Following his death, Colbert's offices were largely taken over by Louvois, except the one that he had really coveted, that of the navy, which went to Colbert's capable son, the marquis de Seignelay.

Colbert's death occurred while Louis was recovering from an accident. He had been riding in the forest of Fontainebleau, and a fall from his horse had left him with a painful dislocated left elbow. The first course of treatment was, of course, to bleed him, but "the cruel vapors that this remedy aroused in the king" prevented his physicians from prescribing it. Instead, it was decided that Louis should go on a special diet, which was expected to produce the same effects as bleeding. He would abstain entirely from eating meat, and he drank almost no wine, a regime he would observe for four or five days. The swelling on his arm was treated with an embrocation made of oil of roses and egg yolks mixed with vinegar and plantain water. On the sixth day, the bruise came up and the inflammation began to cease, at which point the embrocation was stopped and the arm was wrapped each morning and evening in a poultice of strong wine in which had been boiled balustine, myrtle berries, and leaves of wormwood. Next Louis was purged with ordinary bouillon, which produced a satisfying quantity of phlegm and bile. Finally, now that the threat of inflammation and gangrene had been removed, the arm was placed into a plaster of wax and resin, which supported it while the strength and flexibility returned, putting the arm well on the road to recovery.[19]

Even when they were not worried about his health, the eyes of the court were firmly fixed on Louis. Always the topic of conversation, people wondered whether or not he would remarry. "To tell the truth," wrote Liselotte, "I believe that he will do so."[20] As it was, Louis had already made up his mind that he would take a second wife. In fact, he had already chosen her. It was while the court was at Fontainebleau that he began to show increasing favor to Françoise, and his attention caused her to "change the course of her life."[21] Louis had decided that he would marry Françoise.

Before he took such an important step, however, Louis wished to test the opinion of his ministers, and he approached Louvois "as though the thing had not yet been decided." Louvois thought it was an appalling idea: "Ah! Sire!" he cried, "Has Your Majesty seriously considered this? The greatest King in the world, covered in glory, to marry the Widow Scarron: do you wish to be dishonored?" He then realized that he had perhaps gone too far, and he threw himself at Louis's feet, tears streaming down his face, begging Louis to forgive him for the liberties he had taken. He urged Louis to punish him by relieving him of all his offices and casting him into prison. Louis ordered him to get up: "Are you mad?" he demanded before turning on his heel and walking away from the grovelling minister.[22]

When Louis made known to Françoise his intention to marry her, his proposal—or was it a command?—threw her into turmoil. She was filled with uncertainty over her thoughts, her fears, and her hopes. "Her heart was not free," wrote Mme de Caylus, "and her mind was very troubled. In order to excuse her obvious distress, and the tears she freely wept, she complained of the vapors." She spent a lot of time walking in the forest of Fontainebleau with a friend and, when she returned, she appeared to have recovered her composure.[23]

In her confusion, she turned to her confessor, Abbé Gobelin, for advice. He told her, "Do not think of your own feelings, madame, think of your duty to the King and his happiness; and of the great opportunity to which God calls you."[24] The opportunity of which he spoke was for her to accomplish her cherished ambition to lead Louis to salvation. A palpable change now came over Françoise. While once she had hated the court and actively looked for an opportunity to leave it for good, she now saw it as her duty to remain.[25] Louis, meanwhile, moved her into the queen's old apartment at Fontainebleau.[26]

Shortly afterwards, a small group of people—the archbishop of Paris; Père de La Chaise; Alexandre Bontemps, Louis's premier *valet de chambre* and confidant; the marquise de Montchevreuil, Françoise's close friend, and her husband; and one of Françoise's *femmes de chambre*—gathered in the chapel at Versailles. It was dark outside, for the midnight hour was about to strike. Louis then entered, as did Françoise. Vows were exchanged, prayers were said and the blessing given, and Louis and Françoise were pronounced husband and wife.

The marriage was secret because there was no need to make it public;[27] Louis had taken a wife, not a queen. It was not such an extraordinary decision, as morganatic marriages were not uncommon in that day and age. Louis's decision might have been influenced by his council,[28] but it could just as easily have been his own wish, for which he had several reasons. First, he saw no need to found a second royal family. He already had a son and one grandson, while the dauphine was well into her second pregnancy and, indeed, would produce a second son on December 19. Another factor was Louis's past experience. He had grown up amid the turmoil and disorder that could be caused by overambitious family members, and he had no inclination to inflict such horrors on his own son and his family. Françoise, at forty-eight, was too old to produce children, so this danger was removed. Moreover, she was not of royal blood, and so could not be queen.[29]

These were, of course, public or dynastic reasons for not taking another queen, but Louis also had his private reasons. The sudden death of Marie-Thérèse had come as a shock to Louis. He and she were the same age, and if God could take her, why not him? He felt the need to look to his own salvation. A private marriage to a woman of his own choosing would remove from him the temptations to which he had yielded in his youth, and which had endangered his soul. His second marriage, therefore, was not a public affair, it was not registered, and it conferred no official position upon his wife.[30] There would be no Queen Françoise. Indeed, "The only public distinction that discovered her private elevation was, that at mass she occupied one of those little pulpits, or gilded canopies, which seemed to be made for the king and queen."[31] That there would be no queen was confirmed the following year when the queen's official apartments at Versailles were broken up, with much of the space being incorporated into Louis's own apartments.

For both Louis and Françoise, this second marriage followed a less than satisfactory first union. It was to bring happiness, or rather contentment, to both. Louis showed Françoise the respect that was her due, although his courteous manner towards her occasionally bordered on formality. He addressed her as Madame, but he gave her other names too, names that reflected the qualities he saw in her: Reason and Your Solidity.

Louis confessed his love for Françoise: "However much you say you love me, my love for you will always be greater,"[32] and there is no reason not to believe that his sentiment was anything but sincere. Françoise herself believed that the king loved her, "but only so far as he is capable of loving; for if they are not led by passion, men are not very tender in their affection."[33] Perhaps the burning passions that tortured Louis as a young man had mellowed, but Françoise surely had not recognized that Louis's emotions were as still waters: apparently calm on the surface, yet running very deeply.

Whenever they were apart, Louis would leave small notes for Françoise, requesting her company for a walk or hoping for a private meeting, leaving her to decide the time and the place.[34] He would visit her at all hours of the day, attending to his letters and dispatches, and he would read aloud the odd passage and ask her opinion on it. He would linger after supper or when a gambling party left for the night, and Françoise found his constant companionship quite exhausting at times. Her secretary, the demoiselle d'Aumale, often found her mistress tired, anxious, or even ill from the strain of keeping Louis entertained with "numberless little inventions and interests," not to mention their conversations that went on for three or four hours at a time, and the effort it cost her to maintain them. When Louis finally left her apartment at ten in the evening, Françoise was overcome with weariness, and had "only time to say" that she was "quite worn out."[35]

While Louis would make frequent and lengthy visits to Françoise's apartment, she would never go to his unless he was unwell and in need of her care. One day, as Françoise was attending him, Philippe unexpectedly entered the room to find Louis relaxing uncovered on his bed. "You see me in this state and, therefore, you can imagine what she means to me," he told his brother.[36] But what exactly did she mean to him? It is perhaps best summed up this way: "At all times she was a friend ready to listen, a wife prompt to sympathize, a servant quick to do everything for his comfort, and, above all, a counsellor full of wisdom and resource, suggesting or upholding the right course to take, but without pretension or show of superiority."[37]

Being married did nothing to alter the rigidity with which the king's life was regulated. He would still rise between eight and nine each morning to begin his day with the all-important *lever*. Steeped in ceremony, the *lever* was how Louis prepared for the coming day. Certain privileged courtiers would be granted the right of entry to watch as Louis said his morning prayers, was washed, shaved, and dressed. Specially selected courtiers would be designated to hand Louis his shirt, to attach his lace cuffs, or to put on one shoe while another put on the second.

Louis then went to mass, and by nine thirty he would be shut away with one of his councils in a meeting that would go on for some three hours at a time. The king had a great capacity for work, and the different councils would meet on designated days.[38] Sunday was the day of the Conseil d'État, at which the most important business of the state was discussed and major decisions made. Louis maintained the practice of consulting his ministers, allowing each of them to express his views before making up his own mind, which nearly always reflected the majority opinion. The Conseil d'État also met every second Monday, alternating its sittings with the Conseil des despatches, which dealt with the correspondence that passed between the government and the intendants who administered local government in cities and the provinces. Tuesdays were reserved for the royal council of finances, which had replaced the old surintendance des finances. Wednesdays and Thursdays were taken up with the Conseil d'État once again, while Fridays were set aside for the Conseil des consciences. Concerned with ecclesiastical affairs, particularly benefices, the Conseil des consciences, which went back to Mazarin's time, was not strictly speaking a royal council, but Louis continued to maintain it. The royal council of finances held a second meeting each Saturday, which rounded off the formal business of the week.

The councils ended about twelve thirty, at which point Louis would alert the dauphine that he was ready to go to mass. The mass, at which "there was excellent music"[39] and to which he was accompanied by the entire royal household, was an important part of Louis's day and he would never miss it. When he emerged, after about an hour or an hour and a half, he would join the dauphine in her apartments and remain with her during dinner, which was served by the gentlemen of the chamber. Louis's afternoons were then spent at work, or occasionally he would go out for some exercise.

As evening fell, Louis might entertain the court at an *appartement*, a word that had recently been coined to describe a reception, a party, or celebration hosted by the king. It was held in his own apartments, in sumptuously furnished rooms. He had held *appartements* occasionally since 1674, but since the court had moved permanently to Versailles, they had become more frequent and were regularly held on Tuesdays, Thursdays, and Saturdays. At this period, they were still quite innovative, and a medal was struck in 1683 to commemorate them.[40] The legend explained that

> *The King, in order to increase the pleasure of the Court, wished for his Appartements to be opened on certain days of the week. There were large rooms for dancing, games, music. There were others where one would find all sorts of refreshments in abundance, and where one could take pleasure and enjoyment in the presence of so great a King and so good a Master.*

The medal bore the image of a Muse with a lyre to symbolize music, Pomona with a basket of fruit to represent the refreshments that were served, while Mercury presided over the games. The legend read COMITAS ET MAGNIFICENTIA PRINCIPIS, 'signifying the affability and the magnificence of the Prince' and 'the Palace of the King open to the pleasure of His subjects.'

On those days when an *appartement* was held, the salons would open at about seven in the evening. One of Louis's favorite games was billiards, which he would often play until nine o'clock with the comte d'Armagnac, Gramont, or Michel Chamillart of the Paris parlement. As soon as his game was finished, he would withdraw to Françoise's apartments until suppertime, after which there would be a ball to round off the night. The final ceremony was, of course, the *coucher*, in which Louis was prepared for bed watched by those privileged enough to be allowed to witness such an intimate ceremony. As with the *lever*, favored courtiers were selected to hand Louis his nightshirt or hold the candle. It was all highly ritualized, and it brought an ordered end to a much organized day.

The events that took place at Versailles followed a rigid timetable, which was planned months in advance, but life at court was also regulated. "The King was so fond of the old customs of the Royal Household," wrote Liselotte,

> that nothing would have induced him to change any of them. Madame de Fiennes used to say that in the Royal Household they stuck so closely to these old customs and usages that the Queen of England died with a toquet on her head, that is a little bonnet which babies wear when they are put to bed . . . When the King desires anything he would allow no one to reason with him. His orders must be obeyed immediately and without question. He was too much accustomed to 'such is our pleasure' to suffer any suggestions. He was very particular about the etiquette he had established in his household. [41]

Everyone, from the grandest courtier to the humblest servant, observed a strict hierarchy of rank. For the royal family, this was set down in the *Ceremonial*, a large volume that would increase still further in size as the years drew on and the protocols laid down within its pages became more complex. In 1682, prompted by the birth of the duc de Bourgogne, the first of Louis's grandchildren, a new rank was added. The king naturally continued to take precedence, followed by the dauphin, but now came the *petit-fils de France*, the king's grandson, who went before the princes of the blood.[42]

As to the nobility, Louis had accustomed them to accept that their raison d'être was to serve the state, rather than to lead their own lives on their faraway estates. Like moths to a flame, they were attracted to the beauty and grandeur of Versailles and the glamor of life in the presence of the Sun King. On the whole, they came to prefer life at Versailles to the point that they often neglected their own estates and rarely, if ever, saw their tenants. Louis, who was anxious to avoid the conditions that might lead to a new Fronde, used protocol and rank to control and monitor them. It was a system he had used at the Louvre and Saint-Germain, and one that he would continue to use at Versailles.[43] Indeed, Versailles has been described as Louis's revenge for the Fronde,[44] although this is not an entirely fair assessment, given that many leading frondeurs, such as Condé and Turenne, fought valiantly in Louis's wars, with Turenne losing his life for his king. On the other hand, the number of aristocrats who lived at court was relatively low. By the end of Louis's reign, some ten thousand people served at Versailles, of whom five thousand were commoners. The other five thousand were nobles who served in two "quarters," or three-month sessions of service twice a year. In all, the nobility at Versailles comprised only some 5 percent of the entire aristocracy of France.[45]

It is important to note, however, that even the preened and beribboned nobles who served in the king's household were soldiers before they were anything else. While, during the winter months, they gambled, duelled, danced, and attended the king's *lever, coucher,* and *appartement*, once the weather turned, they would be back with their regiments risking their lives for the glory of France. This is why Versailles itself must be seen as more than a gilded royal palace and the seat of government. It must also be understood as an extension of Vauban's *ceinture de fer*, the ring of fortifications that protected France's borders. It was an integral part of Louis's pursuit of power and security for France by war and building.[46] It is no coincidence that Versailles was largely built by soldiers who had also worked on France's fortifications, or that it housed the headquarters of the armed forces.[47]

At Versailles, therefore, the soldier-courtier fulfilled a second function, which was to serve the king in a variety of roles: a master of the wardrobe, perhaps, or a gentleman of the chamber.[48] Discipline was imposed upon them through court ritual as well as art.[49] The greatest sin any courtier could commit was to be absent from court. Even in his youth, Louis would take note of those who absented themselves from his presence,[50] and he would continue to do so. He was instantly aware of who was missing from the crowds that lined the corridors or graced the chambers of Versailles. No excuse was acceptable, and any courtier noted by his absence from courtly entertainments and ballets, or who missed a turn in the gardens, would be scorned with the words "we never see him," the sentence of social death.[51] Given the dual role of the courtier as both soldier and servant, absence could be seen as a form of desertion.

Louis therefore entrapped his nobility within a gilded cage and controlled them with court ceremonial. The ritual that governed life at court, however, did not begin with Louis: it was already elaborate by the time of Henri III over a hundred years earlier, but Louis raised it to new heights, especially upon his relocation to Versailles. Like many who had experienced disorder in their youth, Louis liked regulation, and ceremonial gave him that. It also grounded courtiers in the king's service and in the hierarchy of rank. It ensured that they were too busy to indulge in their personal cabals and intrigues; especially, it prevented them from forming dangerous conspiracies against the king. For the commoner, royal service brought privileges that would otherwise be unavailable to them, elevating them to a level above their lowly status, even if they would never be equal to the aristocracy. In this way, Louis, the sun surrounded by his satellites, watched and controlled those who might rebel against him, while rewarding those whose loyalty was beyond reproach. Versailles was a place of ceremony, service, and discipline, all attributes of the military headquarters that categorized it and justified its existence.

TWENTY-TWO

The Sun Reaches Its Zenith

etween 1679 and 1684, a series of courts were held. Known
as *chambres de réunions*, they sought to establish Louis's
claims regarding the territories he had acquired under the
Treaty of Westphalia in 1648.[1] As with most treaties, Westphalia was
vaguely worded and open to more than one interpretation. The lawyers
Louis sent to the *réunions*, all of whom were French, naturally found
in his favor, with the result that much of the territory between the
Moselle and Rhine, including a large part of Alsace and Luxembourg,
was acknowledged as French. Louis thus had secured large tracts of
economically and strategically important land. The legal foundation
for this had been arranged by Colbert de Croissy, the capable younger

brother of Colbert, while the acquisitions were fortified by Vauban, whose line of fortresses stretched from the Netherlands to Alsace.[2]

Louis's gains, confirmed by the *chambres de réunions*, alienated his former allies, the German princes and the kings of Spain and Sweden. This, however, had not checked his policy of aggrandizement, and he set his sights upon Strasbourg, a free city within the Holy Roman Empire. Louis had no legal claim to the town, but it held a strategic position on the Rhine, and in September 1681, it capitulated under relentless pressure from the royal forces. A new medal was designed with an image of the fortifications Vauban had built surrounding the city and bearing the legend CLAUSA GERMANIS GALLIA, 'France is closed to the Germans."[3]

The following month, Louis and Marie-Thérèse arrived at Strasbourg with the court, and, to music written for the occasion by Lully the king was greeted by his new subjects. However, Louis had even more to celebrate: on the same day that Strasbourg fell, he also obtained Casale, the capital of Monferrat. Casale was one of the major gateways into Italy, and Louis's possession of it checked potential aggression from the duc de Savoy; the duke, who was one of Louis's allies, was offended by the acquisition.[4]

Louis then made his way to Luxembourg, where he laid siege to the town. It was at this point that he received news that Pope Innocent was calling for a new Crusade to assist Emperor Leopold, who was struggling to save Vienna, which was under siege by the Turks. Louis halted his assault on Luxembourg while he considered his options.[5] He was aware that his predecessors, François I and Henri II, had pursued policies of alliance with the Turks, but at the dawn of his own personal rule, such an approach had come to be seen as undesirable. Even so, Louis found himself torn between two opposing views. From a religious perspective, as the Most Christian King, any association with a Muslim power was repugnant to him. Moreover, there was something very attractive about the prospect of attacking the Turks in order to further Christian cohesion in Europe. As a politician, Louis saw that any cooperation with the Turks, however loose, could assist him with his plans for aggrandizement. He was aware, also, that earlier alliances between the French and the Turks had largely been successful. It could not be denied that Louis would benefit from the Turkish invasion of Austria, which would keep the emperor occupied for some time to come. Therefore, even though his fleets were already engaged in a campaign against the North African states in the Mediterranean,[6] Louis decided to ignore Innocent's plea, proclaiming that Crusades "were no longer in fashion."[7]

Spain, meanwhile, had taken advantage of Louis's temporary suspension of the siege of Luxembourg to declare war on France. As he returned to the siege, Louis found himself confronted by Carlos II. The sickly child had grown into a sickly man who suffered fits, was feeble-minded, and whose only real strength lay in his implacable hatred for France.[8] Carlos proved no match for Louis, who easily defeated him before going on to take Luxembourg in June 1684. Louis then turned his attention to Genoa, whose city fathers had offended him by offering a safe harbor for the Spanish to rest and reprovision their ships.[9] The French navy took revenge by mercilessly bombarding the town until it lay in ruins. The Genoese were forced to agree to humiliating terms in order to save what was left of their city.

Then, just as it seemed that Louis's war machine could not be stopped, unexpected and worrying news arrived. John Sobieski, king of Poland, in alliance with Charles, duc de Lorraine,[10] had driven away the Turks and liberated Vienna. Louis had hoped that the siege would last a long time and that it would eventually fail through lack of discipline among the Turks, as well as the inevitable disease that ravaged besieged cities. Louis and his advisors had also expected that the effects of the siege within the Holy Roman Empire would allow them to fulfill their ambitions in Germany. The Venetian ambassador had thought that Louis intended to ally with the Germans and force the Turks to draw back from Vienna, which would have made him the savior of Christendom. Louis would then have received the imperial crown upon the death of Leopold, an eventuality that had been considered, although not entirely seriously, in Louis's youth.[11] As it was, Louis's decision not to come to Vienna's aid left the way open for John Sobieski to win the laurels that might otherwise have gone to the Sun King.[12]

Vienna, therefore, was a missed opportunity for Louis, but his policy of aggrandizement, together with his manipulation of the *chambres de réunions*, alarmed the rest of Europe. Quite simply, Louis was too powerful, and other European leaders feared what he might do next. Under the mediation of the emperor Leopold, the truce of Ratisbon was signed in August 1684. An expedient in the face of French aggression, it recognized Louis's acquisitions as confirmed by the *réunions* for a period of twenty years.

Louis decided to host a great fête at Marly that autumn, at which he intended to give presents to all the ladies. Unfortunately, news of it leaked out, and the court was awash with so many ladies of quality who wished to be included on the guest list that there was scarcely room to move. Many of them had besieged their favorite shops and had bought so much finery and at so great a cost that Louis grew angry. "They will persuade themselves that my presents are so very magnificent, that what I actually give them will appear nothing in comparison," he said. The fête was duly cancelled, and Louis kept the items of jewelry for himself and made Liselotte and the other ladies play among themselves for the brocades, ribbons, and fans.[13]

Shortly after this, Louis went hunting. His first stop was at Chambord, where he stayed from the end of September until October 12, before moving on to Fontainebleau.[14] There was, however, a very special event for which he was determined not to be late. The date was November 15, 1684, and the event was the opening of the Grande Galerie at Versailles. Nothing was allowed to go wrong; Louvois had been sent on in advance to ensure that the work was complete, and Louis was on his way.

Six years earlier, at the conclusion of the Treaty of Nijmegen, Louis's bargaining power had been boosted by significant victories. A council had met to discuss the iconography for the ceiling of a new gallery at Versailles, the plans for which were being drawn up by Louis's new architect, Jules Hardouin-Mansart. Initially, Charles Le Brun had been commissioned to paint themes based upon the Labors of Hercules, but it was decided instead that the ceiling should depict the military glories of Louis's reign.

Situated on the west side of the château and measuring seventy-three meters long by ten and a half wide, the Grande Galerie, better known as the *Galerie des glaces*, or Hall of Mirrors, lay before Louis in all its magnificent glory. Built not for the full light of day, its grandeur can only fully be appreciated in the evening. The setting sun casts its golden rays through seventeen high windows, to be reflected in the tall, arched mirrors that line the wall opposite. The soft, dying light of the day finds new life in the gilded statues within. Positioned up and down the length of the gallery, silver furniture shimmers in the glow of four thousand wax candles. The ceiling, soaring to a height of twelve and a half meters, portrays Louis's martial victories. While gods, fauns, and lovers dance and gaze down at the courtiers below, the Sun King, a celestial warrior in Roman armor, acquires Dunkirk, orders an attack on Holland, takes the town and citadel of Gand in six days, and conquers the Franche-Comté for the second time. The greatest moments are there: *The Passage of the Rhine* and *The Taking of Maastricht*, rendered by Le Brun in spectacular detail. Perhaps the most poignant representation, however, is *Le Roi gouverne par lui-même*. The first to be painted, it depicts Louis taking power into his own hands, so that he is master not only in France but in all of Europe. He wears the blue coronation robes of France over classical armor. Above, a woman representing Glory holds out a crown of stars to the king, whose eyes are fixed only upon her, his hand reaching out to receive the crown, while the lovers, gods, goddesses, and nymphs that surround him are ignored. "Nothing can equal the beauty of this gallery of Versailles," Mme de Sévigné wrote to her daughter, "this sort of royal beauty is unique in the world."[15]

Among the first foreigners to witness this royal beauty was Francesco Mario Lercaro, the doge of Genoa, who arrived at Versailles on May 15, 1685 with four senators. Their mission was to grovel at Louis's feet and plead for his forgiveness for having given refuge to the Spanish.[16] Louis received them in the awe-inspiring surroundings of the *Galerie des glaces*. He had his throne placed at one end of the gallery, which was filled with curious courtiers waiting to see the king's guests. Lercaro and the senators made their way through the château, their route lined with silver furniture, which had been deliberately placed in order to impress them still further. Two days later, Lercaro was due to return to Versailles early enough to attend Louis's *lever*, but one of his senators was so ill that morning that the ceremony was finished by the time the party arrived. Nevertheless, the doge was compensated for his disappointment with a tour of the château. He simply could not believe his eyes. "A year ago we were in hell," he remarked, referring to the bombardment of Genoa by Louis's ships, "and today we descend from paradise."[17] He was served a magnificent dinner in Mademoiselle's apartments, after which he walked in the gardens towards the canal. Louis also received two ambassadors from Moscow, who arrived on May 21 with a small entourage. They were bored by the games favored by the French, but they played chess very well.[18] After their visit, Louis went for a long walk in the gardens before taking a meal with the dauphin and dauphine.

Louis was particularly pleased with his gardens. Like his father before him, he was a keen gardener, and André Le Nôtre, his chief landscape gardener, was more than a servant; he was a friend whom Louis would greet with a bear hug. No garden could function without water, however, and that May, Louis was thrilled to see the reservoir of Versailles filling for the first time. The all-important court entertainments were not forgotten, and although it was still early summer, preparations were already being made for that winter's diversions. The playwright Philippe Quinault presented three works to Louis so he could make his selection. Louis was pleased with all of them, but he selected *Armide et Renaud*, an opera set during the First Crusade and written by Quinault, with music by Lully.[19]

Aware of their propaganda value, Louis was always careful to ensure that his portraits and statues conveyed the right image. One day in November 1685, he was walking in the orangery at Versailles, one of his favorite parts of the garden, when he suddenly came across an equestrian statue of himself. He had commissioned it from Bernini several years ago, and now it had finally been delivered.[20] The Italian had depicted Louis as one of his favorite historical characters, Alexander the Great, but the human figure and the horse had, in Louis's opinion, been very badly formed. Louis "resolved not only to remove it from there, but even to have it smashed up," noted Dangeau.[21] In the end, Louis did not order the work to be destroyed; instead, he commissioned the sculptor François Girardon to transform it into a statue of Marcus Curtius, the mythical Roman hero who saved Rome by sacrificing himself.[22]

TWENTY-THREE
The Edict of Fontainebleau

From early childhood, Louis had been taught—by his mother, by Mazarin, and a succession of Jesuit tutors and confessors—that heresy was nothing less than the road to hell. Louis believed that corruption in the church led to "schism and heresy," which in its turn gravely wounded the church.[1] The schism Louis spoke about here was Huguenotism. The Huguenots promised "an easy and short road to salvation," wrote Louis;[2] he was certain that their doctrine was Satanic.

As Louis understood it, where there was schism in the church, there must also be disunity in the realm as a whole, for religion and politics were inseparable. In the previous century, clashes between Huguenots and Catholics had culminated in the Saint Bartholomew's Day massacre of August 24, 1572. At the siege of Amiens in 1597, Huguenots

310

had come close to betraying Louis's grandfather, Henri IV, to Spain. The following year, Henri signed the Edict of Nantes, which granted freedom of conscience to Huguenots, their rights supported by political and military guarantees. Huguenots had rebelled in the 1620s, most famously at the siege of La Rochelle in 1626, and it could not fail to escape Louis's notice that many of the regions that sided with Condé during the Fronde had large Huguenot populations. Heresy was, therefore, a form of treason. It was Louis's duty, as the king who had been given to France by God, to fulfill the promise he had made in his coronation oath to suppress heresy, to save his people, and unite his kingdom.

For the first few years of his reign, however, Louis did very little other than to appoint ministers to maintain the Edict of Nantes. He also withheld from the Huguenot population certain "graces," although he did this "out of kindness rather than bitterness"[3] so that they might not wonder "if it was with good reason that they willingly deprived themselves of the advantages which they could share with all" his subjects."[4] Louis described his desire to

> *attract, and even to reward, those who might be amenable; to do all I could to inspire the bishops to work at their instruction, and to clear away their scandals, which sometimes separated them from us; finally, to put in the highest places and in all those of which I have the appointment for whatever reason, only persons of piety, application, learning, capable of repairing by an entirely different conduit, the disorders that their predecessors had primarily produced in the church.*[5]

Between 1659 and 1664, Louis closed several Huguenot temples. Those who converted received financial rewards, the money coming from monastic revenues and those of the *régale*. Huguenots were forbidden to emigrate, which many in Europe viewed as a particularly harsh measure.[6] Bibles translated for the benefit of Huguenots were read by some and ignored by others, while catechisms and other texts were designed for indoctrination purposes. These measures did nothing to persuade the most unswerving Huguenots to convert; others, less committed, embraced Catholicism, willingly or otherwise.[7]

Had the matter been allowed to run its course, the Huguenots of France would have died out within two or three generations. However, Louis wanted to be remembered as the king who united France under one religion. It was to be the highest accomplishment of his reign.

Although no longer a state within a state, if indeed they ever had been, Huguenots maintained a sense of particularism that Louis saw as a threat to national identity. Moreover, during the Dutch War, significant numbers of Huguenots had secretly supported William of Orange.[8] As Calvinists, they were believed to be republicans and democrats. In 1679, Louis determined to destroy the Huguenots.

Over the next six years, measures against the Huguenot population became increasingly severe as the guarantees of the Edict of Nantes were systematically eroded away.[9] In the professions, it became illegal for Huguenot women to practice midwifery. Sailors and artisans were forced to remain in France, while certain posts in law and the military were closed to them. Eventually, all legal posts as well as medicine would be closed. In areas of faith and its practice, more Huguenot temples were demolished. It was forbidden for anyone to convert to Huguenotism.

Private worship was banned, while Huguenot ministers were required to move to a new ministry after a maximum of three years. In addition, services could be held only in communities of ten or more families. Any Huguenot minister who accepted a Catholic convert into his flock was forced to make a public apology before being banished from the kingdom. Each temple was required to host a royal agent, who attended the services, studied the congregation, and kept a watchful eye on the pastor.

In private life, mixed marriages were forbidden. Magistrates were sent to the homes of sick Huguenots in a bid to convert them. Louvois, acting on a suggestion by the intendant René de Marillac, authorized the deployment of *dragonnades* in Poitiers. Soldiers who had previously been billeted on tax evaders now moved into Huguenot homes to bully, threaten, and coerce them to convert. However, Huguenots newly converted to Catholicism were spared this horror for two years, presumably to encourage them not to apostatize. In time, the number of *dragonnades* would increase, and their use would spread into other areas of France.

Huguenot children were encouraged to abandon the faith of their parents. From the age of seven, they were granted the right to convert to Catholicism without their parents' consent. Their parents, meanwhile, were required to respect their children's decision and to educate them as Catholics in France. Children were compelled to be taught by Catholic tutors, whether they chose to convert or not. Illegitimate children born to Huguenots were to be forcibly brought up as Catholics.

Lastly, it remained illegal for Huguenots to emigrate, although a great many did. In view of this, a new and sinister law was introduced that awarded half the goods of Huguenots who had emigrated to those who denounced them.

Throughout this period, intendants such as Marillac presented Louis with exaggerated lists of converts. The king, who liked what he saw, did not question the accuracy of the numbers but took them at face value. He concluded that the measures, although harsh, were producing the desired effect. "If God preserves the King," wrote Mme de Maintenon, "there will not be one Huguenot in twenty years." [10]

Encouraged by the apparent success of his policy, Louis continued to apply pressure, so that at the end of six years, few of the rights and guarantees promised by the Edict of Nantes remained. Louis sent missionaries into the newly converted regions. "The courtiers will hear perhaps mediocre sermons," Louis said, "but the Languedociens will learn a good doctrine and a fine moral." [11]

Louis believed that there were so few Huguenots left in the kingdom that the Edict of Nantes became obsolete. It remained only to rescind it, and this is what he now did. The new Edict of Fontainebleau was announced on October 18, 1685, and registered in parlement four days later. Upon the implementation of the new edict, the *religion prétendue réformée*, the 'so-called reformed religion,' was legally no more in France. Pastors were given two weeks to convert or leave the country on pain of being condemned to the galleys.[12] The laity was made to conform or be forced to endure the *dragonnades*. Those Huguenots who had emigrated were granted four months' grace to reclaim their confiscated property.[13] Those who still remained in France were forbidden to emigrate or send goods abroad. Men who broke this law were condemned to the galleys, while women had their worldly goods confiscated.[14] In the end, 1,450 men ended up as galley slaves and some 200,000 people took their wealth and their skills to other countries, including England, Holland, Switzerland, and the New World.[15] "I admire the conduct of the King in destroying the Huguenots," wrote Mme de Sévigné. "The wars they have waged in the past and the Saint-Bartholomew [massacre] have multiplied and given strength to that sect. His Majesty has undermined them little by little, and the edict [of Fontainebleau] that he had just passed, supported by Dragoons and Bourdaloue,[16] was a *coup de grace*."[17] However, the Edict of Fontainebleau is now understood as one of the most criminal and least enlightened acts in the entire reign of the Sun King.

Louis's war on the Huguenots should be seen in the context of his failure to respond to Pope Innocent's call for a Crusade to save Vienna from Turkish aggressors. He felt the need to defend his credentials as a Christian and show that he deserved his title of Most Christian King. The revocation of the Edict of Nantes was also a response to what Louis saw as a fissure in the integrity of the kingdom, which challenged his perception of absolute monarchy and defied his initiative to unite his kingdom under one king, one law, and one faith. He had already begun with Jansenism, and it was inevitable that he would turn his attention to the Huguenots, whose eradication he viewed as necessary to ensure the well-being of the realm.

While the Huguenots were mercilessly persecuted, elsewhere Louis was supporting acts of charity. In March 1684, he authorized the establishment of a new Versailles charity to be directed by the duchesse de Richelieu. It was dedicated to the care of the poor, the crippled, and young girls who were forced to sell themselves on the streets in order to survive.

Françoise, meanwhile, who had often been looked down upon by members of the aristocracy, decided she needed something worthy of her status as the wife of Louis XIV. Since 1681, she had dedicated much of her time to a school she had founded for poor children, particularly girls. Established in Montmorency, it had quickly outgrown its premises and moved first to Rueil and then to Noisy. The school was successful, but Françoise had come to feel that she needed something grander than a charity school for beggar girls. Inspiration came when she contemplated the lot of the sons of nobles whose fathers had been detailed to the frontier to man and maintain the defenses. The education of these boys had been seriously disrupted as a result, and Françoise, encouraged by some caring ministers, established a military academy for them.

Her next step was to found a college for the daughters of impoverished noble families, girls who would otherwise be denied the opportunity to fulfill the expectations of their class. The location selected for the college, which was to be called the Maison Royale de Saint-Louis, was Saint-Cyr, west of Versailles. Mansart was commissioned to design the buildings, while the garden was landscaped by La Nôtre. In May 1686, Louis awarded the new establishment 150 thousand livres in rents and benefices,[18] and on June 6, he "signed the letters patent for the establishment of the community of Saint-Cyr," which he also endowed with a further 50 thousand écus of rentes. Françoise was given the general direction of the school, and her friend Mme de Brinon was appointed superior of the community, with Abbé Gobelin as the ecclesiastic superior.

While the school was a religious establishment, it focused upon giving the students a worldly education. This is reflected in the way the staff and students were referred to. The teachers were addressed as "Madame" with their family name, rather than "Mother" or "Sister," while the girls were called "demoiselles" to reflect their status as aristocrats. Louis also insisted that the demoiselles should be required to take simple vows, rather than the solemn vows initially advocated by Françoise. The king despised the limited education imposed upon women by convents, and he was determined that Saint-Cyr would be different. His confessor, Père La Chaise, agreed:

> Girls are better brought up by people belonging to the [outer] world. The object of the foundation [St. Cyr] is not to multiply convents, which multiply enough of themselves, but to give well-educated girls to the State. There are enough good nuns, and not enough good mothers of families. St. Cyr will bring forth great virtues, and great virtues, instead of being shut up in the cloister, should be used to sanctify the world.[19]

Moreover, Louis took an active interest in every aspect of the creation of Saint-Cyr, even down to the dress worn by the dames. Their habits were to be "grave and modest, without being conventual." Sketches were presented to him, which he modified with his own hand. The demoiselles were divided into four classes distinguished by color: red, green, blue, and yellow. Their uniform was a dress made of brown serge, with a lace or muslin frill around the neck and a little apron trimmed with a ribbon to match. Their hair was dressed according to the latest fashion, although it was held in place by a small linen cap edged with muslin and a ribbon of the appropriate color.

Louis also insisted that each demoiselle should have her own drinking cup, fork, and spoon, all of which were made of silver. They would have proper beds, clean and neatly made, and with curtains as befitting the rank of the young lady who occupied it. He stipulated that gifts were forbidden, as were unexpected visits by the ladies of the court, and no guests were to be allowed to stay for meals. Any princess who wished to would be allowed to visit Saint-Cyr provided they obtained Françoise's permission first; and it was strictly laid down that such visits, which should be rare, would be attended by all due ceremony.[20]

There would be thirty-six dames, twenty-four lay sisters, and 250 demoiselles. The dames and demoiselles were required to provide proof of their nobility over a period of three generations or one hundred years, which Louis verified in person.[21] The king also urged Françoise to keep watch for any suitable husbands for the demoiselles, for each of whom he set aside 3 thousand francs as a dowry to pay for their wedding outfit.[22] That August, the first demoiselles began to arrive at Saint-Cyr from Noisy.[23]

Lessons included religious instruction, the mastery of French, and needlecraft in many forms, especially knitting, lace-making, embroidery, and tapestry work.[24] The elder demoiselles were talented seamstresses, and they made a bed set for Louis of crimson velvet embroidered with gold and silver. They also made vestments to be used at the cathedral at Strasbourg, which Louis had recently annexed to France.[25] In addition to the lessons, Louis required the dames and demoiselles to say two masses daily:

> *That it may please God to give Us and Our successors the necessary light to govern the State according to the laws of justice, and the grace of increasing His worship and exalting the Church in Our Kingdom and the lands and lordships under Our obedience, and to give Him thanks for the graces shed upon Us, upon Our royal house and Our dominions.*[26]

In addition to praying for God to grant Louis the "necessary light" he ardently desired, the demoiselles no doubt also prayed for his good health, for the truth was that the founding of Saint-Cyr coincided with several instances of illness for the now middle-aged king.

The first ailment to afflict Louis was a worsening of the tooth-ache from which he had suffered intermittently since 1676.[27] It had made its first appearance when he was on campaign in Flanders,[28] and while it usually responded well enough to an application of oil of cloves or thyme, the treatment was sometimes overdone, leaving Louis with a burned mouth and feelings of nausea.

Two years after this, Louis suffered a new bout of toothache, which his chief physician, Antoine d'Aquin,[29] attributed to the king's con-tinual hunting in the full heat of the sun. A suppurating abscess caused swelling in Louis's right cheek and gum, which was made worse by the use of a poultice made of breadcrumbs and milk. The abscess eventu-ally had to be lanced, which let out the pus and allowed the condition to clear up.[30] Another time, sugary treatments prescribed by d'Aquin hurt Louis's teeth.[31] However, worse problems were to come.

In 1685, Louis experienced pain in the left side of his upper jaw. D'Aquin recommended the removal of all the teeth in the affected part. However, the operation left a hole in the jaw, which meant that whenever Louis drank or gargled, the liquid in his mouth would flow into his nose, from which "it flowed like a fountain." The jaw itself was decayed, causing it to discharge foul-smelling pus. D'Aquin thought it was possible to repair the hole by cauterizing the gum, to which Louis gave his consent. On January 10, the procedure was carried out, with d'Aquin applying the hot iron fourteen times. The wound was then treated with a concoction of spirits of wine applied as a lotion and a gargle of orange flower water to ward off any further decay, help the scabs fall off, and encourage the regeneration of the gum.[32] Although the treatment worked to the extent that no more fluid flowed from Louis's mouth into his nose, he would continue to have problems with an excess of unpleasant mucus, which obliged d'Aquin to monitor his patient for the possible recurrence of abscesses. The procedure left Louis's jaw sunken on the left side. In the portrait of the king painted by Hyacinthe Rigaud circa 1700, the damage caused to his face is not disguised, although it was possibly played down. As though to compensate, Rigaud painted the legs with the strength and elegance of a younger man, with the feet arranged in the fourth ballet position as a reminder of the king's talent as a dancer.[33]

Louis had not long to enjoy his health, as the following year brought with it a new ailment. In February 1686, the marquis de Dangeau noted that Louis was suffering from a "tumor" on his left thigh, which kept him in his bed all that day. He was still unwell the next day, although the tumor had reduced in size, which gave the hope that it would vanish completely.[34] This hope was misplaced, for the tumor returned on the sixteenth, causing Louis so much pain that he ordered a bed to be placed in the room where he was accustomed to meet his council, in case he was unable to get up.[35] A week later, he was still feeling under the weather; the gout from which he had suffered for some while was bothering him, and the tumor on his thigh showed no sign of diminishing this time. The physicians agreed that the best course of treatment was to cauterize it. The procedure involved applying a hot stone to the tumor and leaving it in place for an hour and a half, before opening the skin with a lancet. It was carried out at ten o'clock on February 23, and it appears to have been successful, for Louis was said to have slept very peacefully that night.[36]

The preceding ten or twelve years had seen an increase in the occurrence of a particularly painful condition, the anal fistula. This was attributed to a variety of causes, such as the feather cushions used in carriages, an excess of stews, or "ultramontane debauchery." In 1687, when Louis developed one, an abscess resulting from his active lifestyle, particularly riding, hunting, walking, and travelling were blamed.[37]

On November 17, Louis toured the gardens of Versailles. He loved his garden, no matter the weather or the season, and he always enjoyed being out in the fresh air, but he was not at all well. He had already made up his mind to undergo an operation for the fistula, which was scheduled for two days' time. Only a handful of people knew of it: Françoise; Louvois; d'Aquin; Félix;[38] and Père de La Chaise, Louis's confessor. The dauphin was also aware that the operation was to take place, but he was not told when. Upon his return from his walk, Louis alerted Françoise, d'Aquin, Louvois, and Félix to be present in his bedchamber at eight the following morning. As to Père de La Chaise, he was still in Paris and was unaware that the operation had been brought forward.[39]

As the clock chimed eight the following morning, the small, select group entered Louis's chamber to find him still sleeping soundly, "a great sign of the tranquillity of his soul, on an occasion where others were in great anxiety," noted the marquis de Sourches.[40] When they awoke the king, he asked if everything was ready and if M. de Louvois was in his antechamber. When he was assured that all was indeed prepared and Louvois was waiting, Louis arose and knelt at the bottom of his bed, where he quietly prayed. His prayers finished, he said in a loud voice, "My God, I put myself in your hands."[41]

Louis now returned to his bed and ordered Félix to begin the operation. Félix, who had practiced on several people suffering from the same condition in order to perfect his technique, worked alongside Bessière, "the most skillful surgeon in Paris." Louvois held the king's hand throughout, while Françoise remained in the room but kept a discreet distance by the fireplace.[42]

The operation was painful, but Louis was as brave at the hands of his doctors as he was on the battlefield, and his cry of "Mon Dieu" when the first incision was made was the only sound he uttered. As the procedure was almost at an end, he urged Félix not to spare him but to treat him "as the least important person in his kingdom." This encouraged Félix to make two more snips, after which he dressed the wound before bleeding Louis by the arm. Félix was pleased with his work, "for he had done it to perfection."[43]

Louis's *lever* had been delayed by only one hour, and as the first gentlemen of the chamber and the officers of the court came in, Louis explained to them that he was unwell. They thought it must be an attack of gout. Then, at ten o'clock, those with right of entry came in and approached the royal bed, and they were astonished as Louis told them all about his operation and the circumstances surrounding it.[44]

As traumatic and painful as the procedure had been, Louis insisted upon presiding over a council meeting as usual.

Louis's health began to improve, and by December 2 he was eating almost normally, taking "a little meat and even a drink of wine."[45] A few days later, however, on the seventh, it was found that Louis's wound was not healing as well as it should. The problem was caused by the formation of calluses, which had to be removed, an operation every bit as painful and unpleasant as the first, and which carried the threat of fever.[46] Nevertheless, Louis agreed to it and the procedure was carried out two days later, on the morning of December 9. Dangeau noted that "the surgeons strongly assured us that there will be no further cutting, and that [the king's] recovery is assured."[47] The operation went ahead, and once again, "the pain suffered by the king did not prevent him holding council and seeing the courtiers as usual." Even so, Françoise noted on December 11 that Louis had "suffered for seven hours as though he had been on the wheel, and I fear that his pains will return tomorrow."[48] Dangeau confirmed the dreadful extent of Louis's suffering, adding that the king's misery was worsened by his grief at news of the death of his cousin, the prince de Condé.

As he was dying, Condé wrote Louis a final letter filled with remorse for all his actions against him. He was thinking of the Fronde. He acknowledged his behavior, which he himself condemned, and expressed his gratitude to Louis for his forgiveness, lamenting that he felt he had not and could never have done enough to merit the goodness that Louis had shown him. He thanked Louis, too, for forgiving his nephew, the young prince de Conti, the knowledge of which allowed Condé to die a happy man. When Louis received the news of Condé's death, he noted sadly, "I have just lost the greatest man in my kingdom."[49]

Louis began to improve on the thirteenth, but his recovery was not fully assured until December 23, when the surgeons advised him to rest for a day or two and, after four days, he would be completely cured without fear of relapse.[50] A *Te Deum* was sung in the parish church of Versailles to give thanks for Louis's convalescence.[51]

TWENTY-FOUR
The League of Augsburg

The truce of Ratisbon had marked a significant victory for Louis, who was then at the height of his power. The other European leaders, however, continued to worry about where his ambition might take him next. They had watched helplessly as Louis grabbed one territory after another, and they came to the conclusion that only strong diplomatic alliances would guarantee the terms of the truce, which would in turn curtail further French expansion. Moreover, the Protestant powers of Europe had been shocked by the revocation of the Edict of Nantes and Louis's treatment of their coreligionists. For his part, Louis wanted to convert the truce into a permanent peace treaty, which would allow him to retain his acquisitions legally and in perpetuity. Such a move would have brought peace to Europe, consolidated France's frontier, increased the reputation of his kingdom, and made Paris, or perhaps more accurately Versailles, the center of a powerful and united Christian monarchy.[1] However, while Louis saw Ratisbon as a prelude to everlasting peace, the rest of Europe used it as a breathing space during which they consolidated their alliances.

On May 27, 1685, Karl II, elector of the Palatinate, died childless. Louis advanced a dubious claim to the Palatine on the grounds that the late elector's sister, Elisabeth-Charlotte, duchesse d'Orléans, was married to Louis's brother, Philippe. The claim sent shock waves throughout Europe. It was believed that Louis would resort to war in order to press his claim, and so, in 1686, the League of Augsburg was formed, an alliance between Emperor Leopold, most of the German princes, and the kings of Sweden and Spain. Louis's response was to strengthen the defenses along his eastern frontier; however, the political landscape in Europe was about to undergo a major upheaval.

It was at this point that Louis found himself in conflict once again with Pope Innocent XI. The pope was horrified at Louis's treatment of the Huguenots, and he was angry about the king's refusal to assist the emperor against the Turks. Innocent had rejected the Four Articles drawn up by the Gallican Church, and he refused to ratify any of Louis's episcopal appointments. As one diocese after another fell vacant, this became a matter of concern.[2]

Innocent also abolished the right of diplomatic immunity for foreign ambassadors to Rome, which Louis took as an act of aggression. When the pope refused to discuss this latest policy, Louis sent the marquis de Lavardin, with a small army. Innocent's response was to excommunicate the marquis. A few months later, in January 1688, he extended the decree of excommunication to include Louis and his ministers. Louis had already consulted Archbishop Le Tellier about his options should such a scenario arise, but the archbishop assured him that the decree would be invalid. Even so, Louis felt uncomfortable with the idea that the Most Christian King should be cast out of the church, and he ordered the news to be kept secret.[3]

As he surveyed his frontiers, Louis identified Alsace as the weakest point because it was vulnerable to attack from Philipsburg in the Palatinate. The electorate of Cologne posed another possible threat. Fortunately, the archbishop-elector of Cologne,[4] Maximilian-Henry, was one of Louis's allies, but he was an elderly man and not expected to live much longer. Louis considered who best to put forward to succeed Maximilian-Henry, and his choice settled upon Wilhelm Egon von Fürstenberg, bishop of Strasbourg. Louis then obtained a cardinal's hat and the post of coadjutor to Maximilian-Henry for Fürstenberg, putting him in Louis's debt. There was another candidate, however: Joseph-Clemens von Wittelsbach, the sixteen-year-old brother of the elector of Bavaria. The emperor favored Joseph-Clemens, who would nevertheless require papal dispensation of age if he was to be promoted to archbishop. Considering the state of relations between Louis and Innocent, Louis had no doubt that the pope would be only too happy oblige the emperor. As Louis considered his options, news arrived from England.

On June 10, 1688, Mary of Modena,[5] the queen of James II, gave birth to a prince, James Francis Edward. King James had acceded to the throne three years earlier following the death of Charles II. He had made it clear that he desired to convert his country back to Catholicism in the event of his becoming king. Now, faced with the prospect of a Catholic royal dynasty, the Anglicans entered into negotiations with William of Orange, inviting him to lead an army to England and assert his wife's and his own claims to the English crown.[6] William, however, was closely watching Louis's activity. He wanted to be available to meet him with armed force if Louis attacked Cologne. William encamped at Nijmegen, a suitable spot from which he could move to England or descend upon Cologne, according to what Louis did next.[7]

In July, Louis made one final attempt to persuade Innocent to support Fürstenberg's candidature to the electorate of Cologne. He sent an ambassador, the marquis de Chamley, to the Vatican with a letter setting out in the strongest terms the consequences should the pope refuse Louis's request. Innocent refused even to receive Chamley.

In September, Louis issued his *Déclaration*, in which he wrote of the treachery and aggression of his enemies who had formed the League of Augsburg against him, denied his rights in the Palatinate, and opposed his candidate to the electorate of Cologne, all of which clearly demonstrated their hostility towards France and their resistance to Louis's very real desire for peace. He then seized Avignon and sent armed forces into Italy before laying siege to Philippsburg. His objective was to force his enemies to come to the negotiating table with a view to converting the truce of Ratisbon into a permanent peace. Having achieved his aim, he would restore the towns.[8]

Of the towns Louis attacked, Philippsburg was the most important, representing as it did a major gap in his defenses on the Rhine.[9] Although the real commander of the army was the experienced maréchal duc de Duras, Louis appointed the dauphin, now aged twenty-six, as nominal head of the army. "The Dauphin has become a warrior," wrote Liselotte as the young man left to join his forces. He told her that after Philippsburg he would take Mannheim and Frankenthal and fight for her interests. "If you would take my advice," she told him, "you will not go because I tell you frankly that it will give me no joy, but only sorrow to know that my name is being used to encompass the ruin of my own unfortunate country."[10] Liselotte's opinion counted for nothing, and the dauphin left Versailles on September 25, arriving at the camp on October 6. Although an attack had been attempted three days earlier, the main assault on Philipsburg took place on October 10 and 11. The town finally surrendered three weeks later, on the thirtieth.

Then, just as the dauphin had promised, the troops next advanced on Mannheim, arriving on November 4. A trench was opened on the eighth, and the town capitulated two days later. Mannheim had been built by Liselotte's father: "My heart bleeds for it," she wrote.[11] The army now pushed on to take Heidelberg, but then the weather closed in. While the army set up its winter camp, the dauphin was obliged to return to Versailles, where he arrived on November 28.

Monsieur de Montausier, the dauphin's former governor, told Liselotte that the dauphin was her champion and that he was going to win back her lands and property. When she made no reply, he noted, "You seem to take my news very coldly." She answered, "Sir, I do indeed hear what you say with indifference, because you are talking of the one thing in the world about which I have the least desire to hear." She went on, saying that she saw no great advantage in ruining her fatherland in her name, and that "far from being overjoyed, I am very much hurt." She explained to him that she could not hide her feelings, nor could she hold her tongue; as she explained to her aunt, the Electress Sophia, "if people do not want me to say what I think about it, they must refrain from broaching the subject to me." Montausier was annoyed by her reaction, and her words eventually reached Louis, who "took the affair very badly."[12]

Louis was displeased about Liselotte's grief for the war in the Palatinate. When she lay ill in Paris for ten days, he never once sent to inquire after her, nor did he reply to any of her letters. Rather, despite her furious protests, Louis was determined to cause as much damage in the Palatinate as possible. When spring came and war could resume, so did the devastation of Liselotte's homeland. Liselotte seemed to believe that Louis continued his campaign to spite her. Confiding in her aunt she wrote, "I am especially heartbroken because the King actually stayed his hand from these devastations until after I craved his leniency for Heidelberg and Mannheim."[13]

Amid such sorrow, more bad news arrived. Marie-Louise, whom Louis had sent to Spain to marry King Carlos ten years earlier, had died. "I expected that you would be sorry to hear of the death of our dear Queen of Spain," wrote Liselotte to her aunt. Although she tried to put on a brave face and "follow the example of her late Majesty's nearest and most highly-placed relations," and attend "all sorts of amusements," she found that her sadness returned the moment she returned home.[14]

In fact, Liselotte took the news very badly. "I agree with you when you say that the dear Queen is now better off than we are," she wrote, but then her letter, melancholy as it was, took an even darker turn: "I should take it as a kindness if anyone were to render me the service they did to her and her mother, and help me from this world to the next in twenty-four hours." Liselotte had revived the belief held by some that Henriette d'Orléans had died of poisoning, and now she suggested that Marie-Louise had died the same way.[15]

Several weeks later, Liselotte wrote again to say that Monsieur de Rebenac, Louis's ambassador in Madrid, was "right in thinking that the dear Queen of Spain was poisoned. It was quite evident when they opened her up, and besides she became purple immediately after her death, and they say that that is a sure sign of poisoning."[16]

While there is no evidence to support the theory that Henriette had been poisoned, in Marie-Louise's case, it is just possible. The comtesse de Soissons had fled France in 1680 at the height of the poisons scandal, having been implicated in the death of her husband. Ending up in Spain in 1686, she had become friends with Marie-Louise, much to Louis's horror. The king asked M. de Rebenac to keep an eye on the comtesse to ensure that Marie-Louise came to no harm. Two years later, King Carlos, who suffered from premature ejaculation, claimed that his affliction was the fault of Mme de Soissons, who he said had bewitched him. He promptly ordered her to leave Spain, upon which she appealed to Marie-Louise for help, only for the queen to support her husband. A successful appeal to Carlos through the imperial ambassador allowed the comtesse to remain in Spain, although she was excluded from the court.[17] Then Queen Marie-Louise became very ill, with continual vomiting and colic, and on February 12, 1689, she died under circumstances that were remarkably similar to those surrounding the death of her mother.

Rebenac was convinced that Marie-Louise had been poisoned, but he placed the blame on two Spanish nobles at court, who acted with the help of one of the queen's ladies. Certainly, Marie-Louise had lived in fear of being poisoned, and she asked her father to send antidotes, a packet of which was said to have arrived at the Spanish court on the day she died.[18] It is possible that a faction at court saw her as an obstacle to an alliance with the Holy Roman Empire and had desired her death for that reason.[19] Alternatively, her death might have been caused by drugs given to her to cure sterility, with the Spanish blaming the couple's childlessness on her rather than her husband.[20] Whatever the case, as she lay on her deathbed, Marie-Louise told Rebenac that she did not believe she had been poisoned after all.[21] Even so, doubts remained.

The death of Marie-Louise was a tragedy, and it would have its political consequences for Louis. For the present, the king justified his actions in the Palatinate by pointing out that they were necessary as a defensive measure. In the face of the League of Augsburg, he saw it as imperative that he should do all he could to prevent the Germans from occupying the land on their side of the frontier. His actions however, exceeded necessity when the Rhine towns of Heidelberg, Mannheim, Worms, and Spire, as well as the surrounding farmlands, were selected for destruction in a "slash and burn" offensive that even his own generals were reluctant to carry out until stern orders from Louvois pressed them into obedience.

William of Orange, meanwhile, content that Holland was safe while Louis was engaged in the Rhineland, responded to his invitation to invade England and sailed across the English Channel on the day that Philippsburg fell. Louis offered to assist James, but the English king refused. He was concerned about how his own naval officers would react should he accept;[22] besides, he thought his forces were more than adequate to repel William. However, when William landed on November 5, many Protestants flocked to his side, including James's younger daughter, Anne. Despite his stronger position, James lost his nerve and fled in the face of the advancing army. William, reluctant to make a martyr of James, allowed him to escape to France.[23]

James remained a refugee in France, and Archbishop Le Tellier, who saw the king's escape as cowardly, poured scorn upon him. Louis, however, welcomed his cousin tenderly and gave him and his family the use of Saint-Germain. Louis was indignant on James's behalf because William, a king who owed his position merely to an act of parliament, had the temerity to depose a divinely appointed ruler.

William of Orange, now William III of England, ruled jointly with his wife, Mary. He was now able to fulfill his ambition to create a Protestant coalition against Louis, the aim of which was to reduce France's borders to the limits imposed upon them by the Treaties of Westphalia and the Pyrenees.[24] The German princes, horrified by Louis's "slash and burn" policy in the Palatinate, were only too happy to join, as was Spain. Sweden and Portugal remained neutral, but the pope's continued hostility towards France left Louis without a diplomatic ally.[25] The War of the League of Augsburg, otherwise called the Nine Years' War, was the inevitable result of Louis's policy of aggrandizement. Much of the fighting was defensive on France's part, with siege warfare being the predominant strategy. As the war dragged on, Louis would be forced to melt down the beautiful silver furniture at Versailles, including a magnificent throne, to finance it.

Louis was eager to assist James in winning back his throne, and in 1689–90, preparations were underway for a naval invasion of England. It was agreed that action in Ireland would distract the English, and in May 1690, James prepared to join his troops. As Louis bade farewell to his cousin, he told him, "The best thing that I can wish for you is that I may never see you again."[26] Six regiments of French troops had already crossed into Ireland, a total of 6,300 men under the command of the comte de Lauzun. The comte had been released from Pignerol nine years earlier, his freedom purchased by Mademoiselle, whom Louis had persuaded to make over her most lucrative estates in favor of his favorite son by Athénaïs, the duc du Maine.

Lauzun had served under James when he was still duke of York, during the Fronde.[27] As the revolution of 1688 unfolded in England,

Lauzun requested Louis's permission to go to James's aid, which Louis was pleased to grant. Lauzun quickly became James's confidant, and as danger threatened Queen Mary of Modena and the prince of Wales, Lauzun was the obvious man to conduct them to the safety of France.[28] This act of gallantry brought him back into royal favor.

A French naval victory at Beachy Head, off the coast of East Sussex, in June 1690 augured well for the battle to come. The Battle of the Boyne took place a month later; however, James's army lacked leadership and morale, both fatal flaws. During the battle, James remained with his guards, and "when he saw his Army everywhere giving ground, was the first that ran for it, and reached Dublin, before the action was quite over."[29] The fallen former king of England returned to France aboard a French ship.

The following March, Louis announced his intention to lay siege to the town of Mons. He would take with him the dauphin and the comte de Toulouse, his legitimized son by Athénaïs. At the same time, he removed his daughter, Françoise-Marie, from Athénaïs's charge and placed her into the care of Mme de Montchevreuil, the wife of duc du Maine's tutor. This was Louis's not-so-subtle way of telling Athénaïs, who had remained at court to take care of her children, that her presence was no longer required. In a fit of pique, she asked Bishop Bossuet, one of her staunchest enemies, to obtain Louis's permission for her to retire to a convent she had founded some time ago, the Filles de la Providence, known as Saint-Joseph's. Perhaps she was hoping that Louis would tearfully bring her back to court as he had previously done with Louise de La Vallière. If so, she was to be horribly disappointed. Instead, Louis simply agreed that her departure would be most convenient. He gave her rooms in the *appartement des bains* to the duc du Maine, while Françoise-Marie moved into her brother's old rooms.[30] So ended the court career of Athénaïs de Montespan, perhaps one of the most vibrant and interesting of Louis's mistresses, whose departure was every bit as unnoticed as her arrival had been.

Louis, unperturbed about the departure of the woman who had captivated his heart and who had been the center of his world for so long, set out from Versailles as planned on Sunday, March 17, 1691, on the first stage of his journey to Mons. Despite suffering from gout, he insisted upon directing the siege and exposing himself to danger. It was almost as though he was tempting fate, taunting the enemy to do their worst while showing the world that nothing could harm the invincible Sun King. The town duly fell on April 9.[31]

The setback came at sea. The French victory at Beachy Head had alerted the English to the weakness of her sea power. The navy had been allowed to decline. It was stated in Parliament that England's power rested solely upon her ships, and efforts were made to restore the navy to its former strength. Their renewed investment paid off in May 1692, when a joint Anglo-Dutch fleet triumphed at the battle of La Hogue, off the coast of Normandy.

Louis had lost his supremacy at sea, but there was still everything to fight for on land. He had identified the town of Namur as the best place to lay siege. It was, he wrote,

> the strongest rampart not only of Brabant, but of the Bishopric of Liège, of the United Provinces, and of a portion of Lower Germany. Besides securing the communications of all these districts, its situation at the confluence of the Sambre and the Meuse makes it mistress of these two rivers; it is well placed, either to arrest the ventures of France . . . and to facilitate those that can be made against France herself.[32]

Once again, Louis led the siege in person at the head of forty thousand men and a powerful artillery force. Vauban travelled with the army, laying the trenches and preparing to work on the fortifications as soon as the siege was won. The maréchal de Luxembourg, meanwhile, stood at the head of a force of twenty thousand, who were stationed nearby to keep watch in case William should seek to defend the town, which fell to France at the end of June.[33] Riding high on his luck, Louis now planned another attack on England and James prepared to set sail, but a terrible, monthlong storm in the English Channel kept the ships in port, and the attack eventually had to be abandoned.

A magnificent victory at the small village of Steinkirk in Flanders on August 3 was destined to go down in history as much for the triumph as for the new fashion it introduced. The Anglo-Scots-Dutch army descended upon the French camp before the maréchal de Luxembourg and his officers had time to complete their toilette. As they rushed out to meet the enemy, their untied cravats flew in their faces, so they twisted them and tucked the ends into a buttonhole. The steinkirk cravat became a favorite fashion item, worn to celebrate the victory. Even women wore one, although they attached theirs to a rever because they had no buttonhole in which to tuck the ends.[34]

The year 1691 also saw the death of the war minister, Louvois; he was poisoned upon the orders of a foreign prince, so some believed.[35] His office was inherited by his third son, the young and inexperienced marquis de Barbezieux. At the same time, Louis reinstated Simon Arnauld, marquis de Pomponne, as secretary of state for foreign affairs. A mild-mannered and diplomatic man, Pomponne initiated tentative steps towards negotiations which would eventually break the Protestant alliance.

Then, in the spring of 1693, Louis travelled to the Luxembourg in Paris. The purpose of his visit was to bid farewell to his cousin, Mademoiselle, who lay dying. As the king approached her bed, she took the opportunity to advance the cause of her kinsman, the marquis de Joyeuse, whom she thought should be made a maréchal of France. Louis obliged his cousin and awarded the maréchal's baton to Joyeuse. Mademoiselle died on April 5, 1693 at the age of sixty-three.[36]

In the early summer of 1693, Louis was once again preparing to join his troops in Flanders. He was now fifty-four years old. Throughout his wars, he shared the often difficult life of a soldier, staying out in all weather and exposing himself to enemy fire. He directed sieges and accepted the humble submissions of city fathers of enemy towns along the Rhine. Louis loved war. By his own admission, he loved war too much, but it was not to be an unconquerable enemy that finally defeated him; it was to be his own failing health. For some time, he had suffered from abscesses, trouble with his teeth, and, most debilitating of all, chronic gout and rheumatism.

On May 18, he set out from Versailles and reached Quesnoy eleven days later. Towards the evening, he complained of pain and tension in the muscles of his neck, which was treated with a rub of sweet almond oil mixed with spirits of wine followed by an application of warm ashes wrapped in linen. The treatment had its effect, and Louis felt much better the next day, but his chief physician, Guy-Crescent Fagon, thought it prudent to bleed him. As so often with Louis, being bled brought on an attack of the vapors, but this time it was "accompanied by much affliction, which recurred several times over the next two or three days, and left His Majesty in this disposition for the rest of the journey."[37] Louis arrived in Flanders on June 2, but he was still unwell. After spending only one week with his troops, he abruptly announced that he was returning to Versailles.

Louis was by no means recovered by the time he arrived home, and as it turned out, he would suffer from intermittent attacks of the vapors, as well as dizziness, until August 5. Only Louis, Françoise, and Fagon were aware of his disposition, and three days after Louis's arrival at Versailles, Françoise wrote to a friend that he was "in perfect health," attributing his untimely return to his decision to send heavily armed forces to Germany to take advantage of the capture of Heidelberg. "I am delighted that the interest of the state forces him to return to Versailles," she added, reiterating once more that "he is very well."[38] As it happened, Louis would never return to the battlefield: to the shock and dismay of everyone, he announced that he would no longer take part in military campaigns.

⚜

It was at this point that a crisis arose in Louis's relationship with Françoise. It began when a certain lady, Mme de Guyon, came into their lives. Jeanne Bouvier de La Motte, Mme Guyon, was widowed at an early age. Rich and beautiful, she was attracted to spirituality and given to episodes of mystical reverie, which inspired her to identify herself with St. Teresa of Avila. She embraced Quietism, a Christian philosophy that preached a childlike innocence of the soul.[39] She claimed to have contracted a mystical marriage with the child Jesus, who placed an invisible ring on her finger. The focus on Jesus as a child provided the essence of Quietism, for it represented a "personal" relationship with Jesus before his ministry, the crucifixion, and the resurrection. It was a personal relationship with God before the existence of the church, and even before the creation. As such, it negated the teaching of the church, dispensed with Holy Scripture, and eliminated the need for the sacraments. It also eliminated the need for priests, for a personal relationship with the divine required no intermediary.

Guided and encouraged by her spiritual advisor, a Barnabite monk named Père Lacombe, Mme Guyon preached self-denial, serenity of mind, the suppression of all desire, the cult of the inner soul, and disinterested love that was not humiliated by fear or inspired by the hope of reward.

Mme Guyon had a cousin, Mme de La Maisonfort, who was a favorite of Françoise, and it was through her subsequent friendship with Françoise that Mme Guyon came to Versailles. Here, she met Abbé Fénelon, tutor to the royal children. A gentle man, well-educated and intellectual, Fénelon was also drawn to the mystical, and in him Mme Guyon found a kindred spirit. It was only a matter of time before she was introduced to the young ladies at Saint-Cyr.

Mme Guyon taught her own brand of spirituality at Saint-Cyr, where the young ladies embraced it passionately. This brought her to the attention of Godet, bishop of Chartres in whose diocese the school fell. He complained of her conduct to the archbishop of Paris, who threatened to take action against her. Françoise now began to realize the danger she was in. She promptly broke off relations with Mme Guyon and refused to allow her to remain any longer at Saint-Cyr.

Françoise was right to worry. When Louis heard how Quietism had spread through Saint-Cyr, he was furious with Françoise for allowing Mme Guyon and Fénelon to preach what he considered to be heresy. He ordered Mme de La Maisonfort and Françoise's closest friend, Mme de Brinon, from Saint-Cyr, while Fénelon was told to withdraw to his bishopric at Cambrai. Louis then reprimanded his wife mercilessly over the affair before leaving her room and refusing to see her.

Bishop Bossuet and Fénelon carried on a spiritual war, attacking each other from the pulpit and in print. Bossuet took pity on Françoise, and he wrote to Louis urging him to give back his confidence "to that excellent partner, filled with the spirit of God, and with tenderness and fidelity to your person." He went on: "I know the depths of her heart, and I will pledge you my word that no one can love you more tenderly and respectfully than she loves you. She will never deceive you, unless she is deceived herself."[40] Bossuet's words were scarcely necessary, for Louis loved Françoise and would do nothing to hurt her. The heart he had tried to harden against her had already softened, and he went to her room to find her worn out with weeping. Moved almost to tears himself, he sat beside her bed and said tenderly, "Madame, are you going to die of this business?"[41]

Their crisis was over, but it is easy to see why Quietism had concerned Louis so much. Fénelon was, from Louis's point of view, a dangerous man.[42] He believed that the king ought to live a simpler, less ostentatious life with a smaller, less expensive court. The king's concerns should be focused not on the pursuit of *gloire* but on the welfare of his subjects. Moreover, Louis should encourage agriculture over massive industry and commerce. Fénelon advocated aristocratic rule as opposed to the absolute monarchy practiced by Louis. He thought France would be better served by being governed by the Estates General, with regular meetings led by the nobility. In other words, France should become a democracy, albeit with certain limits.

Fénelon, a pacifist who believed all wars were civil wars, opposed the War of the Spanish Succession and laid the blame for the conflict firmly upon Louis's shoulders. Wars could be avoided in future, he believed, if the rulers of Europe were to form a league of states and come together in regular summits.

Fénelon's followers formed a small but influential group, while his political importance lay in his position as tutor to the young duc de Bourgogne, who would one day become king. His gentle, mystical philosophy appealed to many high-ranking members of the court, among them the duchesses de Beauvillier and Chevreuse, both daughters of the late Colbert, and their husbands. Mme Guyon's daughter was also married to Nicolas Foucquet's son and heir, the vicomte de Vaux. It is easy to see why Louis worried that Fénelon might provoke factionalism at court. This, even more than the question of heresy, was the reason why he persecuted Fénelon and was resolute in his condemnation of Quietism.

The controversy surrounding Quietism, however, was to continue for some while yet. Fénelon, anxious to retain his offices at court, urged Mme Guyon to seek spiritual council from Bossuet. She received the sacrament and gave him her writings for examination. She did everything he told her to and promised never again to disseminate her teaching. However, she broke her promise, and Louis was forced to order her arrest. She spent her time in the Bastille composing mystical verses.

Bossuet, long considered Fénelon's mentor and master, ordered Fénelon to condemn Mme Guyon and submit to his own pastoral instruction. Fénelon was unwilling to do either, and upon his departure for his own diocese, he published his work, *Maxims of the Saints*, in which he refuted the charges against Mme Guyon and developed a doctrine of holy meditation and spirituality. The outraged Bossuet denounced the book to Louis as he fell to his knees before the king and begged his forgiveness for having allowed a fatal heresy to flourish in his kingdom.

As Louis and Françoise consulted Père de La Chaise for advice, it became a matter of theological discussion as to whether "loving God for Himself" was indeed a heresy. Courtiers sneered at Bossuet, prompting him to write another attack on Fénelon. Both bishops sent their writings to Pope Innocent XII with promises that they would submit to his decision.

Cardinal d'Estrées, Louis's ambassador in Rome, persuaded the king to write to Innocent to demand Fénelon's condemnation. He did so, stating that the *Maxims of the Saints on the Inner Life* had been presented to him as a pernicious work, and urging Innocent to condemn it. After a thorough examination by theologians appointed by the Council of the Holy Office, the propositions expounded by Fénelon were condemned by a majority of votes in Rome on March 13, 1699. Fénelon not only accepted defeat with good grace but he also condemned his own work from his pulpit at Cambrai, while forbidding his friends to defend it. Four years later, Mme Guyon was allowed to leave the Bastille and retire to her own estates, where she spent her time writing and performing acts of charity.

TWENTY-FIVE

"Sire, Marly!"

L ouis was justifiably proud of the gardens at Versailles. Whenever dignitaries visited, he insisted upon showing them the beautiful bosquets, flower gardens, parterres, and fountains. He decided to write *Manière de montrer les jardins de Versailles*, a guide to the best way to view the gardens. There were seven versions in all, the first of which appeared in 1689. The guide was updated as new features were added until the final version was completed in 1705. Some of the editions were written in Louis's own hand, others were the work of various secretaries and corrected by Louis.

Why Louis wrote the guide is not known for certain; it is only known that it was never intended for publication. It might have been written for official receptions or for the king's personal use in later years when painful gout and rheumatism kept him confined to a wheelchair for much of the time. That it could be used by the fountain engineers, to allow them to know which fountains to activate as the king and his guests made their way through the vast park, is equally plausible. Whatever the reason, the itinerary covered several distances depending upon which route was taken. Walks to the menagerie and Trianon were the longest, at some eight kilometers.[1]

Those who ventured through the gardens towards the canal would have been rewarded by the sight of miniature boats, the beginnings of the squadron that would replicate in perfect detail the boats and ships of the royal fleet. Initially, three boats graced the waterways: the *Dunkerquoise*, a replica of a ship used by Dunkirk privateers; the *Réale*, a miniature version of the galleon of the same name and flagship of the Marseilles squadron; and the *Grand Vaisseau*, a small frigate equipped with cannon. Louis would use these ships for cruising on the canal until his physician, M. Fagon, ordered him to stop for fear that the damp air would further aggravate his rheumatism.

Louis was coming up to his fifty-fifth birthday, which, for the period in which he lived, meant that he was swiftly approaching old age. He turned his thoughts to his children, spending more time with them and contemplating the succession. He had already legitimized his children by Mme de La Vallière and Athénaïs and many had been married off, or "established," to use the proper term. In 1680, Louis's daughter by Louise de La Vallière, Marie-Anne de Blois, had married Louis de Conti, nephew of the prince de Condé, although she would be widowed at nineteen. Five years later, his daughter by Athénaïs, Louise-Françoise, Mlle de Nantes, had married Louis III de Bourbon, prince de Condé, a grandson of the prince de Condé. His son by Athénaïs, the duc du Maine, had overcome the illnesses that had afflicted his childhood, although he had been left with a limp. In 1692, at the age of twenty-two, he married Anne-Louise-Bénédicte de Bourbon, one of Condé's granddaughters. By marrying three of his legitimized children into the Condé family, Louis was seeking to ensure their loyalty to the crown, thereby sparing his successor the fear of another Fronde.[2] He still had one more daughter to establish, however: Françoise-Marie. Her marriage to the duc de Chartres, Philippe's son by his second wife, Liselotte, was smoothed by the granting of favors to two of Philippe's friends, the marquis d'Effiat and the chevalier de Lorraine, and the promise of high military office and the governorship of an important province for young Chartres.[3] A large financial incentive further sweetened the agreement, and the wedding went ahead on February 18, 1692.

Louis had one surviving child by Queen Marie-Thérèse, Louis de France, the dauphin, known as Monseigneur. Now aged thirty-two, he was a widower with three fine boys, the eldest of whom, the duc de Bourgogne, was second in the line of succession. Louis took the boy under his wing and instructed him in statecraft, just as Mazarin had taught him. The duc attended councils with the king, and, like him, he learned to listen to petitions and take advice from specialists before making up his mind as to the proper way to proceed in each case.

Bourgogne had been betrothed to Marie-Adélaïde, daughter of Victor Amadeus II de Savoy, who had been won over to France's side during the War of the League of Augsburg. Their marriage would seal the peace agreement between the two states.[4] Now, in October 1696, the eleven-year-old bride arrived at the bridge of Beauvoisin, where she rested in a house on the Savoy side of the border. Having changed her clothes, she went to the bridge, at the entrance of which she was received by her new household, who escorted her to the French house that had been prepared for her on the other side. Here, she spent the night and departed the following morning. She bid farewell to her Italian household without shedding a tear. Only one lady-in-waiting and her physician accompanied her into her new country, but they were not allowed to remain with her for very long.

On November 4, Louis, the dauphin, and Philippe set out in separate journeys for Montargis to receive the new princess. As usual, Louis could not contain his curiosity and excitement, and he rode on ahead so that he was the first to meet Marie-Adélaïde. Their first encounter took place at six in the evening at the door of his carriage. He then took her to the apartment that had been prepared for himself in a house in the town, and here she was presented to the other members of the royal family who had accompanied him.

Louis wrote to Françoise, praising the new princess:

> She has the best grace and the finest figure I have ever seen. Dressed like a picture, and her head to match. The eyes bright and very beautiful; black and admirable eyelashes; the skin smooth, red and white, just as one would have it; the most beautiful and abundant black hair that one can see; a very red mouth, full lips; the teeth white, long, and very irregular; well-made hands, but of the colour of her age. . . . I am quite satisfied. . . . I hope you will be so too. . . . A noble style, polished and pleasant manners. I am glad to speak well of her, for I think, without prepossession or flattery, I am obliged to do so.[5]

Louis decreed that although Marie-Adélaïde would immediately assume her married title, duchesse de Bourgogne, she would be called a princess.[6] She should dine alone, being served by the duchesse du Lude, and would receive visits only from her own ladies and anyone to whom Louis granted his express permission. She would not yet hold court, and would receive visits from her betrothed once every two weeks and his brothers once a month.

By November 8, the whole court had returned to Versailles and Marie-Adélaïde was granted the honor of being installed in the late queen's apartments. Here, she was presented to all the most distinguished persons of Paris. Louis and Françoise instantly fell in love with her. She was the daughter they had never had. They indulged, even spoiled, her, and she, in her turn, "usurped with both a freedom never attempted by any of the children of the king." She called Françoise "aunt" and was, quite simply, enchanting. Marie-Adélaïde's father had been well versed in the ways of the French court, and he had taught his daughter everything she needed to know. She, who had been a willing pupil, "knew so well how to profit by the instruction, and with what grace she did so."

Louis was captivated by Marie-Adélaïde's cleverness, her attentions and graces, which exceeded her age, and he did not want to wait any longer than necessary to marry her to his grandson. He therefore announced that the couple would marry on December 7, the day after the bride's twelfth birthday. He also expressed his wish that the court should wear splendid dress for the wedding. The king, who for some time now had taken to wearing simple clothes, ordered a magnificent suit. No expense was to be spared, and the courtiers competed with each other to see who would be the best dressed on the day; so much so that Louis began to repent having given his order. He "could not comprehend how husbands could be foolish enough to let themselves be ruined for their wives' clothes." Deep down, however, he took great pleasure in the celebrations, and in studying the sumptuousness of the costumes his courtiers wore.[7]

The wedding took place as scheduled on Saturday, December 7. The bridal pair arrived in the king's room just after midday, and Louis led them into the chapel. After the betrothal and the marriage ceremony, the Cardinal de Coislin said low mass. Louis then led the party to dinner. A courier was sent to Turin to inform the new duchesse's father of the marriage, but the rest of the day passed very quietly. That evening, however, the court was joined by King James of England and Mary of Modena. It was a rainy evening, but this did not stop the company from enjoying a fireworks display before they went to supper.

It was now time for the *coucher* of the bride. Louis had ordered that all men were to be excluded from the ritual, but the ladies remained with her, and Queen Mary received the honor of giving the duchesse de Bourgogne her chemise. The duc, meanwhile, undressed in the antechamber, seated on a folding stool. The king and all the princes attended him, while James, in an echo of his wife's role, handed him his chemise.

It was then announced that the duchesse was in bed. The duc entered the bedchamber and climbed into the right side of the bed in the presence of the king and all the court. The king and queen of England withdrew first, then Louis retired to bed, upon which everyone else left the nuptial chamber except the dauphin, the duchesse's ladies, and the duc de Beauvillier, who remained beside the duc's pillow, and the duchesse du Lude, who attended the bride.

The dauphin remained for fifteen minutes or so, during which he told his son to kiss his bride, against the furious protests of the duchesse du Lude. He then made his son get out of bed and return to his own room. As it turned out, the duchesse du Lude was correct to protest, for when Louis found out, he said it was wrong and that "he did not choose his grandson to kiss so much as the tip of his wife's finger till the time came for them to live together."

On the following day, a circle was held for Madame la duchesse de Bourgogne in her apartments. Louis came in towards the end, and he conducted the ladies to a salon near the chapel, where a fine collation awaited them. The evening was filled with music, and the company remained there until nine, when Louis escorted the young couple to the duchesse's apartments. They continued to live as they had done before their marriage; and, although the duc visited his wife every day, her ladies were under strict orders not to leave them alone together. The couple would not be "put together," as the saying went, until shortly after New Year 1699, when the duc de Bourgogne was not yet sixteen and the duchesse was still only thirteen.

Both Louis and William III had come to realize that the war could not be won by either side. The fighting would, nonetheless, continue for some time yet. In the summer of 1695, William's forces threatened Namur, which Louis had captured the previous year.[8] The maréchal de Villeroy,[9] knowing that the fate of the Low Countries rested upon who held Namur, rushed to its defense. On July 13, the French forces encamped before the town and prepared for an assault the next day. The enemy commander, Vaudémont,[10] was in an exposed position, with his only chance of escape being to flee to a wooded area some three leagues distant.

As the morning of July 14 dawned, Villeroy issued orders to the duc du Maine to attack Vaudémont as a delaying tactic designed to allow the maréchal time to position his troops for the main assault and to prevent Vaudémont from escaping. Du Maine was Louis's favorite legitimized son by Athénaïs, and his father, who valued military heroism and courage above everything else, expected much from him.

Some time went by, but Villeroy received no news from du Maine. He issued his orders again five or six times, but still he heard no word. Du Maine claimed to need time to reconnoiter, to go to confession, or to organize his men, but the truth was that he had been ready for a while and his troops were eager to begin the attack. The duke's delay allowed Vaudémont to begin his march, and the French could only stand, watch, and fume as the enemy slipped beyond their reach.

At that point, Montrevel,[11] senior lieutenant-general, was so incensed that he confronted du Maine, reminding him of Villeroy's orders, the victory that would have been theirs for the taking, the damage to the duke's reputation and the risk to the siege, the glories of French success there and the defenselessness of the Low Countries when the only army capable of assisting them had been defeated. Du Maine withstood the onslaught, stammering and procrastinating for so long that any chance of stopping Vaudémont's escape was lost.

As the officers, and no doubt also the men, cursed and vented their anger on du Maine, Villeroy attempted to salvage the situation by detaching three regiments of dragoons, who attacked the enemy's rear. One or two flags were captured and the rear guard of Vaudémont's army was ruffled, but it was little consolation in comparison to the glorious victory it might have been.

Villeroy was too good a soldier and too loyal a courtier to apportion blame to another. He wrote a dispatch to Louis stating simply that Vaudémont had moved too swiftly and had managed to elude him. He gave no further details, but signed and sealed the message and sent it on its way.

At Versailles, Louis waited impatiently for news of the great victory, when he could bristle with fatherly pride at the bravery of his son. When a private gentleman arrived with the dispatches instead of the expected high dignitary, the king was more than a little astonished. His initial reaction turned to concern when he learned that so little action had actually taken place. Louis, meanwhile, moved the court to Marly.

With so little information coming from the front, Louis read all the gazettes he could find from Holland. The first carried a story about the duc du Maine, how he had been wounded and carried off the field on a stretcher, and this is what had allowed Vaudémont to escape. The irony of this irritated Louis, but his annoyance was as nothing compared to how he received the news as written in the next gazette. The duc du Maine, it was announced, had not received so much as a scratch. Louis pondered the contradictory reports, the silence that had followed the battle, Villeroy's laconic dispatch, and his suspicions were aroused. He finally learned the truth from one of his chief valets, Vienne.[12] Louis's "distress was more than he could bear. He felt the weight of the army's contempt for that much cherished son, and the mockery of the gazettes taught him what was being said abroad. His chagrin was great."

Louis rarely lost his temper, and on this occasion, he kept his anger and grief bottled up inside, but his pent-up emotions needed an outlet. He went to dinner as usual with the ladies, and in the presence of the court, he was handed his hat and cane at the end of the meal. Just then, he noticed one of the dessert-waiters placing a sweet biscuit into his pocket. Louis rushed at the man and beat him, abused him, and finally broke his cane across the man's shoulders. Luckily, the cane was made of bamboo and was brittle, but Louis, still holding its shattered remains in his hand, continued to yell curses after the fleeing waiter. He then crossed the salon and disappeared inside Françoise's apartments. His anger—unprecedented and uncharacteristic of the king, who was normally so equitable—had still not abated by the time he emerged an hour later, much to the terror of the whole court. On September 1, 1695, William took back Namur.

The following year, Victor Amadeus II de Savoy agreed to France's offer to give up its ambitions in Italy. Louis, as a gesture of goodwill and a token of his sincerity, returned the fortress of Pignerol to Savoy and gave up Casale to Mantua.[13] For the first time it looked as though an end to hostilities was possible, and Louis was optimistic enough to set out his terms for peace with England and Holland in 1697: he would recognize William as the legitimate king of England, concede defeat over the Palatinate, and surrender all the territories he had acquired since 1679. The Dutch and the English found these conditions acceptable. Emperor Leopold, however, resisted for a time, but the threat of being abandoned by his allies left him with little choice but to accept the terms. In return, Louis was allowed to retain Alsace, Strasbourg, and the electorate of Cologne. The subsequent Peace of Ryswick, which was signed in the autumn of 1697, brought to an end the War of the League of Augsburg at a time when French peasants were at their highest level of poverty and the fiscal system had to be propped up by ministers and tax farmers resorting to the abuses of the past.[14]

Louis attended a fête in the new duchesse de Bourgogne's apartment shortly after her wedding. As he entered the great gallery, he saw that seats had been set out, and all was beautifully decorated. The duc d'Aumont, however, was frantic. There were simply too many people, and he could not cope. Even Louis found himself overwhelmed by the sheer number of people who crowded the gallery, and the fête was spoiled.[15] The rigid etiquette of the court had become stifling even for Louis, whose every waking moment was a matter of public interest. Saint-Simon said that "with a good watch and an almanac, one could know exactly what the king was doing, even if one were a hundred leagues away."[16] Louis needed a retreat.

Some years previously, Louis had demolished the Trianon—the blue-and-white porcelain palace in which he and Athénaïs had shared their love and entertained privileged guests—and built another in its place. Known as the Marble Trianon because of the pink marble panels that adorned the outer façade, it was designed by Jules Hardouin-Mansart under Louis's personal supervision. The new palace was arranged around a central colonnaded gallery, which opened onto a central courtyard on one side and a garden, planted with ten thousand flowers, on the other. Building work had begun in 1687, and although the king held council in the ornate Mirror Room, the Trianon was intended to be a private retreat for Louis and Françoise.[17]

At Trianon, Louis would offer informal entertainments, sharing his table with the ladies and allowing his guests to recline on soft sofas, a luxury quite unheard of at Versailles. Yet however informal it might have been, Trianon was too close to Versailles. Louis longed for a smaller palace where he and a few selected guests could escape the bustle and prying eyes of the court and relax in peaceful seclusion. He had a general idea of where he wanted his new palace to be, and he focused his search on the land that sloped from Saint-Germain towards the Seine as it wound its way through lush meadows and rich pastures. Someone urged him to consider Luciennes, where the marquis de Cavoye[18] had a lovely house, but Louis rejected the idea, saying that the spot had so much potential that it would ruin him. His choice finally fell upon a narrow valley hemmed in by rocky hills that lay behind Luciennes, where a small hamlet called Marly nestled in the shadow of the hills. The ground was marshy, there was no view, and access was difficult. Louis immediately fell in love with it.[19]

Originally, Louis intended to reserve Marly for special occasions, somewhere to withdraw with his family and a few chosen friends from Wednesday to Saturday two or three times a year, with no more than a dozen servants to carry out necessary duties. Visits were strictly by invitation only, and courtiers would drop not-so-subtle hints as the king went past on his way to mass: "Sire, Marly!" The lucky ones would see their names pasted up by midday.

Life was much less formal than at Versailles. Full court dress was not required, so that "everywhere the King goes walking everyone is covered. Men sit in the presence of the Dauphin and the Duchess of Bourgogne. Some even lie full length on the sofa . . ."[20] Louis liked to amuse his courtiers, and occasionally supper parties would end with a food fight. One day, Louis began to throw apples, oranges, and balls of bread at the ladies, and he allowed them to throw similar missiles back at him. Mlle de Viantais, however, got more than she bargained for when she bombarded the king with a bread ball: he took up a plate of salad and hurled it at her.[21] Courtiers still fawned, however. One day the Abbé de Polignac went walking in the gardens with Louis. When it began to rain, the king noticed that the abbé's coat was not suitable for wet weather. "It means nothing, Sire," the abbé assured him. "The rain at Marly is never wet."[22]

As time went by, the estate of Marly inevitably grew larger. The château, or *pavillon du roi*, was a medium-sized building flanked by twelve smaller ones, six on either side, so that the whole complex formed the shape of a capital U. Built by Hardouin-Mansart in an Italianate style, the *pavillon du roi* featured Apollo and Thetis in stucco, while the other buildings were decorated with other Olympian gods, as well as Diana, Hercules, Victory, Fame, and Abundance, and the five known planets: Mercury, Venus, Mars, Jupiter, and Saturn.[23]

The garden at Marly featured tulips, a new innovation for Louis, who had developed a passion for their bright colors. His old favorites were not forgotten, however, and the heavily scented tuberoses, jasmine, and orange also found a place. In the evenings, their scent was sometimes so overpowering that the king and his company were driven indoors to escape it. One of the hills was levelled to provide a view, and a huge set of waterworks was built. Called the Machine de Marly, it comprised an elaborate series of conduits, aqueducts, and reservoirs, which carried water from the Seine to irrigate the gardens and feed the fountains, lakes, waterfalls, and the gilded goldfish pond.

As at Versailles, Louis wanted to look upon full-grown trees when he walked in the garden, so mature trees were taken from Compiègne and elsewhere and replanted at Marly; those that died, and there were many, were immediately replaced with fresh ones. The landscape was changed frequently as dense woodland and dark allées were stripped away to make space for the lakes upon which the courtiers rowed in gondolas; but then the lakes were drained and the woodland returned as dark and dense at it had ever been. In time, visits to Marly would become more and more frequent until, towards the end of the reign, it was almost the permanent residence of the court, but in June 1701, it provided the setting for an event that was to be the prelude to tragedy.

It was Wednesday, June 8, and Philippe came to Marly to dine with Louis,[24] entering the king's study as soon as the king's council meeting ended. It became immediately obvious that all was not well. Louis was angry because the duc de Chartres had been annoying his wife by openly carrying on an affair with a Mlle de Séry,[25] one of Liselotte's maids of honor.

Louis took his anger out on Philippe, who retorted that "fathers who led certain lives could hardly have the grace and the authority to reprove their sons." This stung Louis to the quick, and he angrily retorted that at least his daughter should be spared the indignity of having to witness her husband's bad behavior. This was too rich for Philippe, who reminded Louis that he had shown little concern for the queen's feelings "when he made his mistresses take journeys with her in the same carriage." As the quarrel heated, the brothers began to yell at the top of their voices.

Marly was organized so that the king's room opened onto a small salon, which at this hour was always filled with courtiers waiting to see Louis pass by on his way to dinner. The door to this cabinet always stood open, except when council was sitting. The entrance was concealed by a curtain, which was drawn back by the usher whenever anyone wished to enter. As a result of this arrangement, the raised voices of Louis and Philippe could be distinctly heard, and the usher was obliged to enter and warn them that the courtiers could hear every word they said.

This well-timed warning caused the brothers to lower their voices, but it did nothing to stop the quarrel. Philippe, "off his hinges," reminded Louis of the promises he had made to the duc de Chartres to induce him to marry Françoise-Marie de Blois, none of which had been fulfilled. All the duc wanted, Philippe continued, was some form of service, but since Louis would not oblige, it was not for Philippe to prevent his son from consoling himself by finding amusement elsewhere. As it was, he now saw the truth in the predictions that had been made at the time of the marriage—that the duc would get no profit from the match but only shame and dishonor. Louis now played his ace: the war would soon oblige him to "make certain retrenchments, and that, as Monsieur showed himself so little complying, he should begin by cutting off his pensions before retrenching on himself."

At this moment, dinner was announced. Louis and Philippe sat down to table, but Philippe's face was "flaming scarlet, his eyes sparkling with anger." Several ladies at the table and the courtiers who stood behind them thought that the prince ought to be bled. Still, Philippe ate a hearty dinner, and, when the meal was finished, he took his daughter-in-law, whom he had brought to eat with the king, to Saint-Germain before they returned to Saint-Cloud.

That evening, Louis was working in his cabinet with the dauphin and the princesses when a messenger arrived from Saint-Cloud asking to speak to the king on behalf of the duc de Chartres. He told Louis that Philippe had been seized with faintness during supper. He had been bled and was feeling better, but he had also been given an emetic as a precaution. The message did not quite relate the truth. In fact, Philippe had been taking supper as usual with the ladies, but towards the end of the meal, as he was pouring a glass of liqueur for Mme de Bouillon, he began to stammer and pointed to something with his hand. It was not unusual for Philippe to speak in Spanish, so some of the ladies asked him what he had said; others cried out in alarm. It all happened very quickly, and he fell onto his son in a fit of apoplexy. They carried him to his room, shook him, walked him about, bled him, and administered an emetic, "but without his showing more than a faint sign of life."

Under ordinary circumstances, Louis would have rushed to his brother's side "for mere nothings." On this occasion, he had not been told of the seriousness of his brother's illness and he went instead to Françoise's apartment and woke her up. After a quarter of an hour, he returned and ordered his carriages to be made ready, and then sent the marquis de Gesvres to Saint-Cloud with orders to return and wake him if Philippe's condition worsened. He then went to bed. In Saint-Simon's opinion, Louis thought some ruse was afoot to resolve the difficult position the brothers were in. He had gone to Françoise to seek her opinion: "He would rather, I think, offend all propriety than run the risk of becoming a dupe."

Louis had been in bed for an hour and a half when another messenger arrived from the duc de Chartres. The king was roused from his sleep to be told that the emetic Philippe had been given had taken no effect, and that he was very ill indeed. Louis started out for Saint-Cloud, meeting Gesvres on the way. "No one can imagine the excitement and disorder of that night at Marly, or the horror at Saint-Cloud, that palace of delights," wrote Saint-Simon. Courtiers piled into carriages and flocked to Saint-Cloud, ignoring all ceremony. Louis arrived at three in the morning to find that Philippe had not regained consciousness.

Louis was devastated, and his sadness renewed the love he had always had for his brother. How could this have happened? Philippe was two years younger than he and had always been in good health, better even than the king's. He reproached himself for having hastened his brother's death by their recent quarrel. Naturally given to weeping, he now dissolved in tears. He heard mass at Saint-Cloud, but as the clock struck eight, all hope for Philippe's recovery was lost. Françoise and Marie-Adélaïde begged Louis to return with them to Marly. There was nothing more that Louis could do for his brother in this world. Reluctantly, he allowed himself to be led away. As he turned to leave, he spoke some kind words to the duc de Chartres, both men weeping bitter tears. The young duc asked, "Ah, Sire! What will become of me? I lose Monsieur, and I know that you do not like me." Louis was taken aback. Very touched by his nephew's words, he spoke to him tenderly. As Louis left Saint-Cloud, the crowd of courtiers melted away so that, little by little, the dying Philippe was left on his sofa in his cabinet, surrounded only by weeping scullions and servants.

TWENTY-SIX

The Spanish Succession

L ouis's hopes that his niece Marie-Louise, Queen of Spain, would produce an heir to the Spanish throne—or at least persuade the crown to be passed on to a Bourbon prince following the death of King Carlos—failed when she died childless in 1689. Carlos remarried, but his new queen, unsurprisingly, had so far also failed to produce an heir. The problem of the Spanish succession, therefore, remained unsolved, but there were possible solutions.

The nonpayment of Queen Marie-Thérèse's dowry could be used to annul her renunciation of the Spanish throne. In this case, the dauphin would be the legal heir to the throne of Spain, although it was understood that he would pass his claim to his second son, Philippe, duc d'Anjou. If, on the other hand, the French claim was not accepted, the

Spanish succession would rightfully go to Marie Antonia, the daughter of Leopold I and Margarita Teresa, princess of Spain and electress of Bavaria. Leopold, however, had forced Margarita Teresa to renounce her claim so that he could propose his second son by a subsequent marriage, Archduke Charles. This, then, was the dilemma that faced Louis as he contemplated the problem of the Spanish succession.

Louis did not want another war, and his desire for peace was shared by William III; and so the months between spring and autumn of 1698 were taken up with negotiations that sought to establish the best way forward in the event of the death of Carlos II of Spain. The agreement they reached proposed that the main part of the Spanish inheritance should go to Joseph Ferdinand of Wittelsbach, elector of Bavaria. The Italian possessions would be divided between the dauphin and Archduke Charles, the second son of Emperor Leopold.[1]

The partition treaties agreed between Louis and William would preserve the balance of power in Europe. Although Austria would receive the largest share of the Spanish inheritance, neither the emperor nor Louis would become more powerful than any league that might be formed against them. Moreover, the choice of Joseph Ferdinand was inspired, since he was neither a Bourbon prince nor an Austrian Habsburg. His succession, as both Louis and William recognized, provided the best hope for a peaceful solution to a problem that had threatened for many years. Nevertheless, the proposal was unacceptable to Spain and Austria, but they acquiesced when Carlos made his will in accordance with the treaty. Unfortunately, the elector died suddenly in 1699 at the age of six, and the prospect of war loomed once again.[2]

Louis and William refused to give up, and in March 1700 they returned to the negotiating table to discuss the best way to go forward. The resulting proposal gave Archduke Charles all the possessions that were to have gone to Joseph Ferdinand, with the exception of the Milanais, which would be added to the dauphin's portion. Once again, the arrangement was unpalatable to Leopold because Louis's possession of the Milanais broke up the bloc of territories held by the Habsburgs.[3]

With the balance of power in Europe at an impasse, Louis moved the court to Fontainebleau, where he planned to enjoy the hunting and the verdant beauty of the place he had loved since boyhood. As usual, the business of government continued, and on November 9, the king was holding a meeting with his council of finances when a dispatch arrived from the marquis de Blécourt,[4] his ambassador in Spain. King Carlos II, whose death had been expected for almost forty years, was dead. Carlos's will, which had been witnessed by five or six grandees of Spain, left the entirety of his empire to the duc d'Anjou or his younger brother, the duc de Berry. Should Louis refuse to accept the legacy, Carlos's next designated heir was the Archduke Charles.[5]

Carlos's will offered France much more than Louis could ever have anticipated under the terms of the partition agreements he had concluded with William. He immediately cancelled the hunting expedition that he had planned for that afternoon and ordered his ministers to assemble in Mme de Maintenon's chambers at three o'clock. Beauvillier[6] urged Louis to reject the bequest and maintain the treaty he had agreed with William III. Chancellor Pontchartrain[7] offered a useful summation of the situation as it stood but offered no opinion as to how Louis should proceed. Torcy[8] reasoned that Leopold would never agree to the partition treaty and pointed out that should Louis not accept Carlos's will, the whole of the Spanish succession would go to Archduke Charles. On that basis, he advised Louis to accept the will and declare Philippe, duc d'Anjou, the new king of Spain. The dauphin agreed with Torcy. When the meeting ended after four hours of deliberation, Louis remained undecided, but he took Torcy into his confidence, and the two men held several private discussions over the next few days.

The court returned to Versailles. Immediately after his *lever* the following morning, November 16, Louis invited the Spanish ambassador into his study. He then called for the duc d'Anjou, who was waiting in an anteroom, to enter. Louis turned to the ambassador and said, "You may hail him as your king." The ambassador knelt before the seventeen-year-old and kissed his hand,[9] saying, "What joy! The Pyrenees are no more; they are destroyed."[10] Louis, breaking all royal protocol, then ordered the study doors to be opened wide and commanded the courtiers to come in. He stood for a moment, casting a majestic glance over the large company before pointing to his grandson. "Messieurs, here is the king of Spain. His birth had called him to this crown the late king also by his will; the whole nation [of Spain] wishes it and had commanded it of me. It is Heaven's command, and I accede with pleasure." Turning to his grandson, he told him, "Be a good Spaniard; that is your first duty, but remember that you are born a Frenchman and maintain the union between our two nations; that is the way to make them happy and to preserve the peace of Europe."[11]

Louis and the duc d'Anjou, now Philippe V of Spain, were equals. When the two kings went to mass, Louis offered the new king his hassock, but Philippe did not know how to cope with this breach of tradition, so he refused it. Louis merely put the hassock aside and knelt on the carpeted floor with the rest of his family.[12]

It was decided that Philippe V would travel into his new kingdom on December 1; but Louis, his eyes brimming with tears, had written out some words of advice to give him before he left. Written in haste, the words came straight from Louis's heart:[13]

"Love the Spanish and all your subjects attached to your crown and person. Do not favor those that flatter you most; esteem those who for the common good risk your displeasure. It is in them that you find your true friends."

He urged Philippe to make his subjects happy and not to make war until he was forced to do so. If, however, Philippe was obliged to make war, he should put himself at the head of his armies.

Philippe should never neglect business for pleasure, but to prepare for himself a kind of program which would allow him "some hours of liberty and amusement." There were "few more innocent amusements than hunting and the pleasures of a country house," Louis told him, "provided you do not spend too much on it."

As to business, Louis urged Philippe to "listen carefully to the opening of any business," but to reserve his decision until he had acquired more knowledge. "Remember that it is you who have to decide; but no matter how experienced you are, always listen to every argument of your council, before making that decision."

It was important that Philippe should "always endeavour to have Spaniards" for his viceroys and governors, while keeping "all the French in order."

Louis's sentiments as a grandfather now emerged, and he asked Philippe always to "keep an affection" toward his family. "Remember their sorrow at parting with you," he urged him. "Carry on constant correspondence with them on all matters great and small. Ask us for anything you are in want of or desire to have, and which you lack; we will ask the same of you."

Louis told Philippe: "forget that you are a Frenchman and what may befall you," and, as far as possible, avoid "granting favors to those who lay out money to obtain them. Give opportunely and freely," but "hardly ever accept presents, unless they be quite trifling. If it happen that you cannot avoid accepting them, requite the donors with more generous gifts after a lapse of the few days." In the interests of security, Louis urged Philippe to have a casket in which he could keep "any special thing", and to let no one else have the key. Finally:

> I conclude with the most important advice I can give you. See to it that you are the ruler. You must be master; never have a favorite nor a prime minister. Consult your council and listen to what they have to say, but decide for yourself. God, who had made you a king, will give you the necessary wisdom, so long as your intentions are good.

As Philippe V made his way to Spain, Louis was well aware that his accession cancelled the partition treaty he had agreed on with William. The king of England was equally aware of this, as was Leopold, and they contemplated declaring war on France. Both, however, decided to wait as, one by one, other European powers recognized Philippe's accession.

When he arrived in Spain, however, Philippe found his new country in disarray. There was infighting among the political classes, apathy reigned everywhere, his new subjects were downhearted and in need of strong, stable leadership from a ruler who would reinvigorate the country and bring hope and inspiration to the people. Unfortunately, Philippe was not equal to the task. Louis had never forgotten the behavior of his uncle, Gaston d'Orléans, who had rebelled and intrigued not only against his own brother but also against Louis during his minority. Louis had enclosed the nobility within the gilded refinements of court etiquette and royal service, and that included his own relatives. His own brother, Philippe, had been granted no major role in government or the military. The younger brothers of the duc de Bourgogne, among them the new king of Spain, had been brought up to know their place. As a result, Philippe d'Anjou had not been educated for kingship, and he found the task before him almost impossible. Not knowing what to do, he lapsed into lethargy, rising late in the mornings, arriving hours late to council meetings, leaving letters unopened and rarely even speaking to anyone.[14] He did make a dynastic marriage, however; on September 5, 1701, he married Marie-Louise de Savoy, the twelve-year-old sister of the duchesse de Bourgogne.

Clearly, the situation in Spain could not be allowed to continue. In May 1701, a Monsieur Ozon wrote to Torcy and told him that the people of Spain wanted Louis to govern until Philippe was ready to take over. Louville, chief of King Philippe's French household, warned Torcy that the Spanish expected more of Louis than he could possibly offer them, pointing out that "a kingdom which is rotten from top to bottom cannot be reinstated in a short time."[15]

Louis wrote several letters to Philippe cajoling him to behave like a king, to sort out the problems in his kingdom and see to the welfare of his subjects. When that did not work, he was forced to take matters into his own hands. He reorganized Spain's fiscal system, created a supreme council called the *despacho*, appointed Philippe's gentlemen of bedchamber, sent troops to protect Spanish possessions in the Americas, and appointed merchants to administer Spain's colonial trade.[16]

This was all very well, and other European rulers were prepared to allow that Louis was simply assisting his inexperienced grandson; but then Louis took a step that shattered this hope. By a declaration presented in parlement, he preserved Philippe's provisional claim to the throne of France. This was in clear violation of the stipulation Carlos had placed in his will that the crowns of France and Spain were not to be united.[17] He then took possession of several Flemish towns, which formed a defensive barrier between France and the Spanish Netherlands, as well as two ports, Ostend and Nieuwpoort. Stationing his troops in the towns, he held their Dutch garrisons hostage until the Estates-General declared its intentions. Even though this was a tacit declaration of war, England and Holland were conciliatory. William was happy to accept Philippe V's accession, but he demanded the evacuation of the towns Louis had seized. When Louis refused, the Dutch, fearing for their security, appealed to England for assistance and England responded by preparing for war.

Meanwhile, England, Holland, and Emperor Leopold formed an alliance against Louis, the Grand Alliance of The Hague.[18] Its aims were to address Leopold's claims to the Spanish succession now that Louis's acceptance of Carlos's will had cancelled the partition treaty. Specifically, it wanted Spain's Italian possessions to go to the emperor. It also wanted to secure English and Dutch territories and commerce and, finally, to ensure that captures in the Spanish colonies would be shared by England and Holland. Should Louis fail to satisfy these demands, the allies were prepared to create a barrier between France and the Spanish Netherlands. In addition, they would seek to prevent a union between the crowns of France and Spain. For the moment, they stopped short of declaring war on Louis.

It was at this point that Louis took a step too far. James, the deposed king of England, lay dying at Saint-Germain. Louis called a council to discuss whether or not he should recognize James's son, James Francis Edward, known as the Old Pretender, as the new king of England. The council reminded Louis that the English Parliament had already declared that the crown would go to the house of Hanover upon William's death. France would, therefore, be wrong to recognize the Old Pretender as king.

For Louis, this struck to the heart of the issue. His motives were partly driven by family sentiment, his Catholic prejudices, and his emotions,[19] but he had always held the conviction that kings were appointed by God, not by parliaments. As a divinely appointed king, he had every right to influence royal succession, his choice being guided by God. Kings appointed by parliament, on the other hand, were restrained by the very powers that had created them; and they could control or even destroy him. It was a dangerous road to follow, one that could ultimately lead to the abolition of monarchy.[20] Unfortunately, Louis should have listened to his council; in declaring for the Old Pretender, Louis committed a major error. On May 15, 1702, England, Holland, and the Holy Roman Empire declared war on France. The War of the Spanish Succession had begun.

In this war, which he did not want, Louis was dangerously outmanned and outgunned. France lacked the resources to finance another war, and to further compound the difficulties, Louis had to defend not only France but Spain as well. He adopted the strategy of attacking important towns within the Holy Roman Empire in the hope of forcing Leopold to capitulation.[21] The maréchal de Villars[22] won a significant victory in Friedlingen, after which he pushed on towards the Danube and took Riedlingen the following year. Here, he waited for the elector of Bavaria's army so that they could launch an attack on Vienna together. At the last moment, the elector changed his mind and abandoned Villars, who was so disgusted that he resigned his command.[23]

In 1704, Louis attempted another assault on Vienna; this time his forces were commanded by Marcin.[24] In May of that year, John Churchill, the future duke of Marlborough, began a 250-mile march towards the Danube. In June, he met up with Prince Eugène of Savoy, the son of Louis's former favorite, Olympe Mancini, and together they marched on to meet the French. On August 12, they climbed the church tower at Dapfheim, from which vantage point they could see the French and their Bavarian allies taking up their position before the village of Blenheim. In the ensuing battle, which took place on the thirteenth, the French lost forty thousand of their sixty thousand men. The tides of war had now changed; Louis, no longer the aggressor, was forced to take a defensive position. Leopold erected a statue commemorating the event. The inscription read, LET LOUIS XIV KNOW THAT NO MAN BEFORE HIS DEATH SHOULD BE CALLED EITHER HAPPY OR GREAT.[25] A dispatch carrying the news of the rout at Blenheim was sent to Versailles, but no one except Françoise had the courage to show it to Louis.

Blenheim was a major setback for Louis, but there was more to come. The English took Gibraltar that same month, allowing English ships to sail freely in the Mediterranean, where they could threaten important ports such as Marseilles. It was an English ship that carried Archduke Charles to Catalonia the following year. He captured Barcelona on October 9, made it his capital, and accepted the acclamations of Valencia and Murcia, who declared him king of Spain, supported by England and Holland.

It was now Bourbon against Habsburg as each side struggled to achieve mastery over mainland Europe. Philippe V, who had retreated to Valladolid, attempted to retake Barcelona in 1706, but the English, in alliance with Portugal, thwarted him by lifting the siege on May 11. On that day, there was a total eclipse of the sun; it was to prove an awful omen of the darkness that was about to fall over France. At first, it looked as though the heavens got it wrong, when Vendôme and the duc de Bourgogne launched a surprise attack on Ghent and Bruges, but their advance was halted by Marlborough and Eugène at Oudenarde. The allies then defeated Villeroy at Ramillies, thereby placing the alliance in command of the Spanish Netherlands. Louis moved troops north, but this left his southern flank exposed, and in October, the French under Orléans and Marcin were defeated at Turin. The allies, meanwhile, held on to Barcelona, adding Sardinia, Minorca, and Port Mahon to their growing list of victories.

This was unprecedented. Louis had never before experienced defeat on so great a scale. Comparing the king's tribulations with those of Job, Françoise commented that "God wants to give him the same patience."[26] The year 1707 saw no more military defeats, despite the best efforts of the alliance, but Dutch scouts did manage to reach as far as Versailles, where they captured Béringhen, the dauphin's chief equerry. Fortunately, he was later rescued.[27]

It was now that news arrived of someone long forgotten by all except the *Mercure Galant.* Upon her retirement from court, Athénaïs de Montespan had gone to the convent of Saint-Joseph in Paris, which she had founded. Unable to settle, she travelled frequently between her family estates, Bourbon, where she took the waters, and Fontevrault, where her sister was an abbess at a Benedictine convent. Always a devout Christian, she at last found peace under the guidance of Père de la Tour. Acting upon his advice, she wrote to her husband to apologize for all the wrongs she had done him. She offered to resume their life together or to retire to anywhere he chose for her, whichever he preferred. The marquis, however, would have none of it; he wanted nothing more to do with her for as long as he lived. Despite this, when he died, she mourned him as his widow.[28]

Under la Tour, Athénaïs's penance was harsh, but she willingly submitted to it. Her prayers took precedence over card games, still her favorite pastime. She set aside her beautiful nightdresses for coarse garments of unbleached calico, and beneath her jewelry she mortified her flesh with iron spikes.

Athénaïs had grown very afraid of death, and she employed women to sit by her bedside at night and keep watch over her as she slept with her bed curtains open and the room glowing with nightlights. Her health was generally good, but one night she woke up feeling very ill and sent her watchers to seek help. An emetic was administered and Athénaïs felt better, but the incident frightened her and she made full and public admission of the sins before all her servants and asked for their forgiveness. She then received the sacraments, after which her fear of death faded. It was while she was visiting Bourbon with a friend that she became ill, and it appears to have been the cure rather than the illness that was to be her undoing. She died at three in the morning of May 27, 1707, aged sixty-three.

The following year, Louis embarked upon a disastrous naval expedition to Scotland on behalf of the Old Pretender. As his ships made their way towards the Firth of Forth, Louis thought his offensive would be welcomed; it was a belief predicated on two assumptions. In the first place, he thought that the recent union with the crown of England was unpopular throughout Scotland. Second, he made the mistake of thinking that the Scots on the east coast shared the same religious and political views as those in the west and in the Highlands and Islands.[29] He was wrong on both counts.

The failure of the Scottish expedition was followed by the loss of Lille to the allies. Louis took this defeat hard because the town had been one of his earliest conquests; its loss seemed to take with it the last of the glories of the past. Louis was bereft, but the recent defeats brought out Liselotte's acerbic humor. "Everything is a question of fashion in France, and nowadays it is the fashion to be frightened and run away and be defeated, just as it used to be the fashion to defeat enemies and put them to flight."[30]

An air of despondency now began to stalk the gilded corridors of Versailles. The war was not going well, taxes had to be raised to finance it, Louis's subjects were plunged into deeper poverty than ever before, and now the weather turned. The winter of 1708–9 was particularly hard. Frost gripped the land for two months, rivers froze their entire length, and even coastal waters froze to such a depth that the ice could support fully laden carts.[31] A false thaw melted the snow but quickly froze once more.

The second frost proved more disastrous than the first. At Versailles, bottles holding wines and liqueurs froze and burst, while ice formed in water decanters, even in chambers where fires blazed. People died of the cold, including Louis's confessor, Père de La Chaise, and his former mistress, the princesse de Soubise. Crops were destroyed, seeds rotted, trees perished, and gardens were ruined. People began to hoard what little grain they had, pushing up prices as the harvest failed. In March 1709, Liselotte wrote of the tragedy that befell a family in Paris. A woman had stolen a loaf from a baker's shop and the baker wanted to have her arrested:

> She wept and said, "If you only knew my misery you would not take the bread away from me. I have three small children without any clothes, and they are crying for food. I couldn't endure it any longer, and that is why I stole this loaf." The magistrate before whom the woman was brought told her to take him to her home. He went thither with her and found three little children bundled up in rags sitting in a corner shivering with cold as if they had a fever. He asked the eldest, "Where is your father?" and the child replied, "He is behind the door." The magistrate went to see what the man was doing behind the door and fell back horror-stricken. The poor wretch had hanged himself in a fit of despair. Such things are happening every day.[32]

Wheat was sold at the same price in the provinces, but in Paris the prices were higher. Meanwhile, returns from customs duties and the rentes from the Hôtel de Ville were suspended. Taxes were raised and multiplied, inflation rose; cattle owners, unable to buy food for their stocks, saw them die of starvation. Even people who had assisted the poor in previous years now found themselves in need, and some even took to begging for alms. A blasphemous parody of the Lord's Prayer did the rounds:

> *Our father, who is in Versailles,*
> *Your name is not glorified,*
> *Your kingdom is not great,*
> *Your will is not done on earth or on the waves.*
> *Forgive our enemies who beat us,*
> *And not our generals who let them to do it.* [33]

In spite of this, Louis remained "determined to go on with the war," wrote Liselotte. He did contribute towards the cost when, as he had done in 1689, he sacrificed his treasured possessions. Liselotte noted that he "replaced his golden service with one of porcelain, and he sent everything golden he possesses to the Mint to be converted into *louis*." [34] Other members of the royal family followed suit, as did many of the courtiers, but when Louis found that some were cheating and holding back some of their pieces, he was uncharacteristically sharp, although his complaints had no effect. While the cold never bothered him, he refrained from taking his usual daily walks out of consideration for others.

With France reduced to such a wretched state, Louis barely registered news of the death of Louise de La Vallière, who died in her cell at the Carmelites at midday on June 7. She was sixty-five years and ten months old and had taken the veil as Louise de la Miséricorde some thirty-six years previously. The king's reaction was that from the day she had given herself to God, she was dead to him. [35]

Louis made a difficult decision. At the end of April, he sent Torcy to The Hague to solicit a peace agreement. The allies drew up a list of requirements: Louis must agree to abandon the causes of Philippe V and the Old Pretender; guarantee a strong barrier between France and the Spanish Netherlands; relinquish the French possession of Newfoundland to the English; demolish his fortifications at Dunkirk; surrender Strasbourg and interpret the Treaty of Westphalia in the "German" sense, that is, to restore most of Alsace. While Louis was prepared to consider these demands, the allies added one more clause that the king simply could not accept: to assist the allies in the expulsion of Philippe V from Spain. Louis announced that he preferred to make war on his enemies and not his relatives, upon which the negotiations broke down.[36]

Louis now took the unprecedented step of appealing directly to his people. On June 12, 1709, he addressed a letter to his subjects, which was to be disseminated to every part of the kingdom.[37] In it, Louis acknowledged that his people were harboring hopes of a widespread peace, but he felt he owed it to them to explain why this had not yet come about. Peace had been offered on terms that would have compromised the security of his frontier provinces, and the more he showed himself willing and desirous to allay the suspicions of the enemy, the more they multiplied their demands. These demands, he explained, were not prompted by a wish for lasting peace or international stability but by the desire to surround France and the intention to dismember the kingdom. Louis defended his decision to refuse to remove his grandson from the throne of Spain. He added that he relied upon the support of his subjects, assuring them that he was soliciting the prayers of all the archbishops and bishops throughout the realm. He closed with the assurance that had it been up to himself, his people would now be enjoying the peace that they so much desired, "but which must be acquired by renewed efforts," since the great conditions that he had agreed "are of no use for the reestablishment of public tranquillity."

The war, therefore, had to continue. Louis now removed the duc de Vendôme[38] from his command and replaced him with Villars. In late August 1709, the new commander positioned 100,000 men before the small hamlet of Malplaquet on the French border with the Low Countries. In the ensuing battle, Villars was wounded and had to be stretchered off the battlefield, leaving the command to the seventy-year-old maréchal de Boufflers.[39] At three in the afternoon, the French center collapsed and Boufflers sounded the retreat.[40] The victorious allies allowed the French to withdraw in relatively good order, but their own side had sustained heavy losses. Malplaquet, although an allied victory, could be considered a draw because it left both sides so weak that enemy gains could not be followed up.

Françoise saw in all this the hand of God, who appeared to be punishing Louis just as he had reformed his life and turned away from sin. "The designs of God are incomprehensible," she wrote. "Three Christian kings—namely Louis, the Pretender, James Edward, and Philippe V—appear to be abandoned and heresy and injustice triumph. Let us hope it will not be for long."[41]

Despite her sympathies for Philippe V, Françoise nevertheless thought Louis ought to sacrifice him in order to secure peace. Astonishingly, Louis, who at first rejected the idea, began to view it as a viable option. In the end, he decided to support his grandson, and his decision was vindicated when Philippe V took Vendôme out of retirement and appointed him commander of his armies. The two victories that followed, at Brihuega and Villaviciosa, in December 1710, marked the turning of the tide. Louis's foreign minister, Torcy,[42] was so excited that in a massive breach of protocol, he broke into Louis's cabinet to announce the news. It looked as though Françoise's assessment of God's hand in Louis's affairs had been wrong.

TWENTY-SEVEN
Gathering Twilight

Many years earlier, Mme de Motteville had wondered if Louis had ever considered "how fragile is the grandeur of the great of this earth?"[1] If not, fate was about to ensure that such thoughts never left his mind.

As the enemies of France stood ready to attack, Louis prepared to send forces to meet them. There had been some discussion over whether or not the dauphin should lead the army in Flanders, but Louis decided against it. The dauphin was his only surviving child by Queen Marie-Thérèse, and he was special. The life of the heir to the throne was too valuable to risk on the battlefield.

The dauphin, or Monseigneur, to give him his honorific title, had set up home at Meudon, a little way from Versailles.[2] Following the death of his wife in 1690, he had secretly married Mlle de Choin,[3] a lady-in-waiting to the princesse de Conti.[4] They were happy together, but his eye strayed from time to time. On one occasion he became involved with a Mme de Roure, who, in August 1694, was said to have made certain remarks in Paris that had not gone down too well, and she was ordered to return to her father's estates. Louis, knowing she was not a wealthy woman, gave her two hundred livres to help pay for her journey. The real reason for her dismissal, however, was to get her away from the dauphin.

As had been the case when Louis was a child, the dauphin was a child of France, but this did not mean that there was no affection between father and son. In August 1694, Louis wrote, "I was at Marly today to arrange the accommodation; I hope that when you come back you will be happy with yours."[5] Two weeks later, he wrote to say that he had "not yet come to a decision about the journey to Fontainebleau." He added: "I could not bring myself to pass Choisy[6] while you are not there; but upon your return, I will have the greatest pleasure in staying there for as long as you wish. I shall find myself very lonely at Fontainebleau without you."[7]

One spring day in 1711, as he was returning to his château after Easter, the dauphin encountered a priest carrying the Holy Sacraments. He and the duchesse de Bourgogne, who was travelling with him, got out of the coach and knelt to pay their respects. When the dauphin asked to whom he was taking the sacrament, the priest told him that it was for a man who was dying of smallpox. The dauphin had had smallpox as a child, but it had been a mild case, and he lived in fear of catching it again. He was very alarmed by what the priest told him, and he confided to his chief physician, Boudin,[8] that he would not be surprised if he caught the illness again.

The following day, April 9, the dauphin had planned to go hunting, but as he was dressing he suddenly began to feel very weary and slumped over his chair. Boudin ordered him back to bed and sent a message to Louis, but the incident was related in such a nonchalant manner to the king that he thought little of it and went to Marly as expected after dinner. He was kept informed of his son's progress by Mme la duchesse,[9] who nursed the patient and sent regular reports to Marly.

Although the illness had not yet shown itself, smallpox was suspected, and Louis arranged to go to Meudon the next day. All those who had not had the disease were told to stay away, and Louis took with him only a few necessary personal attendants and ministers so he could continue to work. He visited his son every morning and evening, as well as the occasional afternoon, which he would spend sitting by the patient's bed.

At first it looked as though the fears for the dauphin were ill-founded; he was ill, certainly, but his life did not appear to be in danger. The fishwomen of Paris, who were devoted to him, arrived at Meudon in hired carriages, and he insisted that they should be allowed to enter his chamber. They flooded in and knelt at the foot of his bed, kissing the covers. When they learned that he was expected to make a full recovery, they cheered and promised to spread the good news in Paris and to have Te Deums sung in every church. The dauphin replied, "It is too soon yet, wait until I am quite better."[10] He then ordered his servants to show the women his house, give them dinner, and send them back to Paris with gifts of money.

Louis was in good humor, and he reproved Liselotte for having grumbled so much when she had smallpox. The dauphin does not feel ill at all, he told her. Liselotte replied that he would feel ill when the spots became inflamed, which would be painful.[11] Sure enough, the king's optimism soon gave way to despair when he noticed that his son's face and head had become swollen. Louis was so badly shaken that he stayed only a few minutes, and when he left the room, he could not stop his tears.

The royal physicians, Boudin and Fagon, had no direct experience with infectious diseases, but even as the dauphin's condition worsened, they refused to consult other doctors for advice. Instead, they assaulted their patient with one treatment after another without waiting to see what effects each one might have had. All the while, no one explained the situation to Louis, and although he had been concerned earlier in the day, the absence of further news lulled him into a false sense of hopefulness. He calmly went to supper believing that all would be well, or at least that the condition of his son and heir would not worsen.

As he finished eating and rose from the table, he was astonished to see the distraught Fagon come before him crying that all was lost. Louis rushed to the dauphin's chamber, shoving aside all who stood in his way. As he reached the door, Mme la princesse de Conti barred his way, and, pushing him back with both hands, urged him to think only of himself now. He was kept out of his son's room, said Liselotte, because otherwise "he would only arrive in time to see him die."[12]

Louis was shocked by the sudden change. He sat down in an anteroom, and as each person came out of the sick room, he asked them for news, but no one had the courage to tell him anything; only Mme la duchesse and Mme la princesse de Conti kept him informed of his son's condition. Père Le Tellier was summoned, but the dauphin had lapsed into a coma by the time he arrived. Le Tellier nevertheless assured Louis that he was still able to give absolution. At this moment Françoise came to Louis's side and tried to persuade him to leave Meudon, but, of course, Louis would not go. The dauphin's coma lasted almost an hour; finally Fagon came out and broke the news to Louis that his son was dead.

Louis was in such a state of distress that he lashed out at Fagon, blaming him because the dauphin had not had the chance to make his final confession. He then allowed himself to be led away by Françoise and the two princesses. As Louis stepped out into the courtyard to enter his coach, he noticed the dauphin's berlin standing in front of it. Upset by the sight of it, he signalled for the drivers to bring him another coach.

Despite his grief, the business of governance had to continue and Louis called out to Pontchartrain to notify his father and the other ministers to come later than usual to Marly the next day for the council. Pontchartrain thought it was not right that Louis should work when he had been so recently bereaved, and he said that since the council would be discussing current affairs, perhaps the meeting might be postponed until the king was less harassed. It was a measure of Louis's grief that he gave his consent.

No one expected the king to travel to Marly that night, so nothing had been prepared for his arrival. The door keys were missing, there were no candles, and only a few nightlights pierced the darkness within the château. As the servants bustled about getting everything ready, Louis sat with Françoise in the anteroom of her chamber; there were some other ladies present also, but Louis was so lost in his grief that he might as well have been alone. "He is in such deep sorrow that his plight would melt a rock," said Liselotte. "Nevertheless he does not spare himself. He speaks to everyone with great firmness, but every moment tears rise to his eyes and he chokes back his sobs. I am terribly afraid that he might fall ill himself," she added, "because he looks very bad. I pity him from the bottom of my heart."[13] Louis wept for long periods at a time, and when at last the servants finished preparing the rooms, he went inside with Françoise and the two remained alone. An hour later, the grieving king finally retired to his bed. It was four in the morning.

When the postponed council meeting was eventually held, Louis asked his ministers in a voice breaking with emotion whether the title of dauphin could be given to the duc de Bourgogne. The request was exceptional because the title was strictly reserved for the king's eldest son. Chancellor Pontchartrain, however, said that it should be permitted because Bourgogne was now Louis's immediate heir.[14]

The duc de Bourgogne was still only twenty-eight years old, handsome and intelligent. He had outgrown a tempestuous youth to mellow into a kind and thoughtful young man who excelled in the sciences, philosophy, and Latin. A traditionalist, he believed in the preservation of rank and was incensed by what he saw as the ruin of the nobility, that is, the reduction of their power.[15] Even so, he refused to take the honorific title of Monseigneur, which his father had used, preferring instead to be addressed simply as Monsieur. He even refused the allowance of 12 thousand livres a month that had been offered to him, being content with the much smaller sum of 3 thousand each month.[16] Since their marriage, the duc and duchesse de Bourgogne had gradually grown very close. Although both were still young—the duchesse was still only twenty-five—they evinced a sense of duty, compassion, and responsibility that belied their youth. Courtiers who dared to think such thoughts looked forward to the time when they would become the new king and queen of France.

Early in the morning of Monday, January 18, 1712, Louis travelled to Marly. Accompanying him was the new dauphine, Marie-Adélaïde, despite the fact that she was unwell.[17] She was suffering from severe toothache and inflamed gums, which made her face swell. Upon her arrival at Marly, she went straight to bed, where she remained for most of the day. Louis, however, wanted her to preside over the entertainments in the drawing room that evening, so Marie-Adélaïde rose at seven to prepare. Her teeth were still bothering her, though, so she appeared in her morning dress and with her head wrapped in a hood. When at last the time came for her to retire, she went to see Louis and Françoise in their room before withdrawing to her own bedroom for the night.

Two days later, the dauphine's condition had improved. The swelling had gone down and she began to feel much better. Then, on the night of Monday, February 8, she felt very drowsy. She had been in a high fever with periods of delirium that day, and Louis had been concerned enough to visit her several times. A rash appeared on her skin, and the measles, which were prevalent at that time, announced themselves. The dauphine was treated with an emetic, but it did nothing to help her. The dauphin, who had never left his wife's side throughout, had to be persuaded to go outside into the garden and take some fresh air, but he was so anxious that he returned to his vigil almost at once.

As night fell, Marie-Adélaïde's fever worsened. Louis continued his visits, and Françoise left the bedside only when he arrived. The dauphine's condition had now deteriorated to the point that she was urged to take the sacraments as a precaution. At first she refused, but under gentle persuasion, she finally agreed that she should prepare for death.

Marie-Adélaïde did not want her usual confessor, Père de La Rue, and she asked for M. Bailly, the priest of the mission of the parish of Versailles. Unfortunately, he was unavailable, so instead she asked for a Franciscan friar, Père Noel. As they waited for the friar to arrive, the dauphin could no longer hide his grief, and the doctors persuaded him to go to his own rooms and stay there in order to spare him the awful experience of witnessing his wife's last moments.

At last Père Noel arrived. He heard Marie-Adélaïde's last confession and administered the extreme unction and the last sacraments, which Louis had personally gone to collect at the foot of the grand staircase. An hour later, Marie-Adélaïde asked for the prayers for the dying, but the friar told her that the time had not yet come. Instead, she was urged to try to sleep.

Louis and Françoise waited in the drawing room throughout the sacred ceremony, and when it was over the doctors were summoned into the royal presence. They informed the king that Marie-Adélaïde should be bled from the foot before the fever returned, and that an emetic should be administered before dawn if the bleeding proved ineffective. This was the last thing a doctor should have done to someone in such a weakened state. Liselotte protested, saying that they ought to wait for the sweating to stop before they bled her. The doctors merely mocked her, while Françoise asked if she thought she was cleverer than the physicians. "No, Madame," replied Liselotte, "but one doesn't need to be very clever to know that nature must be followed, and since she is inclined to perspire, it would be much better to allow her to go on as she is, instead of making a sick person in a sweat get up to be bled."[18] As it was, the fever did return, and though it was not as violent as before, Marie-Adélaïde had a restless night. The prescribed emetic was administered, but with no effect.

During the day, Marie-Adélaïde faded into unconsciousness, rousing at rare intervals. As evening fell, many of her servants were so distressed that they were allowed into her room even though the king was present. A few minutes after Louis left, Marie-Adélaïde died.

Louis, Françoise, and Mme de Caylus, Françoise's cousin, drove back to Marly as the court mourned the princess who had been its leading light. Liselotte sympathized with the duchesse de Savoy, for whom the loss of her daughter was irreparable, but the tragedy deeply affected Louis too:

> because he had brought up the Dauphiness to suit himself, and she was his greatest comfort, his only joy. She was so light-hearted that she never was at a loss to find some way of distracting him, however sad he might be. She ran in and out a hundred times a day, and each time she had something funny to tell. The King will miss her everywhere, and it is not to be wondered at that her death has sorely afflicted him. [19]

Louis's grief was profound, but there was more to come. Marie-Adélaïde had often spoken of her death. "A learned astrologer of Turin," wrote Liselotte, "had predicted to Madame la Dauphine all that would happen to her, and that she would die in her twenty-seventh year." While she was still in good health, she often said, "Well, I must enjoy myself, because I cannot enjoy myself long, for I shall die this year."[20] Once she said to her husband that the time was drawing near and she wanted to know whom he would marry after she had gone. He replied that he would marry no one, for he would follow her to the grave within a week.[21]

As it was, the dauphin had become ill while he'd watched over his wife throughout her final illness, and his complaint was made much worse by the intense grief he felt at her loss. He kept to his rooms at

Versailles and allowed no one to see him except his brother, the duc de Berry, his confessor, and the duc de Beauvilliers.

On February 13, he was persuaded to go to Marly to spare him the anguish of hearing the sounds coming from the room above, where the doctors and embalmers were performing their final services for his wife. Although he received visits from Françoise and others, none of them stayed with him for very long, for everyone was so absorbed in their own sorrow that there was no comfort to give or receive.

The dauphin was clearly unwell. His eyes were wild and glazed, and vivid spots had broken out on his face. Still, he waited for the announcement that the king had awoken, then made to go to the *lever* as usual, but the tears that he had been holding back so bravely spilled down his cheeks and he turned away without saying anything. It was only when Saint-Simon pressed him that he left his room and went to the king's apartments.

There were only a few people at Marly, and they had assembled in the drawing room, while those who had the entrée waited in the small room that separated the king's apartments from those belonging to Françoise. She was still in her bedroom, but when she heard that Louis was awake, she went in to see him alone. After a few minutes, the others followed her. Then the dauphin entered. As soon as Louis saw him, he called him to his side and "embraced him tenderly and long, and many times. These first touching moments were passed in broken words mingled with tears."[22]

As Louis looked into his grandson's face, he became alarmed and ordered the doctors to take his pulse. They did so and said that it was not quite normal, although they would later admit that it was, in fact, very bad, and they said that he should go to bed. Louis embraced the young man once again and told him to take care of himself before sending him to his room.

Louis was also feeling unwell. He had spent a bad night and had awoken with a headache, but he carried on as usual, receiving some nobles who had presented themselves. He also visited the dauphin, whose pulse had become more erratic, and who was now showing signs of fever. The dauphin spent his time in prayer and sacred reading. Again, Louis spent a difficult night as his worry for the dauphin increased. He expressed his fears to Boudin that his grandson might not recover.

On Monday, February 15, Louis was bled. Meanwhile, the health of the dauphin had not improved. The king visited him, as did Françoise and the duc de Berry, but the following day the patient's condition worsened. He complained of a consuming fire, as though he was being devoured by flames, which became more violent as the day wore on, while the spots on his face had now spread all over his body. As evening approached, he asked Louis's permission to take communion very early in the morning without ceremony and with no assistants at the mass which would be said in his chamber. Louis granted this request, and immediately after midnight, the sacraments were brought. The dauphin now spent two hours in great communication with God, but he then became very confused. He was given extreme unction, after which he died at half past eight on the morning of February 18. He was only twenty-nine years old.

Saint-Simon hinted that the dauphin and dauphine died by poisoning. He noted that just as the court was settling in at Marly, Marie-Adélaïde's premier physician, Jean Boudin, warned her to be careful, for he had reliable information that certain persons wished to poison her and the dauphin, whom he also warned. He also spoke of the matter openly in the salon, and, needless to say, fear spread among the courtiers. Louis demanded a private word with him. Boudin told the king that his information was sound, although he did not know its origins. This was the first hint of something mysterious afoot, and while his friends told him to keep quiet, the rumor spread into the wider community. As though this was not enough, twenty-four hours had scarcely passed when the dauphin received a similar warning from his brother, the king of Spain. This new message was vague and gave no indication of its provenance, but King Philippe appeared to believe it nonetheless. This one mentioned only the dauphin, although the dauphine was implicated. While everyone at court outwardly dismissed these warnings, inwardly they continued to be disturbed by them, and a feeling of consternation and silence descended upon the court.

A week later, on February 5, the duc de Noailles presented Marie-Adélaïde with a beautiful snuffbox containing Spanish snuff, which she very much enjoyed.[23] She kept the box on a table in her private boudoir. That evening, she was taken ill with a violent fever and went to bed. There she remained until morning, when she felt well enough to get up and go about her daily business. However, the next day she again felt unwell. The fever had returned, and she now began to experience a pain below the temples that was so violent that she begged the king, who was coming to see her, to stay away. The pain could not be relieved by tobacco, opium, or bleedings, but as her fever increased, the pain subsided. The duchess's illness inspired rumors about the snuffbox, but when one of her ladies, Mme de Lévi, went to retrieve the box, it could not be found anywhere.[24]

Elsewhere, however, Saint-Simon suggested that the duc du Maine, protected by Mme de Maintenon, had spread the rumor that Louis's nephew, Orléans, had poisoned the dauphin and dauphine and that Louis had believed it.[25] His motives were easy to find: the duc, knowing that the king was now quite old, feared his loss of status:

> The death of all the princes of the blood of an age to take part in the world had won him his latest and most important grandeur. By crushing this member of the royal family with so fearful a calumny, and by inducing the king and society to believe it, he counted on destroying him forever in the most odious and ignominious manner.[26]

Did Louis believe it, though? Liselotte, who was, after all, Orléans's mother, knew that he did not. The matter was "reported to the king in all seriousness," she wrote, "and he immediately spoke of it to my son.

With unfailing kindness, he assured him that he did not believe it." However, he advised Orléans to "send his apothecary, the poor scholarly Humberg, to the Bastille in order that he might clear himself."[27]

As it turned out, Humberg was not sent to the Bastille, because Louis forbade the officials there to receive him. Louis simply refused to believe what was being said about his nephew, and his feelings on the subject were supported by the results of the autopsies that were carried out on the bodies of the dauphine and the dauphin. No traces of poison were found. "Well, well, Madame," said Louis to Françoise, "didn't I say that what you told me about my nephew was false?"[28] Marie-Adélaïde had died of measles, while "it was the bad atmosphere and grief which were responsible for the dauphin's death."[29]

The young couple was prepared for burial, their hearts being sent to the Val-de-Grâce. On February 25, Louis informed the duchesse de Ventadour, the governess of the couple's two small boys, that the eldest boy, the duc de Bretagne, would henceforth take the name and rank of dauphin.[30] On the following day, the bodies of the dauphine and dauphin were buried together at Saint-Denis, but Louis was forced to relive these tragedies all over again when, on March 5, he received the formal condolences from various institutions.[31] Every last detail of their short lives was read out in speeches that must have wrenched his heart. Little did he know that his grief was about to deepen still further.

The next day, the duc de Bretagne and his younger brother, the duc d'Anjou, developed the measles rash. Although the children had been given a private baptism at birth, Louis now ordered Mme de Ventadour to have them christened in a formal ceremony as a matter of urgency. She was free to choose the godparents, but both boys were to be given the name Louis.

The king's physician, Fagon, and eight colleagues he had brought in from Paris, agreed that the best course of action was to bleed the two boys. Mme de Ventadour thought that the duc d'Anjou, who was only two years old, was too young to be subjected to such treatment. She carried him to her room, wrapped him warmly, and fed him some wine and a biscuit.[32] The child recovered from his illness, but his elder brother was not so lucky. The five-year-old duc de Bretagne was bled, but the treatment had no effect. As his condition worsened, he cried that he did not want to go to Saint-Denis: "That is a horrible journey," he said, "horrible."[33] That night, just before midnight, the little boy died.

Louis reflected upon the terrible events of the past year, during which three heirs to the throne had died, as well as the young princess who had come to his kingdom as a child and whom he had loved instantly as though she had been his daughter. He arrived at the conclusion that God was punishing him: for his vanity, for the hardship he had inflicted upon his people, for his love of *gloire*, which he relentlessly pursued no matter the cost. Now he knew the price of glory: it was to be paid for with the lives of his loved ones, the security of his crown, and the tears he would never stop shedding.

TWENTY-EIGHT
Le Soleil se Coucher

Terrible events had shaken France and broken Louis's heart. The ageing king now longed for nothing more than peace. As it was, events had conspired to grant this desperate wish. The installation of a Tory government in England under Queen Anne had marked a major shift in the political landscape of the country. England no longer insisted upon the restoration of the Habsburgs to the Spanish throne; instead, realizing the futility of the ongoing war, they were desirous to reach an agreement with France that would foster peace and commerce between their two countries.

This possibility was brought a step closer when Emperor Joseph died childless in April 1711. His brother, who still called himself Charles III of Spain, was elected emperor that October. In July of the following year, the maréchal de Villars,[1] as commander of the French forces, orchestrated a daring maneuver to capture the town of Denain in Flanders, close to the border with France. This cut off Prince Eugène's lines of communication so that he had no choice but to lift his siege of the nearby town of Landrecies. Over the next few months Villars swept Eugène away, reestablishing Vauban's *ceinture de fer* and paving the way for Louis to negotiate peace from a position of strength.

The main stumbling block to any treaty was the allies' demand that the thrones of France and Spain must never be occupied by the same prince. However, as Louis stipulated in the letters patent of 1700, when Philippe accepted the Spanish throne, Philippe would not renounce his claim to the throne of France. At that time, this clause was of little consequence. The French line of succession rested safely with the dauphin and his son, the duc de Bourgogne, who, in turn, was the father of two fine boys. The Bourbon line, therefore, was secure for at least the next three generations. Then tragedy struck and only the two-year-old duc d'Anjou remained. Louis, however, worried that young Anjou would not live. Since he firmly believed that the right to the succession was decreed by God and enshrined in the laws of primogeniture, in the event of the duc d'Anjou's death, Philippe V of Spain would become the next in line to the throne of France. Should that happen, Philippe would be succeeded on the Spanish throne by his brother, the duc de Berry.

This scenario was unacceptable to the English, who wrote to Louis to tell him that unless Philippe renounced his claim to the French throne and Berry renounced his rights in Spain, the peace talks would end and the war continue. Louis wrote to Philippe V, pointing out that he had kept the war going long enough to secure him and his queen on the throne of Spain, but "it is not right that I conclude the ruin of my kingdom solely with the view of preserving their rights either to reunite one day the monarchies of France and Spain or to divide them among their children."[2] He then warned Philippe, "It only remains for me to decide whether I want peace at this price or the continuation of war. As the second course is not possible to sustain, I will certainly take the first."[3] Philippe had no choice but to agree, and he announced his decision to Louis on April 22, 1712.[4] The peace negotiations would eventually lead to the Treaties of Utrecht, signed between France and the allies on April 11, 1713, and Rastadt, which Louis signed with the Holy Roman Empire on March 6, 1714.

In May 1714, Louis once again was required to receive the Holy Sacrament for a member of his family. This time, it was his grandson, the duc de Berry, who was in need of the last rites. He had sustained a serious injury while out hunting a few days earlier but had said nothing about it at the time. When he began to pass blood, he put it down to dysentery; but, again, he ordered his valet to say nothing of it, "for fear of being made to swallow heaps of remedies."[5] He was well enough to hunt again that Saturday, and it was then that the secret of his accident came out. A peasant asked one of the king's men how the duc was faring. When told that he was well, the peasant commented, "Princes must have harder bones than we peasants, since I saw him receive a blow on Thursday at the chase while he was pulling up his horse which would have burst open three peasants."

The duc's symptoms were alarming: "a virulent fever, nose bleeding, drowsiness, and sickness accompanied by a high temperature." Worse was to come, for he began to vomit clots of black blood, to the despair of Fagon, who said there was no remedy "because there was already gangrene in his body." The duc died at the age of only twenty-eight. He and his wife, who was pregnant, hoped their child would be a boy. As it was, the duchesse gave birth to a stillborn daughter.[6]

The succession now rested upon two factors: the continuing good health of the king and the survival of his four-year-old great-grandson, the duc d'Anjou. Should Anjou die, the crown would go to Philippe d'Orléans, the son of Louis's late brother, Philippe, and Liselotte. Philippe was a good soldier, a lover of the arts, especially music, a good conversationalist, and quite learned. Perhaps his greatest diversion, however, was women. "I wish that he didn't like them so much," wrote Liselotte, "because he is ruining both himself and his children; besides, his fondness for them leads him into such debauched society that he is weaned away from everything good."[7]

Then there was the rumor that Orléans had poisoned the duc and duchesse de Bourgogne and their son. "I, who would let myself be burned at the stake to testify to his innocence, looked upon the rumor at first as mere folly," wrote Liselotte. While Louis did not believe it, the rumor cast its shadow. Orléans was unpopular in Paris, in the provinces, and at court. His troubles were undoubtedly caused by a cabal against him, perpetrated by the duc du Maine, his wife, and his half brother, the duc d'Antin. This led to an estrangement between Louis and his nephew, which "now became more and more visible to the Court and to those who were producing it."[8] In the face of this, Louis took the step, unique in the history of France, of raising the duc du Maine and the comte de Toulouse, his two sons by Athénaïs, to a rank just below that of princes of the blood and declaring them and their descendants eligible to succeed him should the legitimate line fail.[9]

In doing so, Louis "tempered by a natural law the rigor of the conventional laws, which deprive children born out of wedlock of all rights to the paternal succession." Louis, therefore, did "for his own flesh and blood what he had done on behalf of several of his subjects." He felt especially justified in the case of his own two legitimized sons.[10]

Louis, who was now "ageing visibly" so that people "began to fear that he would not live much longer,"[11] sat down to write his will. In it, he recognized his nephew, the duc d'Orléans, as regent, but decreed that he should not exercise full powers. Instead, he would be chef du conseil, that is, he would sit at the head of a regency council, whose members included the duc du Maine, the comte de Toulouse, the maréchal de Villeroy, and Chancellor Voysin, who was close to Maine and also to Françoise.[12] Orléans was required to conform to the decisions of the council, which would be reached by a majority of votes. Once the duc d'Anjou was old enough to leave the care of his governess, Mme de Ventadour, he would be placed into the charge of the maréchal de Villeroy. The regency council, therefore, would be dominated by the duc du Maine and those of his circle, while the young king would eventually be placed into the care of Villeroy, another of Maine's favorites.

Louis, however, had felt pressed by Maine, Françoise, and the chancellor into writing the will in the way he had. He felt bitter about it, and one day he spoke harshly to Maine: "You would have it; but remember however great I make you in my lifetime, you are nothing after me; it is for you to make a good use of what I have done for you, if you can."[13]

The following morning, Louis sent for the president of the parlement, Henri II de Mesmes, and the *procureur-général*, Henri François d'Aguesseau. As soon as they were alone, the king unlocked a drawer and took out a large package, sealed with seven seals, which he handed to them with these extraordinary words:

> *Messieurs, this is my will; no one knows its contents except myself. I place it in your hands for safe keeping by parliament [sic]; to which I could not give a greater proof of my esteem and confidence than by thus making it the depositary of this document. The example of the kings, my predecessors, and that of the will of the king, my father, do not allow me to be ignorant of what may become of this, my will; but they would have it; they tormented me; they left me no peace, no matter what I said. Oh, well! I have bought my peace at last.*
>
> *There it is; take it away; it will become what it can; but at least I shall have rest and hear no more about it.*[14]

When he finished speaking, he gave a short nod, turned his back, and went into the adjoining cabinet, leaving the astonished d'Aguesseau and Mesmes "almost changed into statues." The two men "looked at each other, frightened at what they had heard, and still more at what they had seen in the eyes and countenance of the king."[15]

Louis's anger had not calmed, however, and the following day, he went to see Mary of Modena, who was visiting Françoise. As soon as he entered his wife's apartments, he addressed the queen of England "in the tone of a man who was full of his wrath":

> *Madame, I have made my will; they tormented me to make it [he then turned his eyes on Mme. de Maintenon]: I have bought my peace. I know its impotence and uselessness. We can do all we choose as long as we exist; after us we can do less than private individuals; one has only to see what became of the will of the king, my father, directly after his death, and that of many other kings. I know this very well; but they would have it; they gave me no peace or rest until I made it. Oh, well! it is done, madame; it will become what it can; but at least I shall not be tormented any longer.*[16]

Mesmes and d'Aguesseau, meanwhile, carried the king's will to the Palais de la Cité. They took some workmen to a tower behind the robing room and the president's cabinet and ordered them to hollow out a space in the wall of the tower, into which the will was placed. The hole was then closed with an iron grille before being bricked up as before.

The parlement was sitting at the time that this work was going on, and Mesmes explained to the assembly the "honor and confidence shown by this deposit, and by the reliance the king placed on the parlement to maintain the provisions of the will it contained."[17]

At the same time, the king's officers presented an edict that had been received from the chancellor that morning. In it, Louis declared that the packet he had entrusted to the president and the *procureur-général* contained his will, "by which he had provided for the care and guardianship of the minor king, and for the choice of a council of regency; which arrangements, for sound reasons, he did not think proper to make public." He asked that the document should be kept in the custody of parlement until the end of his life. He further ordered that, upon his death, the chambers of parlement should assemble, with all the princes of the royal family and all the peers who might be available, and in their presence the will should be opened, read, and the dispositions it contained made public and executed, without power of interference from anyone. Copies of the will were then to be sent to all the parlements of the kingdom to be registered.[18]

As he had already suggested, Louis well knew what became of the last will and testament of kings following their death. His own father, Louis XIII, had willed that France should be governed by a regency council. The first thing Anne of Austria had done was to persuade parlement to set aside this will and leave her with full regency powers, as was her right as the mother of a minor king. Parlement, therefore, effectively possessed the power to appoint the rulers of France. This power had endowed the parlement with an exaggerated sense of its own importance; this had been one of the factors behind the Fronde. Since it was extremely unlikely that Louis XIV would wish to inflict upon his heir the possibility of a repetition of the awful events that had blighted his own minority, it is highly probable, as Saint-Simon asserts, that he was influenced by François and the duc du Maine, acting upon their own interests, in drawing up his will.[19]

In February 1715, Louis received a visit from a most peculiar man.[20] Apparently an ambassador sent from the king of Persia, this man had not been invited to France, and he produced no credentials or powers from his sovereign. He was, in reality, a provincial bailiff of some sort charged by the governor of his province to discuss trade with Chancellor Pontchartrain. Still, he was treated in a manner befitting his alleged rank, and he made his entry into Paris on horseback, escorted by the maréchal de Matignon and the baron de Breteuil. However, he "did so many vulgar things and made such foolish squabbles about the ceremonial that when the procession reached the hotel of the special ambassadors, they left him at the door without accompanying him inside," as normal procedure would dictate. They then went straight to Versailles to complain to Louis, who approved of their actions and "thought the ambassador very uncouth."

It so happened that the man who usually interpreted oriental languages for the king died at about this time, so it was necessary to send for a curé who lived near Amboise who had lived for some years in Persia. The curé was well versed in the manner, customs, and government of Persia and was fluent in the language. He knew from the first that this man's embassy was fictitious. This fact was not related to Louis, however, who continued to believe in the alleged ambassador's integrity. He announced that he would receive this man at Versailles and ordered his courtiers to wear full court dress for the occasion.

The *Galerie des glaces* was selected as the setting for the reception, and a magnificent throne, "raised several steps," was placed at one end. Tiered steps were arranged along each side of the *galerie*, which was superbly decorated, as were all the apartments. The steps nearest the throne were reserved for the ladies, while those farther down were reserved for the gentlemen of the court.

The courtyards, roofs, and avenues of Versailles were filled with people, "which amused the king much as he looked from the windows." He watched for the arrival of the ambassador, who drove onto the avenue at eleven in the morning, accompanied by Matignon and Breteuil. They then mounted horses and rode into the great courtyard, where they dismounted and entered the château through the door of the colonel of the guards. "The suite seemed very wretched in every way," wrote Saint-Simon; "the so-called ambassador was greatly embarrassed, and very badly dressed; the presents were beneath notice."

Louis now went into the *galerie*. He wore the sach of the Ordre du Saint-Esprit over his coat, which was black and gold and "decorated with the finest of the crown diamonds to the value of over twelve millions of francs." The jewels made the coat so heavy that Louis "bent beneath the weight of them and seemed much broken, thinner, and looked very ill in the face." He took his seat on the throne, at the foot of which waited the painter Antoine Coypel and Boze, secretary of the Academy of Inscriptions, one to paint the scene, the other to record it in writing.

The ambassador arrived by the grand staircase, crossed the great apartments, and entered the *galerie* through the salon at the end opposite to where the throne was situated. He was overwhelmed by the splendor of the spectacle, and on two or three occasions he lost his temper with the interpreter, which gave people to think that he knew more Fench than he would admit.

When the audience was over, the ambassador was entertained to dinner, which was held in the late queen's apartments. He then visited Torcy and Pontchartrain before returning to Paris. The presents he left for Louis were "as little worthy of the King of Persia as of the King of France," consisting as they did of "very ordinary pearls, two hundred worthless turquoises, and two gold boxes full of a rare balsam which issues from one rock enclosed in another rock, and congeals after a certain space of time." Saint-Simon adds that this balsam was "said to be marvellous for wounds."

Throughout this visit, Saint-Simon insists that Louis was duped and that he was the only person in his court who believed in the integrity of the false ambassador. It has to be wondered, though: Did Louis know that his visitor was not genuine and was merely taking advantage of the situation to do what he loved to do best: dress up and dazzle courtiers and his visitors alike with his magnificence?

Three months later, on May 3, Louis rose earlier than usual, and after attending mass, he went into the gardens. It was nine o'clock, and he was looking forward to seeing the eclipse, which was due to take place that morning. The ladies had been waiting for an hour by this time, and Cassini had arrived from the Paris Observatory with the special glasses necessary to view the event safely.[21] Notwithstanding his carefree attitude that spring, however, one matter that had exercised Louis for many years was now about to come to a head.[22]

As long before as 1702, the curé of Clermont-en-Auvergne, the abbé Fréhel, had reopened the controversy surrounding the Five Propositions said to be found in the book *Augustinus*.[23] Louis asked Pope Clement XI to settle the question once and for all, and Clement responded by issuing the bull *Vineam Domini*, which condemned Fréhel's work. Cardinal de Noailles, the controversial archbishop of Paris, upheld the pope's condemnation and excommunicated the nuns of Port Royal, who rejected the papal bull. Louis, who also accepted the bull, ordered the destruction of Port Royal. The nuns, all of whom were over sixty years old, were expelled and the buildings razed to the ground.

Then, in 1710, Abbé Fénelon, who was now edging towards Jesuit-influenced orthodoxy, published a pastoral letter, in which he condemned heresies allegedly contained within the *Réflexions Morales sur le Nouveau Testament* by Pasquier Quesnel. Fénelon posted copies of his letter all over Paris for anyone to read. However, Cardinal de Noailles refused to allow the letter to be read in his diocese. Louis appealed once again to Clement XI, this time asking him to condemn Quesnel's work. It took several months, but Clement eventually issued the bull *Unigenitus*, which condemned *en bloc* 101 propositions found in the book. The bull arrived at Versailles on September 25, 1713.

The *Unigenitus* instantly proved controversial and inspired months of argument and debate. The theologians of the Sorbonne, some of the Parisian clergy, and the monastic orders, with the exception of the Franciscans, found it contained certain articles that they could not accept. Louis was determined that the bull should be accepted, but his will was resisted by Noailles and fifteen other bishops, who declared it "a fatal and illegal act of interference in French Church affairs."[24] They demanded the convocation of a national council to settle the matter. Louis agreed that a national council was needed, but he wanted to use it to condemn Noailles. The pope, however, refused to support the king in this endeavor, so Louis decided to hold a council nonetheless. It would meet on September 1, 1715, and Louis would announce its convocation in parlement on August 19. He expected resistance from Noailles's supporters, but in that event, Louis intended to hold a *lit de justice* to enforce his will. Alas, Louis's plan was not to come to fruition.

The king was now in a visible state of decline. His once vigorous appetite was "considerably diminished." Although this had not gone unnoticed by the court, Louis continued to follow the rites and rituals of his everyday life. Beyond France's borders, the king's failing health was also a matter of interest, and bets were being placed that Louis would not live beyond September 1.[25]

Louis was in the habit of asking Torcy to read him the gazettes from Holland. Torcy always took the time to look them over in case there was something printed that he did not want Louis to hear. On one occasion, however, he did not take this precaution, and while he was reading, he suddenly came across a mention of the bets made in London. He stopped, stammered, and skipped the passage, but Louis noticed and asked him what he had skipped and why. Torcy blushed and muttered that the passage was impertinent and not worthy of being read. Louis, however, insisted upon hearing it, and Torcy, "in the greatest embarrassment, read the bets from beginning to end." Louis disguised his feelings, but he was deeply hurt by this, so much so that when he sat down to dinner, he brought up the subject of the gazette. He looked at Saint-Simon, as he did the other diners, but more as if he expected the duc to reply. The duc took care to say nothing; he merely dropped his eyes. Louis "seemed moved, like a man who did not wish to show it." He tried to eat, but it was clear that the news had spoiled his appetite and hurt him more than he cared to reveal.

On Monday, August 12, Louis took medicines for painful sciatica in his leg and thigh.[26] He still managed to work that afternoon with Pontchartrain, and he attended a musical evening with Françoise in her apartments.[27] The following day he went to mass, but he had to be carried in an armchair. That afternoon he received the so-called ambassador from Persia, who was taking his leave before setting off for his own country. Louis held the audience in the throne room, but there was none of the ceremony that accompanied their first meeting. Moreover, the audience, which was rather long, tired the king very much, but he refused to rest and held a council of finances afterwards.

Louis's health had been failing for more than a year. His personal valets had noticed it first, but they were afraid to say anything. Fagon, now laboring under the weight of his own old age, was the only person in Louis's intimate circle who did not see how far the king was declining. His colleague, Maréchal, tried to speak to him several times, but each time Fagon repulsed him. Maréchal felt duty bound to speak to Françoise, assuring her that the king's constitution was sound and that, with the proper remedies, there would be no danger; he added, ominously, that if things went on as they were, he did not hold out much hope. Françoise, however, angrily told him that only Fagon's enemies said such things.

Fagon continued to treat Louis's gout by swaddling him in a mass of feather pillows, which made him sweat so much at night that he had to be rubbed down every morning before the gentlemen of the bedchamber could enter. The physician also made Louis drink aged Burgundy wine with water rather than the champagne he preferred. Louis would joke that "foreign lords were often well taken in by wanting to taste his wine."

On August 14, a group of surgeons arrived from Paris. Their collective wisdom decreed that Louis was suffering from fever, which should be treated with ass's milk. Before it could be administered, however, Fagon countermanded the prescription and gave Louis a cup of bouillon instead. The king held the council of state afterwards, but memories failed when it came to what else the king ate, if anything. Dangeau believes he took a little meat even though it was a feast day, while the Anthoine brothers thought he ate panade, or boiled bread with butter. The pains in his leg and thigh prevented him from walking, and he was carried everywhere in his chair. He spent the afternoon listening to music with Françoise and her ladies in her apartments, and took supper at nine that evening.

The following day was the Feast of the Assumption. Louis, however, was very unwell that morning, and for the first time in his life he did not hold his *lever*. He had slept very badly that night, and he spent the morning in bed drinking copious amount of water. He was well enough to be carried to the tribune of the chapel, where he attended vespers. On his way back to his apartments he passed through the *Galerie des glaces*, which was so crowded with courtiers that he had difficulty getting through. After another musical evening in Françoise's rooms, he retired to bed at ten.

Louis spent another difficult night during which he drank several times. Between three and six in the morning, he felt better, and mass was said in his room. He took dinner at one, after which he was carried once again to Françoise's rooms to enjoy a musical evening with her and her ladies.

A pattern was now forming in which Louis would spend a restless night during which he would drink often, but he would then sleep peacefully during the early hours. He continued to hear mass in his room and hold council or otherwise see his ministers. At one o'clock on August 17, he dressed and took dinner, watched by the courtiers. That afternoon, he held an audience in his cabinet with the general of the order of Saint-Croix before going to Françoise's apartments in his three-wheeled chair, which he steered himself.

On August 18, Louis spent a more peaceful night than he had of late. This time, however, Fagon slept in the king's room, although he was adamant that the king had no fever. Again, Louis heard mass in his room before discussing fortifications with M. Pelletier. After visiting Françoise, he retired to his own apartments, where he ate supper in the presence of the court.

The following day, when Louis should have been addressing parlement, his sciatica was still very troublesome. When the doctors examined his leg, Maréchal noticed a black patch on the left foot and immediately recognized it as a bad sign. He rubbed the leg vigorously with hot cloths, and on the following day, Louis sat in a bath filled with hot Burgundy wine and aromatic herbs for a good hour, after which Maréchal again rubbed the leg with hot cloths, which eased the pain somewhat. After a cup of bouillon, Louis rested.

The doctors came once again from Paris on the twenty-second. After examining the patient, they again prescribed ass's milk, and this time Louis took some. By this time, however, the leg was swollen and burning.

For the next two days, Louis experienced dizziness, which the doctors attributed to the ass's milk. This was immediately stopped. When they examined the leg, they were alarmed to find that the discoloration had spread to the point just below the garter. It was only now that they began to suspect gangrene. They wrapped Louis's leg in linen soaked in camphorated brandy in an attempt to bring back its natural heat.

Even in this state, Louis attended mass, took a cup of bouillon, and held a council of finances until eleven o'clock, when M. Maréchal came to rub the leg in order to relieve the pain. As lunchtime approached, Louis took only bouillon. He held another council afterwards, but again, Maréchal interrupted it to rub the leg. As Maréchal removed the linen, Louis's oldest and closest friend, the maréchal de Villeroy, got his first look at the king's leg. He was horrified to see the extent of the discoloration, although Louis remarked that it did not hurt as much as it had. Villeroy was afraid. He judged the king's condition to be incurable and promptly returned to his apartments to conceal his tears. Louis too was struck by a feeling of melancholy, which he could not shake off. He was helped into his armchair, where he spoke to some of his officers about his illness. Louis knew the end was approaching, and he asked his confessor, Père Le Tellier, to prepare him for death. From that moment on, Le Tellier would never leave the king. As news of Louis's infirmity spread beyond the confines of Versailles, his subjects gathered in the courtyard, where they began their sad vigil.

Sunday, August 25 was the Feast of Saint-Louis, the king's personal saint. Although he had passed a very bad night, he insisted that the drums and oboes should play beneath his windows as usual, and he wanted to hear his orchestra of twenty-four violins playing as he ate dinner.

Louis was then left alone with Françoise and her ladies, but he fell asleep during their conversation. When he awoke his mind wandered, which frightened them so much that they sent for the doctors. They took the king's pulse, which was so weak that they advised him to "make no delay in receiving the sacraments."

Père Le Tellier arrived with the Cardinal de Rohan, grand almoner of France, and the son of one of Louis's minor mistresses, the beautiful princesse de Soubise. Père Le Tellier took the king's confession, while Rohan brought the Holy Sacraments and the sacred oils from the chapel. Throughout the rite, Louis was firm but seemed much moved by what he was doing.

Louis now added a codicil to his will, by which "the whole civil and military household of the king was subjected to the duc du Maine, absolutely and without reserve; and, under his orders, to the Maréchal de Villeroy." Thus he made them "the sole masters of the person and dwelling of the king, of the city of Paris, of the two regiments of the guards and the two companies of mousquetaires, of the whole service of bedchamber, wardrobe, chapel, kitchens, stables etc."[28] He then added a further five or six lines to the document. When he finished, he asked for a drink. He called Villeroy and a few others, who stood at the door, and spoke to them alone for a quarter of an hour. When he had said all he had to say to them, he summoned his nephew, the duc d'Orléans, to whom he gave all the marks of friendship, esteem, and confidence and assured him that there was nothing in his will that would not please the duc.[29]

The following day, Louis awoke after another restless night. His leg was dressed and he heard mass in his room, after which he summoned Le Tellier and Rohan to his side and assured them that "he died in the faith and in submission to the Church." He expressed regret that he had not left the church in better condition, but assured them that he had done all they wished him to do, and that his conscience was clear. He then had dinner in his room, the meal witnessed by all who had the entrée.

When dinner was finished, he requested those present to approach, and he said to them,

Messieurs, I ask your pardon for the bad example I have set you. I have much to thank you for, both for the manner in which you have served me, and for the attachment and fidelity you have always shown. I am very sorry not to have done for you all that I wished to do. The hard times are the reason. I ask of you for my grandson the same devotion, the same fidelity you have always shown to me. Let your example guide the conduct of my other subjects. Follow the orders that my nephew will give you; he will govern the kingdom; I hope he will do it well. I hope also that you will contribute to harmony, and if anyone breaks away from it, that you will endeavor to bring him back . . . I feel that I am moved, and I am moving you; I beg your pardon. Adieu, messieurs, I rely upon the thought that you will sometimes remember me. [30]

He then said good-bye to the maréchal de Villeroy, after which he asked Mme de Ventadour to bring in the dauphin.

The scene that followed was a mirror of that which had occurred between Louis and his own dying father all those years ago. The little boy, only five years old, approached the bed. Louis took him in his arms and said,

You will soon be the monarch of a great kingdom. What I most strongly enjoin upon you is never to forget your obligations to God. Remember that you owe all that you are to Him. Endeavor to preserve peace with your neighbors. I have been too fond of war; do not imitate me in that, neither in my great extravagance. Take council in all things and always seek to know the best and follow it. Let your

*first thought be devoted to helping your people, and do what I have
had the misfortune not to be able to do myself.* [31]

Louis then called for other members of his family. Wrote Liselotte:

*[He bade me] farewell so affectionately that I marvel I did not fall
down in a swoon. He assured me that he had always loved me even
more than I myself imagined, and that he was sorry he had sometimes caused me sorrow. He asked me to think of him sometimes,
adding that he knew I would do so gladly because he was sure that
I had always been fond of him. He said also that he gave me his
blessing and hoped that I would be happy all my life. I threw myself
at his feet, took his hand, and kissed it. Then he embraced me and
turned to the others.* [32]

His farewells had been made. Louis now waited to die.

It was at this point that the doctors decided to try a new remedy they
had heard of, called scarification. As Maréchal made an incision in the
king's lower leg, Louis assured him that he felt nothing at all. Maréchal
cut even deeper to see if he could find the seat of the gangrene, upon
which Louis cried out that the procedure was hurting him. Although
an unpleasant experience, this was a hopeful sign, for it meant that the
leg would suppurate and so release some of the poison. After the operation, the leg was wrapped in cloth soaked in corrosive and swathed in
linen soaked in camphorated brandy. That afternoon, Françoise came to
visit Louis; this was to be the last time husband and wife would speak
together. "I had thought it was more difficult to die," he told her. [33]

It was during this same afternoon that Louis burned many of the
papers that had been kept in a casket in his study. When the surgeons
examined the leg later that day, they were dismayed to find that the
gangrene had worsened.

Louis spent a disturbed night, during which he prayed often. His
attendants saw him beat his breast at the *confiteor*. That morning, he

called Le Tellier to his side, and as the prelate was talking to the king about God, Louis noticed two attendants seated at the foot of his bed silently weeping. "Why do you weep?" he asked them. "Did you think me immortal? I never thought so, and you ought, at my age, to expect to lose me."[34]

There was still hope, however. A Provençal, "extremely rough and common," arrived, claiming that he knew of an elixir from Marseilles that would cure gangrene. Louis was so ill that it was decided to give the medicine a try. Ten drops of this elixir were added to a glass of Alicante wine and administered to the king. Whatever the medicine was, it seemed to work at first, and when the king's pulse weakened again, they asked him to take a second dose. Louis took the glass, saying, "For life or death, as God pleases." As Louis was taking the medicine, Françoise withdrew to Saint-Cyr.

Louis began to look much better. His speech improved and his voice was stronger. The peasant, Le Brun, arranged to have a special bouillon made, which was served to the king every hour. Soon Louis was once again managing to eat solid food. Those around the king began to hope that a miracle would occur.

Alas, this proved to be a false dawn, for Louis relapsed the following day, August 30, when he experienced short periods of unconsciousness. Fagon was furious. He called Le Brun a charlatan and told him he was liable to criminal prosecution for giving the king an unknown remedy. The terrified Le Brun fled Versailles, never to be seen again.

At two that afternoon, Françoise arrived from Saint-Cyr, but Louis was in no condition to speak to her. He lay in his bed with his eyes fixed and wide open. Françoise remained for a short while before returning to her retreat at Saint-Cyr.

The next day, August 31, Louis was calm, although the gangrene had consumed his leg as far as the thigh. Françoise, hoping to speak to him one last time, hurried to Versailles, only to find her husband unconscious. That afternoon, Cardinal de Rohan entered the room and began to recite the prayers for the dying. His words filtered through to

Louis, who said the responses so loudly that he could be heard above all the voices of the priests. When the cardinal finished his prayers, Louis told him, "These are the last favors of the Church." Rohan was the last person to whom Louis spoke. He retreated into himself then, quietly muttering the words *"Nunc et in hora mortis."* He then added, "Oh, God, come to help me; hasten to succor me!" Those were the last words Louis spoke. He lay unconscious throughout the night.

At just after eight on the morning of Sunday, September 1, 1715,[35] four days before his seventy-seventh birthday and in the seventy-second year of his reign, Louis gave a number of short sighs and two gasps. Then quietly, peacefully, Louis XIV—Louis the Great—was dead.

BIBLIOGRAPHY

Airy, Osmund. *Charles II*. London, New York, Bombay: Longmans, Green, & Co., 1904.

Anthoine, Jean and François. *Journal de la Mort de Louis XIV*. Paris: Quantin, 1880.

Arrestation de Fouquet: Mesures Préparatoires in Clément, *Lettres, instructions et mémoires de Colbert*. Paris: Imprimerie Imperiale, 1859.

Barker, Nancy Nichols. *Brother to the Sun King: Philippe, Duke of Orléans*. Baltimore, London: Johns Hopkins University Press, 1989.

Baudrillart, Alfred. *Philippe V et et la cour de France, 1700–1715*. Paris: Bureau de la Revue, 1869.

Beaussant, Philippe. *Lully ou le Musicien du Soleil*. Paris: Gallimard, 1992.

Bély, Lucian, ed. *Dictionnaire Louis XIV*. Paris: Éditions Robert Laffont, 2015.

Benserade, Isaac de. *Ballet des Plaisirs. Dansé par sa Majesté le 4 jour de Février 1655*. Paris: Robert Ballard, seul Imprimeur du Roy pour la Musique, 1655.

Berger, Robert W. "On the Origins of Marly." *Zeitschrift Für Kunstgeschichte* 56, no. 4 (1993): 534–44. doi:10.2307/1482675.

Bertière, Simone. *Le Procès Fouquet*. Paris: Éditions de Fallois, 2013.

Bertière, Simone. *Les Femmes du Roi-Soleil, Les Reines de France au Temps des Bourbons*. Paris: Éditions de Fallois, 1997.

Bibliothèque Nationale. *Mazarin, Homme d'état et collectionneur, 1602–1661, exposition organisée pour le troisième centenaire de sa mort*. Paris: Bibliothèque Nationale, 1961.

Blennerhassett, Charlotte Julia von Leyden. *Louis XIV and Madame de Maintenon*. London: George Allen & Sons, 1910.

Bluche, François, ed. *Dictionnaire du Grand Siècle*. Paris: Librairie Arthème Fayard, 1990.

Bluche, François. *Louis XIV.* Translated by Mark Greengrass. Oxford, U.K.: Basil Blackwell Ltd., 1990.

Bowles, Emily. *Madame de Maintenon.* London: Kegan Paul, Trench & Co., 1888.

Brienne, Comte de. *Mémoires inédits de Louis-Henri de Loménie, comte de Brienne, secrétaire d'état sous Louis XIV.* Edited by F. Barrière. Paris, Leipzig: Ponthieu, 1828.

Brienne, Comte de. *Mémoires de Louis-Henri de Loménie, comte de Brienne, dit le Jeune Brienne.* Edited by Paul Bonnefon. Paris: Société de l'Histoire de France, 1916–19.

Brown, W. E. *The First Bourbon Century in France.* London: University of London Press Ltd., 1971.

Bryant, Arthur. *Charles II.* Revised edition. London: Collins, 1955.

Buckley, Veronica. *Madame de Maintenon, the Secret Wife of Louis XIV.* London: Bloomsbury, 2008.

Burke, Peter. *The Fabrication of Louis XIV.* New Haven, Conn., London: Yale University Press, 1992.

Burnet, Bishop. *History of His Own Time.* London: printed for A. Miller, 1753.

Bussy-Rabutin. *Les Mémoires de Roger de Rabutin comte de Bussy.* Amsterdam: Chez Zacherie Chatelain, 1731.

Bussy-Rabutin. *Correspondance avec ses Famille et Amis.* Paris: Lalanne, 1858.

Campbell, Dorothy de Brissac. *The Intriguing Duchess.* London: John Hamilton Ltd., 1900.

Campbell, Peter Robert. *Louis XIV.* London: Longman Group Limited, 1993.

Carré, Henry. *L'Enfance et la Premiere Jeunesse de Louis XIV.* Paris: Albin Michel, 1944.

Caylus, Marthe-Marguerite, marquise de. *Souvenirs de Madame de Caylus.* Paris: Chez Ant. Aug. Renouard, 1806.

Chatelain, Urbain-Victor. *Le Surintendant Nicolas Foucquet, Protecteur des Lettres, des Arts et des Sciences.* Geneva: Slatkine Reprints, 1971.

Chérot, Henri, ed. *La Première Jeunesse de Louis XIV (1649–1653): d'après la correspondance inédit du P. Charles Paulin.* Lille: impr. de Desclée, de Brouwer et Cie, 1892.

Chéruel, Adolphe, ed. *Mémoires sur la vie publique et privée de Fouquet, surintendant de finances, d'après ses lettres et des pièces inédite, conservées à la Bibliothèque impériale.* Paris: Charpentier, 1862.

Chéruel, Adolphe, ed. *Mémoires complets et authentiques du duc de Saint-Simon.* "Récit officiel de l'arrestation de Fouquet rédigé par Order de Colbert." Paris: Librairie Hachette, 1879.

Chéruel, Adolphe. *Histoire de France sous le Ministère de Mazarin.* Paris: Librairie Hachette et Cie, 1882.

Choisy, M. l'Abbé de. *Mémoires pour servir à l'Histoire de Louis XIV.* Paris: Librairie des Bibliophiles, 1887.

Chouppes, Marquis de. *Mémoires*. Paris: J. Techener, Librairie, 1861.

Clegg, Melanie. *The Life of Henrietta Anne, Daughter of Charles I*. Barnsley, U.K.: Pen & Sword History, 2017.

Clément, Pierre. *Lettres, instructions et Mémoires de Colbert*. Paris: Imprimerie Imperiale, 1859.

Clément, Pierre. *Madame de Montespan et Louis XIV: étude historique*. Paris: Librairie Académique, 1868.

Cooper, J. C. *An Illustrated Encyclopaedia of Traditional Symbols*. London, Thames & Hudson, 1978.

Cornette, Joël. *Chronique du Règne de Louis XIV*. Paris: Editions SEDES 1997.

Coural, Jean. "Gobelins." In *Dictionnaire du Grand Siècle*. Edited by François Bluche. Paris: Librairie Arthème Fayard, 1990.

Cousin, Jules. *L'Hôtel de Beauvais, rue Saint-Antoine*. Paris: Revue Universelle des Arts, 1864.

Créquy, Renée Caroline de Froulay, marquise de. *Souvenirs de 1710 à 1803*. Paris: Garnier Frères, 1873.

Cronin, Vincent. *Louis XIV*. London: The Harvill Press, 1996.

Dangeau, Philippe de Courcillon, marquis de. *Journal du marquis du Dangeau*. Paris: Firmin-Didot Frères, 1854.

Decker, Michel de. *Louis XIV. Le bon plaisir du roi*. Paris: Belfond, 2000.

De Imprimerie royale. *Medailles sur les principaux evenements du regne entier de Louis le Grand: avec des explications historiques*. Paris: De Imprimerie royale, 1702.

De Marly, Diana. *Louis XIV & Versailles*. London: B.T. Batsford Ltd., 1987.

Demouy, Patrick. *Saint Rémi and Our Lady of Reims*. Translated by Carolyn Morson. Strasbourg, France: Éditions du Signe, 1995.

Dent, Julian. *Crisis in Finance: Crown Finances and Society in Seventeenth Century France*. Newton Abbot, U.K.: David and Charles, 1973.

Dessert, Daniel. *Argent, pouvoir et société au Grand Siècle*. Paris: Fayard, 1984.

Dessert, Daniel. *Fouquet*. Paris: Fayard, 1987.

Dethan, Georges. *The Young Mazarin*. London: Thomas and Hudson, 1977.

Du Bois, Marie. *Moi, Marie du Bois*. Rennes, France: Éditions Apogée, 1994.

Dumas, Alexandre. *Le Vicomte de Bragellone*. Paris: Éditions Robert Laffont, S.A., 1991.

Dunlop, Ian. *Louis XIV*. London: Chatto & Windus, 1999.

Dyson, C. C. *Madame de Maintenon: Her life and times 1635–1719*. London: J. Lane, 1910.

Erlanger, Philippe. *Louis XIV*. London: Phoenix Press, 2003.

Erlanger, Philippe. *Monsieur, frère de Louis XIV*. Paris: Libraire Académique Perrin, 1981.

Evelyn, John. *The Diary of John Evelyn*. London, New York: Macmillan and Co., 1901.

Filhol, Emmanuel. "La France contre ses Tsiganes." http://academos.ro/sites /default/files/biblio-docs/249/20100707_tsiganes_filhol.pdf.

Fonck, Bertrand. "Invalides (hôtel royal des)." In *Dictionnaire Louis XIV*. Edited by Lucian Bély. Paris: Éditions Robert Laffont, 2015.

Foucquet, Nicolas. *Recueil des défenses*. No location, 1665–1668.

France, Anatole. *Clio and the Chateau de Vaux-le-Vicomte*. Translated by Winifred Stevens. London: The Bodeley Head, 1923.

Fraser, Antonia. *Love and Louis XIV*. London: Weidenfeld & Nicolson, 2006.

Fraser, Antonia. *King Charles II*. London: Weidenfeld & Nicolson, 1979.

Fumaroli, Marc. *The Poet and the King: Jean de La Fontaine and His Century*. Translated by Jane Marie Todd. Notre Dame, Ind.: University of Notre Dame Press, 2002.

Funck-Brentano, Frantz. *La drame des poisons*. Paris: Librairie Hachette, 1913.

Gazette, Théophraste Renaudot, contributor. Paris: Bureau d'adresse, 1631–1761.

Goulas, Nicolas. *Mémoires*. Paris: Libraire Renouard, 1879.

Gourville, Jean Hérault, sieur de. *Mémoires de Gourville*. Paris: Librairie Renouard, 1894.

Griffet, Henri. *Histoire de La Vie de Louis XIII, Roi de France et de Navarre*. Paris: Chez Saillant, Libraire, 1758.

Guiche, Armand de Gramont, comte de. *Mémoires de comte de Guiche concernant les Provinces-Unies des Pais-Bas*. London: chez Philippe Changuion, 1744.

Hamilton, Antoine. *Mémoires du Chevalier de Grammont*. Paris: Librairie des Bibliophiles, 1876.

Hanley, S. *The Lit de Justice of the Kings of France*. Princeton, N.J.: Princeton University Press, 1983.

Hassall, Arthur. *Mazarin*. London, New York: The Macmillan Company, 1903.

Hassall, Arthur. *Louis XIV and the Zenith of French Monarchy*. London and New York: G.P. Putnam's Sons, 1923.

Hassall, Arthur. *A Short Introduction to the Peace of Westphalia and the Fronde*. San Diego: Didactic Press, 2014.

Hilton, Lisa. *The Real Queen of France: Athénaïs & Louis XIV*. London: Abacus, 2003.

Isambert, Decrusy, Taillandier, eds. *Recueil général des anciennes lois françaises, depuis l'an 420, jusqu'à la Révolution de 1789*. Tome XVIII: Aout 1661–31 Décembre 1671. Paris: Belin-Leprieur, Verdière, 1829.

Jal, A. *Dictionnaire critique de Biographie et d'Histoire*. Paris: Henri Plon, 1867.

Labatut, Jeane-Pierre. *Louix XIV: Roi de gloire*. Paris: Imprimerie nationale, 1984.

Laborde, le Comte de. *Le Palais Mazarin et les Grandes Habitations de Ville et de Campagne au dix-septième siècle*. Paris: Chez A Franck, 1846.

La Bruyère, Jean de. *Œuvres de La Bruyère*. Edited by M. G. Servois. Paris: Librairie de L. Hachette, 1865.

La Fare, marquis de. *Mémoires et Réflexions sur les principaux événements du règne de Louis XIV* in Michaud et Poujoulat, Series 3, volume 30. Lyons, Paris: Guyot Frères, 1854.

La Fayette, Madame de. *Histoire de Madame Henriette d'Angleterre* in Michaud et Poujoulat, Series 3, volume 30. Lyons, Paris: Guyot Frères, 1854.

La Fontaine, Jean de. *Fables et Œuvres Diverses*. Edited by C. A. Walckenaer. Paris: Librairie de Firmin Didot et Cie, 1852.

Lair, Jules. *Nicolas Foucquet*. Paris: E. Plon, Nourrit et Cie, 1980.

Lair, Jules. *Louise de La Vallière*. Translated by Ethel Colburn Mayne. New York: G.P. Putnam's Sons, 1908.

La Porte, Pierre de. *Mémoires* in Michaud et Poujoulat, Series 3, volume 30. Lyons, Paris: Guyot Frères, 1854.

La Vallière, duchesse de. *Réflexions sur la Miséricorde de Dieu*. Paris: J. Techener, Librairie, 1860.

Lemoine, Jean. *Les des Œillets: une grande comédienne, une maitresse de Louis XIV*. Paris: Libraire Académique Perrin, 1938.

Lemoine, Jean and André Lichtenberger. *De La Vallière à Montespan*. Paris: Calmann-Lévy, 1902.

Le Roi, J.-A, ed. *Journal de la Santé du Roi Louis XIV de l'année 1647 é l'anne 1711 ecrit par Vallot, d'Aquin et Fagon*. Paris: Auguste-Durand, Libraire-éditeur, 1862.

Le Roy Ladurie, Emmanuel. *The Ancien Régime: A History of France 1610–1774*. Oxford: Blackwell Publishers Ltd., 1996.

Levi, Anthony. *Louis XIV*. London: Constable & Robinson, 2004.

Lewis, W. H. *The Sunset of a Splendid Century*. London: Eyre & Spottiswoode, 1955.

Locatelli, Sébastien. *Voyage de France: Mœurs et Coutumes Française (1664–1665)*. Translated by Adolphe Vautier. Paris: Alphonse Picard et Fils, 1905.

Loret, Jean. *La Muze historique ou recueil des lettres en vers*. Paris: P. Daffis, libraire éditeur, 1877.

Lough, John. *An Introduction to Seventeenth Century France*. London, New York, Toronto: Longmans, Green and Co., 1955.

Louis XIV. *Œuvres de Louis XIV*. Paris: Chez Treuttel et Würtz, 1806.

Louis XIV. *Memoirs for the Instruction of the Dauphin*. Translated and edited by Paul Sonnino. New York: Free Press; London: Collier-Macmillan, 1970.

Luynes, duc de. *Mémoires du duc de Luynessur la Cour de Louis XV (1735–1758)*. Vol. 2, 1738–1739. Paris: Firmin Didot Frères, fils et Cie, 1860.

Maintenon, Françoise d'Aubigné, marquise de. *Lettres historiques et édifiantes adressées aux dames de Saint-Louis par Mme de Maintenon*. Edited by Théophile Lavallée. Paris: Charpentier, 1856.

Maintenon, Françoise d'Aubigné, marquise de. *Correspondance général*. Edited by Théophile Lavallée. Paris: Charpentier, 1865.

Mazarin, Jules. *Lettres du Cardinal Mazarin pendant son Ministère*. Edited by M. A. Chéruel and V. G. d'Avenel. Paris: Imprimerie Nationale, 1872–1906.

Menin, Monsieur. *Traité Historique et Chronologique du Dacre et Couronnement des Rois et Reines de France*. Paris: Jean-Baptiste-Claude Bauche, 1723.

Mercure Galant. Paris, 1678–1714.

Miller, John. *James II*. Yale: Yale University Press, 2000.

Molé, Mathieu. *Mémoires*. Paris: Chez Jules Renouard et Cie, 1855.

Montglat, François de Paule de Clermont, Marquis de. *Mémoires* in Michaud et Poujoulat, Series 3, volume 30. Lyons, Paris: Guyot Frères, 1854.

Montpensier, Mademoiselle de. *Memoirs of Mademoiselle de Montpensier, written by herself*. London: Henry Colburn, 1848.

Montpensier, Mademoiselle de. *Mémoires de Mlle de Montpensier: Petite-fille de Henri IV*. Edited by A. Chéruel. Paris: Bibliothèque-Charpentier, 1858.

Moote, J. Lloyd, *Louis the Just*. Berkeley, Los Angeles, London: University of California Press, 1989.

Mormondo, Franco. *Bernini: His Life and His Rome*. Chicago: University of Chicago Press, 2011.

Mossiker, Francis. *The Affair of the Poisons*. London: Victor Gollancz, 1970.

Motteville, Mme de. *Memoirs of Madame de Motteville on Anne of Austria and her Court*. Translated by Katharine Prescott Wormeley, with an introduction by C. A. Saint-Beuve. Boston: Hardy, Pratt & Company, 1901.

Murat, Inès, *Colbert*. Paris: Librairie Arthème Fayard, 1980.

Nolhac, Pierre de. *Versailles et la Cour de France: La Création de Versailles*. Paris: Louis Conard, 1925.

Norton, Lucy. *Saint-Simon at Versailles*. London: Hamish Hamilton, 1958.

Norton, Lucy. *Memoirs. Duc de Saint-Simon*. London: Prion Books Limited, 1999.

Ogg, David. *Louis XIV*. London, Oxford, New York: Oxford University Press, 1967.

Orléans, Elizabeth-Charlotte, duchesse d'. *The Letters of Madame*. Translated and edited by Gertrude Scott-Stevenson. London: Arrowsmith, 1925.

Orléans, Elizabeth-Charlotte, duchesse d'. *Life and Letters of Charlotte Elizabeth, Princess Palatine and Mother of Philippe d'Orléans, Regent of France*. London: Chapman and Gall, 1889.

Ormesson, Olivier Lefèvre d'. *Journal d'Olivier Lefèvre d'Ormesson*. Edited by M. Chéruel. Paris: Imprimerie Impériale, 1861.

Palace of Versailles. http://en.chateauversailles.fr/discover/history/louis-xiv-guide -gardens-versailles.

Palace of Versailles. http://en.chateauversailles.fr/discover/estate/estate-trianon

Palmer, John. *Molière, His Life and Works*. London: G. Bell and sons, 1930.

Paris Observatory. www.obspm.fr.

Patin, Guy. *Lettres*. 3 vols. Paris: Chez J.-B. Baillière, 1846.

Pérouse de Montclos, Jean-Marie. *Vaux-le-Vicomte.* Translated by Judith Hayward. London: Scala Books, 1997.

Perrault, Charles. *Courses et Têtes et de Bague, faites par le Roy.* Paris: L'Imprimerie Royale 1670.

Petitfils, Jean-Christian. *L'affaire des poisons: alchimistes et sorciers sous Louis XIV.* Paris: Albin Michel, 1977.

Petitfils, Jean-Christian. *Lauzun, ou l'insolente séduction.* Paris: Librairie Académique Perrin, 1987.

Petitfils, Jean-Christian. *Madame de Montespan.* Paris: Fayard, 1988.

Petitfils, Jean-Christian. *Fouquet.* Paris: Perrin, 1990.

Petitfils, Jean-Christian. *Louis XIV.* Paris: Perrin, 2008.

Pitts, Vincent J. *Embezzlement and High Treason in Louis XIV's France: The Trial of Nicolas Fouquet.* Baltimore: Johns Hopkins University Press, 2015.

Prest, Julia. *Theatre under Louis XIV, Cross-dressing and the performance of Gender in Drama, Ballet, and Opera.* Basingstoke: Palgrave Macmillan, 2013.

Primi Visconti, J.-B. *Mémoires dur la cour de Louis XIV, 1673–1681.* Paris: Perrin, 1988.

Project Gutenberg. *Memoirs of Madame la Marquise de Montespan—Complete.* Project Gutenberg: http://www.gutenberg.org/files/3854/3854-h/3854-h.htm.

Racine, Jean. *Alexandre le Grand.* Paris: Chez Theodore Girard, 1666.

Racine, Jean. *Œuvres complètes de Racine.* Paris: Chez Lefèvre, Libraire, 1822.

Ravaisson, François, ed. *Archives de la Bastille.* 1870.

Renaudot, Theophraste, ed. *Recueil des Gazettes et Nouvelles tant Ordinaires que Extraordinaires.* Paris: au bureau d'Adreffe, 1644.

Retz, Jean Francois Paul de Gondi, cardinal de. *Memoirs.* London, Toronto: JM Dent & Sons; New York: E. P. Dutton & Co., 1917.

Rossi, comte de. *Mercurio Postiglione, di questo e l'autro mondo, Il.* Villa-Franca: Claudio Del Monte, 1667.

Sabatier, Gérard. *Versailles, ou la disgrâce d'Apollon.* Rennes, France: Presses Universitaires de Rennes; Centre de Recherche du Château de Versailles, 2016.

Sablé, Marquise de. *Madame de Sablé, Nouvelle Études sur les Femmes Illustres et La Société du XVIIe Siècle.* Edited by Victor Cousin. Paris: 1882.

Saint-Maurice. *Lettres sur le Court de Louis XIV.* Edited by Jean Lemoine. Paris: Calmann-Lévy, c. 1910.

Saint-René Taillandier, Madeleine Marie Louise. *Madame de Maintenon.* Translated by Mary Sophie Loyd. London: W. Heineman, 1922.

Saint-Simon, Louis de Rouvroy, duc de. *Mémoires completes et authentiques du duc de Saint-Simon.* Edited by Adolphe Chéruel. Paris: Librairie Hachette, 1856–58.

Saint-Simon, Louis de Rouvrou, duc de. *Mémoires de saint-Simon, nouvelle édition.* Edited by Boislisle. Paris: Librairie Hachette, 1879–1931.

Saint-Simon, Louis de Rouvroy, duc de. *Memoirs of the Duc de Saint-Simon on the Times of Louis XIV. and the Regency*. Translated and abridged by Katharine Prescott Wormeley. Boston: Hardy, Pratt & Company, 1902.

Sandars, Mary F. *Lauzun: Courtier and Adventurer: The Life of a Friend of Louis XIV*. New York: Brentano's, 1909.

Sceaux, Nicolas. *Les plaisirs de l'île enchantée*. 2008–2009.

Scott, Virginia. *Molière: a Theatrical Life*. Cambridge: Cambridge University Press, 2000.

Sévigné, Marie du Rabutin-Chantal, marquise de, *Recueil des lettres de Mme la marquise de Sévigné a Madame la Comtesse de Grignan sa fille*. Paris: Chez Rollin, 1754.

Sévigné, Marie du Rabutin-Chantal, marquise de, *Lettres de Madame de Sevigné, de sa famille et de ses amis*. Paris : J. J. Blaise, 1818.

Sévigné, Marie du Rabutin-Chantal, marquise de, *Lettres de Madame de Sevigné, de sa famille et de ses amis*. Paris : J. J. Blaise, 1820.

Somerset, Anne. *The Affair of the Poisons. Murder, Infanticide & Satanism at the Court of Louis XIV*. London: Weidenfeld & Nicolson, 2003.

Sourches, Louis François du Bouchet, marquis de. *Memoires du marquis de Sourches sur le règne de Louis XIV*. Paris: Librairie Hachette et Cie, 1882–1893.

Spanheim, Ézéchiel. *Relation de la Cour de France en 1690*. Paris: Librairie Renouard, 1882.

Steegmuller, Francis. *La Grande Mademoiselle*. London: Hamish Hamilton, 1955.

Tallemant des Réaux, Gédeon. *Les Histoirettes*. Paris: Alphonse Levasseur, 1834.

Talon, Omer. *Œuvres d'Omer et Denis Talon*. Paris: A. Egron, 1821.

Teissier, Octave. *Histoire de la Commune de Cotignac*. Marseilles: A. Gueidon, 1860.

Torcy, marquis de. *Mémoires du marquis de Torcy* in Michaud et Poujoulat, Series 3, volume 30. Lyons, Paris: Guyot Frères, 1854.

Treasure, Geoffrey. *Mazarin. The Crisis of Absolutism in France*. London: Routledge, 1995.

Treasure, Geoffrey. *Louis XIV*. London, Edinburgh: Pearson Education Limited, 2001.

Tucker, Holly, *City of Light, City of Poison. Murder, Magic, and the First Police Chief of Paris*. New York, London: W.W. Norton & Company, 2017.

Vallier, Jean. *Journal de Jean Vallier, Maître d'Hôtel du Roi. 1648–1657*. Paris: Libraire Renouard, 1902.

Voltaire. *The Age of Louis XIV*. London: J.M. Dent & Sons Ltd., 1935.

Wall, Charles Heron. *The Dramatic Works of Molière*. London: George Bell and Sons, 1876.

Walton, Guy. *Louis XIV's Versailles*. Harmsworth, U.K.: Viking, 1986.

Williams, H. Noel. *Five Fair Sisters: An Italian Episode at the Court of Louis XIV*. New York: G.P. Putnam's Sons, 1906.

Williams, H. Noel. *A Rose of Savoy: Marie Adelaide of Savoy, Duchesse de Bourgogne, Mother of Louis XV.* New York, Charles Scribner's Sons, 1909.

Wilkinson, Richard. *Louis XIV,* 2nd ed. Abingdon, U.K.: Routledge, 2018.

Wolf, John B. *Louis XIV.* New York: W.W. Norton & Company, 1968.

Zoete Van Laeke, Philips and Frans. *Journal d'un Voyage à Paris en 1656–1658,* publié par A.P. Faugère. Paris: Benjamin Duprat, 1862.

ENDNOTES

PROLOGUE

1   Henri Griffet, *Histoire de La Vie de Louis XIII, Roi de France et de Navarre* (Paris: Chez Saillant, Libraire, 1758), tome 3, pp. 374–6. This story, as told by the Jesuit Abbé Henri Griffet, first appeared in 1756 and is an elaboration of earlier accounts by the marquis de Montglat (p. 61), an officer in the army of Navarre and grand master of the king's guard, and Mme de Motteville (volume I, p. 60), lady-in-waiting to Queen Anne of Austria.

ONE: A GIFT FROM GOD

1   Marquise de Sablé, Madame de Sablé, *Nouvelle Études sur les Femmes Illustres et La Société du XVIIe Siècle.* Edited by Victor Cousin (Paris: 1882), p. 321.

2   Mme de Motteville, *Memoirs of Madame de Motteville on Anne of Austria and her Court,* trans. Katharine Prescott Wormeley (Boston: Hardy, Pratt & Company, 1901) Motteville, volume I, p. 9.

3   J. Lloyd Moote, *Louis the Just* (Berkeley, Los Angeles, and London: University of California Press, 1989), pp. 84–5; Antonia Fraser, *Love and Louis XIV* (London: Weidenfeld & Nicolson, 2006), pp. 5–6; Dorothy de Brissac Campbell, *The Intriguing Duchess* (London: John Hamilton Ltd., 1900), p. 13.

4   Anne of Austria was known in her native Spain as Doña Ana Maria Mauricia and she married Louis XIII on November 25, 1615. She was styled Anne of Austria because of her Habsburg connections. She was the great-granddaughter of the Holy Roman Emperor Charles V.

5   Moote, p. 85.

6   Fraser, *Louis XIV*, p. 6.

7   Campbell, *Duchess*, p. 18.

8   Vincent Cronin, *Louis XIV* (London: The Harvill Press, 1996), p. 18.

9   Campbell, *Duchess*, pp. 25–6, 55.

10 Motteville, volume I, p. 18.

11 Ibid., p. 15.

12 Ibid., p. 40; Moote, p. 274; Campbell, *Duchess*, p. 172.

13 Campbell, *Duchess*, pp. 173–4.

14   Motteville, volume I, pp. 58–60, 65; Moote, pp. 275–7.
15   Cronin, p. 20.
16   The Feast of the Assumption, August 15, is still celebrated.
17   François Bluche, *Louis XIV*, trans. Mark Greengrass (Oxford: Basil Blackwell Ltd, 1990), p. 10.
18   Octave Teissier, *Histoire de la Commune de Cotignac* (Marseilles: A. Gueidon, 1860), pp. 40–1.
19   Bluche, *Louis XIV*, pp. 10–11.
20   Cronin, p. 20.
21   Quoted in Philippe Erlanger, *Louis XIV* (London: Phoenix Press, 2003), p. 8.
22   John B. Wolf, *Louis XIV* (New York: W.W. Norton & Company, Inc., 1968), p. 4.
23   François de Paule de Clermont, *Marquis de Montglat, Mémoires in Michaud et Poujoulat*, Series 3, volume 30 (Lyon, Paris: Guyot Frères, 1854), p. 216.
24   Motteville, volume I, p. 65.
25   Clovis - Lovis - Louis.
26   Bluche, *Louis XIV*, p. 11.
27   Mathieu Molé, *Mémoires* (Paris: Chez Jules Renouard et Cie, 1855), volume 3, pp. 425–7.
28   Jean Racine, *OEuvres complètes de Racine* (Paris: Chez Lefèvre, Libraire, 1822), volume 5, p. 332. Jean Racine, who was born a year after Louis XIV and would be appointed the king's official historiographer.
29   Quoted in Erlanger, *Louis XIV*, p. 12.
30   Ibid., pp. 12–13.
31   Motteville, volume I, p. 70.
32   Erlanger, *Louis XIV*, p. 18
33   *Recueil des Gazettes*, 1644, pp. 326–7.
34   Cronin, p. 25. The story is almost certainly apocryphal, because kings rarely, if ever, referred to themselves using their regnal number.
35   Motteville, volume I, p. 95; Ian Dunlop, *Louis XIV* (London: Chatto & Windus, 1999), p. 3; Bluche, *Louis XIV*, p. 18; Erlanger, *Louis XIV*, p. 18.

TWO: TO EDUCATE A LIVING GOD

1   Louis's blue eyes, blond hair, and round face hinted at his Austro-Flemish lineage, but the slightly protruding "Habsburg lip" provided the biggest clue to his ancestral heritage.
2   Wolf, p. 12.
3   Olivier Lefèvre d'Ormesson, *Journal d'Olivier Lefèvre d'Ormesson*, ed. M. Chéruel (Paris: Imprimerie Impériale, 1861), volume 1, p. 43.
4   Peter Burke, *The Fabrication of Louis XIV* (New Haven, Conn., London: Yale University Press, 1992) pp. 44–5.
5   It was the duty of the parlement to register policy, not to ratify it.
6   *Gazette* (1643), pp. 427–8.
7   Omer Talon, *OEuvres d'Omer et Denis Talon* (Paris: A. Egron, 1821), volume 1, p. 46.
8   Wolf, *Louis XIV*, p. 16.
9   *Gazette* (1643), p. 428.
10   *Medailles sur les principaux evenements*, p. 4.
11   Motteville, volume I, p. 71.
12   Marquis de Chouppes, *Mémoires* (Paris: J. Techener, Librairie, 1861), pp. 41–4; Motteville, volume I, p. 71.

13 Gédeon Tallemant des Réaux, *Les Histoirettes* (Paris: Alphonse Levasseur, 1834), volume 1, p. 422.

14 Georges Dethan, *The Young Mazarin* (London: Thomas and Hudson, 1977), p. 147; Geoffrey Treasure, *Mazarin. The Crisis of Absolutism in France* (London: Routledge, 1995), p. 25.

15 The suggestion that Anne and Mazarin were lovers and/or that they later married continues to surface from time to time and is most forcefully argued by Anthony Lévi, *Louis XIV* (London: Constable & Robinson, 2004), pp. 17–21, who also suggests that Mazarin, rather than Louis XIII, was the real father of Louis XIV. Most historians have never taken such ideas seriously.

16 Erlanger, *Louis XIV*, pp. 27–8; Comte de Brienne, *Mémoires de Louis-Henri de Loménie, comte de Brienne, dit le Jeune Brienne* ed. Paul Bonnefon (Paris: Société de l'Histoire de France, 1916–19), volume 2, p. 5.

17 Campbell, *Duchess*, p. 248.

18 See, for example, Erlanger, *Louis XIV*, p. 31.

19 Cited in Dunlop, p. 8.

20 *Gazette*, 1643, p. 808.

21 Carré, Henry. *L'Enfance et la Première Jeunesse de Louis XIV* (Paris: Albin Michel, 1944), p. 30; *Gazette*, 1643, pp. 897–908.

22 Carré, p. 30.

23 Comte de Brienne, *Mémoires inédits de Louis-Henri de Loménie, comte de Brienne, secrétaire d'état sous Louis XIV*, ed. F. Barrière (Paris, Leipzig: Ponthieu, 1828), volume 1, pp. 218–22; Dunlop, pp. 7–8.

24 Motteville, volume I, pp. 105, 106–7.

25 Anne of Austria's education strategy for her sons, especially Louis, is outlined in Motteville, volume I. pp. 144–46.

26 Carré, p. 36, quoting Péréfixe's lessons.

27 Ibid., p. 31.

28 Motteville, volume I, p. 146.

29 Ibid., volume I, pp. 154–5.

30 Fraser, *Charles II*, p. 32.

31 Osmund Airy, *Charles II* (London, New York, Bombay: Longmans, Green & Co., 1904), pp. 34–5.

32 Motteville, volume I, p. 169.

33 Ibid., p. 172.

34 Ibid., p. 174.

35 Ibid., pp. 174–5.

36 Ibid., p. 174; Francis Steegmuller, *La Grande Mademoiselle* (London: Hamish Hamilton, 1955), p. 35.

37 Motteville, volume I, p. 125.

38 Ibid., p. 126.

39 Dunlop, p. 9. The term *petit papa* was frequently used by elder brothers.

40 Marie Du Bois, *Moi, Marie du Bois* (Rennes, France: Éditions Apogée, 1994), p. 37.

41 Motteville, volume I, p. 197.

42 Ibid. François Ravaillac assassinated Henri IV, Louis's grandfather, on May 14, 1610.

43 Motteville, volume I, p. 211. Charles's father, Charles I of England, was now a prisoner of the New Model Army, and was currently being held at Hampton Court.

44 Motteville, volume I, pp. 211–12.
45 The course of Louis's illness, including the harsh treatments, is described by Motteville, volume I, pp. 212–15; J.-A Le Roi, ed. *Journal de la Santé du Roi Louis XIV de l'année 1647 é l'anne 1711 ecrit par Vallot, d'Aquin et Fagon* (Paris: Auguste-Durand, Libraire-éditeur, 1862), pp. 1–7.

THREE: THE FRONDE
1   Motteville, volume I, p. 144.
2   A rente was a form of investment for credit, a legal way to make loans for profit.
3   These revolts reflected similar uprisings in Portugal, Naples, England, and, later, the Netherlands, all of which began as protests against excessive fiscality, see Le Roy Ladurie, Emmanuel. *The Ancien Régime: A History of France 1610–1774* (Oxford: Blackwell Publishers Ltd., 1996), p. 99.
4   Le Roy Ladurie, pp. 96–100; John Lough, *An Introduction to Seventeenth Century France* (London, New York, Toronto: Longmans, Green & Co., 1955), pp. 127–9.
5   Cronin, p. 39.
6   Geoffrey Treasure, *Mazarin. The Crisis of Absolutism in France* (London: Routledge, 1995), p. 350 n1.
7   Cronin, p. 38; Lough, p. 130.
8   Bluche, *Louis XIV*, p. 37; Jean-Christian *Petitfils, Louis XIV* (Paris: Perrin, 2008), pp. 81–2.
9   Formerly the duc d'Enghein, Louis II de Bourbon inherited the title of prince de Condé upon the death of his father two years earlier. He would be known to history as le Grand Condé.
10 The Battle of Lens, fought on August 20, 1648, was the last major battle in the Thirty Years' War.
11 Motteville, volume I, p. 311.
12 According to Motteville (volume I, p. 312), the French army had 14,000 men, while that of the enemy comprised some 15,000 or 16,000.
13 Wolf, p. 38.
14 Cronin, p. 41.
15 Today, Rueil is called Rueil-Malmaison. It is a small commune to the west of Paris.
16 Motteville, volume I, p. 344.
17 Among other libels, the *Mazarinades* suggested that Mazarin and Anne of Austria were lovers, with the unspoken implication that Louis was their illegitimate son. Despite this, the frondeurs continued to insist that their anger was directed primarily at Mazarin and not the king.
18 Motteville, volume II, p. 40.
19 Ibid., p. 38.
20 The fullest account of Louis's escape to Saint-Germain is that of Mme de Motteville (volume 2, pp. 41–7). The incident is also mentioned by Montglat (p. 203), Jean Francois Paul de Gondi, cardinal de Retz, *Memoirs* (London, Toronto: JM Dent & Sons; New York: E.P. Dutton & Co., 1917) pp. 102–3, and Talon (pp. 248–9).
21 Montpensier (1848), volume I, pp. 121–2.
22 Motteville, volume II, pp. 48–9.
23 Ibid., pp. 49–50. Mme de Motteville kept a copy of Louis's letter, which she included in her *Mémoires*. The letter was also signed by de Guénégaud.
24 Ibid., p. 104.

25   *Le Custode du Lit de la Reine* is reproduced in le Comte de Laborde, *Le Palais Mazarin et les Grandes Habitations de Ville et de Campagne au dix-septième siècle* (Paris: Chez A Franck, 1846), p. 157.

26   The name Dieudonné was sometimes given to children of dubious paternity, euphemistically referring to them as gifts of God.

27   Carré, pp. 75–6.

28   Motteville, volume II, p. 144.

29   Ibid., p. 139.

30   Carré, pp. 76.

31   Motteville, volume II, p. 143.

32   Ibid., p. 144.

33   Known today as Saint-Paul-Saint-Louis.

34   Motteville, volume II, p. 144.

35   Jean Vallier, *Journal de Jean Vallier, Maître d'Hôtel du Roi* (1648–1657) (Paris: Libraire Renouard, 1902), volume 1, pp. 389–90.

36   Motteville, volume II, p. 145; Carré, pp. 78–9.

37   Mademoiselle was the formal title of the duchesse de Montpensier, who was also known as the Grande Mademoiselle.

38   Vallier, volume 1, p. 396.

39   Mme Le Feron was the wife of the *prévôt des marchands*, the nearest equivalent of a mayor.

40   Vallier, volume 1, p. 397. The occasion is also described in *Gazette* (1649), pp. 757–68.

41   Motteville, volume II, p. 149.

42   Ibid., p. 149.

43   Ibid., p. 145.

44   Lough, pp. 131–31; Motteville, volume II, p. 66.

45   Henri Chérot, ed. *La Première Jeunesse de Louis XIV* (1649–1653): *d'après la correspondance inédite du P. Charles Paulin* (Lille: impr. de Desclée, de Brouwer et Cie, 1892), pp. 68–9.

46   Ibid.

47   Ibid., p. 54; *Gazette*, p. 1200, p. 1649.

48   Chérot, p. 59.

49   Ibid., p. 60.

50   *Gazette*, 1649, pp. 1273–80.

51   *Gazette*, 1650, pp. 60, 92; Chérot, p. 67.

52   Pierre de La Porte, *Mémoires in Michaud et Poujoulat*, Series 3, volume 30 (Lyon, Paris: Guyot Frères, 1854), p. 47.

53   Ibid.

54   *Gazette*, p. 60.

55   Motteville, volume II, p. 218.

56   Ibid., p. 211.

57   Cronin, p. 72.

58   Carré, p. 83.

59   Arthur Hassall, *A Short Introduction to the Peace of Westphalia and the Fronde* (San Diego: Didactic Press, 2014), loc.162.

60   A treaty of unity was signed on January 30, 1651.

61   Motteville, volume II, p. 332.

62   Ibid., p. 335.

63   Ibid., p. 344. It was later discovered that Orléans was being incited by Retz to take custody of Louis, shut Anne into a convent, remove Mazarin permanently, and make himself regent. Fortunately, Orléans resisted the pressure exerted upon him.

64   Montglat, volume 2, pp. 276–7; Motteville, volume II, pp. 345–6.

65   Motteville, volume III, pp. 345–6.

66   Montglat, volume 2, p. 277.

67   Motteville, volume II, p. 349.

68   Cronin, p. 53.

69   Erlanger, *Louis XIV*, p. 63; Cronin, p. 60.

70   This section follows Motteville, volume III, pp. 44–51.

71   The account of the ceremonies surrounding Louis's coming of age is mainly taken from Motteville, volume III, pp. 44–51, which is based upon a newspaper report.

72   In this context, the caduceus is a symbol of peace and protection.

73   The word used by Evelyn was *semée*: sown with, powdered.

74   John Evelyn, *The Diary of John Evelyn* (London, New York: Macmillan and Co., 1901), volume II, p. 41.

75   Louis is often described as being tall. Estimates vary, but he is believed to have been anywhere between five feet nine and six feet tall. See Petitfils (*Louis*, p. 171 and note), who explains how the myth that Louis was short came about. Of course, Louis's high-heeled shoes and, later, his tall wig gave the impression that he was even taller than this.

76   Vincent J. Pitts, *Embezzlement and High Treason in Louis XIV's France: The Trial of Nicolas Fouquet* (Baltimore: Johns Hopkins University Press, 2015), p. 23.

77   La Porte, p. 49.

78   Ibid., p. 51.

79   Montpensier (1848), volume I, pp. 264–5.

80   Montpensier (1848), volume I, pp. 273–4. The princess later told Mme de Motteville (volume III, p. 78) that this had not been done on her orders. "I know, however," said Motteville, "that the king and queen were convinced to the contrary, and perhaps with reason."

81   Motteville, volume III, p. 75.

82   Ibid., pp. 86–7.

83   Ibid., p. 87.

84   Ibid., p. 88. The arrest of Retz could have gone so differently. At first, the order was given to Pradelle, the captain of a company of the infantry of the Gardes. He begged Louis to sign it with his own hand "because he felt that, as this stroke ought not to fail, he might perhaps be forced to kill him [Retz] rather than to allow him to escape." As it was, Queen Anne could not consent to such an "act of vengeance and cruelty." She and Louis waited until "God was pleased, in blessing their good and just intentions, to give them the means of making sure of his person in a more gentle manner; which came to pass, at last as they wished," at Christmas 1652 (Motteville, volume III, pp. 87–8).

85   Burke, p. 45; *Jeane-Pierre Labatut, Louis XIV: Roi de gloire* (Paris: Imprimerie nationale, 1984), p. 43.

FOUR: "THE ANOINTED OF THE LORD"

1   The *Ballet de la Nuit* was first performed on February 23, 1653.

2   Carré, pp. 188–9; *Gazette*, 1653, pp. 222–3.

3   The Cour des Miracles, a medieval Parisian slum, was situated in the district surrounding the now lost Filles-Dieu convent, near Notre-Dame des Victoires, and was the haunt of beggars, vagabonds, and prostitutes.

4   Le Roi, ed., p. 14.

5   Ibid., pp. 14–15.

6   Ibid., pp. 15–16.

7   Julia Prest, *Theatre under Louis XIV, Cross-dressing and the performance of Gender in Drama, Ballet, and Opera* (Basingstoke, U.K.: Palgrave Macmillan, 2013), p. 107.

8   The first anointed coronation to take place at Reims was that of Louis the Pious, son of Charlemagne, in 816. After that, coronations might be held at Soissons, Saint-Denis, or Noyon. From 1027 onwards, all kings of France were crowned at Reims, the first being Henri I, with Charles X as the last, in 1825. There were two exceptions, Louis VI and Henri IV. (Patrick Demouy, *Saint Rémi and Our Lady of Reims. trans.* Carolyn Morson (Strasbourg, France: Éditions du Signe, 1995), pp. 10–11.)

9   The general chronology of the coronation service and the ceremonies surrounding it are taken from Menin, pp. 195–316. However, Louis's ceremonies differed in certain respects, and these will be highlighted in the notes.

10   The bishop of Soissons would officiate at Louis's coronation. Normally the officiate would have been the archbishop of Reims, but the titular holder, Henri de Savoy, was not in holy orders, so the task fell to his senior suffragan, Simon Le Gras, bishop of Soissons (Dunlop, p. 33).

11   The archiepiscopal palace is the Palais de Tau, next door to Notre-Dame de Reims. It is so named because the building is in the shape of the Greek *T*.

12   Archbishop Hincmar was the first to assert that the holy oil had been brought from heaven in the beak of a dove (Demouy, p. 11).

13   Louis XIV, King of France and Navarre, the most Christian King.

14   The Edict of Nantes of 1598.

15   At this point, Louis had no intention of persecuting the French Protestants, known as Huguenots; the time would come, however, when he would be less tolerant.

16   Menin, p. 328.

17   Cronin, pp. 70–72.

18   Guy Patin, *Lettres*. 3 vols. (Paris: Chez J.-B. Baillière, 1846), volume 2, p. 140.

19   Louis XIV, *OEuvres de Louis XIV* (Paris: Chez Treuttel et Würtz, 1806), volume II, p. 95.

20   Joël Cornette, *Chronique du Règne de Louis XIV* (Paris: Editions SEDES 1997), p. 25.

FIVE: LOUIS IN LOVE

1   Motteville, volume III, p. 96.

2   Isaac de Benserade, *Ballet des Plaisirs. Dansé par sa Majesté le 4 jour de Février 1655* (Paris: Robert Ballard, seul Imprimeur du Roy pour la Musique, 1655), p. 24.

3   The events of this evening are recounted by Mme de Motteville, volume III, pp. 98–9.

4   Jules Cousin, *L'Hôtel de Beauvais, rue Saint-Antoine* (Paris: Revue Universelle des Arts, 1864) pp. 12–13, dates the incident to the winter of 1654.

5   Jean de La Bruyère, *OEuvres de La Bruyère. ed. M. G. Servois* (Paris: Librairie de L. Hachette, 1865), p. 490, note 2. Similarly, Saint-Simon (Boislisle, volume 1, p. 291) described Mme de Beauvais as the woman who had taken the king's virginity; see also M. l'Abbé de Choisy, *Mémoires pour servir à l'Histoire de Louis XIV* (Paris: Librairie des Bibliophiles, 1887), volume 1, p. 99.

6 Elizabeth-Charlotte, duchesse d' Orléans, *The Letters of Madame*. trans. and ed. Gertrude Scott–Stevenson (London: Arrowsmith, 1925), volume II, pp. 131–2: Montglat, p. 247.

7 Motteville, volume III, p. 96. Olympe first arrived at court with her sisters in 1647, when Mme de Motteville (volume 2, p. 201) noted that she was brunette, with a "long face and a pointed chin. Her eyes were small but lively, and it might be expected that when fifteen years old she would have some charm. According to the rules of beauty it was impossible at this time to grant her any, except that of having dimples in her cheeks." Time would change her opinion of Olympe. Brienne (1916–19, volume 1, pp. 278–81) introduces his readers to the Mazarinettes, as the cardinal's nieces were called.

8 Motteville, volume III, p. 96.

9 Ibid., p. 97.

10 Ibid., p. 95.

11 This section follows Adolphe Chéruel, *Histoire de France sous le Ministère de Mazarin* (Paris: Librairie Hachette et Cie, 1882), volume 2, pp. 254–7 (Louis's speech, p. 255); Montglat, p. 306; Patin, p. 168.

12 Bluche, *Louis XIV*, pp. 79–80.

13 Chéruel, *Histoire de France*, volume 2, p. 257; Bluche, *Louis XIV*, pp. 79–80.

14 Du Bois, pp. 110–12.

15 Louis's bedchamber comprised an antechamber, a *grande chambre*, where he received those who had right of entry, and a *chambre de l'alcôve*, or recess, which contained his bed and the commode. A rail or bannister divided the *grande chambre* from the alcove, while the space between the bed and the wall was called the *ruelle*, a very private area to which only specially selected persons had entry.

16 Louis would learn statecraft by example. In Mazarin's chambers, he would read the day's dispatches, which he would then copy out, the hands-on approach being deemed the best way for him to practice formulating ideas. Louis would also attend council meetings, beginning with those dealing with simple matters that required a straightforward solution. Gradually, the business would become more complex. As time went on, Louis's attendance increased so that he was present at meetings in which even the most important decisions were made and the most secret affairs of state were discussed. At this stage, however, the king always deferred to Mazarin's judgment.

These lessons served Louis well. Throughout the reign he would consult his council and hear the advice of his ministers, but the final decision would always be his own. Louis would face every problem by reasoning and thinking it through. He would then compare his solutions with those of "able and experienced people" (Louis XIV, *Œuvres*, volume I, pp. 23–4).

17 The Petit-Bourbon was a town house that lay between the Louvre and the cloister of Saint-German-l'Auxerrois.

18 This game resembles one made popular by the marquise de Rambouillet in her famous salon.

19 Louis's apartment at the Louvre featured a tapestry of Scipio and a white satin bed embroidered in gold, which had been left to Louis by Cardinal Richelieu (Motteville, volume III, p. 104).

20 Motteville, volume III, pp. 99–101; Montglat, p. 314.

21 Motteville, volume III, p. 102.

22 Louis liked to make unexpected appearances because he preferred to see people as they really were, rather than as they wanted him to see them.

23 Motteville, volume III, p. 105.

24 Ibid., p. 105.

25 Montpensier, volume II, pp. 51–2.

26 Motteville, volume III (1848 edition), p. 113–14. Olympe had recognized that Louis's friendship for her had only been his way of amusing himself and that since neither of them had much regard for the other, they would soon have fallen out anyway. Moreover, she felt that her uncle was keeping her in order to serve his own interests, rather than seeking to marry her for her own advancement.

27 Prince Eugène's mother was a daughter and co-heir of the comte de Soissons; Eugène took the title to become comte de Soissons. Soissons was a branch of the house of Bourbon, to which Louis belonged.

28 H. Noel Williams, *Five Fair Sisters: An Italian Episode at the Court of Louis XIV* (New York: G.P. Putnam's Sons, 1906), p. 44.

29 The young man, Armand de la Porte, having seen Marie and her sister, Hortense, when they first arrived in France, fell passionately in love with Hortense despite the fact that she was only a child. He declared that if he could not marry her, he would marry no one and would, instead, spend the rest of his days as a monk. Mazarin, indignant, announced that he would rather marry his niece to a lackey than to him. He would later change his mind, and the two would marry in 1661, just ten days before Mazarin's death (Williams, pp. 48–50, 228).

30 Williams (*Sisters*), p. 56.

31 Ibid.

32 Motteville, volume III, p. 115.

33 Montpensier, volume II, pp. 75–6.

34 As Louis was travelling back from Montmédy, he was passing through a part of the woods known as Le Trou de Souris when the coach containing two of the king's gentlemen was suddenly fired upon and the coachman was wounded. The gentlemen immediately got out and, getting on horseback, rode into the woods, where they found ten or twelve fusiliers. They killed one or two of them and took the rest prisoner (Montpensier, volume II, p. 76).

35 It is difficult to date when Louis first noticed Mlle de La Motte-Argencourt: she had recently come to court in the service of Anne of Austria, and Louis appears to have known her for a short while (Jules Lair, *Louise de La Vallière*, trans. Ethel Colburn Mayne (New York: G.P. Putnam's Sons, 1908), p. 26). Mme de Motteville (volume III, pp. 116–18) dates the beginning of Louis's relationship with her to 1657, while Mademoiselle, who confuses her with the similarly named Mlle de la Motte-Houdancourt, (pp. 87–8) links it to the time of the death of Mazarin's nephew, Alfonso Mancini, who died in 1658. He attended the prestigious Jesuit Clermont College in Paris. One day, as the boys were playing the game of being tossed in a blanket, he fell and fractured his skull, dying of his injury. He was only twelve years old.

36 Motteville, volume III, p. 117.

37 Ibid.

38 Ibid.

39 Montpensier, volume II, p. 88.

40 Motteville, volume III, pp. 117–18. Returning to Paris after a brief stay at Vincennes, Louis was firm in his resolve never to see La Motte-Argencourt again, but his will was tested at a ball a few days later when the young lady went to him to

take him as her partner. Louis turned pale, then red, and, later, La Motte-Argen-court told her friends that the king's hand "trembled all the time that it held hers." Mlle de La Motte-Argencourt left court soon afterwards and retired to the convent of the Filles-de-Sainte-Marie at Chaillot.

41 Mazarin and King Philip IV of Spain had both sought to make an ally of England. At first Cromwell favored Spain, but Philip's conditions were too high, and when England seized Jamaica, England and Spain went to war. With Spain now fighting two enemies, Mazarin proposed an alliance with Cromwell in which English troops would capture Gravelines, Mardyck, and Dunkirk, the main sources of provisions to the Spanish forces. In return, England would keep Mardyck and Dunkirk, an attractive proposition for Cromwell, as the latter gave him a major port in continental Europe. The treaty was signed in 1657. Louis had inspected the Ironsides, as Cromwell's army was called, and was impressed by them.

42 Le Roi, ed., pp. 52–66; Motteville, volume II, pp. 144–5; Montpensier, volume II, pp. 102–3; Patin, pp. 407–8; Montglat, p. 331.

43 Jules Mazarin, *Lettres du Cardinal Mazarin pendant son Ministère*, ed. M. A. Chéruel and V. G. d'Avenel (Paris: Imprimerie Nationale, 1872–1906), volume 8, p. 489.

44 Philips and Frans Zoete Van Laeke, *Journal d'un Voyage à Paris en 1656–1658, publié par A.P. Faugère* (Paris: Benjamin Duprat, 1862), p. 291; Arthur Hassall, *Mazarin* (London, New York: The Macmillan Company, 1903), pp. 138–40.

SIX: A ROYAL WEDDING

1 Montpensier, volume II, pp. 106–8.

2 Montpensier, volume II, p. 108. Gaston avenged himself later when he walked in the garden with Mazarin. He made the cardinal remain uncovered for an equal length of time before telling him he could put on his hat. Both of these incidents were remarked by the courtiers.

3 Motteville, volume III, p. 148.

4 Ibid., p. 149.

5 Scaramouch was the stage name of Tiberio Fiorilli. He performed on the most prof-itable days of the week: Tuesdays, Fridays, and Sundays, with Molière making do with the remaining four days.

6 Geoffrey Treasure, *Louis XIV* (London, Edinburgh: Pearson Education Limited, 2001), p. 256.

7 Motteville, volume III, p. 151.

8 Christine de France had governed Savoy as regent on behalf of her son, Charles Emmanuel II, since the death of her husband in 1637.

9 Montpensier, volume II, p. 111. It has been speculated that Marie Mancini had influenced Louis's decision to ask his mother to accompany him to Lyons, knowing that she would be asked to join the queen's entourage. This way, she could persuade Louis not to marry Marguerite, which would have been Anne's preferred outcome. Similarly, Mazarin saw Marie as useful in this regard; he thought that if Philip IV decided at the last moment to offer the Infanta to Louis, and Louis had fallen in love with Marguerite, his niece could persuade him to change his mind, see Williams, *Sisters*, pp. 85–6. Mme de Motteville (volume III, pp. 154–5) asserts that Anne consented to travel to Lyons "in order to try to break [the marriage] off." However, Anne trusted in the will of God and was

resolved that if Louis found Marguerite to his taste and wanted to marry her, she would not stand in his way.

10   Montpensier, volume II, p. 112.

11   Ibid., p. 115. The Estates, or States, was the representative assembly of certain regions, comprising the clergy, nobility, and the bourgeoisie. Aside from the Estates, there was also the Estates General, which covered the whole of France. It met but rarely, and while it could pass resolutions, it could not legislate (W. E. Brown. *The First Bourbon Century in France* (London: University of London Press Ltd, 1971), p. 11).

12   *Rissolles* were a type of minced pie.

13   Montpensier, volume II, p. 115.

14   Ibid., p. 119. The princess of England was, of course, Henriette.

15   Ibid., p. 120.

16   Motteville, volume III, p. 149.

17   Montpensier, volume II, p. 121. Louis spoke enthusiastically to Marguerite about his musketeers and other regiments, their number and their commanders, and he asked Marguerite about her brother's guards. The conversation then changed to extolling the virtues of their respective capitals, Paris and Turin.

18   Montpensier, volume II, p. 122.

19   Motteville, volume III, p. 159. When Maria-Teresa came to France, she told Mme de Motteville that her father's words had pleased her, for she had been concerned about Louis's journey to Lyons. She said that she "had in her heart a presentiment which told her that the King was to be her husband, and she knew that she alone was entirely worthy of him."

20   Montglat (p. 337) suggests that Mazarin initially thought that Philip IV's offer was a "ruse on Spain's part, designed to make the court of Savoy leave France discontented and offended, so they would return to Piedmont to treat with Spain and abandon France in order to avenge the contempt they had been shown, and would no longer wish to give the Infanta to the King." It soon became apparent, however, that Philip was sincere.

21   Motteville, volume III, p. 160. Pimentel travelled incognito and, having no passports, he was in danger of being arrested. He remained in the shadows throughout his stay in Lyons.

22   Montpensier, volume II, p. 124; Williams, *Sisters*, p. 91. Mademoiselle (volume 2, p. 131) thought that Louis's coldness towards Marguerite resulted from "the hopes held out by the King of Spain."

23   Motteville, volume III, p. 163.

24   Montpensier, volume II, p. 132.

25   Montglat, p. 337.

26   Montpensier, volume II, p. 133.

27   Motteville, volume III, p. 171.

28   A handsome building had been especially erected on the island, designed to accommodate the strict protocols demanded by both nations. Mademoiselle (volume II, pp. 171–2), who made a point of visiting it, left the following description. "We reached it by a bridge formed and tapestried like a gallery. At the termination of this was a saloon, which opened by a door to another bridge, built in the same manner on the side of Spain, as was this on the side of France. It had a large window, looking towards the river on the side of Fontarabia. There were two doors; the one on the side of France, the other on the side of Spain, by which you entered two rooms, magnificently

furnished, and ornamented with fine tapestry. There were also small rooms with their cabinets, and, in the center, the Hall of Assembly. It appeared to me very large, but with no other windows than those which overlooked the river, where two sentinels were stationed while the Kings were there, the *corps-de-garde* not having come over to the island. There were, besides, guards in the hall near the vestibule of which I have spoken; each chamber had only one door, except the Hall of Conference, which had two, placed opposite each other, and which, as I have said, was very large, having really formed two rooms, which had been thrown into one. The tapestry, both on the side of France and that of Spain, was admirable. The Spaniards had laid down Persian carpets, the groundwork of which was of silver and gold, remarkably beautiful. On our side, the carpets were of crimson velvet, decorated with gold and silver lace; as for the chairs, I do not recollect of what they were framed. There were two *ecritoires*, I know not of what material, but I think the locks were of gold; and, if I am not deceived, there was a clock on each table. Everything was in duplicate, and equal to its duplicate in value."

29 Madame de La Fayette, *Histoire de Madame Henriette d'Angleterre in Michaud et Pou-joulat*, Series 3, volume 30 (Lyons, Paris: Guyot Frères, 1854), p. 178.

30 Montpensier, volume II, pp. 143–4.

31 Brienne (1916–19), volume 2, pp. 10–11. According to Mme de Motteville, Mazarin was tempted by the prestige that a marriage between Louis XIV and his niece would bring to his house and his name. He spoke to Anne about it in a manner that was light-hearted but which concealed the seriousness of his ambition. His words elicited a firm response: "I do not believe, Monsieur le cardinal, that the king is capable of such base-ness; but if it were possible that he should think of it, I warn you that all France will revolt against you and against him; and that I will put myself at the head of the rebels to restrain my son" (Motteville, volume III, pp. 171–2). On the other hand, the abbé de Choisy (volume 1, pp. 67–8) suggests that Mazarin was considered too timid to allow the match, fearing that it would make an implacable enemy of Queen Anne.

32 Motteville, volume III, p. 178; La Fayette, p. 178. Williams (*Sisters*), (p. 118) quotes Marie's words as "Sire, you are king, you weep, and I leave."

33 Racine's Emperor Titus chooses his duty to Rome over his love for the Palestinian queen, Bérénice. When he tells her he will not marry her, Bérénice tells him, "You are Emperor, Sire, and you are weeping?" (*"Vous êtes empereur, Seigneur, et vous pleurez?" Bérénice*, Scene V).

34 Williams (*Sisters*), p. 116.

35 Motteville, volume III, p. 179.

36 Ibid.

37 Williams (*Sisters*), p. 117.

38 Motteville, volume III, p. 179.

39 Treasure, *Louis XIV*, p. 258.

40 Bluche, *Louis XIV*, pp. 86–7.

41 Roughly £500,000, or $395,000.

42 Bluche, *Louis XIV*, p. 87.

43 Williams (*Sisters*), p. 145.

44 Lair, *Louise de La Vallière*, pp. 41–2; Louis XIV, *Œuvres*, volume V, p. 6.

45 *Gazette*, January 1660, pp. 39–40.

46 Talc is a transparent, translucent, or shimmering material chosen to replace silver thread, which was forbidden in Spain.

47 Mme de Motteville (volume III, p. 201) describes the *guard-infanta*, or farthingale, which was worn by the Spanish ladies, as "a semi-round and monstrous machine, which seemed to be made of several barrel hoops sewn inside their petticoats; except that ordinary hoops are round, while their *guard-infantas* were flattened a little before and behind, and projected wider at the side. When they walked, this machine moved up and down, giving them a most ugly appearance."

48 Motteville, volume III, p. 200.

49 Ibid., p. 204.

50 Ibid., p. 205.

51 Ibid., p. 206.

52 Ibid., pp. 206–7.

53 Mademoiselle de Montpensier (volume II, p. 206) could not remember what Louis wore, since all eyes were on the young queen, but she believed that his costume was richly embroidered with gold.

54 The duchesse de Navailles served Maria Teresa as lady of honor and lady-in-waiting on this occasion.

55 Motteville, volume III, p. 215.

56 Ibid., p. 216.

57 Montpensier, volume V, p. 161; Loret, volume 3, p. 231.

58 Motteville, volume III, p. 220.

59 Petitfils, *Louis XIV*, pp. 184–5.

SEVEN: A NEW DAWN

1 John Palmer, *Molière, His Life and Works* (London: G. Bell and sons, 1930), p. 116.

2 The *galerie des rois* was so named because portraits of kings were held there.

3 Montpensier, volume II, p. 219.

4 Motteville, volume III, p. 228.

5 Brienne (1828), volume 2, pp. 115–16. Brienne's observations are supported by Motteville (volume III, p. 225).

6 Estimates of Mazarin's personal wealth vary, but it was probably about 39 million livres, of which about a third was in hard cash (Treasure, *Mazarin*, p. 279).

7 Colbert was employed to look after Mazarin's business affairs and administer his vast personal fortune.

8 See Treasure, *Mazarin*, p. 279.

9 Choisy, volume 1, pp. 70–1.

10 The *taille* was a direct tax imposed upon households. In theory, the level of the *taille* was supposed to reflect the taxable wealth of the household, but in practice it was much heavier, see Pitts, p. 27.

11 Bluche, *Louis XIV*, p. 93.

12 Motteville, volume III, p. 228.

13 The *Religion Prétendu Réformée* was the official term for the Huguenots or Calvinist Protestants. Their rights had been enshrined in the Edict of Nantes, signed April 1598 by Henri IV.

14 Brienne (1916–19), volume 3, pp. 35–38.

15 Petitfils, *Louis*, p. 191.

16 Motteville, volume III, p. 230.

17 Choisy, volume 1, p. 100.

18 For this section, see Cronin, pp. 116–18. For comparison, the population of England was five and a half million, while that of Russia was fourteen million.

19 Louis XIV, Œuvres, volume I, p. 6.

20 Ibid., p. 20.

21 Ibid., pp. 9–10.

22 Ibid., pp. 10–11.

23 Ibid., pp. 11–12.

24 Ibid., p. 12.

25 Jules Lair, Nicolas Foucquet (Paris: E. Plon, Nourrit et Cie, 1980), volume 2, p. 3.

26 Nicolas Foucquet, Recueil des défenses (No location, 1665–1668), volume VII, p. 387.

27 Motteville, volume III, p. 258.

28 Louis XIV, Œuvres, volume I, pp. 24–26, 33.

29 Ibid., p. 33.

30 Prest, p. 122.

31 Philippe Beaussant, Lully ou le Musicien du Soleil (Paris: Gallimard, 1992), p. 250.

32 Pitts, pp. 33–4.

33 On occasion, Foucquet was obliged to raise large sums of money urgently to maintain the armies in the field and to pay for necessary provisions, some of which were supplied by Mazarin as a contractor, see Pitts, p. 35.

34 Pitts, p. 35.

35 Mazarin married his niece, Hortense Mancini, to Armand-Charles de la Porte, duc de La Meilleraye, provided he took the title duc de Mazarin. The couple inherited some 28 million livres.

36 Daniel Dessert, Fouquet (Paris: Fayard, 1987), pp. 228–9.

37 Clermont, which was founded by the Jesuits in 1563, changed its name to the Lycée Louis-le-Grand after Louis XIV gave it his official patronage in 1682. Situated in the rue Saint-Jacques in the Latin Quarter of Paris, its alumni include Richelieu, Condé, Foucquet, Molière, Voltaire, and Victor Hugo. More recently, it was attended by the future presidents Georges Pompidou, Valéry Giscard d'Estaing, and Jacques Chirac.

38 Petitfils, Louis XIV, pp. 204–5.

39 Petitfils, Louis XIV, pp. 205–6.

40 Montpensier, volume II, p. 226. The Innocents, or Holy Innocents, was a Parisian cemetery dating back to the 12th century. Originally graves were separate, with individual sepulchres, but as it filled, the dead were increasingly buried in mass graves. The cemetery was closed in 1780, the remains relocated, and the area, in the Les Halles district, was gradually developed.

41 Montpensier, volume II, pp. 91–2.

42 Motteville, volume III, p. 244.

43 Louis XIV, Œuvres, volume I, p. 62.

44 Motteville, volume III, p. 244.

EIGHT: THE SUMMER OF 1661

1 At this stage, the rituals surrounding the lever and coucher of the king were less elaborate than they would be later in the reign.

2 Louis's daily routine at this stage of the reign is described by Mme de Motteville, volume III, pp. 242–3.

3 Motteville, volume III, p. 243.

4   Ibid.
5   Ibid., p. 216.
6   Ibid., p. 217.
7   Marie-Thérèse became pregnant in early February 1661.
8   Motteville, volume III, p. 246.
9   Ibid., p. 244.
10   La Fayette, p. 183.
11   Motteville, volume III, p. 249.
12   Motteville, volume III, p. 252.
13   Motteville, volume III, p. 250.
14   Motteville, volume III, p. 252.
15   La Fayette, p. 184.
16   Lair, *Louise de La Vallière*, pp. 3, 11.
17   Ibid., p. 19.
18   Ibid., p. 54. The grateful Louis later granted Mme de Choisy a pension.
19   Ibid., p. 55.
20   Ibid., p. 58.
21   Cronin, p. 122.
22   Ibid., p. 124; Lair, *Louise de La Vallière*, pp. 70–1. Louis first performed the ballet at the Louvre the previous February (Jean Loret, *La Muze historique ou recueil des lettres en vers* (Paris: P. Daffis, libraire éditeur, 1877), volume 3, p. 32).
23   One anonymous chronicler tells of Louis and Louise being caught in a shower of rain while out walking together. The gallant Louis "sheltered the girlish head with his own hat, and brought her back to the Palace, braving the jealous eyes of the Court" (Lair, *Louise de la Vallière*, pp. 69–70). This scene proved irresistible to Dumas, who included it in *Le Vicomte de Bragelonne* (Paris: Éditions Robert Laffont, S.A., 1991), volume 2, p. 2. Sadly, it comes from a questionable source and is not supported by any reliable contemporary writer.
24   Brienne (1916–19), volume 3, pp. 40–6.
25   Robert Lefebvre (1608–1675/7) was called de Venise because of his long sojourn there.
26   Prest, pp. 90–1.
27   Lair, *Louise de La Vallière*, pp. 71–2.
28   Motteville, volume III, p. 248.
29   Ibid., p. 260.
30   Dunlop, p. 103.
31   Ibid., p. 104.
32   Bluche, *Louis XIV*, pp. 205–6.
33   Ibid., pp. 206–7.
34   Ibid., p. 207.
35   Pascal's final two *Lettres Provincials* were a defense against Father Annat's accusations of heresy against him.
36   Bluche, *Louis XIV*, pp. 210–11.
37   Louis XIV, *Œuvres*, volume I, p. 83.
38   *l'Écureuil* means 'the Squirrel,' or *foucquet* in the Breton dialect.
39   Louis explains his decision to bring about the fall of Foucquet in his memoirs (*Œuvres* volume I, pp. 101–3). This section had originally been drafted by Colbert, who used notes taken at the time, and which reflected his own opinion. Later,

when Louis edited the text, he allowed this version of events to stand because he believed it to be correct. By that time, Colbert's version had become Louis's own.

40   Louis XIV, *Œuvres*, volume I, p. 33.

41   Brienne (1916–19), volume 3, p. 50.

42   Chrétien de Lamoignon was president of the Parlement of Paris.

43   La Fayette, pp. 185–6.

44   Lair, *Foucquet*, volume 2, p. 36.

45   Jean-Christian Petitfils, *Fouquet* (Paris: Perrin, 1990), p. 349.

46   This story is found in an anonymous letter held in the collection of Valentin Conrart, a man of letters and first secretary of the Académie Française. The collection contains many letters and documents, some of which are of questionable authenticity or are heavily redacted. This story does, however, find support in a contemporary publication, *Il Mercurio Postiglione* p. 76, in which Foucquet is said to have offered Louise 25,000 "doppie," or doubles. The abbé de Choisy also knew of Foucquet's approach to Louise, stating that the go-between was Foucquet's confidante, Mme du Plessis-Bellière (*Mémoires*, volume 1, p. 131).

47   The representative assembly of Brittany, which was composed of the clergy, the nobility, and the bourgeoisie.

NINE: AT VAUX-LE-VICOMTE

1   For an account of the fête given by Foucquet at Vaux, see Urbain-Victor Chatelain, *Le Surintendant Nicolas Foucquet, Protecteur des Lettres, des Arts et des Sciences* (Geneva: Slatkine Reprints, 1971), pp. 471–81.

2   Chatelain, p. 472.

3   Cronin, p. 133.

4   Jean de La Fontaine, *Fables et OEuvres Diverses. ed. C. A. Walckenaer* (Paris: Librairie de Firmin-Didot et Cie, 1852), p. 540.

5   Ibid.

6   Petitfils, *Fouquet*, p. 356.

7   The rocks, shells, and other special effects were designed by Giacomo Torelli and painted by Le Brun.

8   The ballets were choreographed by Pierre de Beauchamps.

9   Molière is known to have played more than one of these characters, although it is not certain which. Charles Heron Wall, *The Dramatic Works of Molière* (London: George Bell and Sons, 1876), p. 283, suggests Molière played Lisandre, Alcandre, and Alcippe.

10   Petitfils, *Fouquet*, p. 358.

11   Choisy, volume 1, p. 136.

12   Brienne (1916–19), volume 3, p. 49.

13   Jean-Marie Pérouse de Montclos, *Vaux-le-Vicomte*, trans. Judith Hayward (London: Scala Books, 1997), pp. 137–8. Foucquet's motto is sometimes given as *Quo non ascendam?*—'Whither will I not climb?' but this is incorrect.

14   Choisy, volume, 1, p. 136. This, however, does not appear in the section of Jean Hérault Gourville's *Mémoires de Gourville* (Paris: Librairie Renouard, 1894) that deals with the fête at Vaux-le-Vicomte.

15   La Fayette, p. 136.

16   The *ordonnance de comptant* was a cash account of the treasury which made expenditure of matters of state that were to be kept secret from the public, see Julian Dent,

Crisis in Finance: Crown Finances and Society in Seventeenth Century France (Newton Abbot: David and Charles, 1973), p. 84.

17 Choisy, volume 1, p. 137.

18 Palmer, p. 176.

19 Virginia Scott, *Molière: A Theatrical Life* (Cambridge: Cambridge University Press, 2000), pp. 136-7.

20 For Petitfils (*Fouquet*, p. 360), this was proof that Louis had "decided to finish with his superintendent and seize Belle-Isle."

21 The Chambre des Comptes was a royal accounting agency and one of the oldest institutions of the French monarchy (Dent, p. 100).

22 There are several accounts of the arrest and subsequent imprisonment of Nicolas Foucquet, the official version being *Récit officiel de l'arrestation de Fouquet rédigé par Ordre de Colbert*, which is printed in volume 8 of the *Mémoires complets et authentiques du duc de Saint-Simon* edited by Chéruel (Paris: Librairie Hachette, 1879) pp. 447–453. Another version, *Arrestation de Fouquet: Mesures Préparatoires*, is printed in Pierre Clément, *Lettres, instructions et Mémoires de Colbert* (Paris: Imprimerie Imperiale, 1859) volume 2, part 1, pp. cxcix-cxcvi. Brienne, who was present at Nantes, includes the event in his *Mémoires* (1916–19, volume 3, pp. 53–77). His account is particularly poignant as it highlights the still unwell Foucquet's sense of helplessness in the face of forces beyond his control. The abbé de Choisy, who was not present but was otherwise well-informed, wrote about the arrest in his *Mémoires*, volume 1, pp. 137–151.

23 Foucquet's fever was such that he was relatively well for two days and ill on the third. The exact nature of the illness is not known, although it is described as ague in some sources and malaria in others.

24 Brienne (1916–19), volume 3, pp. 62–3.

25 Ibid., p. 61.

26 Charles de Batz Castelmore, sieur d'Artagnan, was the historical figure who inspired Dumas's famous hero. Although often referred to as Captain d'Artagnan, he was not the real captain of the musketeers, as that post was held by the king.

27 Chéruel, *Saint-Simon*, p. 448.

28 Letter from Louis to his mother, dated September 5 (Louis XIV, *Œuvres*, volume V, p. 50).

29 Letter from Louis to his mother, dated September 5 (Louis XIV, *Œuvres*, volume V, p. 51).

30 Chéruel, *Saint-Simon*, p. 448.

31 Letter from Louis to his mother, dated September 5 (Louis XIV, *Œuvres*, volume V, pp. 53–4).

32 Chéruel, *Saint-Simon*, p. 449.

33 Brienne (1916–19), volume 3, p. 72.

34 Louis XIV, *Œuvres*, volume V, pp. 50–54.

35 Inès Murat, *Colbert* (Paris: Librairie Arthème Fayard, 1980), pp. 110–111.

36 Brienne (1916–19), volume 3, p. 73.

TEN: THE SUN KING

1 Louis XIV, *Œuvres*, volume I, p. 104.

2 Ibid., p. 105.

3 Murat, pp. 109–110. Louis (*Œuvres*, volume I, pp. 108-9) claimed the idea as entirely his own, but this was not true. However, he and Colbert were as one on this subject, as they were with many others.

4   Louis XIV, *Œuvres*, volume I, pp. 111–12.
5   Ibid., p. 112.
6   Ibid., pp. 113–15.
7   Cronin, pp. 159–160. Louis's measure is reminiscent of that of his grandfather, Henry IV, who insisted that every peasant should have a chicken in the pot on Sundays.
8   Cronin, pp. 160–161.
9   Loret, volume 3, pp. 417–18.
10 Louis XIV, *Œuvres*, volume I, p. 121.
11 Ibid., p. 127.
12 Louis (*Œuvres*, volume I, p. 129) refers to him as the comte de Fuensaldagna, although he was actually the marquis de La Fuente.
13 Louis XIV, *Œuvres*, volume I, pp. 129–30.
14 Ibid., p. 140.
15 Motteville, volume III, p. 268.
16 Loret, volume 3, p. 423.
17 Louis XIV, *Œuvres*, volume I, p. 141. Louis added the warning that if princes did not fulfill expectations, their people would reproach them forever.
18 Ibid., p. 153.
19 Anne-Constance de Montalais. She had been a companion to the d'Orléans princesses at Blois, and was maid of honor to Henriette, duchesse d'Orléans.
20 When Louise first arrived at court, she attracted the attention of several young beaux, among them the comte de Guiche. Upon seeing the king take an interest in her, he had the good sense to withdraw, but he exacted his revenge on Louis by paying court to Henriette. Louis exiled him from court for his insolence, although he soon allowed him back.
21 La Fayette, pp. 189–90.
22 Ibid.
23 Ibid.
24 Motteville, volume III, pp. 284–85. The story of the anonymous letter is related by several writers, including Motteville (volume III, pp. 283–5), La Fayette (pp. 190–2) and d'Ormesson (p. 330–2). All vary in their details. The version given here is taken from La Fayette, whose narrative was related to her by Louise's mistress, Henriette.
25 Lair, *Louise de La Vallière*, pp. 99, 100.
26 Ibid., p. 101.
27 Ibid., p. 102.
28 Charles Perrault, *Courses et Têtes et de Bague, faites par le Roy* (Paris: L'Imprimerie Royale, 1670); Loret, volume 3, pp. 511–12; Dunlop, pp. 94–6; Lair, *Louise*, pp. 104–5.
29 The carousel provided the arena for an early spat between Colbert and Louvois. Louvois had suggested to Louis that he hold the carousel, his motive apparently being to embarrass Colbert, who, as intendant of finances, would be responsible for raising the money to pay for it. If so, Louvois's plan failed, because Colbert asked Louis to keep the carousel secret for a week, during which time he temporarily transferred to *octroi* (a tax levied on the goods entering the city) of Paris to the royal treasury. The carousel was then announced, which attracted people from other parts of France and abroad. Colbert then asked for the carousel to be delayed for a further two weeks, during which time the hordes of visitors spent their money on food and other provisions, thereby filling the royal coffers and paying for the entire celebration, see Louis XIV, *Œuvres*, I.195 note; Dunlop, p. 96.

30   Perrault, p. 44.
31   Louis XIV, *Œuvres*, volume I, p. 195.
32   Ibid., p. 190.
33   Louis XIV, *Œuvres*, volume I, p. 196.
34   Ibid., p. 196. Sun iconography was not unique to Louis, although he is the king
     most closely associated with it. The sun had been part of the iconography of the
     royal House of France for some time, the first Sun King being Charles VI, who
     reigned between 1380 and 1422 (Erlanger, *Louis XIV*, p. 83).
35   Louis XIV, *Œuvres*, volume I, p. 197.

ELEVEN: *LE CHÂTEAU DE CARTES*
1   Motteville, volume III, p. 276.
2   Bussy-Rabutin. *Les Mémoires de Roger de Rabutin comte de Bussy* (Amsterdam: Chez
     Zacherie Chatelain, 1731), volume 2, p. 205.
3   Catherine de Menneville was one of the queen-mother's young ladies. Famed at
     the court for her beauty, the twenty-five-year-old was the mistress of Nicolas Fouc-
     quet at the time of his arrest. Disgraced, she would spend the rest of her life in a
     convent.
4   Antoine Hamilton, *Mémoires du Chevalier de Grammont* (Paris: Librairie des Biblio-
     philes, 1876), p. 81; Lair, *Louise de La Vallière*, p. 107 note 1. Gramont was exiled to
     England, where he arrived in June 1662.
5   Montpensier, volume II, p. 253.
6   Lair, *Louise de La Vallière*, p. 107.
7   Ibid., p. 108. Louis was annoyed by the duchesse de Navailles's attachment to
     Marie-Thérèse. He did not realize that she was faithful enough to him to defend
     him to the queen (Motteville, volume III, p. 292).
8   Motteville, volume III, p. 293.
9   Ibid., p. 294.
10   Montpensier, volume II, p. 253.
11   Ibid.
12   Lair, *Louise de La Vallière*, p. 108. Louis was eventually forced to deal with the com-
     tesse de Soissons. In the spring of 1665, she and her husband were ordered to retire
     to one of their estates for having said disrespectful things about Henriette. Vardes
     was also punished. Having already been exiled, he was imprisoned in the citadel of
     Montpellier (Motteville, volume III, pp. 315–18).
13   Simone Bertière, *Les Femmes du Roi-Soleil, Les Reines de France au Temps des Bourbons*
     (Paris: Éditions de Fallois, 1997), p. 116.
14   Motteville, volume III, p. 285. Motteville qualifies Louis's happiness with "if
     anyone in this world can be happy."
15   Ibid., pp. 287–90.
16   Ibid., p. 288. Of course, Anne of Austria was Marie-Thérèse's mother-in-law as well
     as her aunt, but she made no such distinction.
17   Ibid., pp. 288–9.
18   This exchange is recounted in Motteville, volume III, p. 290–91.
19   Le Roi, ed., p. 80.
20   The Concordat of Bologna was an agreement, signed between François I and Pope
     Leo X in 1516, involving the regalian rights of the French church. The *régale*, or

regalian rights, referred to the king's right to receive the revenues of vacant bishop-rics in certain parts of France.

21   The Three Bishoprics comprised Metz, Toul, and Verdun.

22   Bluche, *Louis XIV*, p. 211; Dunlop, pp. 99–103; Louis XIV, *Œuvres*, volume V, pp. 91–2.

23   Dunlop, p. 99.

24   Louis XIV, *Œuvres*, volume V, pp. 91–2.

25   Clément, volume V, pp. lix-lx; Petitfils, *Louis*, p. 292; Cornette, p. 105.

26   Jean Coural, "Gobelins." In *Dictionnaire du Grand Siècle, ed. Bluche* (Paris: Librairie Arthème Fayard, 1990), pp. 660–1.

27   Pérouse de Montclos, p. 36.

28   Ibid., p. 44.

29   Coural, p. 661.

30   Guy Walton, *Louis XIV's Versailles* (Harmsworth, U.K.: Viking, 1986), p. 54.

31   The *Gazette* (1651, p. 672) records Louis having visited Versailles in July 1651; Pierre de Nolhac, *Versailles et la Cour de France: La Création de Versailles* (Paris: Louis Conard, 1925), p. 29 notes that the young king had also hunted there the previous April.

32   Louis de Touvroy, duc de Saint-Simon, *Memoirs of the Duc de Saint-Simon on the Times of Louis XIV. and the Regency*, trans. and abridged Katharine Prescott Wormeley (Boston: Hardy, Pratt & Company, 1902), volume III, p. 304.

33   Nolhac, p. 33 and note.

34   Walton, p. 55.

35   Clément, volume V, pp. 268–70, where it is dated 1665; Nolhac, pp. 49–50, who dates it to 1663.

36   The course of Louis's attack of measles and his various treatments can be followed in Le Roi, ed., pp. 82–7.

37   Lair, *Louise de La Vallière*, p. 123.

38   Ibid., pp. 122–3. While the king was honorary captain of this regiment of veterans and the young dauphin lieutenant, there is some dispute as to whether or not La Vallière was the actual commander. Lair says not.

39   Lair, *Louise de La Vallière*, p. 124.

40   Motteville, volume III. p. 283; Bussy-Rabutin, *Mémoires*, volume 2, p. 204.

41   Bluche, *Louis XIV*, pp. 236–7.

42   The modern-day rue Richelieu covers the area where the Palais Brion was situated.

43   Over the next fifty years, Louis would spend some 95 million livres on Versailles. His wars, on the other hand, would cost 3,000 million (Erlanger, *Louis XIV*, p. 153 note). During the twenty years it would take to build Versailles, 227 people would die (Erlanger, *Louis XIV*, p. 153). Louis would live at Versailles in 1674, 1675, and 1677 before moving in permanently in 1682 (Bluche, *Louis XIV*, p. 183).

44   Nolhac, p. 47, quoting an account written by Colbert.

45   Ibid., p. 48.

46   After Louvois's death, his son, Courtanvaux, would take over this function.

47   Bluche, *Louis XIV*, pp. 185–6.

48   Midwives could be male or female: Boucher was a man.

49   duchesse de La Vallière, *Réflexions sur la Miséricorde de Dieu* (Paris: J. Techener, Librairie, 1860), volume 2, pp. 201–6; Lair, *Louise de La Vallière*, pp. 131–2. Charles died when he was about two years old, the victim of one of many childhood illnesses.

50   Motteville, volume III, p. 295.

TWELVE: THE PLEASURES OF THE ENCHANTED ISLE

1   Walton, p. 55.
2   Motteville, volume III, p. 295.
3   Louise was already pregnant with her second child by this time (Fraser, *Louis XIV*, p. 88).
4   Bussy-Rabutin, *Mémoires*, volume 2, p. 224.
5   Known in French as *Roland furieux*.
6   Nicolas Sceaux, *Les plaisirs de l'île enchantée* (2008–2009), p. 5.
7   Ibid., p. 5.
8   Ibid., pp. 6–11.
9   Ibid., pp. 21–84.
10 Ibid., pp. 83–95.
11 Lair, *Louise de La Vallière*, pp. 140–1.
12 Palmer, p. 279.
13 *Gazette*, May 21, 1664, cited in Palmer, p. 280.
14 Cited in Palmer, p. 280.
15 Ibid.
16 Wall, volume 2, p. 292.
17 Cited in Palmer, p. 281.
18 Nancy Nichols Barker, *Brother to the Sun King: Philippe, Duke of Orléans* (Baltimore, London: Johns Hopkins University Press, 1989), p. 88; Palmer, p. 285. Louis became Molière's patron on August 14, 1665.
19 The account of the Brancas incident is given in Motteville, volume III, pp. 295–8. Suzanne de Brancas, née Garnier, and her husband had been clients of Foucquet, whose arrest had proved detrimental to them. Suzanne, it appears, was trying to cultivate Louise's friendship as a means to restore their fortunes.
20 Dunlop, p. 101.
21 Voltaire, *The Age of Louis XIV* (London: J.M. Dent & Sons Ltd., 1935), pp. 10–11.
22 A commemorative tapestry was begun in 1669, but by this time, Louis's anger had cooled and he had ordered the pyramid in Rome to be demolished, Dunlop, p. 103.
23 Lair, *Louise de La Vallière*, p. 141.
24 Motteville, volume III, pp. 298–303. Mme de Motteville's account of the cause of the animosity between Louis and Anne is vague, but the details can be followed, and she is in no doubt about the consequences.
25 Motteville, volume III, p. 303.

THIRTEEN: THE DARK SIDE OF THE SUN

1   Motteville, volume III, pp. 305–6.
2   Ibid., p. 306.
3   Clément, *Lettres*, volume V, p. 467.
4   Anatole France, *Clio and the Chateau de Vaux-le-Vicomte*, trans. Winifred Stevens (London: The Bodley Head, 1923), pp. 259–61.
5   The Anqueil is the river that flows through the park at Vaux, and which was diverted to form the canal.
6   Orontes was the name given to Foucquet by La Fontaine in the *Songe de Vaux*. Orontes's palace was a sanctuary for artists.
7   Henri IV, Louis's grandfather.
8   See above, p. 181.

ENDNOTES

9   Chéruel, volume 2, pp. 260-3.
10   Louis carried the sword of justice at his coronation, a symbol of one of his royal qualities.
11   Charles de La Porte, duc de La Meilleraye, was the governor of Brittany, and
     another of Foucquet's enemies.
12   Chéruel, volume 2, pp. 263-70; an abridged version appears in Lair, *Foucquet*,
     volume 2, pp. 107-8.
13   D'Artagnan was serving as Foucquet's jailer.
14   Lair, *Foucquet*, volume 2, p. 108.
15   Pitts, p. 61.
16   Pitts, p. 61; Chéruel, volume 2, pp. 334-5.
17   The *Chambre de justice* was a special court believed to have been inaugurated during
     the reign of François I to investigate corruption in public finances and to try those
     involved. It acted as a buffer between the populace and the crown, protecting the
     latter from the people who were angry with the tax system, but it was also a means
     by which financiers could be forced to make reparation on their excessive profits
     through fines or threats of prosecution (Pitts, p. 61; Dent, pp. 103-4).
18   Foucquet had been loyal to the crown and to Mazarin during the Fronde; neverthe-
     less, Louis always associated him with that dark period of his life. The discovery of
     the *Projet de Saint-Mandé* merely confirmed Louis's fears.
19   The reason for Séguier's hostility is difficult to explain, although it is thought that
     he blamed Foucquet for his exclusion from the royal council (see Pitts, p. 52; Petit-
     fils, *Fouquet*, p. 327; Lair, *Foucquet*, volume 2, p. 6).
20   Bluche, *Louis XIV*, p. 201.
21   Foucquet's accounts would not be examined until the 20th century. *Daniel Dessert,
     Argent, pouvoir et société au Grand Siècle* (Paris: Fayard, 1984), pp. 305-6, 310.
22   Foucquet's assertion that he had shown no one the plan was not true if his friend, Gour-
     ville, is to be believed. Gourville claimed that Foucquet showed him the document and
     that he urged the superintendent to destroy it (*Mémoires*, volume 1, pp. 171-3).
23   Lair, *Foucquet*, volume 2, p. 175.
24   Ibid., pp. 318-25.
25   Motteville, volume III, p. 308.
26   Marie-Anne de France would die on December 26, 1664, after only a few weeks of life.
27   Motteville, volume III, pp. 308-9: Sévigné, Marie du Rabutin-Chantal, *marquise
     de, Lettres de Madame de Sevigné, de sa famille et de ses amis* (Paris : J.J. Blaise, 1820),
     volume I, pp. 66-8.
28   The mass Locatelli attended took place on November 11, 1664.
29   Sébastien Locatelli, *Voyage de France: Moeurs et Coutumes Française* (1664-1665),
     trans. Adolphe Vautier (Paris: Alphonse Picard et Fils, 1905), p. 126.
30   Petitfils, *Fouquet*, p. 428.
31   Lair, *Louise de La Vallière*, pp. 148-9.
32   Philippe de Courcillon, marquis de Dangeau, a memorialist, was one of Louis's
     close friends.
33   The story of the maréchal and the madrigal is told by Mme de Sévigné (1820),
     volume I, pp. 82-3.
34   Pitts, p. 146.
35   François Ravaisson, ed. *Archives de la Bastille* (1870), volume 2, pp. 390-92.
36   Sévigné (1820), volume I, p. 100.

37 Chéruel, volume 2, p. 334.
38 Pitts, p. 158.
39 Lair, *Foucquet*, volume 2, p. 406; Patin, volume 3, p. 503.
40 Ormesson, *Journal*, volume 2, p. 278.
41 Ravaisson, ed., volume 2, p. 393.
42 Pitts, p. 159.
43 Sévigné (1820), volume I, p. 102.
44 Pignerol is known today by its Italian name, Pinerolo.
45 The only clemency Foucquet would receive came in 1679, some eighteen years after his arrest, when he was allowed to talk to a fellow prisoner, the comte de Lauzun. Also that year, his wife and children, all now grown up, would be allowed to travel to Pignerol to visit him. He died in 1680, and a few weeks later, his wife was given permission to bury his body where she wished. The following year, Foucquet's mother died at the age of 91, just as her son's coffin was making its way back to Paris. Mother and son were buried together in the convent of the Visitation on the rue Saint-Antoine.

FOURTEEN: MARS AND ATHENA
1   Motteville, volume III, p. 342.
2   Ibid., p. 344.
3   Ibid., p. 345.
4   Ibid., p. 348.
5   Ibid., p. 349.
6   Ibid.
7   Ibid., p. 350.
8   Ibid., p. 355.
9   Ibid.
10 Louis XIV, *Œuvres*, volume II, p. 50.
11 Ibid., p. 51.
12 Ibid., p. 52.
13 Ibid., pp. 52–3.
14 Ibid., p. 53.
15 Louis XIV, *Œuvres*, volume V, p. 361. Louis's letter is dated February 11, 1666.
16 Lair *Louise de La Vallière*, p. 168.
17 *Gazette*, 1666, pp. 341–4. Mouchy-le-Châtel is in the Département Oise, north of Paris.
18 For the text of the letters patent and analysis, see Lair, *Louise de La Vallière*, pp. 195–201.
19 Département Indre et Loire.
20 Marie-Anne was born at Vincennes on October 2, 1666, the first of Louis's illegitimate children to be born after his mother's death.
21 Lair, *Louise de La Vallière*, p. 197.
22 Ibid., p. 199. At this point, Louise was again pregnant with the king's child, but this child was excluded from the inheritance (Lair, p. 201). Louise had previously given birth to a son at noon on January 7, 1665. Following the usual procedure, he was secreted away nine hours later by Colbert, who handed the child to Bernard, the husband of the demoiselle du Coudray, both former servants in Colbert's household. The following day, at Louis's command, the baby was baptized in the church of Saint-Eustache as Philippe, the son of François Derssy and Margaret Bernard,

his wife. Philippe, like his elder brother, Charles, was not destined to live long; he would die at the end of June 1666.

23 Louis, *Œuvres*, volume II, p. 291.

24 Ibid., pp. 290–1.

25 Arthur Hassall, *Louis XIV and the Zenith of French Monarchy* (London, New York: G.P. Putnam's Sons, 1923), pp. 138–9.

26 Treasure, *Louis XIV*, p. 163.

27 Hassall, *Louis XIV*, p. 139.

28 Montglat, p. 357.

29 Hassall, *Louis XIV*, pp. 140–41. Franche-Comté operated a system of gavelkind, in which a deceased man's property would be divided among his sons. In Luxembourg, two thirds of a man's property would go to the son, with the final third going to the eldest daughter. In this scenario, Charles II would have inherited the main part of the inheritance, with the rest going to Marie-Thérèse. Louis's claim, therefore, would be upheld in a few locations only.

30 Treasure, *Louis XIV*, p. 163.

31 A treaty of alliance with the Dutch (1662) obliged Louis to wage war on England, but his navy was unequal to the task, and he was unable even to assist Ruyter in his assault on England.

32 Saint-Maurice, volume 1, p. 115.

33 Motteville, volume III, p. 258.

34 Saint-Maurice, volume 1, p. 110.

35 Ibid., p. 56.

36 This incident is airbrushed out of the official history (*Gazette*, 1667, p. 582).

37 Montpensier, volume II, pp. 305–6.

38 Ibid., p. 306.

39 Tonnay-Charrante was one of the titles held by Athénaïs's family.

40 Since neither family had anything material to gain from the marriage, it is generally accepted that this was a love match.

41 Lisa Hilton, *The Real Queen of France: Athénaïs & Louis XIV* (London: Abacus, 2003), p. 42.

42 Montpensier, volume II, p. 305.

43 Ibid., p. 306.

44 Catherine de Neufville-Villeroy, contesse d'Armagnac, was one of Marie-Thérèse's ladies. Known for her mischief, she would be dismissed from court.

45 Montpensier, volume II, p. 311.

FIFTEEN: THE TRIPLE ALLIANCE

1 Bluche, *Louis XIV*, pp. 242–3.

2 Ibid., pp. 243–4.

3 Ibid., p. 244.

4 Peter Robert Campbell, *Louis XIV* (London: Longman Group Limited, 1993), p. 62.

5 Bluche, *Louis XIV*, p. 243.

6 Campbell, *Louis XIV*, p. 62. Under the terms of the partition treaty, which was intended to be implemented in the event of Carlos II's death, France would receive Naples, Sicily, Flanders, Franche-Comté, and Navarre. Austria would take Spain, the remaining Italian territories, and most of Spain's overseas empire. As it was, the treaty was never implemented because Carlos defied all expectation and

lived, and because it was compromised when France occupied Lorraine in 1700, with Leopold being forced to defend the province, which was part of the Austrian Empire.

7   Cornette, pp. 173–4.

8   Marc Fumaroli, *The Poet and the King: Jean de La Fontaine and His Century*, trans. Jane Marie Todd (Notre Dame, Ind.: University of Notre Dame Press, 2002), pp. 94–5.

9   Lair, *Louise de La Vallière*, pp. 233–4.

10 Ibid., p. 236; Bussy-Rabutin, *Correspondance avec sa Famille et Amis* (Paris: Lalanne, 1858), volume 1, p. 382.

11 Pierre Clément, *Madame de Montespan et Louis XIV: étude historique* (Paris: Librairie Académique, 1868), p. 13; Jean Lemoine and André Lichtenberger, *De La Vallière à Montespan* (Paris: Calmann-Lévy, 1902), pp. 256–7.

12 Lemoine and Lichtenberger, p. 258; see also Ravaisson, ed., vol. IV, p. 16. Mme de Montausier never recovered from the shock of her encounter with Montespan. She rapidly declined and on her deathbed begged forgiveness for her part in facilitating the king's affair with Athénaïs (Hilton, p. 92). According to Saint-Simon, Montespan had even physically attacked his wife.

   Although not always the most reliable memoirist, Saint-Simon appears to have been accurate on this occasion. The document formalizing the separation of Montespan and her husband refers to his ill-treatment towards her, see Anne Somerset, *The Affair of the Poisons. Murder, Infanticide & Satanism at the Court of Louis XIV* (London: Weidenfeld & Nicolson, 2003), p. 91.

13 The people of Gascony were well known for their eccentricity, and boastful or exaggerated behavior was often referred to as *gasconnade*.

14 A *lettre de cachet*, or letter under the signet, was a notorious instrument by which the king could order the imprisonment of anyone who displeased him without his having to give a reason and without the prisoner facing trial.

15 Guy Patin, cited in Lair, *Louise de La Vallière*, p. 230. The For-l'Eveque was demolished in the early 19th century. The building at 19 rue Saint-Germain-l'Auxerrois now stands on the site.

16 Lemoine and Lichtenberger, p. 269; J.-B. Primi Visconti, *Mémoires dur la cour de Louis XIV, 1673–1681* (Paris: Perrin, 1988), p. 26.

17 C. C. Dyson, *Madame de Maintenon: Her life and times 1635–1719* (London: J. Lane, 1910), p. 76.

18 *Gazette*, 1668, p. 1010.

19 Cronin, p. 175; Lair, *Louise de La Vallière*, p. 231.

20 Hilton, p. 87.

21 Ibid., pp. 87–8.

22 Bluche, *Louis XIV*, pp. 213–14.

23 Ibid., pp. 303, 215.

24 *Medailles sur les principaux evenements*, p. 114. The medal is dated 1669.

25 Louis XIV, *Œuvres*, volume I, pp. 142–3.

26 *Recueil général des anciennes lois françaises*, XVIII, pp. 44–5; *Louis XIV. Memoirs for the Instruction of the Dauphin*, trans. and ed. Paul Sonnino (New York: Free Press; London: Collier-Macmillan, 1970), pp. 115–16: Bluche, *Louis XIV*, pp. 113–15.

27 Sévigné (1820), volume I, p. 154.

28 Bluche, *Louis XIV*, p. 114.

29 The French populace was divided into the first, second, and third estates. The first estate comprised the clergy, who were exempt from paying taxes because they served the country through prayer and charitable works. The second estate comprised the nobility and the royal family, but not the king, who stood above the estates. The nobility served in the military and the royal household, and were exempt from most forms of taxation. The third estate was made up of everyone who did not belong to the first two estates. Comprising some 98 percent of the population, they were liable for all forms of taxation.

30 Bluche, *Louis XIV*, p. 144.

31 Ibid., p. 115.

32 Hassall, *Louis XIV*, pp. 156–61, 163, 168.

33 Brown, p. 163.

34 Fraser, *Charles*, p. 272.

35 Arthur Bryant, *Charles II*, Revised edition (London: Collins, 1955), p. 203.

36 For the palace of Trianon, see Hilton, p. 151.

37 See Hilton, pp. 152–3.

38 Melanie Clegg, *The Life of Henrietta Anne, Daughter of Charles I* (Barnsley, U.K.: Pen & Sword History, 2017), p. 180.

39 Bryant, p. 211 note. Among the ladies who accompanied Henriette to England was Louise de Kérouaille. Charles was instantly attracted to the beautiful Breton, only to be discouraged by Henriette, who reminded him of her responsibility to the lady's family. The English king would have to wait a while longer before he could add the fair Louise to his collection of mistresses.

40 Montpensier, volume III, p. 61.

41 Ibid., p. 65.

42 Ibid.

43 Ibid., p. 66.

44 Ibid.

45 Ibid., p. 67.

46 Ibid., p. 68.

47 Ibid., p. 72.

48 Ibid., p. 70. Despite the findings of the physicians, there were those who continued to believe that Henriette had been poisoned, among them her brother, Charles II of England.

SIXTEEN: MARRIAGES AND INTRIGUES

1 Montpensier, volume III, p. 69.

2 Ibid., p. 76.

3 Ibid., p. 81.

4 Lair, *Louise de La Vallière*, pp. 283–4.

5 The unhappy Louise looked upon her continued residence at court as God's way of helping her atone for her sin in loving Louis (duchesse de La Vallière, *Réflexions sur la Miséricorde de Dieu* (Paris: J. Techener, Librairie, 1860), volume 1, p. 52).

6 Elisabeth-Charlotte von der Pfalz was the great-granddaughter of James I of England though his daughter, Elizabeth Stuart.

7 Barker, p. 126.

8 However, as shall be seen, Louis would later assert Liselotte's claims for his own ends.

9   Elizabeth-Charlotte, duchesse d'Orléans, *Life and Letters of Charlotte Elizabeth, Princess Palatine and Mother of Philippe d'Orléans, Regent of France* (London: Chapman and Gall, 1889), p. 17.

10   Elizabeth-Charlotte, duchesse d'Orléans, *The Letters of Madame*, trans. and ed. Gertrude Scott-Stevenson (London: Arrowsmith, 1925), volume II, p. 21.

11   Petitfils, *Lauzun*, p. 15; A. Jal, *Dictionnaire critique de Biographie et d'Histoire* (Paris: Henri Plon, 1867), p. 749.

12   The date at which Lauzun inherited his title is disputed, with sources variously stating 1660, 1668, or 1671; for convenience, he will be referred to as Lauzun throughout.

13   The festivities took place between April 6–15, 1666.

14   Saint-Simon (Cheruel), volume 20, p. 46.

15   Alexandre Bontemps, the king's chief valet and confidant.

16   One would scratch at the door, not knock. Courtiers often grew the nail on the little finger longer for the purpose.

17   Saint-Simon (Chéruel), volume XIX, p. 174.

18   Montpensier, volume III, p. 101.

19   Ibid.

20   Ibid., p. 116.

21   Ibid.

22   Ibid., p. 121.

23   Ibid., p. 120.

24   Ibid., p. 123–4.

25   Ibid., p. 127.

26   Ibid., p. 130.

27   Now part of Paris, Charenton was still a rural village in the 17th century.

28   Montpensier, volume III, p. 133.

29   Ibid., p. 134.

30   Ibid., p. 135.

31   Ibid., p. 144.

32   This date is established in the *Gazette*, October 28, 1671.

33   Saint-Simon (Chéruel), volume XIX, pp. 172-3.

SEVENTEEN: THE DUTCH WAR

1   Saint-Maurice. *Lettres sur le Court de Louis XIV*, ed. Jean Lemoine (Paris: Calmann-Lévy, c. 1910), volume 2, p. 58.

2   Sévigné (1820), volume II, p. 195.

3   Sévigné, volume I, pp. 198–9.

4   Ibid.

5   Ibid., p. 200.

6   Burke, p. 74.

7   Only the ranks of colonel and captain could be obtained by purchase. Those available by promotion were ensign, lieutenant, major, lieutenant-colonel, and brigadier. Cadets were required to serve a minimum of two years before they were eligible to purchase a commission. See Brown, p. 159.

8   Brown, p. 159.

9   Ibid., pp. 159–60.

10   Ibid., p. 160.

11   Ibid., p. 152.

12   Saint-Maurice, volume 2, p. 68.

13   Ibid., pp. 209–10.

14   Ibid., pp. 219–20 and note.

15   Ibid., p. 241 and note.

16   Ibid., pp. 278–9.

17   Ibid., p. 286.

18   Ibid., p. 290.

19   Ibid., p. 294.

20   Louis XIV, *Œuvres*, volume III, pp. 183–4.

21   Saint-Maurice, volume 2, pp. 314–15.

22   Armand de Gramont, comte de Guiche, *Mémoires de comte de Guiche concernant les Provinces-Unies des Pais-Bas* (London: chez Philippe Changuion, 1744), p. 397.

23   Guiche, p. 409.

24   Louis XIV, *Œuvres*, volume III, p. 199.

25   Cronin, p. 196.

26   Dunlop, p. 228.

27   Hassall, *Louis XIV*, pp. 176–77.

28   Sévigné, Marie du Rabutin-Chantal, marquise de, *Recueil des lettres de Mme la marquise de Sévigné a Madame la Comtesse de Grignan sa fille* (Paris: Chez Rollin, 1754), volume II, p. 290.

29   Hassall, *Louis XIV*, p. 178.

30   Ibid.

31   Ibid., p. 177.

32   Cornette, p. 208.

33   Grimarest, cited by Palmer, pp. 403–4. Grimarest recorded the memories of Michel Baron some thirty years after these events.

34   François de Harlay de Champvallon had become archbishop of Paris in 1671 following the death of Hardouin de Péréfixe. Whereas Molière had died in the arms of two nuns, Harlay de Champvallon would die in the arms of his mistress after a life of debauchery. Mme de Sévigné would never invite him into her house, saying that she had no daughters young enough for his entertainment.

35   Brossette, cited in Palmer, p. 407.

36   Ibid.

37   Candia is known today as Crete.

38   Cronin, p. 198.

39   Louis XIV, *Œuvres*, volume III, p. 373.

40   Dunlop, p. 231.

41   Bluche, *Louis XIV*, p. 251.

42   Louis XIV, *Œuvres*, volume III, p. 402.

43   Hassall, *Louis XIV*, p. 181.

44   Louis XIV, *Œuvres*, volume III, p. 453.

45   Ibid., pp. 473–9.

46   *Medailles sur les principaux evenements*, pp. 132–5.

47   César de Vendôme was the son of Gabrielle d'Estrées, while Antoine de Moret's mother was Jacqueline de Bueil.

48   Lair, *Louise de La Vallière*, p. 313.

49   Ibid., p. 316.
50   Ibid., p. 237.
51   Clément, pp. 233–4; Lair, *Louise de La Vallière*, pp. 316–17.
52   Hilton, p. 137.
53   This was a separation and not a divorce, since divorce was not recognized by the Roman Catholic Church. Marriage was a sacrament and could not be undone. Athénaïs could separate in bed and board from her husband, but she could not remarry.
54   La Vallière, *Miséricorde*, volume 1, p. 126.
55   Bussy-Rabutin, *Correspondance*, volume 2, p. 344.
56   Lair, *Louise de La Vallière*, pp. 324–5.
57   Ibid., p. 327.
58   Dunlop, p. 234.
59   Ibid., p. 235; La Fare, pp. 284–5.
60   Ibid., p. 235.
61   marquis de La Fare, Mémoires et Réflexions sur les principaux événements du règne de Louis XIV in Michaud and Poujoulat, Series 3, volume 30 (Lyons, Paris: Guyot Frères, 1854), p. 285; Dunlop, p. 236.
62   Richard Wilkinson, *Louis XIV*, 2nd ed. (Abingdon, U.K.: Routledge, 2018), p. 155.
63   Voltaire, pp. 124–15.
64   La Fare, p. 267.
65   Voltaire, p. 126.

EIGHTEEN: LES FEMMES

1   Primi Visconti, pp. 99–100. A few days later, Athénaïs confided to her lady-in-waiting, Mlle Desœillets, that she had dreamed that all her hair had fallen out.
2   Ibid., p. 100.
3   Ibid., p. 103.
4   Ibid., pp. 103–4.
5   Sévigné (1754), volume III, p. 346.
6   Primi Visconti, p. 100.
7   Hilton, p. 265.
8   Jean Lemoine, Les des OEillets: *Une grande comédienne, une maitresse de Louis XIV* (Paris: Libraire Académique Perrin, 1938), p. 49; Somerset, p. 179.
9   Somerset, p. 103.
10   The story of Athénaïs's golden dress is told by Mme de Sévigné, Sévigné, Marie du Rabutin-Chantal, *marquise de, Lettres de Madame de Sevigné, de sa famille et de ses amis* (Paris : J.J. Blaise, 1818). volume V, pp. 54–5.
11   Sévigné (1818), volume V, p. 66. Actually, the word *oisons* should be translated as 'goslings,' but 'geese' fits better in this context.
12   Primi Visconti (p. 246) goes further, suggesting that Louis had harbored an inclination for Mme de Soubise for fifteen years.
13   Lucy Norton, *Saint-Simon at Versailles* (London: Hamish Hamilton, 1958), volume I, p. 412.
14   Saint-Maurice, volume 1, p. 256.
15   Ézéchiel Spanheim, *Relation de la Cour de France en 1690* (Paris: Librairie Renouard, 1882), pp. 11, 130.

ENDNOTES

16   See Somerset, p. 103; Saint-Simon (Wormeley), volume III, p. 313. Bertière, *Les Femmes* (p. 244) suggests that Mme de Sévigné was also aware.
17   Somerset, p. 104; Saint-Simon (Norton), volume 1, p. 264.
18   Montpensier (Chéruel), volume IV, pp. 419–20; Marthe-Marguerite, marquise de Caylus, Souvenirs de Madame de Caylus (Paris: Chez Ant. Aug. Renouard, 1806), p. 108. Mme de Sévigné, volume IV, p. 467.
19   Sévigné (1818), volume IV, p. 467
20   Sévigné (1818), volume V, p. 82.
21   Ibid., pp. 82–3.
22   Sadly, Mme de Soubise's looks were marred when she lost a tooth (Sévigné (1818), volume V, p. 112).
23   Decker, p. 152.
24   Hilton, p. 209.
25   Somerset, p. 104.
26   Saint-Maurice, volume 1, p. 503, note 1.
27   Sévigné (1818), volume III, p. 156.
28   Primi Visconti, p. 155, Somerset, p. 105.
29   Michel de Decker, *Louis XIV. Le bon plaisir du roi* (Paris: Belfond, 2000), p. 153; Sévigné, volume V (1818), p. 97 note.
30   Sévigné (1818), volume V, p. 88.
31   Bussy-Rabutin, *Correspondance*, volume IV, p. 21.
32   Somerset, p. 106.
33   Bussy-Rabutin, *Correspondance*, volume III, pp. 354, 381; Somerset, p. 106.
34   Bussy-Rabutin, *Correspondance*, volume IV, p. 45; Clément, *Montespan et Louis XIV*, p. 97; Somerset, p. 106.
35   Bussy-Rabutin, *Correspondance*, volume IV, p. 106.
36   Somerset, p. 107.
37   Ibid.; Primi Visconti, p. 172.
38   Marie-Louise (1662–1689) was the eldest daughter of Philippe d'Orléans and the duchesse Henriette d'Angleterre.
39   Fraser, *Louis XIV*, p. 171.
40   Orléans, duchesse d', *Letters* (Scott–Stevenson), volume I, pp. 33–4.
41   Mademoiselle (volume III, p. 181) cautioned Philippe, duc d'Orléans not to bring his daughter to court so often, for "it will give her a disgust for all other matches, and if she does not marry the Dauphin, it will embitter the rest of her life."
42   Barker, p. 210.
43   Montpensier, volume II, p. 182, note.
44   Fraser, *Louis XIV*, p. 172. The Most Catholic Queen would be Marie-Louise's official title as queen of Spain.
45   Fraser, *Louis XIV*, p. 172.
46   Orléans, duchesse d', *Letters* (Scott–Stevenson), volume I, p. 78.
47   Montpensier, volume III, p. 181.
48   Ibid., p. 182.
49   Orléans, duchesse d', *Letters* (Scott–Stevenson), volume I, p. 38.
50   Montpensier, volume III, pp. 182–3.
51   Orléans, duchesse d', *Letters* (Scott–Stevenson), volume I, p. 38.
52   Montpensier, volume III, pp. 183–5.

53   Orléans, duchesse d', *Letters* (Scott–Stevenson), volume I, p. 34.
54   Choisy, volume 2, p. 35.
55   Orléans, duchesse d', *Letters* (Scott–Stevenson), volume II, p. 169.
56   Ibid.
57   Ibid., p. 125.
58   Hilton, pp. 224–5.
59   Bussy-Rabutin, *Correspondance*, volume IV, p. 333.
60   Somerset, p. 108.
61   Montpensier, volume III, p. 183.
62   Somerset, p. 109.
63   Bussy-Rabutin, *Correspondance*, volume IV, pp. 344, 345; Somerset, p. 109.
64   See Hilton, pp. 19, 59–60, 181, 330–34, 350–52.
65   Bussy-Rabutin, *Correspondance*, volume IV, p. 345.
66   Ibid., pp. 386, 419.
67   Hilton, p. 229. This story also appears in the apocryphal *Memoirs of Madame la Marquise de Montespan—Complete*: "At the chase, one day, his nymph, whom nothing could stop, had her knot of riband caught and held by a branch; the royal lover compelled the branch to restore the knot, and went and offered it to his Amazon. Singular and sparkling, although lacking in intelligence, she carried herself this knot of riband to the top of her hair, and fixed it there with a long pin. Fortune willed it that this coiffure, without order or arrangement, suited her face, and suited it greatly. The King was the first to congratulate her on it; all the courtiers applauded it, and this coiffure of the chase became the fashion of the day. All the ladies, and the Queen herself, found themselves obliged to adopt it."
68   Sévigné (1818), volume VI, p. 203.
69   Bussy-Rabutin, *Correspondance*, volume IV, p. 424.
70   Ibid., p. 428.
71   Primi Visconti, p. 173.
72   Hilton, p. 227; Somerset, p. 110.
73   Sévigné (1818), volume VI, p. 180; Somerset, p. 111.
74   Ibid., p. 242.
75   Ibid., p. 369.
76   Mme de Sévigné (1818), volume VI, p. 273, described Cabrières as a *médecin forcé*, not really a doctor, although he seemed to have helped Mlle de Fontanges, at least for a while.
77   Bussy-Rabutin, *Correspondance*, volume V, pp. 109–110.
78   Ibid., p. 108.
79   Primi Visconti, pp. 254–5.
80   It would later be claimed that Mlle de Fontanges's last words were that she died content because she had seen the king weep for her. Sadly, this was not the case, see Jean-Christian Petitfils, *Madame de Montespan* (Paris: Fayard, 1988), pp. 172–30. Mme de Sévigné (1818), volume VII, p. 73, marked the event with the comment *"Sic transit gloria mundi."*
81   See Frantz Funck-Brentano, *La drame des poisons* (Paris: Librairie Hachette, 1913), p. 250; Somerset, pp. 291–2; Holly Tucker, *City of Light, City of Poison: Murder, Magic, and the First Police Chief of Paris* (New York, London: W.W. Norton & Company, 2017), p. 208; Francis Mossiker, *The Affair of the Poisons* (London: Victor Gollancz, 1970), pp. 260–61.
82   There are several books on the Affair of the Poisons, with the fullest treatments being that of Somerset (in English) and Petitfils (in French). Tucker's book combines a study

of the Affair with a life of La Reynie, the chief of police who investigated the case. Mossiker's work is somewhat outdated, although it is still an interesting read.

NINETEEN: THE AFFAIR OF THE POISONS

1   It was widely believed (e.g., La Fare, p. 291; Ravaisson, ed., volume, VI, p. 396; Primi Visconti, p. 228) that the marquise de Brinvilliers had learned the art of poisoning by experimenting on paupers in the public hospitals, whom she visited out of charity. She was alleged to have fed them poisoned biscuits and studied the effects so that she could calculate the correct dosage when she administered poison to members of her family. However, this was probably not true, but the fact that many believed it speaks to the horror with which her crimes were viewed, especially as they were perpetrated by a wealthy aristocratic lady: see Somerset, p. 7.

2   See above, p. 219.

3   Primi Visconti practiced palmistry, cartomancy, and astrology.

4   Primi Visconti, p. 232.

5   Somerset, p. 153; Ravaisson, ed., volume VI, pp. 31, 37.

6   Somerset, p. 151; Ravaisson, ed., volume, V, p. 348.

7   Somerset, p. 151.

8   Aged fifty-one at the time of his appointment, La Reynie had been a provincial governor before becoming a master of requests in the Parlement of Paris. Colbert had been so impressed with his work that he would have offered him a position in the admiralty had not fate intervened. Louis, who was equally impressed with La Reynie, created the post of lieutenant-general of the Paris police, to which he appointed La Reynie on March 15, 1676 (Somerset, p. 126).

La Reynie's responsibilities were wide-ranging and included public order, public health, regulating food supplies and prices, traffic control, and improving and maintaining regulations governing inns and hostelries. Street lighting and hygiene also came under his jurisdiction, as did addressing emergencies, such as fire and floods. He was also responsible for combatting debauchery and tracing unfaithful wives. He transformed Paris, turning it from a dangerous and dirty city into a clean, safe, and pleasant place where people were not afraid to go about their business (Somerset, p. 126; Tucker, pp. 15, 18, 19–25).

9   Somerset, p. 151. Among Colbert's other posts was that of minster for the département of Paris, and it was in this capacity that he countersigned the commission for the establishment of the Chambre d'Arsenal.

10 Torture was known to be an unsatisfactory method of extracting information because victims usually said what they thought their interrogator wanted to hear. There had been calls for the practice to be stopped. Even so, it continued to be used in order to make victims reveal the names of accomplices and clients.

11 Funck-Brentano, pp. 165–6.

12 Ravaisson, ed., volume VI, pp. 372–4.

13 Ibid., pp. 214–15.

14 Ibid., p. 305.

15 Le Roi, ed., pp. 125–6.

16 Funck-Brentano, p. 183. Romani and Bertrand, friends of La Voisin, were implicated in the plot to murder Mlle de Fontanges.

17 Ravaisson, ed., volume VI, pp. 290–1.

18 Ibid., pp. 198, 242–3.
19 See above, pp. 228-9.
20 Hilton, pp. 114–15.
21 Ravaisson, ed., volume VI, pp. 244, 291.
22 Guibourg referred to this ritual as a *messe sèche*, or 'dry mass,' meaning one without consecration (Ravaisson, ed., volume VI, p. 420).
23 Ravaisson, ed., volume VI, pp. 420–1. It has been speculated that Mlle Descœillets, wittingly or otherwise, and the English lord had been part of a wider international conspiracy to assassinate Louis, see Hilton, pp. 267–8.
24 Somerset, p. 307.
25 The Château de Suisnes is in the département de la Seine-et-Marne, southeast of Paris.
26 Somerset, p. 304.
27 Unbeknownst to Louis, Le Reynie kept a secret record of the poisons affair, thus providing a great service to historians.

TWENTY: MME DE MAINTENON
1 De Imprimerie royale, p. 110.
2 Hôpital Général (1656–1790) (http://archives.aphp. fr/hopital-general-1656–1790/).
3 Dunlop, p. 248.
4 Emmanuel Filhol, "La France contre ses Tsiganes." http://academos.ro/sites/default /files/biblio-docs/249/20100707_tsiganes_filhol.pdf
5 Franco Mormondo, *Bernini: His Life and His Rome* (Chicago: University of Chicago Press, 2011), pp. 255–6.
6 Claude Perrault was the brother of the author, Charles.
7 Paris Observatory (www.obspm.fr). Gabriel La Hire's map showed France to be slightly smaller than had originally been thought, upon which Louis commented, "You have taken from me more of my kingdom than I have won in all my wars." Quoted in Cronin, p. 305.
8 Dunlop, pp. 250–52; Bertrand Fonck, "Invalides (hôtel royal des)." In *Dictionnaire Louis XIV*, ed. Lucian Bély (Paris: Éditions Robert Laffont, 2015), pp. 670–2.
9 Emily Bowles, *Madame de Maintenon* (London: Kegan Paul, Trench & Co., 1888), p. 15.
10 Ibid., p. 15; Françoise d'Aubigné, marquise de Maintenon, *Lettres historiques et édifiantes adressées aux dames de Saint-Louis par Mme de Maintenon*,.ed. Théophile Lavallée (Paris: Charpentier, 1856), p. 77.
11 Bowles, p. 15; Maintenon (1856), p. 77.
12 Bowles, p. 18.
13 Ibid., pp. 18–19.
14 Ibid., p. 20.
15 Ibid., p. 21.
16 Ibid., p. 23.
17 Madeleine Marie Louise Saint-René Taillandier, *Madame de Maintenon*, trans. Mary Sophie Loyd (London: W. Heineman, 1922), p. 43.
18 Abbé Gobelin was a doctor of theology at the Sorbonne. Known for his severity, Françoise chose him because she hoped he would help her lead a "stricter life."
19 Usually described as Françoise's niece, Marthe-Marguerite was, in fact, a distant cousin. She would marry the comte de Caylus and would recall Françoise in her memoir, *Les souvenirs de Madame de Caylus*.

20 Referring to the difficulties involved in running her secret household, Françoise wrote, "The strange kind of honor cost me an infinitude of pain and trouble. Often I was standing on ladders, doing the work of upholsterers and workmen, who might not be allowed to come into the house." She did everything herself, rather than tire out the wet nurses and risk harming their milk; at the same time, she walked the streets in disguise as she sought one nurse after another, or carry linen or meat under her arm. "I would often spend the whole night with one of the children who was ill in a little house outside Paris. In the morning I would go home by a little back-gate, and, after having myself dressed, would go out at the front door to my coach, and drive to the Hôtels de Richelieu or d'Albret." Her friends had no idea that she had a secret to keep. "Everybody saw how thin I became, but no one guessed the reason." She saw her position as divinely ordained: "This is how God makes use of everything to fulfill His plans, and how He leads us insensibly, without our knowing when we are led" (cited in Bowles, p. 32).

21 Françoise's preferred attire was a gown of *etamine*, a woollen material favored by gentlewomen of modest means. It was austere but practical.

22 Bowles, p. 37; Françoise d'Aubigné, marquise de Maintenon, *Lettres historiques et édifiantes adressées aux dames de Saint-Louis par Mme de Maintenon*, ed. Théophile Lavallée (Paris: Charpentier, 1856), p. 137.

23 Caylus, pp. 89–90.

24 Mme de Sévigné, cited in Bowles, p. 35.

25 Sevigné, volume III, p. 76.

26 Château de Maintenon is about 35 miles, or 50 kilometers, west of Versailles.

27 Maintenon (1856), p. 135; Bowles, pp. 35–6.

28 Bowles, p. 38.

29 Ibid., p. 37.

30 Ibid., p. 39.

31 Veronica Buckley, *Madame de Maintenon, the Secret Wife of Louis XIV* (London: Bloomsbury, 2008), pp. 167–8; Bowles, p. 36.

32 Buckley, p. 168; Bély, *Dictionnaire*, p. 825.

33 Bowles, p. 44.

34 Ibid., p. 53.

35 Caylus, p. 42.

36 Buckley, p. 195.

37 Ibid.; Bély, *Dictionnaire*, p. 825.

38 Bussy-Rabutin, *Correspondance*, volume V, p. 94.

39 Sévigné (1818), volume VI, p. 465.

40 Cited in Charlotte Julia von Leyden Blennerhassett, *Louis XIV and Madame de Maintenon* (London: George Allen & Sons, 1910), p. 68.

41 Ibid., pp. 67–8; see also Bluche, *Louis XIV*, p. 479.

42 Cited in Bowles, p. 58.

43 Ibid., p. 61.

44 Caylus, p. 168; Bowles, p. 61.

45 See above, pp. 211–12.

46 Bluche, *Louis XIV*, p. 303.

47 Dunlop, p. 267.

48 Ibid.; Bluche, *Louis XIV*, pp. 303–5; Cornette, p. 302; Wilkinson, pp. 169–70.

49 Dunlop, p. 267.

TWENTY-ONE: VERSAILLES

1 Louis François du Bouchet, marquis de Sourches, *Memoires du marquis de Sourches sur le règne de Louis XIV* (Paris: Librairie Hachette et Cie, 1882–1893), p. 101.
2 *Mercure Galant*, août, 1682, pp. 15–16.
3 Ibid., p. 27.
4 Ibid., p. 28.
5 The duc de Bourgogne was born on August 6, 1862.
6 Bluche, *Louis XIV*, p. 148.
7 *Gazette*, 1683, p. 396.
8 Bowles, p. 66.
9 Orléans, duchesse d', *Letters* (Scott–Stevenson), volume I, p. 62. The letter is incorrectly dated January 19, 1683.
10 Orléans, duchesse d', *Letters* (Scott–Stevenson), volume II, p. 133. In this letter, dated October 29, 1716, Liselotte spoke of the unhappiness of the queens of France: "We have had few Queens of France who have been entirely happy. Marie de Medicis died in exile. The mother of the King and Monsieur was miserable as long as her husband lived. Our own Queen, Marie-Thérèse, said on her deathbed that in all her life since she became Queen she had had only one really happy day."
11 Bowles, p. 67.
12 Wilkinson, p. 232.
13 "The populace were so aroused against him," wrote Liselotte, "that at his funeral they would have liked to have torn his poor corpse into ribbons, and the King's footguards had to line the road from his house to where they buried him. Even then they couldn't help innumerable lampoons, in verse as well as prose, being stuck on the walls of the chapel where his tomb is." (Orléans, duchesse d', *Letters* (Scott-Stevenson), volume I, p. 64.) Colbert was buried in the Église Saint-Eustache in Paris.
14 Murat, p. 417.
15 Ibid., p. 420.
16 Ibid., p. 422.
17 René-Robert Cavelier, Sieur de La Salle, 1643–87.
18 Brown, pp. 148–52.
19 Le Roi, ed., pp. 159–60.
20 Orléans, duchesse d', *Life and Letters*, p. 23.
21 Caylus, p. 178.
22 Choisy, volume 2, p. 93.
23 Caylus, pp. 189–90.
24 Dyson, pp. 128–9.
25 Caylus, pp. 190–1.
26 Buckley, p. 242.
27 Liselotte, even years later, had been unable to discover whether or not the marriage had taken place (Orléans, duchesse d', *Letters* (Scott–Stevenson), volume 1, pp. 79–80).
28 The council, which met on August 13, two weeks after Marie-Thérèse's death, agreed that second marriages were "unfortunate" (Fraser, *Louis XIV*, p. 203; Wolf, p. 332).
29 Bély, *Dictionnaire*, p. 857.
30 Fraser, *Louis XIV*, p. 204. The secrecy surrounding the wedding and the fact that it was not registered means that the date on which it took place is not known. Historians have, nevertheless, offered their own opinions, although their conclusions

vary. Blennerhassett (p. 75), for instance, offers January 1684; Bowles (p. 73) and Dyson (p. 128) narrow it down to January 12, 1684. Buckley (p. 246) offers the night of October 9–10 1683, as does Bély (*Dictionnaire*, p. 857). A letter from Françoise to her spiritual advisor, Abbé Gobelin, dated September 26, 1683, could offer a clue that would support this earlier date. In it, she requests him not to forget her before God, for, she wrote, "I greatly need strength to make a good use of my happiness" (cited in Saint-René Taillandier, p. 130). It might be inferred from this that Françoise had already decided to accept Louis's proposal of marriage. With no reason to wait, the couple probably married soon afterwards.

31 Voltaire, p. 300.
32 Cited in Cronin, p. 301.
33 Cited in Bowles, p. 78.
34 Blennerhassett, p. 75; Françoise d'Aubigné, marquise de Maintenon, *Correspondance général*, ed. Théophile Lavallée (Paris: Charpentier, 1865), volume 3, pp. 208–9; Bluche, *Louis XIV*, p. 485; Maintenon (1856), volume 2, p. 198.
35 Bowles, pp. 78–9.
36 Blennerhassett, p. 76.
37 Bowles, p. 78.
38 Bluche, *Louis XIV*, p. 375; Dangeau, volume 1, pp. 88–9.
39 Philippe de Courcillon, marquis de Dangeau, *Journal du marquis du Dangeau* (Paris: Firmin-Didot Frères, 1854), volume 1, p. 87.
40 De Imprimerie royale, p. 194.
41 Orléans, duchesse d', *Letters* (Scott–Stevenson), volume II, p. 127.
42 Bluche, *Louis XIV*, p. 349.
43 Ibid., p. 351.
44 Ibid., p. 352.
45 Ibid., p. 354.
46 Wilkinson, p. 104.
47 Ibid., p. 89, 104.
48 Bluche, *Louis XIV*, p. 351.
49 See, for example, Louis's creation of the Académie Royale de Danse above, p. 109.
50 See p. 30.
51 Wilkinson, p. 87.

TWENTY-TWO: THE SUN REACHES ITS ZENITH
1 Campbell, *Louis XIV*, p. 64.
2 Ibid., p. 65.
3 De Imprimerie royale, p. 195. The medal would be struck in 1683.
4 Campbell, *Louis XIV*, p. 65.
5 Hassall, *Louis XIV*, pp. 223–26.
6 In 1684, Louis would receive envoys from Algiers, who had been sent to Versailles to beg him for mercy.
7 Wilkinson, p. 159.
8 Ibid., pp. 159–160.
9 Bluche, *Louis XIV*, p. 300.
10 Charles Léopold Nicolas Sixte (1643–1690).
11 See above, p. 84.

12 Hassall, *Louis XIV*, p. 226. Sobieski was formerly a client of France, and Louis's attempts to persuade him not to go to the aid of Vienna had been unsuccessful. The Turks drew back to Budapest, which fell to them in 1685.
13 Orléans, duchesse d', *Letters* (Scott–Stevenson), volume I, p. 66.
14 *Gazette*, 1684, pp. 668, 692.
15 Sévigné (1818), volume VII, p. 260.
16 Dangeau, volume 1, pp. 171–2. A personal and public apology from the doge was one of the conditions of Louis's cease-fire.
17 Ibid., p. 174.
18 Ibid., p. 176.
19 Ibid., pp. 172–3.
20 Bernini had worked on the statue between 1671 and 1677. He died in 1680.
21 Dangeau, volume 1, p. 252.
22 Ibid., p. 134, note.

TWENTY-THREE: THE EDICT OF FONTAINEBLEAU
1 Louis, *Œuvres*, volume I, p. 85.
2 Ibid., p. 86.
3 Ibid., p. 87.
4 Ibid., pp. 87–8.
5 Ibid., p. 88.
6 France held the view, shared by the rest of Europe, that the ruler decided the religion of the people. Unlike France, however, other countries usually let dissidents emigrate.
7 Bluche, *Louis XIV*, p. 403.
8 Ibid., p. 402.
9 For this section, Bluche, *Louis XIV*, pp. 403–5.
10 Maintenon (1865), volume 2, p. 162.
11 Dangeau, volume 1, p. 233.
12 Wilkinson, p. 174; Bluche, *Louis XIV*, p. 405.
13 Bluche, *Louis XIV*, p. 406.
14 Ibid.
15 Wilkinson, p. 174.
16 Père Bourdaloue was one of the missionaries sent to preach to the newly converted.
17 Sévigné (1818), volume VII, p. 353.
18 Dangeau, volume 1, p. 332. The school would be disbanded during the Revolution. Napoleon would later establish a military academy, the *École Spéciale Militaire*, for the training of young officers. It replaced the earlier *École Royale Militaire* based at Fontainebleau. Napoleon would later move the academy into the premises formerly occupied by Françoise's school.
19 Cited in Bowles, p. 97.
20 Saint-René Taillandier, pp. 178–79.
21 Dangeau, volume 1, pp. 346–7; Bowles, p. 102.
22 Saint-René Taillandier, p. 179.
23 Dangeau, volume 1, p. 364.
24 Bowles, p. 87.
25 Ibid.
26 Cited in Bowles, p. 100.

27 Along with smallpox, toothache was one of the curses of Louis's day.

28 Le Roi, ed., pp. 135–6.

29 Louis had five chief physicians during his lifetime: Jacques Cousinot (1638), François Vaultier (1646), Antoine Vallot (1652), Antoine d'Aquin (1672) and Guy-Crescent Fagon (1693).

30 Le Roi, ed., p. 140.

31 Ibid., p. 145.

32 Ibid., pp. 162–3.

33 Burke, p. 33.

34 Dangeau, volume 1, p. 291.

35 Ibid., p. 296.

36 Ibid., pp. 300–1

37 Bluche, *Louis XIV*, p. 467.

38 Charles François Tassy, known as Félix, was Louis's surgeon and premier valet of the garderobe.

39 Sourches, p. 457.

40 Ibid.

41 Ibid.

42 Ibid.

43 Ibid., pp. 457–8.

44 Ibid., p. 458.

45 Ibid., p. 461.

46 Ibid., p. 463.

47 Dangeau, volume 1, p. 426.

48 Maintenon (1865), volume 3, p. 49. An instrument of execution, the victim would be tied to the wheel and his limbs broken, after which he was left to die in agony.

49 Cited in Dunlop, p. 323.

50 Dangeau, volume 1, p. 435.

51 Sourches, p. 470. According to the marquise de Créquy, Madame de Brinon, who was noted for her poesy, wrote a prayer for Louis's recovery and for the souls of those who did not survive Félix's earlier operations:

> *Grand Dieu, Sauvez le Roi!*
> *Grand Dieu, Sauvez le Roi.*
> *Venger le Roi!*
> *Que toujours glorieux,*
> *Louis victorieux*
> *Voye ses enemies*
> *toujours soumis.*
> *Grand Dieu! Sauvez le Roi!*
> *Grand Dieu! Sauvez le Roi!*
> *Vive le Roi!*

The prayer was then set to music by Lully and sung to Louis when he visited the school upon his recovery. Mme de Créquy notes that the song found its way to England, where the lyrics were translated into English as 'God Save the King' and adapted into a patriotic song which became the British national anthem.

The veracity or otherwise of this story cannot be established. It is very late, it is not supported by any contemporary evidence, and the only source for it is the ninth volume of Mme de Créquy's *Souvenirs*. Mme de Créquy, a lady of letters, was born in 1714 and married Louis-Marie de Créquy, marquis d'Hemont, in 1737, only to be widowed four years later. Among her friends were Jean-Baptiste le Rond d'Alembert and Jean-Jacques Rousseau. She was not a contemporary witness, and, indeed, there is no reference to the song in the text of the *Souvenirs*; it appears only in a *piece justificative* written and signed by three former nuns and dignitaries of the convent of Saint-Cyr, who recalled hearing the song and the story associated with it while at Saint-Cyr: Anne Thibault de La Noraye, P. de Monstier, and Julienne de Pelagiey. The *piece justificative* is dated September 22, 1819 (Renée Caroline de Froulay, marquise de Créquy, *Souvenirs de 1710 à 1803* (Paris: Garnier Frères, 1873), pp. 157–9. The song appears on p. 158. For background information on Mme de Créquy see http://data.bnf.fr/11986767/renee _caroline_de_froulay_crequy/#documents-about).

TWENTY-FOUR: THE LEAGUE OF AUGSBURG

1 Hassall, *Louis XIV*, pp. 228–9.
2 Dunlop, p. 306.
3 Ibid., pp. 306–7.
4 Cologne was an ecclesiastical principality within the Holy Roman Empire.
5 Mary of Modena was the daughter of Laure Martinozzi, the eldest of Mazarin's nieces. Louis had endorsed her marriage to James, who was then duke of York, in 1673.
6 William of Orange's claim came through his mother, who was the eldest daughter of Charles I of England. He also had a claim in right of his wife, who was the eldest daughter of James II by his first wife, Anne Hyde.
7 Dunlop, p. 308.
8 David Ogg, *Louis XIV* (London, Oxford, New York: Oxford University Press, 1967), pp. 79–80.
9 Dunlop, p. 309.
10 Orléans, duchesse d', *Letters* (Scott–Stevenson), volume I, pp. 81–2.
11 Ibid., p. 82.
12 Ibid., pp. 82–3.
13 Ibid., p. 83.
14 Ibid., p. 83.
15 Ibid., pp. 83–4.
16 Ibid., p. 86.
17 Somerset, p. 211.
18 Sourches, volume III, pp. 39–40; Somerset, p. 211.
19 Somerset, p. 211.
20 Fraser, *Louis XIV*, p. 231.
21 Ibid., p. 231.
22 John Miller, *James II* (New Haven, Conn.: Yale University Press, 2000), p. 194.
23 Miller, p. 208.
24 Ogg, p. 81; Campbell, *Louis XIV*, p. 66.
25 Ogg, p. 81.
26 Hassall, *Louis XIV* p. 274.
27 Mary F. Sandars, *Lauzun: Courtier and Adventurer: The Life of a Friend of Louis XIV* (New York: Brentano's, 1909), volume 1, pp. 36–7.
28 Ibid., volume 2, pp. 468–77.

29 Bishop Burnet, *History of His Own Time* (London: printed for A. Miller, 1753), volume III, p. 69.
30 Dangeau, volume 3, p. 300; Hilton, p. 327; Bély, *Dictionnaire*, p. 946.
31 Dangeau, volume 1, pp. 302, 320.
32 Louis XIV, *Œuvres*, volume IV, pp. 344–5.
33 Namur would be the last siege that Louis would direct personally.
34 Diana De Marly, *Louis XIV & Versailles* (London: B.T. Batsford Ltd., 1987), p. 88; Voltaire, p. 155.
35 Dangeau, volume 3, p. 450. According to Liselotte, a servant "has already been arrested under suspicion of having poisoned a silver mug from which Monsieur de Louvois drank during the afternoon." A month later, she confided to a friend that she did not believe that Louvois's sons had poisoned him, "bad though they may be. I prefer to think that it was done by some doctor who did the deed in order to please a certain old woman." The "old woman" was Mme de Maintenon. Several weeks later, she had lost interest: "Monsieur de Louvois is now so completely forgotten that no one bothers to find out whether he was poisoned or not." (Orléans, duchesse d', *Letters* (Scott–Stevenson), volume I, pp. 101, 102).
36 Saint-Simon (Wormeley), volume I, pp. 58, 58. Louis had taken advantage of Mademoiselle's abiding love for Lauzun, who had been languishing in Pignerol. He had prevailed upon her to make over some of her most valuable properties to the duc du Maine. The young duc, therefore, acquired the magnificent châteaux of Eu, Aumale, and Dombes, and in return Lauzun acquired his freedom. Lauzun and Mademoiselle, who were believed by some to have married, later quarrelled, and she refused to have anything more to do with him. She died without ever seeing him again.
37 Le Roi, ed., p. 205.
38 Maintenon (1856), pp. 303–4.
39 For this section, see Voltaire, pp. 441–47; Bluche, *Louis XIV*, pp. 508–11; Saint-René Taillandier, p. 202–4.
40 Cited in Saint-René Taillandier, p. 204.
41 Ibid.
42 See Brown, p. 215.

TWENTY-FIVE: "SIRE, MARLY!"

1 Palace of Versailles (http://en.chateauversailles.fr/discover/history/louis-xiv-guide-gardens-versailles). See also Bluche, *Louis XIV*, pp. 366–69;Gérard Sabatier, *Versailles, ou la disgrâce d'Apollon* (Rennes, France: Presses Universitaires de Rennes; Centre de Recherche du Château de Versailles, 2016), pp. 247–57. The fountains had to be turned on and off as Louis and his guests moved through the gardens until the Machine de Marly brought water from the Seine. Although some of the features Louis highlighted in his guide have since disappeared, it is still possible to follow in his footsteps and see many of the views he and his visitors used to enjoy.
2 Another of Louis's sons by Athénaïs, the comte de Toulouse, did not marry in his father's lifetime.
3 Barker, p. 217.
4 This section follows Saint-Simon (Wormeley), volume I, pp. 144–48.
5 Cited in Bowles, p. 167.
6 Orléans, duchesse d', *Letters* (Scott–Stevenson), volume I, p. 144.

7   Saint-Simon notes that the clothes he and his wife bought for the occasion cost 20 thousand livres between them.
8   This incident is recounted in Norton, *Saint-Simon at Versailles*, pp. 25–29.
9   François de Neufville, duc de Villeroy, 1644–1730.
10 Charles-Henri de Lorraine, prince de Vaudémont, 1649–1723.
11 Nicolas Auguste de la Baume, marquis de Montrevel, 1645–1716.
12 François Quintin de la Vienne, a masseur, was one of Louis's four chief valets.
13 Campbell, *Louis XIV*, p. 67.
14 Ibid., p. 68.
15 Saint-Simon (Wormeley), volume I, pp. 144–48.
16 Cited in Wilkinson, p. 88.
17 Palace of Versailles (http://en.chateauversailles.fr/discover/estate/estate-trianon).
18 Louis d'Auger, marquis de Cavoye (1640–1716), grand sergeant of the king's household.
19 For Marly, see Saint-Simon (Wormeley), volume III, pp. 307–9; Robert W. Berger, "On the Origins of Marly." Zeitschrift Für Kunstgeschichte 56, no. 4 (1993): 534–44. doi: 10.2307/1482675, pp. 534–44; Cronin, pp. 301–4.
20 Orléans, duchesse d', *Letters* (Scott–Stevenson), volume I, pp. 254, 227, 256.
21 duc de Luynes, *Mémoires du duc de Luynes sur la Cour de Louis XV (1735–1758)*. Vol. 2, 1738–1739 (Paris: Firmin Didot Frères, fils et Cie, 1860), volume 2, p. 244.
22 Quoted in Cronin, pp. 303–4.
23 Berger, p. 537.
24 This section follows Saint-Simon (Wormeley), volume I, pp. 224–28.
25 Mlle de Séry later became the comtesse d'Argenton. She would have three children by Chartres, although only one, the chevalier d'Orléans, would be legitimized.

TWENTY-SIX: THE SPANISH SUCCESSION
1   Campbell, *Louis XIV*, p. 68.
2   Ibid., p. 68.
3   Ibid., pp. 68–9.
4   Jean-Denis, marquis de Blécourt, d. 1719.
5   Dangeau, volume 7, pp. 411, 412.
6   Paul, duc de Beauvillier, duc de Saint-Aignon (1649–1714) was first gentleman of the chamber, minister of state, and governor of the royal grandchildren.
7   Louis Phélypeaux, comte de Pontchartrain (1643–1727), was *contrôleur-général* of the finances, secretary of state for the navy and the royal house, and chancellor of France.
8   Jean-Baptist Colbert, marquis de Torcy (1665–1746), a grandson of the late minister Colbert, was secretary of state for foreign affairs.
9   Dangeau, volume 7, p. 418.
10 *Mercure Galant*, November 1700, p. 237; see also Dangeau, volume 7, pp. 418–19. In time, the ambassador's words would be attributed to Louis, see for example Voltaire, p. 310.
11 Orléans. Duchesse d', *Letters* (Scott–Stevenson), volume II, p.26.
12 Louis's early morning prayers were said as he knelt at his prie-dieu, but at mass he was accompanied by the rest of the royal family, who all knelt side by side at a carpeted balustrade. Louis alone had a hassock (Norton, *Saint-Simon at Versailles*, p. 35).
13 Voltaire, pp. 312–14.
14 Dunlop. p. 363.

15   Ibid., p. 365.
16   Cronin, p. 313. Some of Louis's letters can be found in Louis XIV, *Œuvres*, volume VI.
17   Ogg, pp. 85–6.
18   Ibid., p. 86.
19   Bluche, *Louis XIV*, p. 521.
20   Cronin, p. 316.
21   Ibid., p. 317.
22   Claude Henri, duc de Villars (1653–1734), maréchal de France.
23   Cronin, p. 317.
24   Ferdinand Marcin or Marsin (1656–1706) was an ambassador and maréchal of France.
25   Cited in Cronin, p. 318.
26   Ibid.
27   Ibid., pp. 318–19; Saint-Simon (Wormeley), volume II, pp. 18–22.
28   For the death of Athénaïs, see Saint-Simon (Wormeley), volume II, pp. 31–37; Hilton, pp. 355–6.
29   Ogg, p. 90.
30   Orléans, duchesse d', *Letters* (Scott–Stevenson), volume I, p. 276.
31   The harsh winter was described by Saint-Simon (Wormeley), volume II, pp. 106–12.
32   Orléans, duchesse d', *Letters* (Scott–Stevenson), volume II, p. 23.
33   There are several variants of this parody. This one is translated from the version printed by Brown, p. 217. Brown (p. 217) also notes that a crowd of starving people marched on Versailles to demand bread, only to be turned back by troops as they approached the château. It was a chilling presentiment of the so-called women's riot of October 5, 1789. The events in 1709 had a happier ending.
34   Orléans, duchesse d', *Letters* (Scott–Stevenson), volume II, p. 26.
35   Lair, *Louise de La Vallière*, pp. 384, 385.
36   Ogg, p. 91.
37   The text of the letter is printed in Sources, volume 11, pp. 356–58.
38   Louis-Joseph, duc de Vendôme (1654–1712), was general of the galleys, viceroy of Catelonia, and generallisimo of Spain.
39   Louis François, marquis then duc de Boufflers (1644–1711), maréchal de France.
40   Cronin, pp. 321–2.
41   Cited in Hassall, *Louis XIV*, p. 389.
42   John-Baptiste Colbert, marquis de Torcy (1665–1746), was the grandson of the late minister, Colbert.

TWENTY-SEVEN: GATHERING TWILIGHT

1   Motteville, volume III, p. 295; see above, p. 165.
2   For this section, see Saint-Simon (Wormeley) volume II, pp. 241–4, 247–53, 267; Orléans, duchesse d', *Letters* (Scott–Stevenson), volume II, pp. 39–42.
3   Marie-Émilie Thérèse de Joly de Choin (1670–1732). Her name is sometimes rendered as Chouin.
4   Like that of his father, the dauphin's marriage was morganatic. Marie-Anne, princesse de Conti, was Louis's legitimized daughter by Louise de La Vallière.
5   Louis XIV, *Œuvres*, volume IV, p. 458.
6   Choisy was the dauphin's country seat.
7   Louis XIV, *Œuvres*, volume IV, pp. 465–6.

8   Jean Boudin (d. 1728) was the king's apothecary and a student of Fagon.
9   Louise-Françoise de Bourbon, Louis's legitimized daughter by Athénaïs.
10   Orléans, duchesse d', *Letters* (Scott-Stevenson), volume II, p. 39.
11   Ibid., p. 40.
12   Ibid., p. 39.
13   Ibid., p. 41.
14   Cronin, p. 325.
15   Saint-Simon (Wormeley) volume III, p. 59.
16   Cronin, p. 325.
17   This section follows Saint-Simon (Wormeley), volume II, pp. 34–39.
18   Orléans, duchesse d', *Letters* (Scott–Stevenson), volume II, p. 130.
19   Ibid., p. 49. Saint-Simon's tribute is particularly touching (Wormeley, volume III, p. 45):

> With her, all joy, all pleasure, all amusements even, and every species of grace were eclipsed; darkness covered the whole Court; she had animated, she had lighted every corner of it; she had filled it, she had pervaded its most inward parts. If the Court existed without her it was only to languish. Never was a princess so regretted, or so deserving of it; and thus it is that regrets have never passed away; involuntary and latent sorrow has remained, with an awful void which has never been diminished.

20   Cited in Williams, *Rose of Savoy*, p. 449, note.
21   Cronin, p. 326.
22   Saint-Simon (Wormeley), volume III, p. 47.
23   Marie-Adélaïde often used tobacco products for toothache, either as snuff, a chew, or smoked in a pipe.
24   Saint-Simon (Wormeley), volume III, pp. 32, 35, 36.
25   Ibid., pp. 73–77; see also Orléans, duchesse d', *Letters* (Scott-Stevenson), volume II, p. 57.
26   Saint-Simon (Wormeley), volume III, pp. 74.
27   Orléans, duchesse d', *Letters* (Scott-Stevenson), volume II, p. 50.
28   Ibid., p. 57.
29   Ibid., p. 51.
30   Saint-Simon (Wormeley), volume III, pp. 65–66. In the interests of clarity, this child will continue to be referred to as the duc de Bretagne, rather than the dauphin. He was, incidentally, the second duc de Bretagne. An elder brother, who bore the same title, had been born to the duc and duchesse de Bourgogne in 1704 but died the following year.
31   Cronin, pp. 328–29.
32   Orléans, duchesse d', *Letters* (Scott-Stevenson), volume II, p. 52. According to Saint-Simon (Wormeley, volume III, p. 67), the young duc d'Anjou was given medicine brought from Turin by the comtesse de Verue. The comtesse was a mistress of Victor Amadeus, who had sent her the medicine after she had been poisoned and lay dying at Turin. She brought some of this antidote with her when she returned to France.
33   Cited in Cronin, p. 329.

TWENTY-EIGHT: *LE SOLEIL SE COUCHER*
1   Claude-Louis-Hector, duc de Villars (1653–1734), maréchal de France.
2   Alfred Baudrillart, *Philippe V et et la cour de France, 1700–1715* (Paris: Bureau de la Revue, 1869), p. 479.
3   Baudrillart, pp. 480–81.

4   The renunciations were registered in parlement on March 15, 1713 (*Gazette*, 1713, pp. 131–32).

5   Orléans, duchesse d', *Letters* (Scott-Stevenson), volume II, pp. 71–4.

6   Ibid., p. 75.

7   Ibid., p. 21.

8   Saint-Simon (Wormeley), volume III, p. 158.

9   Orléans, duchesse d', *Letters* (Scott-Stevenson), volume II, p. 76; *Gazette*, 1714, pp. 371–2. In time, even this small distinction would be removed and du Maine and Toulouse would be fully equal to legitimate princes of the blood (Voltaire, p. 306).

10   Voltaire, p. 306.

11   Saint-Simon (Wormeley), volume III, p. 156.

12   Jean and François Anthoine, *Journal de la Mort de Louis XIV* (Paris: Quantin, 1880), p. 86.

13   Saint-Simon (Wormeley), volume III, p. 163.

14   Ibid., p. 164.

15   Ibid.

16   Ibid., pp. 164–5. Saint-Simon (p. 165) felt obliged to assure his readers of his sources for these two speeches by the king:

I hold those [words] said by the king to the president and the procureur-général, *who could never forget them, from the first-named; it is true that this was a long time after they were said; for one ought to be exact in reporting such things. I also heard them from the* procureur-général, *who repeated them to me, apart and at another time, in precisely the same language, and such as I have here written down. With regard to what the king said to the Queen of England, which is even stronger and more explicit because he was more free with her, perhaps also because Mme. de Maintenon was present, on whom the greater part of the reproaches were intended to fall, I knew it two days later from M. de Lauzun, to whom the Queen of England told it while still in her first surprise.*

That Louis was coerced into writing his will in favor of the duc du Maine and his circle is supported by Saint-Simon's assertion that Louis had wanted to entrust the young king's education to the duc de Beauvillier, who had served as governor to the royal grandsons. Beauvillier requested Saint-Simon to help him with this charge: see Saint-Simon (Wormeley), volume III, pp. 169–71.

17   Saint-Simon (Wormeley), volume III, p. 166.

18   Ibid., p. 166.

19   See the argument in Dunlop, p. 455.

20   This section follows Saint-Simon (Wormeley), volume III, pp. 206–10.

21   Dangeau, volume 15, p. 411.

22   Dunlop, pp. 456–60.

23   See above, pp. 122–3, 211.

24   Blennerhassett, p. 293.

25   This event is described by Saint-Simon (Wormeley), volume III, pp. 210–11.

26   This section follows Saint-Simon (Wormeley), volume III, pp. 264–79; Dangeau, *Journal*, volume 16, pp. 11–12, 95–137 and the account written by the Anthoine brothers, pp. 5–77. Quotations and additional information are as indicated.

27   Dangeau, volume 16, p. 11.

28   Saint-Simon (Wormeley), volume III, pp. 270–1.

29   The duc d'Orléans told his mother that Louis "had told him that he had made a will about which he would have no complaints to make, and this will was found to

ENDNOTES

be entirely in favor of the Duc du Maine." Orléans, duchesse d', *Letters* (Scott-Stevenson), volume II, p. 97. At a *lit de justice* which followed the king's death, Orléans was recognized as regent, see Orléans, duchesse d', *Letters* (Scott-Stevenson), volume II, pp. 95, 97.

30   Saint-Simon (Wormeley), volume III, pp. 273–4. Saint-Simon assures his readers that these words were written down within the hour.

31   Voltaire, pp. 307–9. Louis XV had these words inscribed and hung in his bedroom, where Voltaire found and copied them.

32   Orléans, duchesse d', *Letters* (Scott-Stevenson), volume II, p. 93.

33   Voltaire, p. 307.

34   Saint-Simon (Wormeley), volume III, p. 275; cf Voltaire, p. 307.

35   Dangeau (volume 16, p. 136) gives the time of Louis's death at eight forty-five; Saint-Simon (Wormeley), volume III, p. 275, places it as eight fifteen.

INDEX